WINDOW ON CONGRESS

Barber B. Conable Jr. in front of the U.S. Capitol, 1965 (Credit: Barber B. Conable Jr.)

WINDOW ON CONGRESS

A CONGRESSIONAL BIOGRAPHY
OF BARBER B. CONABLE JR.

James S. Fleming

UNIVERSITY OF ROCHESTER PRESS

First published 2004
by the University of Rochester Press

The University of Rochester Press
668 Mt. Hope Avenue, Rochester, NY 14620, USA
Boydell & Brewer, Ltd.
P.O. Box 9, Woodbridge, Suffolk IP12 3DF, UK
www.urpress.com

ISBN 1–58046–128–X

Library of Congress Cataloging-in-Publication Data
Fleming, James S., 1943–
    Window on Congress: a congressional biography of Barber B. Conable, Jr. / James S. Fleming.
        p. cm.
    Includes bibliographical references and index.
    ISBN 1–58046–128–X (hardcover : alk. paper)
    1. Conable, Barber B.   2. Legislators–United States–Biography.
3. United States. Congress. House–Biography.   4. United States–Politics and government–1945–1989.   I. Title.
E840.8.C65F57 2004
328.73'092–dc22   2003027554

British Library Cataloging-in-Publication Data
A catalogue record for this item is available from the British Library

Printed in the United States of America
This publication is printed on acid-free paper

To my wife, Chris, and our two sons, Bren and Jay,
without whose love and support this biography
would not have been possible.

Contents

List of Photographs   *viii*

List of Doodles   *x*

Foreword   *xi*

Acknowledgments   *xiii*

1. Introduction   *1*

2. Roots in Western New York   *14*

3. Becoming a Lawyer and Politician   *33*

4. Mr. Conable Goes to Albany   *52*

5. A Freshman in the Eighty-Ninth Congress   *75*

6. Appointment to the Ways and Means Committee   *108*

7. Support for Richard Nixon   *130*

8. The Watergate Betrayal   *156*

9. Toughest Reelection   *179*

10. A Friend in the White House   *197*

11. Republican Leader of Ways and Means   *234*

12. Cutting Taxes   *266*

13. Saving Social Security   *309*

14. Concluding a Congressional Career   *339*

15. Life After Congress   *373*

Notes   *385*

Index   *417*

Photographs

Frontispiece: Barber B. Conable Jr. in front of the U.S. Capitol, 1965

After page 32:

1. The Conable Brothers, 1930
2. Barber as a senior at Cornell, 1942
3. Barber and John during World War II, 1943
4. Mother and Father in 1964
5. With Nelson Rockefeller, 1964
6. Barber, Charlotte and Children in Washington, D.C., 1965
7. With Gerald R. Ford, 1965
8. At Iwo Jima dedication, 1965
9. Meeting von Braun, 1965
10. Reading constituent questionnaires, 1966
11. With Girl Scouts, 1966
12. With Mills and Byrnes, 1967

After page 308:

13. Meeting with Richard M. Nixon, 1967
14. With Richard F. Fenno, late 1960s
15. With Rumsfeld's Raiders, 1969
16. Showing map of district to interns, 1969
17. Advising Ford at the White House, 1975
18. Typing newsletter, 1978
19. At presidential signing of Social Security Reform legislation, 1983

20. With Republican House Leaders, 1983
21. Speaking with Moynihan, 1984
22. In office with administrative assistant, 1984
23. Back at home in Alexander, 1985
24. Meeting with President Bush as World Bank President, 1989
25. Meeting with author and students, 1992

Doodles

Conable frequently doodled on stationery provided during congressional committee meetings, and during meetings at the White House, the World Bank, and various other locations. When asked if he doodled to steady his hand, Conable responded, "No, to steady the mind." The doodles were quite popular among his constituents, colleagues, and friends. To that end, each chapter begins with a doodle. The following is a list of the included doodles with their dates and locations where they were drawn.

Dust jacket	Committee on Ways and Means, February 21, 1980
Chapter 1, page 1	Committee on the Budget, May 19, 1980
Chapter 2, page 14	World Bank, September 24, 1990
Chapter 3, page 33	National Committee on U.S.–China Relations, May 15, 2001
Chapter 4, page 52	Committee on Veterans Affairs, May 8, 1980
Chapter 5, page 75	Committee on Ways and Means, March 25, 1981
Chapter 6, page 108	Committee on Ways and Means, December 4, 1979
Chapter 7, page 130	Committee on Ways and Means, August 1, 1981
Chapter 8, page 156	Honeywell Corporation, June 17, 1986
Chapter 9, page 179	Committee on the Budget, March 6, 1980
Chapter 10, page 197	The White House, March 9, 1982
Chapter 11, page 234	Committee on Ways and Means, September 20, 1983
Chapter 12, page 266	Committee on the Budget, March 5, 1980
Chapter 13, page 309	Unknown, March 15, 1986
Chapter 14, page 339	Committee on Standards of Official Conduct, May 18, 1983
Chapter 15, page 373	World Bank, December 13, 1990

Foreword

Members of the United States House of Representatives come in many varieties. Few biographies have been written about them, however. And fewer still have been especially penetrating or praiseworthy. When a first-rate congressional biography comes along, therefore, it is a special gift to people who think about the practice of politics in America. This is all the more true when the book illuminates a distinctive kind of representative. In this case, the distinction lies in the analytical sophistication and the explanatory skills of one who was also a "master teacher." Barber B. Conable Jr. of New York was as highly and widely respected as any member of Congress in the last half of the twentieth century. James S. Fleming's rich legislative biography explains why—why Conable's constituents trusted him, why his colleagues relied on him, why journalists admired him, and why educators (like myself) made him the very model of what a good congressman should be. This book is, therefore, a special gift.

It traces Barber Conable's life from his small-town upbringing in western New York through his twenty years (1965–85) in Congress. (In a final chapter on Conable's "retirement" it also touches on his presidency of the World Bank.) It covers his election contests, his leadership within a powerful committee, his role as a party leader, his relationship with presidents, his window on Watergate, his legislative work on taxes and Social Security—and all of it as a member of the Republican minority in the House. Whether, how, and to what degree Conable's stellar reputation was related to his minority party status is, perhaps, something for readers to ponder. And there is a wealth of material, much of it newly unearthed, to use in answering that question—and many others concerning this individual and this time in American political history.

Four elements of Fleming's biography are especially noteworthy. First, there are Conable's regular newsletters to constituents, in which he analyzes the events of the day, and through which he lays

out his philosophy of representative government. Second, there are
Conable's career-long private journals in which he confided his
thoughts, opinions, and emotions concerning political events, problems, and people. Here, we find the worries and frustrations of a
dedicated policy activist denied the opportunities he would have
enjoyed had his party controlled the chamber. Third, there are sixty
hours of taped conversations between author and congressman—
checking sequence, adding nuance, and updating information.
Taken separately, any one of these first-person commentaries would
be exceptional. Taken together, they are a biographer's—and a
reader's—treasure trove.

The fourth special element is the biographer himself and his
particular angle of vision. As a representative, Barber Conable must
be understood in terms of his personal attachments—to his prominent family, to his small town beginnings, and to his regional,
western New York values. Jim Fleming—a small-town southerner
from a locally active and respected family—carries similar personal
connections. And from them he draws a valuable working base of
empathy with his subject. In addition to which, political scientist
Fleming is, like Conable, both an intellectual and a teacher. This
combination helps explain the political acumen and the scholarly
care the author brings to his work.

Barber Conable was an especially admirable United States
Representative; and Jim Fleming has written an especially
admirable congressional biography.

RICHARD F. FENNO JR.
William R. Kenan Professor Emeritus of Political Science
Distinguished University Professor Emeritus
University of Rochester

Acknowledgments

Many people helped make this biography possible. First and foremost, I would like to thank the University of Rochester political scientist, Richard F. Fenno Jr., and Theodore J. Lowi of Cornell University for originally suggesting that I write a biography of Barber B. Conable Jr. Without their continual support and encouragement, I probably never would have begun, and I certainly never would have finished. To both of these wonderful scholars and friends, I say thank you.

Early conversations I had with my graduate school mentor and friend, Charles O. Jones, were also very helpful to me in shaping the research design of this book. Much of what I know about the United States Congress, I first learned as Chuck Jones's graduate student at the University of Arizona.

Paul Miller, noted sociologist, former president of the Rochester Institute of Technology, and my colleague in the College of Liberal Arts for many years, was also quite helpful to me in beginning this project. Paul and I have had many conversations over the years on the challenges of writing biographies, and like many others who have come into contact with Paul Miller, I was always enriched and inspired by his friendship and wise counsel.

Several others at RIT have also assisted me in writing this biography. The two provosts with whom I have served, Tom Plough and Stan McKenzie, have both been kind and supportive of this effort, as have three consecutive deans in the College of Liberal Arts—Mary Sullivan, Bill Daniels, and Andrew Moore. I am also indebted to my department chairmen, Paul Brule, Paul Ferber, and John Murley.

In researching Conable's early years growing up in western New York, I have been notably assisted by Barber's brother, John, and the long-time historian of Wyoming County, John G. Wilson. Both of these very colorful men were gold mines about Conable family history and what it was like to grow up in the Conable household in the 1920s and 1930s.

For background on Conable's law school days at Cornell, I am grateful to the dean of the Cornell Law School, Russell Osgood, for granting me access, with Conable's approval, to his law file. I am also indebted to Matthew Trail, the administrative director of the Telluride Association at Cornell, for providing me a copy of Conable's file at the Telluride House, where he lived during law school from 1946 to 1948, and for the names of several of his housemates, with whom I subsequently communicated. Particularly important were the correspondence and interviews I conducted with Conable's fellow Telluride members: Donald E. Claudy, Norton T. Dodge, Robert F. Gatje, Eric Pell, Bertil L. Peterson, and Allen S. Whiting. Correspondence with two other law school classmates, Donald S. Day and James E. Bennett, was also illuminating, as was an interview with Conable's former Buffalo law partner and future Assistant Secretary of Treasury Donald C. Lubick with whom he practiced law briefly in Buffalo in the late 1940s.

Karl Buchholtz, the former owner of the Genesee Hardware Store and one of Conable's first friends when he moved to Batavia in 1952, helped me understand the beginnings of Conable's life as a small-town lawyer and politician in Batavia in the 1950s. My former Scottsville, New York, neighbor and dear friend, Marge Gray, who along with her husband, Norm, had been friends and law clients of Conable in the 1950s, first introduced me to Conable in the summer of 1985 and provided me many valuable insights into Conable's life and career. Tom Benton, one of Conable's oldest friends and most trusted advisers, who served as his legislative assistant in the New York State Senate in 1963 and 1964 and later assisted him with district affairs during his congressional career, was also helpful in understanding Conable's early legislative life and connections to his district. Robert McEwen, a four-term Republican state senator from Ogdensburg, New York, and Conable's colleague in the New York State Senate, and later his colleague in Congress, also provided me a fascinating personal glimpse into Conable's early legislative life.

The historians in Genesee, Livingston, Monroe, Ontario, and Wyoming counties—a most valuable source of knowledge on local history in New York—were also helpful in locating and verifying information about Conable's early life and political career in western New York.

For insight into Conable's congressional office and his relationship with his staff, I have benefitted enormously from conversations with Harry Nicholas, Conable's administrative assistant for twenty years, and Linda McLaughlin, his receptionist, secretary, and office manager. Both have provided me valuable insights on the way Conable organized his Washington office and his overall role and operating style as a congressman.

For glimpses into Conable's political opposition, I have relied on interviews with two of Conable's toughest electoral opponents: Rochester attorney Neil Bubel, who waged a vigorous campaign against Conable in his first congressional election in 1964, and the former Rochester vice-mayor and presidential advisor, Margaret "Midge" Costanza, who gave Conable his toughest reelection campaign in the post-Watergate election of 1974. Through their eyes and the eyes of Peter Regenstreif, a University of Rochester political science professor, Costanza's 1974 campaign manager, I was able to get a good sense of what it was like to be on the other side of a Conable campaign.

I am also indebted to the many fine journalists and scholars who reported on Conable's congressional career and presidency of the World Bank. Too numerous to mention by name here, but cited throughout the book, they have all contributed significantly to my understanding and documentation of Conable's career. I am particularly indebted to the splendid reporting of the *Congressional Quarterly* for helping me provide the historical context and legislative detail of Conable's career.

I am also grateful to the following libraries for their assistance in documenting Conable's career: Brighton Memorial Library, Buffalo and Erie County Library, Division of Rare and Manuscript Collections at the Cornell University Library, Gerald R. Ford Library, George Bush Presidential Library, Jimmy Carter Library, Richmond Memorial Library in Batavia, RIT's Wallace Library, Rochester Public Library, and the Rush Rees Library at the University of Rochester.

Along the way, I also received several grants and fellowships to facilitate the research and writing of this biography. In 1988, with the assistance of Dick Fenno and Paul Miller, I received a research grant from the Everett McKinley Dirksen Congressional Center to write a paper on Barber Conable's congressional newsletters, which was eventually published in the spring 1993 issue of *Congress and the Presidency*. In 1994, Congressman Amo Houghton helped me obtain a grant from the Corning Foundation which provided me time to work on the biography. Throughout the 1990s, I also received several faculty research and development grants from RIT. In 2000 I received the first Paul and Francena Miller Faculty Fellowship in the College of Liberal Arts at RIT to complete the biography.

A number of colleagues and friends read the manuscript from start to finish, and I benefitted from all their comments. For their kind assistance and comments, I would like to thank Frank Annunziata, Tom Benton, John Brademas, Dick Fenno, Burdett Loomis, Ted Lowi, Harry Nicholas, Andrea Quagliata, Anne Rider, Joel Silbey, and Aaron Wicks.

Several other people provided commentary on individual chapters or were of assistance in other ways. They include John Bouchard, Mike Colosi, Linda Coppola, Tom Cornell, Brett Daley, Gilbert Forbes, Roger France, Craig Grau, Ed Hall, Terry Hollenbeck, Ann Howard, Jim Hutchings, Bruce Jacobs, Don Londorf, Bob Manning, Sue Maher, Joe Mason, John Marcham, David Murdoch, Jackie Pastore, Ben Peterson, Peter Regenstreif, Christine Reilly, John Riedman, Sue Rogers, Phil Simpson, Murli Sinha, Max Stoner, Shannon Taggart, Mike Vernarelli, Jeff Wagner, and Ken Williams.

One of my most valuable sources of support and assistance in this project were my students. I recognized early on that Barber Conable was, at heart, a teacher who loved explaining things to students. Almost from the beginning, I invited two or three students to go with me to Conable's home in Alexander, New York to tape record conversations on his career. Over the course of the fifteen years it took for me to complete this biography, I invited more than thirty students to make the trip with me to Alexander, and each of these students, many of whom did independent study projects with me on Conable's career, contributed significantly to this biography. Watching Conable's interaction with the students and hearing his answers to their questions gave me a personal insight into the educational quality and humanity of Conable's career I would not have had otherwise.

None of this would have been possible, of course, without the full support and cooperation I received from Barber Conable himself for this biography. I am especially grateful to him for giving me access to the personal journal he kept during his congressional career, which has provided us with a rare look inside the mind of a congressman and greatly enriched the overall quality of the biography. I am also grateful to Mr. Conable for reading a completed version of the manuscript. He made no substantive changes, but was very helpful in catching certain factual, typographical, and spelling errors.

I am also indebted to Charlotte Conable for the warm hospitality she extended to my students and me on our many trips to Alexander and for her personal assistance to me in other ways.

In all the hard work it took to put this book together, I have been greatly assisted by my neighbor and friend, Louise Novros, who typed transcripts of sixty hours of interviews and multiple drafts of the manuscript. Through it all, Louise has been not only a highly competent secretary and typist but also a close confidant on the project.

I also wish to thank Tim Madigan, the editorial director of the University of Rochester Press, and his colleagues—John Blanpied, Louise Goldberg, Lisa Mauro, Susan Dykstra-Poel, Amy Powers, Sue Smith and others—for their assistance in publishing this book. They have all made the process of publishing the book a more efficient, enjoyable, and educational experience than it might have been otherwise.

Finally, most especially, I would like to recognize my family for their continual support. My wife, Chris, and my older son, Brendon, provided me with invaluable editorial assistance throughout this project. My younger son, Jay, offered me many happy and constructive diversions from the rigors of writing this book. My mother, an insightful historian and a member of the Conable Great Depression–Second World War generation, helped me more fully understand Conable's formative years. My father, who was a revered educator and Victorian gentleman (in many ways much like Barber B. Conable Sr.) in small-town eastern North Carolina in the 1950s, also inspired and helped me better understand the environment in which Barber B. Conable Jr. grew up and the values that sustained his life.

To all my family, friends, colleagues, scholars, journalists, students, and others who helped make this biography possible, I say thank you. I hope you will recognize in the pages and footnotes of this biography your contributions to my understanding of one of the most distinguished and exceptional men ever to serve in the United States Congress.

Chapter 1

Introduction

Barber B. Conable Jr., a third-generation western New Yorker, represented a Rochester-area district of western New York in Congress from 1965 to 1985. Though Conable spent his entire twenty-year congressional career in the minority, his colleagues voted him the "most respected member" of the House from either party in 1984. Conable was praised at the time by his Republican colleague, Guy Vander Jagt from Michigan, as a "statesman-legislator," as someone who had "dedicated his talents not to political advantage but to the country. Few members, if any," Vander Jagt said, "can walk in Barber's footsteps." In achieving this honor, Conable outpolled such other well-known congressional leaders as the Democratic Majority Leader Jim Wright, Speaker Tip O'Neill, the esteemed Democratic congressman from Arizona, Mo Udall, and the Republican Minority Leader Bob Michel.[1]

The high regard in which Conable was held by his House colleagues was shared by others in and out of Congress. "There never has been a better congressman," in the opinion of George Will.[2] "Some men meet standards; others set them. Barber Conable has been one of the others," Senator Daniel Patrick Moynihan said at the time of Conable's retirement.[3] Political scientist Charles O. Jones expressed the opinion of many when he observed that "Barber Conable was just about everybody's idea of what a congressman should be."[4]

In this biography of Barber Conable's congressional career, I will explore the reasons for Conable's high reputation and success as a congressman. My thesis about Conable, and the underlying theme of the biography is that Conable owed his reputation and congressional success primarily to his pedagogical skills, as a gifted teacher-legislator, to explain to others the complex issues of the day and the inside workings of Congress as an institution. The Greek and Latin roots of pedagogy, *paidaggos* and *paedaggus*, were used to describe the slave who escorted the children to and from school. Conable was by no means a slave, but he certainly was a servant, leading his constituents through the murky waters of tax cuts and Social Security reform, among other complex legislative issues, and the labyrinth of the legislative process. A pedagogue is an educator, and Conable saw his position in Congress as an opportunity and a responsibility to educate his constituents and others on the institution's function.

With an undergraduate degree in medieval history and a law degree from Cornell, Conable was not trained as a teacher. But inspired early on by his educationally-minded parents and his mentors at Cornell, Conable had acquired a distinctive academic perspective on life and politics by the time he arrived in Congress in 1965 at the age of forty-two. He thought and communicated philosophically, as the best teachers do, in clear, concise terms about complicated legislative and political issues. His highly developed, pedagogical style, particularly when mixed with Conable's folksy, down-to-earth manner, was enormously appealing to his colleagues and constituents and others who observed and learned from his congressional career.

Educating the public about congressional activities is widely seen as one of the primary responsibilities of a congressman.[5] But rarely has a congressman taken the educational responsibilities of his job as seriously as Barber Conable. Conable would be the first to admit that his way was not the only way to be a successful congressman.[6] "Don't imitate others," Conable liked to advise would-be successors, paraphrasing the Danish philosopher, Soren Kierkegaard. "Every personality and constituency is different, and success ultimately depends on finding a truth that's true for you."[7] But the truth that Barber Conable found—the need to explain to others his own thinking and activities as a legislator and how Congress functions as an institution—worked very well for him and accounts for the sterling reputation Conable enjoyed.

As a congressman, Conable strongly disagreed with the often-cited Washington adage, that "if you have to explain anything, you're in trouble." Conable, in fact, so frequently and publicly disagreed with this standard advice on how to succeed in Washington that the *New York Times* columnist William Safire cited Conable as the source of this quotation in his dictionary on politics.[8] On the contrary, Conable believed, as he often said in talking with the press and others, that "congressmen are going to have to carry a greater burden of explanation than they have historically enjoyed."[9] For Conable, explaining things always seemed to be more of a joy and felt necessity than a burden.

Barber Conable, in short, had an unmistakable "pedagogical instinct for doing things," as his administrative assistant for twenty years, Harry Nicholas, said, summing up the essence of his career. "Barber thought it was very important to explain to people his reasons and thinking on controversial issues. He had a strong belief that people could disagree with your position on an issue, but respect the process and thinking you went through in reaching the conclusion you did. And he thought it was important to try to explain that most issues were complex, that a lot of elements went into discussing them, and that it was important to understand the broad perspective."[10]

A close examination of Conable's congressional career shows that he tried to explain things about Congress and about his thinking on the issues to four primary groups: his colleagues, his constituents, the press, and the academic community of political scientists. These groups played a major role in establishing Conable's high reputation in Congress. Each group was drawn to Conable's explanations for different reasons. But all four groups saw Conable essentially the same way: as a teacher-legislator, as someone who could help them understand the complexities of public issues and the legislative process. By looking briefly here at how each of these groups saw Conable, one can begin to grasp the profound and exceptional pedagogical dimension of Conable's career and why he was an ideal representative.

Conable's House colleagues paid special tribute to the intellectual and educational qualities that distinguished his congressional career in an hour-long salute at the end of his career in October 1984. Indicating the widespread respect in which Conable was held in both political parties, Jake Pickle, a colorful, seventy-one-year-old Democrat from Texas, who served with Conable on the Ways and Means Committee, noted:

> If you were asked to raise your hand and name five of the most outstanding members to serve in Congress in the last generation, Barber Conable would be one of the first mentioned.
> He has what it takes—insight, courage, and compassion. He can see through a problem quicker than a shaft of light penetrating the dark. And he can arrive at a conclusion and recommendation while most members are still scratching their heads and asking: "What was that?"
> In Texas, we would say he is quick as a cat, sharp as a tack, and tough as a boot—and that's saying a lot for a New York Yankee.[11]

Describing Conable as "the think tank of the Republican Party," "the epitome of what an ideal legislator should be," "a brilliant thinker and legislator," "an intellectual giant," and "a genuine scholar with the ability to understand the whole and its parts," Conable's House colleagues took special note of his educational talents as a teacher-legislator.

"I have the greatest respect and admiration for Barber Conable," Sam Hall, another Texas Democrat, said. "He is both a student and a teacher of the legislative process. . . . He is a polished academic with a unique ability to reduce complex issues to a form and substance that can be generally understood."[12]

Conable's unique ability to clarify complex legislative issues—the distinguishing pedagogical quality of his career—was particularly appreciated by his colleagues on the highly specialized Ways and Means Committee, where he served as the ranking minority member from 1977 until his retirement in 1985. According to his friend and fellow Republican committee member, Bill Frenzel from Minnesota, Conable was viewed more as a "tax philosopher" than a "tax technician" on the Ways and Means Committee. "Barber had wide-ranging, thoughtful views on everything we did," Frenzel said, "but particularly on the tax work to which he was assigned on the Ways and Means Committee. He was both our philosopher and our conscience."[13]

Off the committee, too, throughout the House, on both sides of the aisle, Conable was considered to be one of the House's foremost authorities on tax policy and other economic matters that came before the Ways and Means Committee. "To his great credit," the Republican Congresswoman Marge Roukema from New Jersey noted, "Barber has always been the member his colleagues turn to for advice and counsel on tax-related issues because his is the voice of substance, experience, and reason."[14]

As a teacher-legislator, deeply committed to representative government, Conable also took a special interest in helping new members learn about the House of Representatives. "Barber has always been there, always willing to teach junior members about the House," one of his Republican colleagues from New York, Bill Green, observed.[15] "As a junior member in Congress in my first year, I was unfamiliar and tentative over the workings of this great body," another Republican colleague, Thomas J. Bliley from Virginia, said. "I remember the kindness and patience of my senior colleague from New York who took the time to lend a helping hand to this very new colleague from the Commonwealth of Virginia."[16] "The respect that those of us in this House feel for Barber Conable," a young Democratic congressman from Kansas, Dan Glickman, added, "stems in large part from the respect he has shown for this institution."[17]

The studious, pedagogical style Conable adopted in his relations with his colleagues was equally apparent in his dealings with his constituents. In the final analysis, Conable concluded, as he wrote his constituents at the end of his career, "a realistic expectancy of government and an understanding of how it functions are probably more important than any of the specific things government does."[18] To this end, Conable regularly wrote his constituents a highly informative newsletter throughout his congressional career, describing for them the details of the legislative process and explaining to them his own activities in Congress. These newsletters were an important part of what Conable often called the "dialogue of representation," by which he meant the "two-way communication" or "exchange of ideas" between a representative and his constituents, which he believed was the "lifeline of the representative process."[19]

Unlike most congressmen who rely on their staffs to write their newsletters, Conable personally wrote his own. He considered this to be an important part of his style, an important part of the way he tried to explain things to himself by explaining things to others.[20]

At the mid-point of his career Conable explained why he wrote his own newsletters. "Originally, I thought I would establish a newsletter pattern, then let someone else do it to free my time, but

I have become hooked on the process and rationalized the arguments for continuing it to the point where I think it is personally one of the most rewarding activities I perform. In my job it would be easy to spend all my time simply reacting to the pressures on me, but the newsletter forces me to sit down at regular intervals for the purpose of ordering my thoughts about the issues, reflecting on the patterns of government and explaining (at least to my satisfaction) the significance of my analysis of what I'm doing."[21]

Like many reflective and academically oriented people, in other words, Barber Conable wrote in large part to clarify his own thinking. He approached the process of writing newsletters much in the same way a university professor might approach the process of converting his lecture notes into a publication. "The things I set down on paper come out of my mouth when I make speeches," he explained to his constituents, "but more important, putting views in concise form tests and sometimes changes their outline and their significance in the mind of the writer. I have said to my staff that I would continue to do this for subjective reasons, even if I thought nobody read what I wrote."[22]

Conable's newsletters were particularly useful to him in helping him clarify his own thinking about complicated tax issues. "I didn't know anything about tax law when I got on the Ways and Means Committee," he recalled. "I always refused to practice tax law as a lawyer. I didn't like it. The only way I learned the tax law was to reduce it to simple terms so I could explain it to my constituents. That was one of the advantages of the newsletters. They made me think about things more clearly."[23]

Conable's newsletters were also educationally valuable to his constituents, as they were continually drawn to his accounts of activities in Washington and to his explanations of his own thinking as a congressman. By using his newsletters to clarify his own thinking, Conable also gave his constituents a rare look inside his mind. "I used to look forward to the heart-to-heart discussion Conable had in his newsletters," one constituent recalled. "It was almost like a one-on-one conversation with Conable, where he sat down in the living room with you in a fireside chat and tried to explain to you how things worked."[24] Another constituent likened Conable's newsletters to the *Kiplinger Washington Letter*, a popular financial newsletter. "It contained good general information. It wasn't 16 pages long, and it didn't contain a lot of malarkey."[25]

To some constituents, of course, Conable sounded "too much like a professor."[26] But to most constituents, Conable was, as one faithful newsletter reader described him, "a very intellectual man we could all trust, who had a way of presenting very complex ideas in simple terms so everybody could understand."[27]

The journalists who covered Conable's career, both in Washington and in his district, were also continually impressed with the educational quality of his newsletters and newspaper columns which he also wrote for newspapers in his district. They were particularly impressed, as were Conable's colleagues and constituents, with his ability to clarify and explain the complicated issues in the Ways and Means Committee.

Albert R. Hunt, for example, who reported on the Ways and Means Committee for the *Wall Street Journal*, relied extensively on Conable's newsletters and press interviews with him for his coverage of the committee's activities in Congress.[28] Describing Conable's newsletters as "political science at its best," Hunt noted: "If the representative's role is to educate, Congressman Barber Conable . . . [is] among the best ever."[29]

In the spring of 1974 David Broder devoted an entire column in the *Washington Post* to Conable's newsletters and press interviews. Describing Conable as "one of the best minds in Washington," Broder praised Conable's newsletters for being "at the opposite pole from most of the puffery which flows from Congress." Broder, like others, admired the way Conable "cuts through the puffery to the fundamentals."[30]

In 1974, Conable was a valuable source of inside congressional information for Bob Woodward and Carl Bernstein, the *Washington Post* journalists, while they were researching and writing about the final days of Richard Nixon's presidency. During his congressional career, Conable wrote regularly in a personal journal that he rarely shared. At Woodward and Bernstein's request, Conable read them sections of the journal. As a result, Woodward and Bernstein were able to reconstruct many of the important congressional events leading to Nixon's resignation from the presidency on August 9, 1974.[31]

Significantly, William Safire of the *New York Times* also credits Conable as being the first congressional leader to use the phrase "smoking gun" to describe the incriminating June 23, 1972, White House tape that forced Nixon from office.[32]

Long after he left Congress, the Washington press corps still recalled the clarity and incisiveness with which Conable discussed issues with the press. Godfrey Sperling of the *Christian Science Monitor*, for instance, who invited Conable to be a guest in his famous *Monitor* breakfast series several times, years later could not remember any specific thing Conable told members of the Washington press assembled for these regular question-and-answer sessions, but he recalled "how charming and articulate Conable was. He was always such a good guest and could explain issues and programs so well. For reporters," Sperling said, "that was a treat."[33]

In addition, Conable was a valuable source of information on the Congress for the reporters in his district. Always anxious to explain the inner workings of Congress to the local press, Conable hosted a luncheon for district reporters at the beginning of each year to explain the year's legislative agenda and take questions from reporters on life inside Congress. These press dinners, which were widely reported in the media, as well as Conable's newsletters and newspaper columns in the district, all helped establish his local reputation as a thoughtful observer and informant on the legislative process.

"Make no mistake," the editorial page editor of the *Rochester Times-Union*, Read Kingsbury, concluded at the end of Conable's career, "Barber Conable is, above all else, a teacher. He seems to enjoy nothing so much as describing to his neighbors of the 30th Congressional District the strange workings of Congress and the complex issues of the day. . . . Readers of his newsletters and columns must be among the best-informed citizens in the nation, not only because Conable has so often been at the center of matters but because he can make the complex clear."[34]

Another group impressed with Conable's power of explanation, and continually drawn to the insights he provided them on the inner workings of Congress, were political scientists. It was only natural that someone who excelled in explaining things to his colleagues, constituents, and journalists would also find an attentive audience among the very people who specialize in explaining Congress to the academic community.

Particularly influential in establishing Conable's reputation among political scientists was the congressional scholar, Richard F. Fenno Jr., at the University of Rochester. Impressed with Conable even as a freshman congressman in 1965 and recognizing Conable as a valuable source for his own participant-observation studies of Congress, Fenno followed Conable around his freshman year to study how a new member is inducted into the legislative life of the House of Representatives.[35] Then in the early 1970s, Fenno selected Conable as one of the eighteen congressmen he included in his classic study on how House members relate to constituents in their districts.[36]

Over the years of closely following Conable's congressional career and developing a close personal relationship with him, Fenno came to view Conable as his "most valued participant analyst of legislative life" in Congress.[37] He regarded Conable, along with the former Democratic Speaker Tom Foley, as the "best of the breed" of the dozens of congressmen he has studied in over four decades of congressional research.[38]

What most impressed Fenno about Conable from the outset was the academic way in which he answered his questions. "He would answer my questions from day one in a way a political scientist could understand them," Fenno recalled. "He was always reflective. He had a framework," an academic framework for understanding and communicating his congressional experiences that greatly appealed to Fenno.[39]

Other political scientists too were drawn to Conable's academic explanations of Congress. He was frequently cited in the political science literature as an articulate and thoughtful observer of legislative life.[40]

In the early 1980s, Paul Light relied on extensive interviews with Conable to write an informative account of the Social Security reforms of 1983 in which Conable played a key role.[41] Always recognized by political scientists as a splendid teacher and informant on life inside Congress, Conable was featured in a 1984 American Political Science Association telecourse on how Congress works.[42] Even Conable's announced retirement from Congress in 1984 sparked political science interest, as two scholars from Syracuse University, Linda L. Fowler and Robert D. McClure, used the occasion to write a book on the politics of replacing Conable in Congress.[43] Widely admired in academic circles for his expertise on tax policy, Conable was invited to give a series of lectures on Congress and the income tax at the University of Oklahoma after his retirement, which were later published as a book.[44] And in the ultimate tribute by the academy to his academic prowess, Conable was offered several academic appointments in political science—at Harvard, Yale, Stanford, Xavier University, and the University of Virginia—before accepting a position on the political science faculty at the University of Rochester after his retirement from Congress in 1985.[45]

Thus, Barber Conable, by drawing on his remarkable intellectual and pedagogical abilities, appealed to a diverse assortment of colleagues, constituents, journalists, and political scientists. Each of these four groups had different interests and motivations propelling them toward Conable. Conable's congressional colleagues were attracted to the broad intellectual and philosophical perspective he brought to his analysis of legislative problems. His constituents liked the way Conable kept them connected, and gave them a sense of involvement in the legislative process through his newsletters and newspaper columns. Journalists, too, grew dependent on Conable's analysis and insights for their own reporting on Congress. And political scientists sought Conable out to help them test and confirm their own academic theories on how Congress works. But all four groups were attracted to Conable for essentially the same reason. He was a master teacher, a master at explaining things to them, in a way that made sense within their own frame of reference, giving their own participation and observations about politics greater meaning and perspective. With equal ease, through the skills of a graceful and talented educator, Conable spoke the language and responded to the divergent needs of colleagues, constituents, journalists, and political scientists alike.

Hence, Barber Conable becomes for this and future generations a valuable educational resource. He has left a record of his own career and the important issues with which he dealt. This biography follows Conable's congressional career from beginning to end, pausing with him along the way to reflect on the larger meaning of his experiences. It is not necessary to agree with all the interpretations and lessons Conable drew from his own experience to recognize that he was a remarkably observant and conscientious congressman, thoroughly committed to the principles of representative government, and determined to do his part to make the system work.

Conable has left behind a vast body of material from which to construct such a biography, including a large collection of public papers at Cornell University.[46] There are also 254 congressional newsletters and some six hundred newspaper columns Conable wrote his constituents during his twenty years in Congress.[47] In addition, there are hundreds of newspaper articles and press reports about his days in Congress, a large number of congressional documents, several valuable political science publications about his career, and an insightful book Conable wrote on Congress and the income tax after his retirement from Congress.[48]

To this impressive assortment of data, I have conducted over sixty hours of interviews with Conable on his congressional career that have been taped and transcribed. I have also conducted extensive interviews with many of Conable's friends, associates, and constituents. Of special value, Conable has also given me access to a voluminous personal journal he kept during his years in Congress. Conable's journal offers a rare and highly instructive opportunity to see a reflective, congressional practitioner at work.[49]

Barber Conable, of course, did not somehow just suddenly become the brilliant teacher-legislator he was the first day he set foot in Congress in 1965. The intellectual and communication skills which formed his distinctive style as a congressman had been in the making for years prior to his arrival in Congress.

Recognizing the importance of Conable's early years on his congressional career, I spend the first three chapters of the biography exploring the circumstances and influences that shaped Conable's life prior to his arrival in Congress in 1965. In the next chapter I trace Conable's roots growing up in the small town of Warsaw, New York, in the 1920s and 1930s, the three years he spent at Cornell University from 1939 to 1942, and the four years he spent as a Marine in World War II from 1942 to 1946. Then in chapter 3 I follow young Barber Conable as he returned to Cornell for law school after the war and began his legal and political career, first in Buffalo and then in Batavia, New York, in the 1950s. In chapter 4 I describe the important two years Conable spent learning to be a legislator in the New York Senate in 1963–64 before going to Congress in 1965.

In the next ten chapters, I trace Conable's congressional career from its beginning in 1965 to its conclusion in 1985. In chapter 5 I follow Conable as a freshman in the historic Eighty-ninth Congress of 1965–66 as he begins his legislative career in the House of Representatives and establishes relations with constituents back in his western New York district.

Chapter 6 recounts how the House minority leader, Gerald R. Ford, recruited Conable to the prestigious Ways and Means Committee in 1967 and how Conable and another newcomer to the committee, freshman Congressman George Herbert Walker Bush from Texas, learned to write the tax laws of the country from two of their legislative heroes: Wilbur Mills of Arkansas, the Democratic chairman of the committee, and John Byrnes of Wisconsin, the ranking minority member on the committee.

I devote three chapters to Barber Conable's turbulent association with Richard Nixon. Conable did not know Nixon well personally, but he was one of the Nixon program's strongest supporters in Congress. In chapter 7 I explain why Conable was such a strong supporter of Nixon's domestic and foreign policies in Congress. Chapter 8 draws upon Conable's personal journal to recount the deep personal and political anguish he felt at Richard Nixon's betrayal of the Republican Party and the nation in the Watergate scandal of 1974. And in chapter 9, I follow Conable through his most difficult reelection campaign in the fall of 1974, as he fought off the determined efforts of the popular vice mayor of Rochester, Midge Costanza, and the Democratic presidential candidate, Jimmy Carter, to link Conable to Richard Nixon and the Watergate coverup.

In chapter 10 I describe the important institutional changes the Democrats made in the Ways and Means Committee and House of Representatives in 1975, the intensive behind-the-scenes efforts Conable made to help his friend Gerald Ford in the White House, and the bitter disappointment Conable felt at Ford's defeat by Jimmy Carter in the 1976 presidential election.

With Carter's election to the presidency, Conable also began a new phase of his congressional career, becoming the ranking minority member of the Ways and Means Committee, a position he held for eight years. I devote chapter 11 to some of the frustrating legislative and political challenges Conable faced as he led the Republican opposition on the Ways and Means Committee during the Carter presidency. I continue to look at his minority leadership of the Ways and Means Committee in chapter 12 by examining the reluctant but pivotal role Conable played in the passage of Ronald Reagan's historic tax cut in 1981. Then in chapter 13 I review the influential role Conable played—along with Daniel Patrick Moynihan, Bob Dole, Alan Greenspan, and others—in saving Social Security in 1983, an accomplishment Conable considered "the high point" of his legislative career.[50]

Chapter 14 brings the story of Conable's congressional career to a close by examining the reasons for his unexpected retirement from Congress in 1984 and his return home to western New York in 1985. I also discuss the congressional and public reaction to Conable's retirement, the politics unleashed in the district for choosing his successor, and some of the larger, educational lessons Conable learned about representative government from his twenty years in Congress.

Chapter 15 provides a brief postscript on Conable's life after Congress, a life that included a five-year presidency of the World Bank from 1986 to 1991 and then a happy return once again to his beloved western New York, where he continued to pursue, as a private citizen, the goals and values that sustained his public career.

After his retirement from Congress, Conable often brooded about the impact of his legislative service in Congress. "Your work in Congress is written on the wind," he lamented in a 1992 interview.[51] So quickly were the laws changed that he helped craft during his years in Congress that Conable wondered in retirement if he had made any difference at all in Congress. He was also limited in his legislative effectiveness by his minority status. He very much wanted to be chairman of the Ways and Means Committee, which could have put him in the position to have the kind of legislative impact he wanted. "If I could have been in the majority for just one term," he said in another interview, "it would have made a big difference in my career."[52] But that was not his fate. For twenty years, he was relegated to minority status, always hoping in vain, with each new election, that his fate and that of his party would change. But throughout his legislative career, Barber Conable was faithful to his personal mission of helping others better understand representative government and his own life as a congressman, which inspired both his contemporaries and this biography of his congressional career.

Chapter 2

Roots in Western New York

Searching for the forces that shaped Barber Conable's life prior to his arrival in Congress in 1965, we begin with his growing up in western New York. Always conscious of his ancestral history and western New York identity, Conable reaffirmed his roots with a humorous anecdote he told a group of Rochester community leaders in 1990 on a trip back to the city after he retired from Congress and was president of the World Bank.

> I used to come home 40 times a year and spend a lot of my time up in Rochester, and it was, for me, a source of strength and understanding, and extremely valuable. I miss it now in the World Bank, where I seem to work around the clock most of the time, and I feel as though I have somehow been diminished by not being able to be back here more often.

> They tell a story of a young man who was hired for duty by the highway department painting a line up the center of the highway. He did very well the first day. He painted a couple miles. The second day, he only had a couple hundred yards, and the third day, only a few feet. And his boss called him in and said: "I can't keep you. There's something wrong. You're not doing as well as I thought you were going to do. What happened?" The young man said: "It isn't my fault. Everyday I get farther from the paint can."

"Well," Conable told his smiling audience, "I feel as though I'm quite a ways from the paint can nowadays. And I regret it."[1]

Indeed, there was something about being away from home, away from the paint can, away from his roots in western New York, that Barber Conable always regretted. The first time I met him was in the summer of 1985 at his home in Alexander, New York, a small village of only four hundred people in rural Genesee County, near Rochester. We chatted about life in Congress and his plans for retirement. As Conable walked me back to my car, he looked up at a beautifully clear western New York sky and exclaimed, "Even the sky in Washington is oppressive!"—the thoughts and sentiments of a man who was obviously glad to be back in western New York, the place that had always been "a source of strength and understanding" for him, as it had been for generations of Conables before him.[2]

In the winter of 1821, Conable's great-grandfather, Rufus Conable, and his pregnant wife, Sophia Barber, set out by ox cart from western Massachusetts to settle in the small town of Gainsville, New York, about fifty miles southwest of Rochester. Rufus had gone to Gainsville the year before to build a cabin for his family. The winter's journey from Massachusetts to Gainsville was so bumpy that the jostling of the ox cart caused the premature birth of Sophia's son, whom she and Rufus named Benjamin Barber Conable.

The "runt of the family," at five-and-a-half feet, Benjamin Barber Conable never got along with his father, whom John S. Conable, Barber's brother, described as a "ne'er-do-well, a drinker and frontier drifter." In his lifetime, Rufus Conable went as far west as Ames, Iowa, and died in Ripon, Wisconsin. Benjamin Barber's relations with his father were so bad that when he was seventeen, he borrowed three hundred dollars from an uncle to buy his time until he was twenty-one so he could be free of his father. Benjamin sheared sheep for his uncle and was a cattle drover to Buffalo. He saved so much money that when he was twenty-one, he got married and bought a farm the same day.[3]

In 1877, after thirty-four years of marriage, Benjamin Barber's wife died. The next year—and this is a part of family history the Conable brothers relish telling—Benjamin Barber, now fifty-six, married "a little, sixteen-year-old Irish girl, named Minnie McCaffery, who was keeping house for him and living next door in a family of a bunch of alcoholics."

Barber remembered his grandmother as "quite a girl. She was illiterate, but my grandfather taught her. She learned French and was left a rich young widow with over a $100,000 fortune at the age of thirty-six [in 1902]."[4]

Benjamin Barber Conable and his young second wife, Minnie McCaffery, had two children: Maud, born on July 12, 1879, and Barber Benjamin Conable (Congressman Conable's father), who was born on February 19, 1881.

From all accounts Barber Benjamin Conable lived happily with his father, who was sixty-two years old when he was born, and his young mother and sister. They divided their time between a large, two-story frame house in Warsaw, New York, a small town near Gainsville in Wyoming County where they moved in 1888, and their family farm on the outskirts of town. Though young Barber would spend much of his youth on his family's farm, he never did much farm work because of the terrible asthma and hay fever which he suffered from all his life. He excelled, though, in his school work and was widely regarded by his proud parents and friends as a brilliant young man with a promising future.

In 1901, the year before his father's death, Barber Conable Sr. graduated from Cornell University in Ithaca, New York, about one hundred miles southeast of Warsaw, beginning a long family association with Cornell. Two years later, he received a law degree from New York University and returned to Warsaw to practice law.

Within a few years of returning home, Conable Sr. fell in love with a beautiful young woman named Agnes Gouinlock, five years his junior and the sister of one of his friends. The Gouinlock family, originally from Scotland, had emigrated from the Gatlin area of Ontario, Canada, in 1883 when prospectors discovered salt in Wyoming County.

Agnes's father, William C. Gouinlock, a physician, had been in the salt business in Canada before establishing a salt factory in Wyoming County. Agnes's mother, Margaret, was a well educated and progressive woman, active in the women's suffrage movement and a close acquaintance of Susan B. Anthony in nearby Rochester. One of the Gouinlock daughters, in fact, humorously recalled a time when the famous suffrage leader came to the Gouinlock home for dinner. Though the Gouinlock children had been excited to meet the "great woman," in the end they remembered mainly being "appalled by the size of her feet and . . . disappointed when she ate all the olives at dinner."[5]

Agnes, a highly intelligent and determined young woman in her own right, entered Cornell University in 1904, but returned home to care for her ailing mother, who died in 1906. Feeling the more pressing obligations of family, Agnes stayed in Warsaw to care for her father and five younger siblings.

Barber Conable Sr. was totally taken by the lovely and independent-minded Agnes and proposed to her in 1910. But Agnes, with family responsibilities and her own interests to consider, did not know if she should marry the young lawyer. She "felt her family needed her more since her mother's death," according to a family historian, "and she also wanted to carry on her mother's work in the women's civil rights movement." To complicate her decision even more, Agnes's father, Dr. Gouinlock, at first "did not approve of Barber because of his asthmatic conditions," which he thought "might lead to the premature widowhood of his beloved daughter." Finally, after a tempestuous three-year courtship, during which they were engaged and separated at least five times, the determined and patient Barber Conable Sr. married Agnes Gouinlock on May 22, 1913.[6]

Growing up in Warsaw

Barber and Agnes Conable had three sons: two sons born during World War I—William on June 28, 1915, and John on October 31, 1917—and their third son, Barber B. Conable Jr., named for his father, born on November 2, 1922.

"I was fortunate," John Conable recalled. "My older brother was named William after my mother's father. Mother wanted to name me Barber B., but Dad never liked his name and said, 'No son of mine is going to have that name.' So I got John. The day Barber arrived, Mother sent Dad down to the drugstore to get some supplies and then told the registrar of births the boy's name was to be Barber."[7]

The year after Barber was born, his father, worn out from practicing law for two decades and with an ulcerated stomach from caring for his clients too much, decided to seek refuge on the bench by running for Wyoming County Judge. The year before, the Republican incumbent judge had resigned to accept a seat on the New York

Supreme Court. Alfred E. Smith, the Democratic governor of New York, had appointed a Warsaw Democrat to fill the vacancy, the first time a Democrat had ever held a judgeship in the predominantly Republican Wyoming County. Sensing an opportunity for a new career, Conable announced that he would seek the Republican nomination for Wyoming County Judge in the fall 1923 general election.[8]

A life-long Republican, like most of his neighbors in Wyoming County, Barber Conable Sr. sought his party's nomination in a three-way contest with two other well-established local attorneys. He proved to be a tireless and effective campaigner, passing on campaign stories to his sons that would help shape their attitudes toward politics.

"Barber was a little too young to remember the campaign," John Conable recalled.

> But one of my early memories as a child was licking stamps to put on fliers in that primary campaign and riding around the county with Dad and hearing stories about campaigning.
>
> I remember one story, in particular, Dad told about going out in a hay field to call on a couple farmers, and of course this was during Prohibition. And an old farmer pulled a jug out from under the hay stack—hard cider— and offered Dad a pull on it. And Dad said, "No thanks, I don't drink." And Dad made his sales pitch and got ready to leave, thinking he probably didn't have a vote there, and as he turned to walk away, the old farmer said, "I'll vote for you. Woodworth and Walker [the two other Republican candidates in the primary] were up seeing me too, and they both took a pretty good pull on the jug. I want my county judge to be himself at all times.[9]

Drawing on this and other campaign experiences, Barber Conable Sr. was full of advice for his sons on how to win elections. "When you talk with somebody in a campaign," he told his sons, all three of whom became active in politics, "if you sense any hesitation, count them against you. You may be pleasantly surprised. People will almost always be polite and courteous, but don't think just because they're that way that they're going to vote for you."[10]

To the surprise of many, Conable outpolled his two well-known rivals in the Republican primary, receiving almost half of the Republican vote. He easily defeated the Democratic incumbent in the November general election, becoming the new judge of Wyoming County, a position he would hold for twenty-eight years until his retirement from the bench in 1951.[11]

Growing up in the Conable family was a happy and stimulating experience for all three Conable boys. Barber, who was affectionately called Bunt, after the nursery rhyme "Bye Baby Bunting," recalled a very happy childhood.

> My parents were fine people—very different but very fine. My father was an original thinker, highly intellectual with a photographic memory. My mother was a strong person, but a very warm person. The two of them were very different. I don't know how they lived together, but they did quite successfully.
>
> I very much admired my brothers, particularly my oldest brother, Bill, who died of a brain tumor [in 1966] when he was fifty-one [after a lustrous career as a corporate lawyer in Buffalo]. He was a brilliant fella with a photographic memory with the ability, for example, to recite all the Mother Goose nursery rhymes by the time he was twenty months old. And John had a genius IQ. . . . I was the dumb one in the family, as a matter of fact. I really was.[12]

"But, you know," Conable remembered, with nostalgia for the small-town values that shaped his early life, "Warsaw was a happy place to grow up in back in those days, even though the Depression was on. Small towns were very sustaining. I was active in Boy Scouts and was a leader in the high school class, graduated when I was sixteen and went off to college green as grass."

Because Conable's mother was from a family of nine children, most of whom settled around Warsaw, Bunt grew up near many of his first cousins. "And I obviously had no wants," he said. "With my father making $4,000 a year as a judge, we were among the wealthiest people in town during the Depression."[13]

In addition to hearing campaign stories, Conable also learned his political philosophy from his father. The senior Conable was an historically minded man, inspired by the sacrifices and lessons of his forebears. "We were reminded as boys," John Conable recalled, "that one of our ancestors [Samuel Conable, Rufus's father] had fought in the American Revolution to achieve a constitution of a limited form of government, which Dad thought Franklin Roosevelt was going to destroy. Dad hated Roosevelt and thought he was going to ruin the country."[14]

Franklin Roosevelt's New Deal represented a direct challenge to Mr. Conable's decentralist political philosophy, reminiscent of early nineteenth-century, agrarian, Jeffersonian democracy and still very popular in the farming communities and small towns of western

New York. Like most of his neighbors in rural Wyoming County, Judge Conable still believed in a very limited federal government with most of the power and responsibility for policy-making residing at the local level. He vehemently objected to the concentration of political power in the federal government, which he thought the New Deal represented.

Within his own community, however, Mr. Conable strongly believed in and continually emphasized to his sons the fundamental importance of political equality in American democracy. He was true to the rural, Jeffersonian values that inspired him. "Everybody has one vote," John Conable remembered his father telling him and his brothers. "Nobody is more important than anybody else. We all have the same amount of say in this government." Mr. Conable regularly instructed his sons on the principles of American democracy.[15]

All three of the Conable boys apparently took to heart and learned their father's lesson on equality very well. "One quality that stayed with all the Conables," John Wilson, the Wyoming County historian who knew all the Conable family, observed, "was their very common demeanor. They never made themselves out to be aristocrats, though they had every reason to be. If you saw Judge Conable coming down the street," Wilson said, "you would have thought he was just another farmer coming to town."[16]

Mr. Conable also encouraged his sons to get involved in a political party when they were in high school and college. John Conable remembered his father telling them: "You boys get active in your political party. If you don't, if decent citizens don't get active in a political party, the people with special interests that want something will control it."

Judge Conable was particularly fond of poetry as a means of exploring the inner truths of the human heart. "Father was a Victorian gentleman," John Conable remembered, "and I think poetry was quite important to that generation." John resisted his father's efforts to teach him poetry, saying "I'll learn when I go to school." But Bunt took a particular delight in his father's poetry as a preschooler and learned to recite poetry with his father as they milked the family cows together—one of their favorite father-son activities—in the mornings and evenings in the barn behind their Jefferson Street home.[17]

Judge Conable was particularly fond of Thomas Gray, an eighteenth-century history and modern language professor at Cambridge and the most scholarly of the early English Romantic poets. Gray liked to travel about the English countryside and write descriptions of what he had seen. And Mr. Conable taught his young son and pupil Barber to recite the most beautiful and famous of Gray's poems, "Elegy Written in a Country Courtyard," which Barber was always fond of reciting.

And "we read out loud a lot at home" too, Conable recalled with a glow of affection and appreciation for his father's eccentricities.

> Father was an agnostic and was greatly impressed by Robert Ingersoll and he used to read him to me when I was a little boy. He read William Thackeray, and I remember we read Rudyard Kipling a lot until 1930 when Britain repudiated her war debt, and then Father prohibited any more Kipling in the house. And I used to say to him, "Father, he poked fun at the Empire." And Father would say, "but he never broke with it. He never broke with it."[18]

"But I knew it all by heart by then anyway," Conable added. "It was a funny thing, a strange, but warm and close relationship."

If Judge Conable was a major role model for his sons, introducing them to politics and poetry and showing them early in life the virtues of an independent mind and intellectual curiosity, Agnes Conable proved to be a softer, more conciliatory, but no less important influence on the early development of her children. "A strong, but very warm person, very much into her children," Barber Jr. remembered, Agnes Conable tended to the every need of her children and provided them a wholesome and happy childhood. Despite her own plans and ambitions for carrying on her mother's work in the women's suffrage movement, Agnes quickly made her adjustment to marriage and became a devoted wife and proud mother.[19]

Like her husband, Agnes Conable took a special interest in her children's education, always encouraging and supporting them, overseeing their homework, meeting with and thanking their teachers, often with a bouquet of flowers from her garden, surrounding her children with books at home, and in the age before television dominated family entertainment, frequently reading aloud to her children in the evenings for both entertainment and education. An accomplished horticulturist, Mrs. Conable was especially fond of teaching her children about the flowers and plants of her garden and western New York, instilling in them a love of nature and a lasting commitment to the environment. In addition, she was very knowledgeable about the Indian culture and history of western New York, helping young Bunt, for example, start an arrowhead collection, which he liked to display with other Indian artifacts. This began a lifelong study of Indian history for which Conable was well known in the region.[20]

On the personal level, "Mother was very good at handling people, and Barber got that from her," John Conable observed. "Mother was the sort of lady who would remain quiet in a meeting with her friends and associates while they debated some issue. And at a certain point, Mother would get up and say, 'I think we've talked about this long enough. I move that we do thus and so.' Somebody else would second it, there would be a vote, and that would be the end of it. Mother had a good sense of timing and was much better than Father at handling people." John stressed how his brother Barber acquired his mother's tact with people, while at the same time assuming his father's intellectual and political interests.[21]

Thus, Barber and Agnes Conable reared their children in the same rural, small-town values of western New York into which they themselves had been born in the late nineteenth century. The Conables were like their friends and neighbors in many ways: in their strong sense of family, in their politics and identification with the Republican Party, and in their attachment to their region and local community. But the Conables also differed from most of their friends and neighbors in important ways. The strong emphasis the family placed on education, the commitment to public service Judge Conable exemplified and instilled in his children, and the social status the Conables enjoyed as the family of the county judge set them apart from many others in the community and made them one of the most prominent families of Wyoming County.

With the strong influence Barber and Agnes Conable had on the early development of their children, it is not surprising, therefore, that all three sons followed similar paths into adulthood. All three sons, like their parents, went to Cornell University for their under-graduate education. All three also graduated from the Cornell Law School and practiced law within fifty miles of where they grew up in Warsaw. All three became civic leaders and active in local Republican politics. John, the middle son, succeeded his father as Wyoming County Judge when he retired from the bench in 1951, and today lives in the same house at 38 Jefferson Street in Warsaw where he and his brothers were born. Conable practiced law for ten years with his father in Batavia, New York, a small town very much like Warsaw in neighboring Genesee County, after his father retired as Wyoming County Judge.

In 1933, in the midst of the Great Depression, the oldest and most brilliant of the three sons, Bill, graduated from Warsaw High

School and headed off to Cornell University. Then in 1936 John graduated from high school and joined his older brother at Cornell.

About this same time, in the mid-1930s, the Conables bought a farm outside Warsaw. "Convinced that Roosevelt was going to ruin the country," Mr. Conable wanted to provide his family more self-sufficiency from the government and protection from the Depression. "So during my high-school period," Conable recalled, "I grew up in the country and I was a farmer. I hoed beans and admired plants."

"We also kept cows in the village," where the Conables spent most of their time at their Jefferson Street home in Warsaw, "and Father and I milked them, and I peddled milk up and down the street," Conable added.[22]

Milking the family cows, of course, by this time had become an important ritual for both father and son, the significance of which went far beyond just providing milk for the family and neighbors. It had become an important daily opportunity for Bunt and his father to show off their mastery of poetry, delve into the mysteries of life, and enjoy each other's company. Judge Conable's fondest hope—that one of his sons would someday adopt his love of poetry—was now realized as his youngest son and namesake could recite almost as much poetry as he could. Browning, Shakespeare, Gray, whatever the moment seemed to demand, father and son would spend their mornings and evenings together reciting poetry as they tended the family cows.

In 1939, at the age of sixteen, Conable graduated from high school and went to Cornell. In high school he had been an "A" student, president of his junior and senior classes, and captain of the football team. At Cornell, the values and skills he had learned growing up in Warsaw were extended and tested as he began an important new phase in his life.

Leaving home for Cornell was a major event not only in the life of young Bunt Conable, but also in the lives of his parents as they saw their youngest son depart for college. "The day Barber left for college," John Wilson, the Wyoming County historian, remembered, "his father sold the family cows." There would be no point in keeping them now that Bunt was gone. It would be too much of a chore and not nearly as much fun to try to milk the cows without Bunt along to recite poetry. So, with Barber's departure, Mr. Conable sold the family cows, marking the end of the cow-milking and poetry-reciting sessions that began with his youngest son as a little boy. But the poetry Bunt Conable learned from his father would stay with him and inspire him for the rest of his life, as he would continually emulate his father's Victorian quest to see life and politics through the eyes of a poet.[23]

Going Off to College

Conable received $500 in scholarships at Cornell for his outstanding high school record, which was more than enough to pay the $400 tuition. He also worked part-time at the information desk at the Student Union for fifty-five cents an hour, showing himself to be a most energetic young man. "My father could have afforded to send me to college," he said, "but I worked my way through just the same, which was an ego trip for me to make a little extra money on the side."[24]

Continuing to emulate his older brothers, both of whom were then enrolled in the Cornell Law School, Conable had the same undergraduate faculty adviser as his brother John, Frederick G. Marcham, a popular English history professor who advised more students in his seventy years at Cornell than anyone else in the university's history. As with many other students, Marcham had an important influence on Conable's intellectual development at Cornell.

"Your college career has now begun and you are experiencing a new chapter in your life," Marcham liked to tell his new freshman advisees in his "Letter to a Freshman," where he summarized his advice on getting the most out of college and life. "You see around you new faces by the thousand and you are aware of having joined a vigorous community; old in its Cornell traditions, ancient in its purpose as a university, yet at this moment just as young as you are because you and your fellow freshmen have started the university on another four-year cycle of teaching.

"What a variety of courses!" Marcham exclaimed to the students. "What a miracle that here on this campus you can find the answer to almost any question.

"By entering the university," Professor Marcham told his students, "you have in a sense made a decision to be what we may call an intellectual; that is, a person whose happiness and success in life will come in large part from his mental abilities. You have come to the university to develop your mind. I believe that a basic mental quality is what I call alertness. To be alert," the professor instructed his new advisees,

> you should look and listen more carefully than you have done in the past. When you walk to class in the morning,

look at the sky and note the quality of the light or the formation of the clouds, look at the shape of the trees, the
principal characteristics of the buildings, and the dress of
the people you pass in the streets. Find things of interest
in what you see. . . . In general . . . treat the sights and
sounds which you experience throughout the day as full
of life, color and interest. Do not take them for granted.
Believe with me what one of our professors used to say—
that there are no uninteresting things, only uninterested
people.

Clear writing and thinking on what one saw in life were particularly important to Marcham as he advised Barber Conable Jr. and
other students on the importance of the English language in communicating with others. "You should use language which is clear to
others," Marcham told the students, "and, before you say or write
anything of a serious nature, you should ask yourself not what it
means to you, but what it means to the person you are addressing.
In other words, your task now is to express your thoughts in such a
way that others will readily understand them."

Fred Marcham exerted an important influence on Barber
Conable's formative years at Cornell. Marcham provided Conable
and other impressionable young men and women entering college
an exemplary role model on the life and virtues of an intellectual.
A brilliant scholar and gifted teacher, with a compassionate regard
for his students, Marcham had a special way of always reminding
his students that the mastery of their own lives was as important as
the mastery of the subjects they were studying. "Recognize that
what counts in the long run," Marcham told his students, "is not the
ups and downs you experience from day to day but your poise and
steadiness through the months and weeks. To be a student," he
said, "is a great joy, a joy worth all the sacrifice and the occasional
setbacks which go with it."[25]

"I always felt that he was trying to make me a better person.
And the memories we hold of Fred will continue to make us better
people," John Conable said at the time of Marcham's death in
1992.[26]

Following the example of Fred Marcham and his own love of
history instilled in him by his parents and early teachers growing
up in Warsaw, Conable decided to major in medieval history at
Cornell. More important, though, than his major, Cornell provided
Conable the wide-ranging liberal arts foundation that shaped and
influenced him for the rest of his life. Ideally suited for a liberal arts
education by his own temperament and background, the general

education Conable received at Cornell—emphasizing the intellectual and observational skills he learned from Marcham and his other teachers—placed him in good stead in the years ahead and enabled him to master, not only himself, but a wide variety of complex and specialized fields of knowledge.

Conable's years at Cornell were, of course, clouded by the outbreak of World War II in Europe. On September 1, 1939, just a few days before Conable began his freshman year at Cornell, Germany invaded Poland. France and Great Britain quickly responded and Europe found itself on the brink of a second great war.

Influenced by his father's pacifism and opposition to American involvement in the war in Europe, Conable became an active member of the Cornell Committee Against Intervention in the War. "My father was a real isolationist and pacifist too," he said, explaining his father's influence on his attitude about the war. "He really did not believe in war at all, and of course I was very much influenced by him at that point.

"I remember when Pearl Harbor occurred," he said of the attack, which happened in the middle of his junior year, on December 7, 1941. "All the boys in my fraternity were marching around with brooms over their shoulders, shouting, 'We're going off to war, we're going off to war.' I lay down in my bed and cried."

The isolationism and pacifism which Conable had acquired from his father was severely tested in the days and weeks after Pearl Harbor as he saw many of his friends and classmates leave for war. Gradually, by the spring of 1942, as the war intensified in Europe and Asia, Conable remembered, "I really got scared and decided it was my war too and that I'd better participate." But how would he participate in the war without offending his father and violating his own pacifist views? This became a pressing question for the college junior as he pondered his future.

"I thought, well, I don't want to go in the service. I'm a pacifist. And so I looked around and discovered they were starting an intensive Russian language school at Cornell. I got myself accepted for it. I went home and told my dad, 'I want to become a Russian language specialist,' and he immediately thought I would become a communist and thought my association with the Russians would taint me. He said, 'I'd rather have you dead than red.' I said, 'All right, I'm going to go in the service.'

"And Dad accepted that," Conable recalled, "even though he thought Roosevelt got us in the war. He hated Roosevelt. He thought Roosevelt had deliberately antagonized the Japanese and refused to give the warning necessary to prevent the attack on Pearl Harbor."

Back at Cornell in the late spring of 1942, now with his father's permission to enter the war, Conable went to the Registrar's Office and upon checking his record discovered he had nearly enough academic credits to graduate. As a result, at the end of his junior year in August 1942, after picking up four remaining required credits in summer school, Barber Conable Jr., the transformed pacifist, graduated from Cornell University, three months short of his twentieth birthday. He filled out his papers to enter the Army Enlisted Reserve Corps and went home to Warsaw to wait to be called up.[27]

A Marine in World War II

Back home in Warsaw, the new college graduate went to work in a nearby canning factory, canning apples sixteen hours a day, while he waited to be notified for active duty. Impatient to enter the Army and do his part in the war, he kept calling the Reserve Corps asking when his papers would be processed, and they kept stalling him. Finally, in November, frustrated after repeated and unsuccessful attempts to finalize the Army paperwork, Conable wrote the Reserve Corps a "real nasty letter" saying: "I've given up a wonderful senior year at Cornell [where he had been elected president of the Student Union and president of the Senior Men's Honor Society] to go into the war. And I've been wasting my time in a damn canning factory while you fuss around with papers."

In response, Conable got a letter back saying, "We regret to inform you that the colonel who swore you into the Enlisted Reserve Corps had not been empowered to do so, and therefore we suggest that you take the matter of your enlistment up with your draft board."

Conable was so angry in December he joined the Marine Corps, not even knowing what it was. He would soon find out, as he and hundreds of other young recruits were shipped off to twelve weeks of boot camp at the Marines' basic training school in Paris Island, South Carolina. Because he had a college degree, following boot camp he was sent to the Marine Corps Officers Training School in Quantico, Virginia.

After nine weeks of training, Conable ranked second in his class and was offered a regular commission in the Marine Corps. "But I turned it down," he recalled, with the ambition of someone who did not want to spend the rest of his life in the Marine Corps. "I said I thought I had a higher calling in life than being a regular Marine. And I remember the drill instructor who was interviewing me said,

'Whoops,' because he was a regular Marine. I dropped from second to eleventh in class overnight.

"I then was horrified," he said, "to find that because I had good mathematical abilities, measured by the regular testing they give you, that they had assigned me to artillery school." Though Second Lieutenant Conable was frightened at the thought of becoming an artillery specialist, the mathematical skills that propelled him into artillery school probably saved his life early in the war. "The rest of my class went right out to Guadalcanal and Bougainville," he said, referring to two bloody battles in the Pacific in 1943. "Almost half of my class was dead by the time I got out of artillery school. Second lieutenants were terribly expendable in the Marine Corps."

Lieutenant Conable was then chosen to join the artillery school staff at Quantico to help train other second lieutenants. "I didn't like that at all and I raised hell about it," he said, "until they finally sent me out to be with the Fifth Marine Division on the west coast. And I stayed with them through the rest of the war, until they were disbanded when we were in the Occupational Forces in Japan."

Shortly after arriving on the west coast in late 1944, Lieutenant Conable was sent to the Pacific to prepare for the invasion of Iwo Jima in February 1945. A half century later, Conable did not want to remember many of the details of the battle, or even want to talk about it. "It's hard to think about," he said in a 1994 interview. "I don't remember much about it. I lost a lot of friends. My outfit had 57 percent casualties."

But thanks to a journal which Conable kept during the war, it is possible to understand what it must have been like to be a young, frightened Marine storming the beaches of Iwo Jima. "I had the horrid thought that the four years I would spend in the Marine Corps would be a terrible waste of time. So I read a lot and wrote some to try to improve my writing skills," he said. Those skills played an important role in enabling Conable to discipline his thinking and later establish his legislative career.[28]

At the forty-fifth anniversary commemoration of the Battle of Iwo Jima on February 19, 1990, Conable read from his war-time journal.

"Forgive me if I pick out four poems I wrote, full of the pretentiousness of youth, to read today," Conable, then 67 years old and in the third year of his presidency of the World Bank, told his fellow Marines as they assembled at the Washington National Cathedral. "They are not successful efforts. I long ago learned to limit myself to doggerel at office parties and family picnics. I offer these poems today only as modest windows on what at least one of us was thinking, forty-five years ago.

"The first poem I wrote during that long trip out from the Island [Hawaii]. Do you remember the days full of calisthenics and fabricated activity, memorizing the facts about Iwo and the operation—and the long quiet nights?"

> A mast sways dark against the Milky Way,
> Slowly it moves from port to starboard and then
>   back again.
> It mutely counts the swells beneath our bow,
> And marks the measure of the ocean's restlessness.
>
> The smoking lamp is out, along the deck,
> But every now and then a little glow defies authority
> And makes its statement.
> Soft voices rise around me in the night,
> With talk of girls, or home, or family:
> These sounds are half-thought phrases, telling half-
>   filled hopes within our half-lived lives.
> Will there be more?

"Then we got to Saipan," he recalled, "and what a surge of pride to see that great Pacific fleet going by single file, headed north. The power looked so impressive we actually tried to put ourselves in the enemy's shoes, imagining what he would think when those cruisers came up over the horizon. It was a jingo period," he acknowledged, "and I tried to express the hype and excitement with of all things, an Elizabethan sonnet:"

> The pallid fingers of another dawn
> Are beckoning our landing craft ashore.
> We breathe as if we've never lived before.
> The time for doubts and fears is nearly gone.
>
> The island writhes in hopeless agony,
> Explosive tears its evil soul away.
> This is the price all tainted soil must pay,
> In harboring the sons of infamy.
>
> No stubborn atoll ringed with sudden death
> Can halt the tide of our illimitable power.
> Nor can the jungle, with its poisoned breath,
> Delay the stroke of our appointed hour.
>
> With thoughts like these before the day's begun
> Who doubts that, even now, the battle's won?[29]

As twenty-two-year-old Lieutenant Barber Conable led his men ashore the next day, February 19, 1945, his father's sixty-third birthday, he could not help but be struck by the irony of the moment. "My God, I'm going to be killed on my father's birthday," he remembered saying to himself as he landed on the beach at Iwo Jima. But Conable was not even scratched—one of his many lucky breaks during the war—in what turned out to be one of the bloodiest battles of World War II, with over 4,000 Marines killed and another 16,000 wounded or missing in action.

There were, though, scary moments for Lieutenant Conable and the 150 or so men under his command as they landed in the afternoon of February 19. "My outfit went ashore right at the base of Mt. Suribachi, which commanded the whole island. I was the executive officer of the Battery, the man in charge of the guns, the big 105 mm howitzers. I was in charge of the emplacements. I took some risks to get in early at night, went up over the top of the island and went into the position that we were scheduled to go in with my guns.

"We didn't realize at that point that we were all ahead of the infantry," he said. "If there had been a banzai attack, as there were in all other island battles the first night, we would've all been killed. But General Kuribayashi, the Japanese commander, did not believe in banzai attacks; it wasted men. And the result is that I survived."[30]

There was not much time for journal entries over the next twenty-eight days it took the Marines to capture the island. As he looked back over his journal half a century later, Conable could find only four lines written then.

> More desolate the spot, now that the flower has grown,
> A savage irony that tender blossom brings.
> Beauty sprung up where jagged steel was sown,
> And loveliness among exploded things.

"Forgive the poetic license: Iwo was not the kind of place where a flower could grow, but I suppose I wanted to express the paradox of still finding things to admire in the midst of carnage," he told his fellow Marines.

On the way back to Hawaii after the battle was won, "when there was some time for grieving, or at least wondering about our dead friends," Conable wrote another poem in his journal, marked only with the initials "L. B.," which he read to the surviving Marines.

> They say that bullets don't discriminate.
> Well, he was the nicest one of all,
> The brightest, most responsive face in the whole squad
> His smile was never slow, or late,
> His friendship never known to pall.
> His faults were only known to God.

"Now, I've been wracking my brain to try to remember what I can about this 'L. B.,'" Conable told his audience. "I had better friends who were killed, and I actually didn't know that much about him except that I liked him. He was from Texas, I think. I suppose he was nineteen or twenty like the rest of us. Unlike most of us, he was married, probably to his childhood sweetheart. I hope she married someone else nice, later. We don't think much of nineteen or twenty-year-olds now, but then we knew they were old enough to die."[31]

"We were so badly shot up after Iwo that they sent us back to Hawaii to regroup. We were due to go to Amami, up the Ryukyu chain from Okinawa," Conable said, as he described how he spent the final months of the war, "but the division was so badly shot up they felt they couldn't do that. So they sent us back to Hawaii instead to pick up some replacements from the States."

President Truman's decision to drop atomic bombs on Hiroshima and Nagasaki on August 6 and 8, 1945, as the Fifth Marine Division was on its way to invade Japan, probably once again saved Barber Conable's life, as he discovered later in conversations with his brother John. "My brother was the G-4 [chief quartermaster] of the Eleventh Airborne Division at that point and he was helping plan the invasion of Japan, the so-called Olympic Operation," Conable recalled. "These divisions of Marines were going in abreast at Kagoshima, the southern point of Kyushu and we were going to take a coastal plain there surrounded by mountains. It would have been just like Anzio. I saw the area later and the mountains were full of dual purpose coastal defense guns. They would've just kicked the hell out of us. I wouldn't have survived it."[32]

For the rest of his life, Barber Conable felt fortunate to have survived Iwo Jima and the war in general. And with the luck of survival, Conable, like many others in what Tom Brokaw has called "the greatest generation," felt a special obligation to make a contribution to society.[33]

"You can all think of somebody fine who would be with us today," he told the Iwo Jima survivors on February 19, 1990, "if forty-five years ago he had stayed in his foxhole a minute longer, or moved his head eight inches to the right at that critical moment, or if the Japanese sniper's hand had wavered. That friend would have had the chance to be a good father, or have his own business, or serve on the school board. Our good fortune carries with it an obligation to do a little of his work as well as our own, to make the world a little better than it otherwise would be. . . .

"We're still not too old," Conable reassured himself and his aging audience, "to make a contribution to this world of ours. . . . Like you, I am proud to be a Marine who served at Iwo. . . . And like you, I shall probe the meaning of today's remembrance for the inspiration to make a contribution in the future beyond my own individual normal daily duty."[34]

At the war's end, the twenty-three-year-old Barber Conable Jr. was not yet the fully formed individual he was when he entered Congress in January 1965, but he was well on his way. As we look back on the early years of Conable's life—the years he spent growing up in Warsaw, his days as a student at Cornell, and his stint as a Marine in World War II—we can see that these years were profoundly important in the formation of his character and values he took with him into adulthood.

The first sixteen years of his life spent growing up in Warsaw gave Conable personal and intellectual security, political conservatism, and a deep attachment to family and the rural, small-town values of western New York. The three years he spent at Cornell, in the midst of World War II, stimulated and expanded his intellectual abilities, saw the budding of a young politician, and most importantly saw him slowly and painfully break from his father's pacifism and volunteer for service in World War II. And the four years he spent as a Marine in World War II not only tested his physical courage, but also strengthened his resolve to contribute to society and do something meaningful with his life.

Figure 1. Young Barber Conable, at the age of 8, with his older brother, John, standing to the right, and Bill seated next to him, around 1930. (Credit: Barber B. Conable Jr.)

Figure 2. Barber just before graduating from Cornell University at the age of 19, summer 1942. (Credit: Barber B. Conable Jr.)

Figure 3. Barber and his brother John on a brief leave home from World War II, fall 1943. (Credit: Barber B. Conable Jr.)

Figure 4. Following a long-standing tradition in the Conable household of reading to each other, Barber's father is pictured reading to his mother in their home in Warsaw, New York, in 1964. (Credit: Barber B. Conable Jr.)

Figure 5. New York State Senator Barber B. Conable Jr. announcing his support for New York Governor Nelson Rockefeller for the Republican presidential nomination in 1964. (Credit: Barber B. Conable Jr.)

Figure 6. Newly-elected Congressman Barber B. Conable Jr. and his wife, Charlotte, with their four children (from left to right, Anne, Jane, Emily, and Sam) shortly after their arrival in Washington in 1965. (Credit: Barber B. Conable Jr.)

Figure 7. Conable and his political mentor, House Minority Leader Gerald R. Ford, celebrate a happy moment together in 1965. (Credit: Barber B. Conable Jr.)

Figure 8. Conable at the dedication of the Iwo Jima memorial in Washington, D.C. on February 19, 1965. Former Marine Lieutenant Barber Conable reminisced with the division commander, General Keller Rocky, to the left, and on the right, General H. M. ("Howlin' Mad") Smith, the Task Force commander of the Battle of Iwo Jima. (Credit: Barber B. Conable Jr.)

Figure 9. As a member of the Science and Astronautics Committee, Congressman Conable meets with NASA scientist, Dr. Wernher von Braun, at the testing of the Apollo engine at the Space Center in Huntsville, Alabama, March 1965. (Credit: Box 80, Barber B. Conable Papers, #2794, Division of Rare and Manuscript Collections, Cornell University Library.)

Figure 10. Congressman Conable reviewing the results of constituent questionnaires, March 1966. (Credit: Barber B. Conable Jr.)

Figure 11. In one of his favorite constituent activities, Congressman Conable takes time out from his legislative business to pose with a group of Girl Scouts from Rochester on the Capitol steps, June 1966. (Credit: Box 80, Barber B. Conable Papers, #2794, Division of Rare and Manuscript Collections, Cornell University Library.)

Figure 12. Conable with two of his most important legislative mentors, Wilbur Mills, Democratic chairman of the Ways and Means Committee, and John Byrnes, ranking Republican member on the committee, shortly after Conable's appointment to the Ways and Means Committee in 1967. (Credit: Barber B. Conable Jr.)

Chapter 3

Becoming a Lawyer and Politician

After World War II, Conable returned to Cornell to carry on his family's tradition in the legal profession—something he had intended to do before the interruption of the war. His parents had always felt that education in law was the best education they could give their sons. Bill and John had both graduated from the Cornell Law School in 1940. Now, in September 1946, after spending the previous six months with the U.S. occupational forces in Japan, it was Conable's turn to take his place studying law at Cornell.[1]

The strong reputation Conable's brothers had set as students at Cornell, plus his own exemplary record as an undergraduate, stood him well in his application to law school. "I doubt that the third of the Conable brothers needs any introduction or recommendation from me," the assistant dean of the College of Arts and Sciences at Cornell wrote in recommending Conable for law school prior to his sudden and unexpected entry into the Marine Corps in 1942. "He is living up to the excellent reputation his brothers William and John made here, and in some ways he is outdistancing them, I think. Enough to say that he is a very able and a very admirable and likable young man."[2]

Conable's mentor, Frederick G. Marcham, also favorably compared him to his older brothers in recommending him to law school and commented on his ambition, already apparent as a young college student, to become a politician. "I write to recommend to you Mr. Barber B. Conable Jr. who is an applicant for admission to the Cornell Law School," Marcham wrote in his letter of recommendation. "I can do this in a few words, by saying that Mr. Conable is, in my opinion, the most promising person I have been asked to recommend to you for the past six years or so. He has the same background and qualities of personality as his brothers. He differs from them, perhaps, in having more drive and perhaps, in having more intellectual ability."[3]

Conable quickly discovered, though, that he was "not much interested in the intellectual problems of the law." He was too restless and wide ranging in his interests to be content with an exclusive focus on the law. His quick mind and writing abilities, which he had worked to perfection during college and off and on during the war, enabled him to become editor of the *Cornell Law Quarterly* his second year. And, without working too hard, he recalled, he graduated third in his class in 1948 and first among his forty-one classmates on the final comprehensive exam. But generally, Conable found law school to be too confining for the broad intellectual and political interests he had developed since college.

When Conable talked about his law school days, he was actually more interested in talking about where he lived and his diverse group of intellectual friends outside the school. "When I went back to law school," he recalled, still with the excitement he felt fifty years earlier, "I was accepted in the Telluride Association," an educational experiment founded in the early twentieth century by Lucien L. Nunn, the entrepreneurial and idealistic head of the Telluride Power Company, now the Utah Power and Light Company.[4]

The guiding principle of the Telluride Association was Nunn's "belief that practical work and accomplishment, as well as abstract study and intellectual growth, are important to the development of character and judgment" in young people. To further this belief, Nunn built the Telluride House on the Cornell University campus in 1910, just down the hill from the Law School, to allow twenty-four undergraduate and graduate students and a few faculty members to live there, with free room and board, in exchange for managing the practical affairs of the Telluride House. Nunn believed that this atmosphere would provide some of Cornell's most able students an ideal place to live and develop their intellectual abilities.

As Nunn envisioned the Telluride House, students would organize formal programs of public speaking and, with invited faculty members, conduct seminars on a wide variety of topics. Much of the Telluride House's "special import," though, Nunn believed, would occur "informally in daily life" as students from a wide range of disciplines would "share in an atmosphere of rigorous intellectual exchange and draw on each other for advice, support, and inspiration." Members of the Telluride House would also be given special opportunities to develop themselves in practical ways by handling the ongoing maintenance of the house through a committee system and weekly democratically organized house meetings.[5]

For almost a century, some of Cornell's brightest students have benefitted from the Telluride experience and gone on to distinguished careers in law, medicine, business, engineering, government service, and education. This was exactly the kind of intense intellectual and social atmosphere that Conable yearned to have as an undergraduate at Cornell before the war.

Conable had applied for membership in the Telluride House as an undergraduate, but he had not been successful in his application. "I had come very close," he recalled, "but I had not made it, and that bothered me." So he tried again. In 1946–47, during his first year in law school, he lived in the Telluride House as a non-member of the association. He reapplied for formal membership in the Telluride House for his second year. This time, he was successful.[6]

In his Telluride application, Conable explained how membership would offer him a much needed "escape from the confining influences of professional study" and improve his understanding of social issues. "I have always supported the organizations I considered worthy of my loyalty with all my energy, and I feel that Telluride is such an organization. My background is somewhat different from that of most of the present members of the branch, and anyone tending to broaden the cultural basis of a group contributes to its social impact."

Members of the Telluride House were impressed with his application this time. A brief, unsigned note attached to his application in the Telluride House provides a frank and succinct summary of how he was seen by other members of the house.

> Conable—friendly, benevolent, honest—most of all honest. Sense of responsibility, based on honesty. A positive, easily adjustable personality, with a streak of modesty. . . . With regard to problems of public life, Conable is rather on the side of cautious appreciation in a conservative mood, than on the side of criticism. Still, he listens carefully to arguments, and he does it in the most objective manner. He admits, quite often, a critical point of view, if presented fairly and quietly. . . . A former fraternity man, Conable is highly critical of social snobbishness. He certainly deserves attentive consideration.

In his application Conable also provided some insights about the broad intellectual interests that were shaping his thinking. Asked to list a few books he had read during the past year outside his course assignments, he listed a diverse assortment of historical and literary works, including Will Durant's *Our Oriental Heritage*, Aldous Huxley's *Brave New World*, Thomas Wolfe's *The Hills Beyond*, Jacques Boulenger's *The Seventeenth Century*, L. H. Myers's *The Pool of Vishnu*, and Ernest Hemingway's *A Farewell to Arms*.

On why he had decided to study law, Conable wrote: "I have chosen the law, both because of the lawyer's position in society, and because my inclinations and qualifications seem to indicate that I can make my best contributions in this field."

But as Conable made clear in his Telluride application, becoming a lawyer involved more than the formal practice of law. He saw law as an entry into public service, his real interest and motivation. "One of the fine things about the law," he wrote, "is that it not only is itself an instrument of public service, but also places a person in such a position in the community that other extra-legal forms of service are expected of him. I expect to show a contributive interest in these social activities which I think play a constructive part in the community."

"What have you gained, outside the financial return, from any practical work you have done?" the Telluride Association also asked prospective members. Conable replied that from farming with his father in Wyoming County, he had learned "patience and physical strength." And from the Marine Corps, he had learned "self-confidence in a greater degree and tolerance for organizational and individual stupidity."

The final vote on Conable's reapplication for membership in the Telluride House was seven to zero, with a short sentence attached to the application explaining the selection committee's unanimous endorsement of his application and anticipating the course his early legal career would take: "The committee was impressed with a maturity and stability of character, resulting probably from his war experience, and with the belief that he is probably the type who will be a leader in civic enterprises, while pursuing his work in law ably if not spectacularly."[7]

As a full-fledged member of the Telluride House in his second year of law school, Conable became a leader of the House, serving as president and organizing a series of lectures, presentations, and social events for the members. Recalling his time at the Telluride House, Conable noted, "This was a very salubrious environment for somebody studying in a confining discipline like law studies, because this was a very broadly based, highly intellectual group of young men. The average in the House was far above that required for Phi Beta Kappa. One of the guys living there was Dick Feynman, the great nuclear physicist who won the Nobel Prize in physics [in 1965]. People like that were associated with the Telluride House. It was a great experience and I had a good time there."[8]

Living at the Telluride House also put Conable back in touch with people on a close personal and social level, which had been so important to him as a boy. There were dances and social occasions in the evenings and public speaking once a week when someone in the House would give a talk. Conable thrived in this personal and intellectual mixture, having the chance to interact daily with some other brilliant students from diverse backgrounds.

Conable's friends at the Telluride House, such as Eric Pell, a graduate student in physics, were particularly impressed with his "remarkable memory," and "how he used to paste up a piece of poetry on the bathroom mirror in the morning to memorize while he shaved."

Pell also remembered Conable for his engaging personality. "Barber was one of the friendliest guys in the House," Pell recalled, "one of my particular friends, who invited me to go home with him once, where I met his father, a very gentlemanly man, and his mother, who was very warm, and we picked raspberries and went swimming in Silver Lake."[9]

So back at Cornell after the war, Conable prepared for dual careers in law and politics. For him, the two careers went hand-in-hand. His studies at the Cornell Law School equipped him with a first-rate formal education from which to launch a legal career. His extracurricular activities in the Telluride House expanded his knowledge of social and political issues and gave him a friendly, stimulating environment within which to further develop his intellectual and political skills.

Big City Lawyer

After graduating from law school in the summer of 1948, Conable accepted a position with the large, prestigious Buffalo law firm of Hodgson, Russ, Andrews, Woods, and Goodyear. It was the same law firm that had counted two United States presidents among its partners. Millard Fillmore had organized the firm in the early 1800s, and Grover Cleveland managed the firm during the Civil War.

Conable's law practice was abruptly interrupted, however, with the outbreak of the Korean War in 1950. His Marine Corps Reserve unit was called for active duty. Conable spent six months at Fort Sill, Oklahoma, preparing to become a Marine Corps intelligence officer. Then he spent a year as a legal and intelligence officer at Camp Lejeune, North Carolina.

Eighteen months later, in December 1951, Conable returned to Buffalo to resume his law practice with Hodgson, Russ, Andrews, Woods, and Goodyear. While successful in his work, with the potential of becoming a partner, Conable increasingly found he had serious questions about whether he wanted to stay with the firm. The partners wanted him to specialize in corporate tax law, and he "hated it." He also found he didn't like living in the city. "I was living in a crummy little rooming house. The law firm was full of a lot of Harvard people who looked down their noses at a Cornellian. And I hadn't learned a thing," he said.

So, early in 1952, unhappy with the big city life of Buffalo and the prospect of becoming a corporate tax lawyer, Conable decided to resign from his Buffalo law firm and set up a private law practice with his father. Conable Sr. had retired the previous year from his thirty-year judgeship of Wyoming County, and was succeeded by Barber's brother, John. To avoid a possible conflict of interest with the new Judge Conable, Barber and his father established their practice in the town of Batavia, the county seat of rural Genesee County, only twenty miles north of his family's home in Warsaw.

There Conable returned to the same small-town, rural environment that had shaped his growing up in the 1920s and 1930s.

Shortly before he left for Batavia, the State Supreme Court Judge, Carlton Fisher, invited Conable for lunch at the Buffalo Athletic Club. Judge Fisher, who was originally from Alexander, a small village of about four hundred people near Batavia, surprised Conable by saying, "Young man, I have my eye on you, and you have a bright future in politics. I've arranged with the district attorney for you to be the special prosecutor in the pin ball case that is coming up."

The case involved a state assemblyman and four Buffalo councilmen who had been accused of taking payoffs for the placement of pin ball machines around Buffalo, which were the subject of a lot of side gambling. Because of its notoriety, the trial would have given Conable great visibility in the city.

Without hesitation, Conable replied, "Judge Fisher, I'm sorry, but I've decided to go out to Batavia. I'm going out to the country. I don't like Buffalo, and I'm not going to stay here. So I can't accept your kind offer."

Totally exasperated, the judge yelled, "Oh don't do that, Barber. I was born in Alexander, and I couldn't wait to get out of there. You've got a bright future. If you go out there, you'll be buried. We'll never hear from you again. It's just a frightful little bucolic backwater." Undeterred, Conable packed his bags for Batavia.

Although he did not like Buffalo, it was a place of great importance for Conable. A few weeks before he left for Batavia in March 1952, he met a young, attractive graduate of Cornell, Charlotte Williams (nicknamed "Tinker" by her parents for her love of tinker toys as a child), who in a few short months would become his wife. "When I got back from the Korean War," Conable recalled, "I was in the Cornell Club in Buffalo. They had a glee club concert. I was put in charge of tickets, and she was one of my ticket salesmen." The only child of a disabled war veteran, whose mother worked as a secretary with the local Red Cross, Charlotte had graduated from Cornell in 1951 with a degree in home economics. After graduation she took a job in Buffalo as the director of Christian Education at the Holy Trinity Lutheran Church. A college politician like Barber, Charlotte had served as president of her junior and senior classes at Cornell and president of her sorority. Conable, now thirty years old and interested in marriage, took an instant liking to this bright young woman seven years his junior, who shared many of his social and political interests. At first Charlotte resisted Barber's overtures, but finally after three tries Conable succeeded in getting a date with her. He continued to drive to Buffalo to see Charlotte after moving to Batavia. They became engaged in May and married in Buffalo on September 13, 1952.[10]

Return to Small Town Life and Politics

In Batavia, Conable lived in "a little rooming house and boy did I starve," he recalled. "I did collection work—collecting on bad debts—and everything else to try to make a living while Dad and I set up the business."

Conable's legal experience with the Buffalo law firm had not prepared him for the kind of work he would have to do as a small-town, country lawyer. "When I came down here," he said, "I had never closed a real estate deal. I'd never drawn a will. That's one reason I wanted my father around, to keep an eye on me, because he was a very bright lawyer . . . a very successful lawyer before he got ulcers and had to go on the bench as a kind of refuge."

One of Conable's first acquaintances in Batavia was Karl Buchholtz, owner of the Genesee Hardware Company, just down the street from the new Conable law office. Trying to economize, the Conables had rented a poorly maintained office for fifty-five dollars a month. Conable took on the task of fixing up his new location, knowing for the price he was paying he could expect little help from the landlord.

In search of a paintbrush, hammer, and nails, Conable went three doors down to the Genesee Hardware Company. As he walked in, the man behind the counter looked at him and turned white, saying "My God, you must be related to George Gouinlock."

"Well, as a matter of fact I am. What's it to you?" Conable replied. (Gouinlock was Conable's first cousin killed on the Normandy beachhead at Omaha Beach during World War II.)

"He was my best friend," the man said. "What are you doing here in Batavia?"

To which Conable said, "I'm going to open a law office down the street, three doors down."

"You'll be my lawyer," came the reply.

"Well, that's very nice," said Conable. "Excuse me, what's your name?"

"Buchholtz, Karl Buchholtz," he said.

Buchholtz, fifteen years older than Conable and a native of Genesee county with many business and social connections in the community, struck up a fast friendship with Conable that lasted half a century. Soon they were meeting with another merchant friend, Al Walkley, an insurance man, for a coffee break on Saturday mornings. As Buchholtz tells the story, "Barber would walk up the street Saturday mornings to Al's insurance office, whistle at the foot of the stairs for Al to come down from his upstairs office, and they'd go get me, and we'd all go to the little restaurant next door for a coffee. None of us had any money," Buchholtz recalled, "and we'd flip dimes to see who would buy for the others."[11]

This threesome of Buchholtz, Conable, and Walkley enjoyed their social get-togethers so much that they soon expanded their meetings into more organizational get-togethers. They invited a dozen or so other merchants and civic leaders in the community—a local doctor, an artist, the local YMCA director, a bank president, a farmer, a minister, a local judge, and several other community-minded citizens—to join them for coffee and donuts every Saturday morning to catch up on the local gossip and community developments. They called themselves the Saturday Morning Club and agreed to keep their Saturday morning discussions private. At first they met at the local restaurant and later they moved to a little donut shop next door. Eventually they settled on the back room of Buchholtz's hardware store for their regular meetings.

These weekly meetings were important to Conable. The Saturday Morning Club provided him a small, close-knit group of friends from diverse professional backgrounds with whom he could associate.

Buchholtz's friendship was critical to Conable's success in his new job and life. He also helped Conable become a member of the Batavia Rotary Club, an important organization for a young lawyer looking for clients and contacts in Batavia. Within three months of their first meeting, Conable recalled, Buchholtz "rammed me into the Rotary Club of Batavia over the dead bodies of a lot of well-established lawyers who wanted to be in the Rotary Club. And almost all my first clients came from the Rotary Club."

Being a small-town lawyer, which Conable described as a "sociological experience," appealed to his generalist orientation and provided him valuable preparation for his career in Congress. As he later explained: "A country lawyer takes on whatever business walks in. He's not an expert on anything. Country lawyers are very well trained to become congressmen, because they have to shift gears constantly. They have to skate across the surface of a wide range of law with a surface credibility. They have to live in a close society with their constituents. They represent people and not corporations.

"But the most important thing about it," he said, "was that it put me in close contact with people instead of sitting at a desk somewhere writing memoranda and filing papers and doing things of that sort. So I never regretted being a country lawyer. I thought it was a much more interesting experience and of course I wound up a generalist and not a specialist. That's what representatives have to be too."

His new life was not worry free, however, as he was concerned about having enough money to live on. He and his father agreed that Barber should take three-fourths of the profits and his father, who had a pension from his judgeship, would take one-fourth. At first, it seemed difficult to imagine how he would get by.

As he had for so many years while they were milking the cows together back in Warsaw, Conable's father offered him advice on how to get ahead in Batavia. "Bunt," he said, "You've got to put a lot into the community if you're going to take a lot out of it."

So Conable threw himself whole-heartedly into Batavia's community affairs, running three major fund drives in the first six months he was there. By the end of his first year in Batavia, in December 1952, he also became involved in local Republican Party politics.

He had been married for three months when a fellow met him on the street and said, "Are you a Republican?"

"Of course I am," Conable replied. "My whole family is."

"I thought so," exclaimed the man. "I've been a committeeman here for a long time, and I'm really fed up with it. Would you like to be a committeeman?"

"Well, I'd have to get elected," Conable responded.

"Nobody wants to be a committeeman around here. If you want to be a committeeman, you can be one," assured the fellow Republican.

About six months later, in the summer of 1953, the chairman of the Republican Committee in Batavia resigned, creating an opportunity for Conable to become more deeply involved in local Republican politics. "Nobody wanted the job," he recalled.

> And so I said I'd take it. And I worked out a deal with the Democratic leader, a guy by the name of Joe Ryan, to overhaul city government. We had a weak mayor form of government, and we set up a charter commission and agreed that each of us would support the results of the charter commission's work. They came up with a strong city administrator form of government.

> Then I went around with the Democratic chairman,
> and we sold the commission's work as a kind of constitu-
> tional convention in the city of Batavia and supported the
> new charter. And in the process, I got the city, which had
> a Democratic mayor forever and a Democratic council,
> solidly Republican.

In the six years Conable served as a Batavia Republican committeeman from 1953 to 1959, he recalled with some amusement
later, "I never got more than seven votes, because nobody ever ran
against me. Nobody ever ran against anybody who was a committeeman, and nobody would vote in the election. Anybody with a
large family could have knocked me off as Republican city chairman. And they didn't. In other words, I could do what I damn
pleased. I didn't feel that it was a big deal, and I didn't care about
offending people. So I took the job seriously and worked hard at it."

His political and civic involvement at the local level resulted in
Conable being chosen, along with Brooklyn Dodgers baseball star,
Jackie Robinson (the first African-American to play major league
baseball), as one of the five "outstanding young men" in New York
by the Junior Chamber of Commerce in 1953. "I was the one
that nobody knew," Conable recalled, "and I don't know why I got
chosen for that, but somehow, because I had an impressive list of
community activities, I was chosen."[12]

A few weeks later Conable and the four other outstanding
young men of New York state were honored at a Junior Chamber of
Commerce awards dinner in Buffalo. The speaker that evening,
Walter Mahoney, the Republican Senate majority leader from Buffalo
and a man known throughout the state for his oratory skills, made
a speech that greatly impressed Conable. "All those community
activities are fine and great public service," Conable remembered
Mahoney telling them, "but what we really need is good people in
politics"—words that would eventually inspire Conable to run for
the New York Senate in 1962.[13]

Conable continued his community activities and partisan
responsibilities as chairman of the Batavia Republican Committee
until 1959, when he and his wife made an important family decision
that seemed at the time to lessen the possibility of a future in
politics. Conable resigned from the chairmanship of the Batavia
Republican Committee. He and Charlotte and their three small
children moved to the small village of Alexander near Batavia.[14]
They bought a restored early nineteenth-century farmhouse in the
middle of the village. There the Conables created a new home,
removed from the social and political life of Batavia which had been

such an important part of their early marriage. Conable continued to commute back and forth to his law office with his father in Batavia, and he still met with "the boys" at the Genesee Hardware Store every Saturday morning for coffee and donuts. But at the time Conable remembered thinking that his move to Alexander would probably be the end of his career in politics, as Judge Carlton Fisher had warned him before he left Buffalo.

But word of Conable's political skills as a party organizer had traveled with him from Batavia to Alexander. Shortly after he arrived in Alexander, Conable recalled, there was a vacancy on the Genesee County Republican Committee, and somebody said, "You're the guy whose been working in Batavia for the Republican Party, aren't you?"

"Yeah," Conable replied.

"Would you like to be a committeeman here?" the man asked.

"It was a crazy kind of thing," Conable remembered. But he quickly threw himself into the politics of the Genesee County Republican Committee. The following year he was appointed by the county chairman, Jim Beach, a businessman in Corfu, to head the Republican campaign in Genesee County for the 1960 presidential election. That year, Conable helped the Republican presidential nominee, Richard Nixon, carry Genesee County with a 59 percent majority over the Democrat, John F. Kennedy. Through his organizational skills, Conable was also instrumental in securing the reelection of a number of local Republican candidates, including the incumbent state senator, Austin Erwin, the powerful chairman of the Senate Finance Committee.[15]

Deciding to Run for the State Senate

Though Conable had helped reelect Austin Erwin to the New York Senate in 1960, he came to have serious reservations about Erwin's qualifications and integrity as a public servant. This opened the door for Conable's own bid to replace Erwin in the state Senate in 1962. From neighboring Livingston County, Erwin, a man now in his mid-seventies, had represented this region of western New York in the Senate since 1946. In 1954, as the personal choice of the Republican governor, Thomas E. Dewey, Erwin had been named chairman of the Senate Finance Committee, regarded by most observers as the most powerful committee in either house of the legislature. Erwin was very popular with western New York constituents and had easily won reelection in each succeeding election.[16]

But Austin Erwin was not popular with Barber Conable and some of the younger members of the Genesee County Republican Party, who wanted to broaden and democratize participation within the party. While working in the Republican election campaign for Genesee County in 1960, Conable and his younger colleagues had come to detest Austin Erwin and saw him as an anathema to the kind of above-board Republican party they wanted to build for the future.

Conable objected specifically to the way Senator Erwin used his public office as chairman of the Senate Finance Committee to advance his own financial position and reputation as a lawyer. "I was a lawyer," Conable said, "and one thing that very much offended me was the generally known practice Austin Erwin had of conducting most of his law practice in the Court of Claims. Then, using his position as chairman of the Senate Finance Committee," Conable explained, "he would gain big settlements from the state departments that were targets of lawsuits. He also greatly increased the pay of Court of Claims judges and had a special relationship with them so that he got big settlements from the state.

"Here was a man, a legislator, working for the state," Conable said, "yet, as a lawyer, he was suing the state and getting big settlements from them on a contingency fee arrangement. So the bigger the settlement, the more he got. He got a third of whatever settlement he got. People from all over the state were bringing claims against the state to him, knowing that the chairman of the Senate Finance Committee, who controlled the budgets for the state departments, was going to be their lawyer, advising them about how to get claims from the state.

"Now, I thought that was plain dishonest."

Conable also strongly objected to the political favoritism and nepotism Erwin used to arrange the appointment of personal friends and his own son to important positions in the New York state government. "For instance," Conable recalled, "Erwin's law partner was Marc Welch. Marc Welch was the chief counsel to the majority leader of the Senate. The chairman of the Republican Party in Wyoming County [one of the counties in Erwin's five-county senatorial district and the county where Conable himself had been born in 1922] was Bob Bentley. Bob Bentley was the counsel for the Senate Finance Committee.

"Then, of course, Erwin got [Governor Nelson] Rockefeller, who needed his support in the Senate, to appoint his son Livingston County Judge to fill the vacancy after Judge [George D.] Newton suddenly resigned. And that was after the Republican County

Committee over there [in Livingston County] had voted by a wide margin against recommending him to the governor. But still," Conable recalled, "Erwin pulled strings with the governor and got Austin Jr. appointed. That was pretty arrogant."

Conable's criticism of Erwin reached a breaking point in early 1962, when Jim Beach, the Genesee County Republican chairman, asked him once again to head the Republican campaign efforts in Genesee County for the forthcoming November elections. "I'm not going to do it," Conable remembered telling a shocked Beach, "if that old bastard [Austin Erwin] is on the ticket. I have too much self-respect to be in a position to support somebody like that, and the party ought to be able to find somebody else."

Word of Conable's conflict with party chairman Jim Beach over the reelection of Austin Erwin spread quickly throughout the city of Batavia. Within a few days of Conable's conversation with Beach, the editor of the local Batavia newspaper, John Connor, came to see Conable and said: "I hear you and Jim have had a real fight over Austin Erwin. Well, I want to tell you, I agree with you. Why don't you run for the state Senate yourself?"

"Me run for the state Senate?" Conable replied. "I've never even been to Albany."

"Well," Connor said, "I just want to tell you, if you run for the state Senate, we'd support you in our paper."

"Well, that's very interesting. I'll think about that," Conable said.

Conable gathered his friends—young Republicans who, along with Conable, had been challenging Beach's "one man dictatorship" of the party—and asked them: "What shall I do? John Connor said I should run for state Senate."

Conable's colleagues, aware of the difficulties of challenging Erwin for the party nomination, advised him to go around and talk to some of the other four county leaders and see what they said.

"Well, I went around and unanimously," Conable recalled, "they'd say: 'Barb, come on. Erwin's a powerful man. Don't get into that. Don't cause problems. Go home and take a cold shower.'"

One day when Conable returned to his office after traveling around to see other county leaders, there was a phone call from Jim Beach. He said, "Barber, I'm over at the County Building [just across the street from Conable's law office]. Would you come over and see me?

"I understand you're considering running against Austin Erwin for the state Senate," Beach said when Conable arrived at the County Building a few minutes later.

"I'm thinking about it, Jim. Why?" Conable asked.

"Well, I've heard about this," Beach replied. "I just called Austin Erwin, and he's got some things he wants to resolve down at the state Senate. If you'll support him this year and be our campaign chairman, he'll support you for the state Senate two years from now."

"Well, that's interesting," Conable responded. "I'm surprised, but I'll consider it."

Conable went back to his friends and had another meeting. "Now look," he said, "I've got some bargaining power. I don't want to run for the state Senate, but suppose we use the bargaining power to get Jim Beach to change the structure of the Republican County Committee, so we'll have a real functioning party government here instead of one man deciding everything?"

And Conable's friends all responded: "Barber, if they're scared of you, they're scared of you for a reason. You should run for the state Senate. That's the way to get these guys in trouble, and then really bring about some real changes."

Conable and his friends "talked about that pretty late one night" and finally Conable decided: "Well, what have we got to lose? I don't care if I'm a state Senator or not, and maybe we can rock the boat in some constructive way."

Thus, Barber Conable, the conservative politician, known through his later legislative career as a faithful party man, ironically began his career as a maverick, challenging one of the most powerful men in the Republican establishment, not so much with the expectation of winning as with the hope of shaking up the status quo.

The idea that the New York Senate Republican majority leader, Walter Mahoney, had first planted in Conable's mind at the 1954 Junior Chamber of Commerce award dinner—the idea, the exciting possibility that "what we need are some good men in politics"— had found the opportunity for practical expression. Conable, buttressed by the moral and political support of his young Republican friends in Batavia, set out to unseat the powerful chairman of the Senate Finance Committee, Austin Erwin.[17]

Moving swiftly to mount the party support he would need to challenge Erwin in the Republican primary in September, Conable sent a letter on April 16 to four hundred Republican committeemen in the five-county senatorial district announcing his candidacy and telling them that he would personally ask for their support. Conable made a pledge, "if elected, not to use my public position for private gain. This means," Conable said, in an unmistakable reference to Austin Erwin's habit of practicing law before the New York Court of Claims, "that I will not serve as a lawyer for private individuals in matters involving the public interest, as in law suits where the state is a party." And in a jab at Erwin's habit of rewarding his friends and family with political positions, Conable promised: "I will do everything in my power to advance the Republican Party on all levels, regardless of my personal interests or the interests of my relatives."

Ideologically, there was not much difference between Conable and Erwin. Both were fiscal conservatives and both were decentralists in the typical western New York tradition, favoring, as Conable said in announcing his candidacy, policies which encourage "responsibility in our localities, rather than vesting additional power in our distant seats of government."[18]

Conable's campaign received mixed reactions from the press and local Republicans. "I remember going around to the *Buffalo News* and the Rochester papers, and they threw me out," Conable recalled. "What kind of brass do you have, young man, thinking you can run against a man like Austin Erwin? Why he's one of the most powerful men in the state! Look at the Erwin road program, look at all these things, and who are you? You ever run for office before? 'No sir, no sir.' Ever been to Albany? 'No, never been to Albany.'"

As he campaigned throughout his rural district, Conable was received more positively. Many of these folks had never been to Albany either. He had a particularly positive response in nearby Wyoming County, where his brother John continued to serve as county judge. He also counted on the support of his many friends and acquaintances in Batavia and throughout Genesee County.

As support for Conable's candidacy mounted, Senator Erwin unexpectedly began to reconsider his own reelection bid.[19] Five weeks after Conable entered the race, Austin Erwin announced that, after nineteen years in the New York Senate and fifty-two years in public office, he would retire from public life and not seek reelection to the Senate. A local newspaper reported that Erwin was under "pressure from members of his family to give up the challenging duties of the state Senate" and that the senator himself wanted "to devote full time to his Geneseo law practice." Importantly, the paper said Senator Erwin was also "genuinely concerned that the appearance of two Erwin names on the ballot [where his son, Austin, Jr. was seeking the Republican nomination for Livingston County judge] could hurt his son's chance for nomination and election to a full-term as Livingston County judge."[20]

With Austin Erwin out of the race, Conable became the odds-on favorite to win the Republican nomination and succeed Erwin in the New York Senate. Livingston County Republicans, caught off guard by Erwin's sudden retirement, spent the better part of the next three weeks finding an acceptable replacement for Erwin from their county. After some initial uncertainty, they finally settled on the popular, thirty-one-year-old sheriff of Livingston County, Jim Emery, as their nominee. With the "strong support" of Erwin himself, Jim Emery immediately became the old-guard Republican establishment's choice.[21]

Determined to have Sheriff Emery and not Barber Conable succeed him, Erwin arranged for his close friend and law partner, Marc Welch, to be Emery's campaign manager. "The next day," Conable said, as he recalled the deal Emery had made to ensure Erwin's endorsement, "Jim announced his support of Austin Erwin Jr. for county judge, shifting from opposing Austin Jr. to support him. And concurrently," Conable remembered, "all the sheriff's departments announced for Jim because he was sheriff and they thought there were too many lawyers in the legislature.

"And I knew right away," Conable said, "that I had an interesting race on. All that long hot summer, every time there was a dog fight, Jim Emery and I were there in the area, passing out cards. My wife [who, ironically, was Emery's third cousin] was my campaign manager, and she stayed home with our four small children, helped plan the campaign, and talked on the phone, while I ran my legs off."[22]

Through his personal contacts and extensive campaigning, Conable received the party endorsements of three of the five counties in the district: Genesee County, where he lived and practiced law, Wyoming County, where he was born, and Orleans County to the north on Lake Ontario. With the strong support of the retiring Senator Austin Erwin, Sheriff Emery received the endorsement of Livingston County, his home county and the one with the largest number of registered Republicans, slightly more than the number of Republicans in Genesee County. Eugene Forhan, the mayor of Wellsville, received the endorsement of his native Allegheny County.[23]

Forhan's support was confined mainly to Allegheny County. But Conable and Emery had substantial support throughout the district, and both of these young, ambitious politicians, criss-crossed the district in the closing days of the campaign searching for the votes they needed to win.[24] With the outcome of the election in doubt, the day before the election the Batavia *Daily News* predicted a "very close contest between Mr. Conable and Sheriff Emery" and urged a big voter turnout in Genesee County to assure a Conable victory. "The onus . . . is on Genesee County," the paper warned on election eve, as it encouraged all Republicans in the county to vote for Conable the next day. "They must turn out a tremendous advantage for Mr. Conable if they want to assure Genesee having the distinction of being the home of the district's state senator."[25]

The week before the election, Conable shrewdly sent out letters to all of the 50,247 registered Republicans in his district in what *The Daily News* called "one of the largest mailings of its type ever undertaken." On election eve, 175 Genesee County Republican women organized a telephone campaign to get out the vote in Genesee County. Telephone committees were also set up in Wyoming and Orleans counties where Conable had been endorsed.

Although Conable deplored Austin Erwin and looked askance at Emery's political deal to gain Erwin's support, he never criticized or personally attacked Emery. Instead, beginning a practice he would employ throughout his legislative career, he focused on his own qualifications for office.

"I have made no promises and have no commitments," Conable said on election eve. "I have based my campaign on my qualifications and have carried my campaign to every part of the district," he said. And acknowledging the importance of widespread voter participation for a successful outcome, he appealed "for a large voter turnout everywhere in order that a majority of those eligible may decide the outcome."[26]

The voting results surprised nearly everyone. Rather than the close contest that most had expected, Conable easily defeated his opponents. "Riding the crest of a fantastic show of strength in his home county, Barber B. Conable Jr. of Alexander swept to the Republican nomination in the 53rd Senatorial District," the jubilant Batavia *Daily News* reported the next day. "In a vote-getting display that left veteran political observers gasping," the paper said, "Conable crushed three opponents and turned what had been a close contest into a shambles." Among the 44 percent of registered Republicans who voted, Conable received 54 percent of the primary votes, nearly twice as many as his nearest competitor.[27]

Recognizing those who had worked on his behalf, Conable expressed his appreciation to all who campaigned and voted for him. He expressed special thanks to his campaign advisory committee and to the dozens of people who had telephoned voters on election eve. The circumstances of the election, forcing a powerful Republican incumbent from the race and defeating his hand-picked successor, without making any commitments or promises to individuals or special interests, were particularly important to Conable. As he had learned from his father, this was the way elections should be fought. "I am happy to be in a position where I can be completely independent," he said after the election. "But I am also pleased to be in the Republican line-up, because the Republican Party stands for what I stand for." Like his father, Conable would seek to balance his political independence with party loyalty.[28]

With his victory in the Republican primary in the predominantly Republican Fifty-Third District, Conable's election to the New York Senate was virtually guaranteed in the November general election. "Although there was a good Democrat nominated against me," Conable recalled, "he tested the water and found so much support for me among Democrats that he didn't even try."[29]

As a result, four days after his fortieth birthday, Barber Conable won the general election to the New York Senate by the largest margin of any contested Senate election in the state that year. In a few short weeks, he would become the first New York state senator elected from Genesee County since 1916.[30]

Chapter 4

Mr. Conable Goes to Albany

Arriving in Albany as a state senator in January 1963—in a scene reminiscent of Frank Capra's classic 1939 film *Mr. Smith Goes to Washington*—the newly elected Senator Conable found the "Albany scene a confusing one for a newcomer." But he was determined, as he wrote a friend back home, "to give the job all I've got."[1]

On seeing the chamber of the New York Senate for the first time, an exuberant Barber Conable asked the security guard stationed outside the door: "Is this the Senate chamber?"

"Yeah," the guard replied.

"Well, do you mind if I look around? I'm a senator," Conable said.

"The guy thought it was the most hilarious thing he'd ever heard of," Conable recalled, laughing at his own naiveté years later.

Anxious to get off to a good start with the leader of the Republican Party in the Senate and the man who had first inspired him to run for public office back in 1954, Conable went down the hall to reacquaint himself with the majority leader of the Senate, Walter Mahoney from Buffalo.

"Senator," Conable explained as he entered Mahoney's large office in the state Capitol, "you may not remember, but you spoke at the Junior Chamber of Commerce dinner in Buffalo back in '54 and said, 'We need good people in politics.' Well, here I am," Conable said as he presented himself to his leader.

A bit startled, Conable recalled, Mahoney, a close friend of the ousted Austin Erwin and one of the most powerful men in Albany, "cleared his throat and backed up with his cigar and let me know that there was more to being a state senator than just getting a few more votes than the other guy. So, I started off under rather bad circumstances."

Conable's bumpy introduction into the ways of the New York Senate continued with his maiden speech on the Senate floor a month later. In a test of the new senator's legislative skills and party loyalty, Majority Leader Mahoney assigned Conable responsibility for opposing a Democratic motion to discharge from the Republican-controlled Judiciary Committee a bill which would have made "permanent personal registration" mandatory for all voters throughout New York. Long advocated by the New York League of Women Voters as an effective way to increase voter participation in the state, the Democratic bill would have eliminated the legal requirement that some counties still maintained for the permanent residents of communities to re-register to vote between elections. Permanent personal registration (known as PPR) has since been adopted for all of New York. But at the time of this debate in the state Senate in 1963, each county in New York had the option of retaining the old system. As of February 1963, forty-five of New York's sixty-two counties had permanent personal registration systems. But the other seventeen counties, mostly in the rural, small town Republican regions of western New York, had retained the old system. The Senate Republican leadership, led by Majority Leader Mahoney, was opposed to mandating permanent personal registration for all the counties in the state and asked Conable to lead the Republican opposition to the Democratic proposal for PPR on the floor of the Senate.

"Senator Barber B. Conable, Jr. isn't going to win any bouquets from the League of Women Voters for a while," a Rochester newspaper reported. "As three League ladies glowered at him from the first row of the gallery, Conable argued that PPR should be a matter of local option."[2]

"No Republican," Conable asserted during the floor debate, "opposes, in principle, permanent personal registration or any other method extending the franchise to the greatest number of people at the most reasonable cost." But he pointed out to his colleagues that "all of the cities, villages and counties [which have adopted PPR] have done so at local option, [which] is the way it should be. Decisions such as this, concerning, as they do, a right that is at the heart of our democratic system, should be kept as close to the people as possible."[3]

"I'm surprised that a senator from the Bronx [the liberal Abraham Bernstein who was leading the Democratic fight for a mandatory, state-wide PPR law] would tell us how to run an election in western New York." Conable added.

The Republican Senate rejected Bernstein's motion in a straight party vote. But in the process, the *Rochester Times-Union* observed, the freshman senator from western New York "learned something about the legislative process."

"I'm new here," an inexperienced Barber Conable told Bernstein during the floor debate on the Democratic motion to discharge the PPR bill from the Judiciary Committee. "What's your reason for making this motion at this particular time?" Conable asked, suggesting that the Democrats hoped to increase their state-wide voter registration through adopting a mandatory permanent personal registration law for the state.

Veteran Senator Edward J. Speno from Long Island, who was occupying the majority leader's chair during the floor debate on the Democratic motion, interrupted with some advice for the new senator from Genesee County. "I've learned never to ask [the partisan] reasons for legislation," Speno admonished Conable. "I suggest that you proceed to another aspect of the argument."[4]

Though Conable had some awkward moments in dealing with his party's leadership during his early days in the state Senate, he was generally well liked by his colleagues. "I liked and admired Barber from the first day I met him," Robert McEwen, a four-term Republican senator from Ogdensburg, recalled from first meeting Conable in January 1963. "He had sort of a country-boy image which fooled a few people at first. He never took himself seriously. He said he had no background for the Senate and didn't know how he was going to handle the job. But people could see he was very bright. Like all the Conables, his brains are bowed out, he's so smart.

"Of course, Barber came into the Senate with a good deal of attention for knocking off Austin Erwin, a real power, a real autocrat, a fixture in the Senate," McEwen added. "People were interested in who is this guy Conable who knocked off Austin Erwin."[5]

McEwen quickly discovered, as others would, and as Conable's constituents already knew, that he made up with hard work and sheer force of intellect what he lacked in experience. He may have seemed like "a country boy" to some, and indeed often referred to himself as "just a country boy from western New York," but beneath his folksy, down-to-earth image and self-depreciating humor was a piercing intellect and a driving ambition to make something of his life and contribute to the public affairs of his state.

Communicating with Constituents

As a new senator, Conable not only had to learn to deal with his colleagues in the legislature, but if he was to stay in the Senate, he knew he would also have to sustain and cultivate the good relationships he had begun to develop with his constituents during the campaign.

To facilitate relations with his constituents, Conable decided early in his senatorial term to write a weekly newspaper column for the newspapers in his district, describing the activities of the state legislature and what he was doing to represent his constituents in Albany. Rather than delegating the news column to his legislative assistant, Tom Benton, his old friend from home and former Associated Press reporter who could have easily written these columns, Conable decided to write them himself.

"The basic factor in representative government is communication between a legislator and the people he represents," Conable wrote in his first "Albany Report" on January 17, 1963. "This is the reason for this column. I hope in succeeding weeks to be able to tell you what is going on in Albany, how it affects us in our district, and how I am reacting as your representative in making your point of view known in our state government."[6]

From the outset, Conable adopted a very distinctive pedagogical style in these newsletters, interweaving lessons on the legislative process with a discussion of his own activities in Albany. A natural born teacher and story teller, Conable was interested in explaining how the system worked, in being his constituents' educator on the inner workings of the system, as well as recounting his own legislative activities.

In his second "Albany Report" from January 24, 1963, for instance, the new senator showed a particular fascination with the large number of bills that were introduced in the state legislature each year. Conable combined an informative essay on bill introduction and the legislative process with an opportunity to explain the importance of his own committee assignments for the people in his district.

"Every year we are treated to the news photograph of a pretty girl sitting on top of a mountain of bills introduced in the legislature," Conable began. "This year's mountain will include 10,000 or more, although few more than a thousand will become law.

"The obvious question for most of us," he said, "is how all these bills can be considered and acted upon in a legislative session that lasts only three months. The answer is the committee system."

Senator Conable explained to his constituents, much as a professor would explain to his students, how the system worked. "The committee system is at the heart of our legislative process, I am most pleased with my four committee assignments—Agriculture, Banking, Penal Institutions, and Public Health. Each one is of real interest to our district or fits in with my own experience."[7]

Three months into his term as a state senator, Conable "pause[d] for a moment" in his "Albany Report" to give his constituents some of his "impressions as a new legislator . . . on the way things are in Albany.

"First of all, I'd like to say that legislation is a very human process. The personalities of my colleagues affect what they are doing. There is nothing impersonal or inexorable about the making of laws, as you might imagine if you didn't see the interplay of personalities." Seeing this interplay of personalities up close affirmed for Conable the importance of individual personalities and the human dimension of the legislative process. This important lesson stayed with Conable throughout his legislative career and he repeatedly communicated it to his constituents.

"Next," Conable said, "I don't believe this political life has affected my own personality much. When I was elected, people told me, 'Oh, after you've been down there awhile, you'll be like all the rest of them.' Well, everyone of 'them' is different." Reflecting on his own experience in local government, he said he didn't see "any essential difference between the law-making process in Albany and the same process on the Board of Supervisors or the Town Board."

Wanting and perhaps finding a reason to believe he could work within the system and still be his own man, Conable noted that the political pressures from lobbyists and party leaders, both in Albany and at home, were more subtle and indirect than usually imagined. "Nobody, I must say, has twisted my arm to get me to follow some particular course. The Senate leadership, is very restrained about the suggestions it makes to rank-and-file members." And he noted "there is virtually no contact between the governor and the legislators except on a social basis. The governor's attitudes and the feelings of the legislators are exchanged through consultation between the governor and the legislative leaders. Party leaders in our home counties too have been notably restrained about urging any particular view on my part.

"The biggest problem I have," Conable continued, "is time. I am determined to answer as many of the personal letters I receive as possible, and believe me, the volume is tremendous. It is a really time-consuming job, too, to read all bills that come before the Senate and to be prepared to vote on them intelligently."

Conable also reported to his constituents on "the many social events in the evening, given by individuals or by state organizations of one sort or another. I am trying to attend all I can," he said, "so I will have more idea of the relative importance of each group."[8]

As Conable made his way through the social events in the evenings, Tom Benton recalled that Conable was "a little leery and socially naive" at these gatherings. "My job during those events," Benton remembered with a chuckle, "was to go over and get a ginger ale for him, so he could hold it in his hand, and nobody would come over and push drinks on him."[9]

"All of these affairs," Conable explained to his constituents, "are sponsored by somebody with an ax to grind. But I must say that lobbyists for special interests are not as pesky as I thought they might be. I see nothing wrong with listening to their views. Studying all sides of an issue is the only way to learn its true value. Besides, in a very real way everyone who writes his legislator is a lobbyist, if only for his own personal viewpoint. And that's the way it should be."[10]

As a reflective, philosophically oriented politician, Conable also used his "Albany Report" to reflect on the practical implications of his own political philosophy. "A person cannot conscientiously serve in the legislature for long," he wrote his constituents on March 21, 1963, "without wondering where his political philosophy is taking him. Many legislators react to pressures on specific bills. But unless they have some philosophy of government to guide them, they are likely to be pulled many different ways, falling into inconsistencies and contributing more to confusion than to a rational social pattern.

"Several conclusions have been impressed upon me by the impact of office. I believe these fit into a pattern which may eventually influence . . . voters to identify themselves with me, or to oppose me.

"First," as a rural, western New York conservative, where the suspicion of concentrated power runs deep, "I expect generally to encourage diffusion of power, whether it is the power of big labor or big government. Power is destructive of freedom. The essence of our Constitution is to minimize the concentration of governmental power by checks and balances within the framework of the federal system. Big government is the biggest threat to our freedom today."

Reflecting a value first instilled in him by his civic-minded father, Conable then said, "I expect to represent all the people in our district, not just those who are organized." Discovering first-hand the pressure group bias of American politics from the evenings he spent with lobbyists in Albany, the new senator was "dismayed to find how many organizations exist solely for the purpose of getting something for their members, whether it is costly to their neighbors or not. But nobody tries to get anything for the little man," Conable lamented, "particularly the little businessman or the little taxpayer, and because he is not organized, his interests are frequently not represented."

Finally, Conable reiterated his Jeffersonian commitment to strong local government, a belief that he also acquired from his father and from growing up in a rural, small-town culture that valued self-sufficiency and independence. "Governor Rockefeller is right in his 'new federalism' to the extent that he tries to concentrate social services at the state level rather than the federal level," Conable wrote.

> But if this promotes freedom, how much better is freedom promoted by the solution of problems at the local level, where our individual voice amounts to something and the legislator is our neighbor. And how much less expensive it is!
>
> We must stand for and fight for strong local government, managed by responsible people, if our democracy is to remain vital. This means that we have to make it our mission to get the strongest possible leaders—people whose responsibility to the public good is unquestioned— into our town boards, boards of education and boards of supervisors. We must encourage by every possible means responsible and thoughtful local government. If we do, we will have gone a long way toward bringing the same responsibility and thoughtfulness into state and federal government.[11]

After the legislative session ended in the first week of April in 1963, Conable asked the newspaper editors in his district for some feedback on his "Albany Reports." He recalled that three months earlier he had promised to deliver a weekly column to newspapers in his district "to keep voters in the 53rd Senatorial District informed about the things going on in their state government. It's hard to imagine now the appalling effrontery that must have been behind that rash promise," Conable said. He confessed to "a high degree of amateurism" in the columns and that he had not been "too happy with some of the efforts," but he said he was pleased that he "had not missed a deadline." And now that the session was over, he said he would "be most grateful" for their comments and "to know if [they] consider it was worthwhile."[12]

One small town newspaper editor in Dansville, in the Genesee Valley, impressed with the high quality of Conable's reporting, wrote back to Conable with these comments on his newspaper columns.

> Dear Senator:
> You know what caused the lady of easy virtue to finally forsake her chosen profession?
> Too much amateur competition, she finally decided.
> If your column was amateurist, you're going to drive a lot of pros out of business.
> The column was well received here; we appreciated your constant effort; we think such a column hurts the writer not at all when it comes to cementing relations with his constituents.[13]

Back home in his district after the legislative session ended in April, Conable continued the informative, educational style of communicating with his constituents that he had begun in the "Albany Report." In constant demand to speak to groups and organizations in his district about what was going on in Albany and to elaborate on his own political views, Conable reported to a friend that there was "one four week period in early spring" when he "did not miss a single night except Sundays" speaking to a group in his district. Modestly describing his "speaking technique" as "not very high powered," he found "that most people prefer a talk which is primarily a chatty recounting of what goes on in Albany viewed from a fresh and comparatively unsophisticated point of view."[14]

But whatever the audience—the Rotary Club in Batavia or a Republican clambake in Rochester—the emerging public image of Conable was always the same: that of a folksy, but highly intelligent, articulate senator, with keen powers of observation and analysis, who relished in explaining to his constituents how things were in Albany and what it was like to be a state senator. With his speeches, as with his "Albany Report," Conable opened a window on state government for his constituents, and they liked the way he told them what he saw, and, in the telling, made them part of the process.

In a speech Conable gave to the Batavia Rotary Club on July 30, 1963, for example, he tried to give his friends and fellow Rotarians a sense of how constituent mail could influence legislative decisions. "A legislator's mail is a real help to him in forming judgments as well as assessing the mood at home," Conable said.

> Sometimes the mail reaches the proportion of deluge. In the two weeks after last winter's auto license dispute [over a proposal to increase fees] arose, I received more than 1,200 communications.
>
> Even when a legislator doesn't agree with all the people who write to him, his mail offers him a means of testing the value of his own views. And I'll say this, if you vote against the views of a constituent, you'd better have a good, clear-cut reason. . . .
>
> Among other pressures on a state legislators is the pressure brought by his own associates within the legislature. The give-and-take of open discussion among legislators of varying points of view is one of the most important factors in helping a senator or an assemblyman determine his own position on any issue. It is both a perfectly proper means of forming judgments and an inevitable part of the legislative process.
>
> I went to Albany with a determination to apply certain principles to all matters and to act within their limits with as much independence as possible. I am more than ever · convinced that this is a basically valid point of view.

But, as a practical matter in the Senate, Conable said that he had also learned that "principles are not always easy to apply, because nice little rules-of-thumb have a way of popping up on both sides of a question." On the proposal to encourage dairy farmers to voluntarily limit their milk production for the year, he noted, for example, "it would have been easy to vote 'no' by applying my belief in a free economy. It was equally logical to vote 'yes' by applying my belief in home rule, since the legislation would have left the ultimate decision to the dairy farmers themselves."

From his first year in the New York Senate, Conable concluded, "Nothing is all black and white" in legislation, making him, in truth, very different from Frank Capra's crusading and simple-minded Mr. Smith in the United States Senate. "There are shades of gray in every issue [and] I have to conclude that legislation is not a simple matter and that it is easy to suspect people who say it is."[15]

But the studious Conable found that he liked the job of dealing with the complexity of legislative issues. "I enjoy my job and find it not only stimulating but downright challenging," he wrote a friend shortly after the legislative session ended in April 1963. "My law practice has taken second place to the problem of government, and I expect that is the way it will be as long as the people see fit to return me to Albany."[16]

Barber Conable's first year in the New York Senate, 1963, was an important year in his development as a legislator. It was also, on a larger scale, an important year in the history of the country. Just as Barber Conable's legislative career was beginning, another prominent political career was ending. On November 22, 1963, as the country was preparing to celebrate Thanksgiving, John F. Kennedy was suddenly gunned down in Dallas, Texas. Profoundly moved by this tragic event, the new senator from Genesee County was asked to participate in a memorial service at a Batavia church for the slain president, who at forty-six was only six years older than Conable. With his gift for words, Senator Conable eloquently captured the grief he and his community were feeling, offering a lesson on what the president's death meant for the country.

"Happily for us, history touches our lives rarely," Conable began.

> From a tragic and apparently senseless event like the death of our president, we must learn many things if we are to continue to believe that history has meaning for its participants.
>
> First, we must learn that our American traditions, the stability of our government and the leadership which we take so for granted are tremendously important to us—a part of our consciousness which can be explained only in terms of the great sense of personal loss which we all feel today.
>
> Next, we must learn that nothing in the world is certain, because all men are mortal, no matter how widely known, how gifted, how vital, how confident of self and destiny.
>
> Next, we must learn how much we owe to those who bear our burdens and accept the risks of leadership in the causes of decency, peace and freedom.
>
> And last, we must learn that the things which divide us as rich man and poor man, as Protestant and Catholic,

as northerner and southerner, as negro and white man, as
Republican and Democrat, are not of any consequence
compared to the things which unite us in universal broth-
erhood.

"From these lessons," Conable concluded, "let us draw new
personal dedication to our fellow man, our country and our God."[17]

An Unexpected Opportunity

As Conable was settling into his second year in the New York
Senate in February 1964, fully hoping and expecting to be in Albany
for some time to come, he was suddenly presented with an unexpected opportunity to run for Congress. But this time his opportunity to run for public office came from within the Republican Party
establishment, not in opposition to it.

Early in 1964, Harold Ostertag, the seven-term incumbent
Republican congressman from the district, unexpectedly retired.
Representing the district since 1951, Ostertag was from the small
town of Attica in rural Wyoming County, only a short distance from
where Conable lived. The county Republican leaders who had
opposed Conable's run two years earlier against Austin Erwin for
the state Senate now went to see Conable urging him to run for
Congress. The county chairmen, representing the four rural counties in the congressional district (Wyoming, Genesee, Livingston,
and Orleans counties, the same counties Conable represented in the
New York Senate) were afraid that if they could not find a popular
replacement for Ostertag from the rural portions of the district, they
would lose the congressional seat to a candidate from Rochester
and suburban Monroe County, which comprised two-thirds of the
population of the congressional district.

Conable initially told the party leaders he was not interested in
seeking Ostertag's seat in Congress. He had just been elected to the
state Senate and wanted to stay there.

"On what basis would you run for Congress?" the county
chairmen asked Conable.

"Well, there's one thing that would be very interesting," Conable
replied, aware of the demographic importance of Rochester and
Monroe County in the district, "and that is if I got organizational
support from Monroe County."

Three days later, on February 24, the day before Ostertag planned
to announce his retirement from Congress, the chairman of the

Monroe County Republican Committee, Donald Foote, came to see Conable at his Batavia law office and told him he would support his nomination. "Harold Ostertag is going to announce his retirement from Congress tomorrow," Foote told Conable, "and I want you to run for his seat. I think I can deliver Monroe County for you. I don't know you from Adam, but I know that if Harold Ostertag announces he's not running, Paul Hanks [a state Republican assemblyman] from Brockport [a small Monroe County town on the Erie Canal northwest of Rochester] and Vince Tofany [the Republican majority leader of the Board of Supervisors] in Greece [the largest suburb of Rochester, home to many Eastman Kodak employees] are going to get into a terrible fight over which one is going to be congressman, and they're going to split the vote in Monroe County.

"I don't know you," Foote told Conable, "but . . . from what I've been told by the other county leaders, and the way you've conducted yourself in the state Senate, and the way you ran your campaign, and the way you beat them all, I am quite confident you would win the primary, because Hanks and Tofany would split the Monroe County vote which is only half of the Republicans, and you would have solid support out here [in the rural counties]. And I don't want to get into that kind of party fight. We've got enough problems in Monroe County the way it is.

"So when Ostertag announces tomorrow," Foote proposed to Conable, "I will announce my support of you, and it will lop Tofany and Hanks off at the ankles. They won't be able to run, because the other committeemen will go along with me, since they don't know anything about it. They aren't prepared for this. They don't know Ostertag is going to resign."

Conable had to decide, and decide quickly, whether to seize the new opportunity. That night, he and Charlotte sat up all night trying to decide what to do. He liked Albany and wanted to continue in the state Senate. "I thought I was going to be a big frog in a small pond, and I looked at Congress and I said, the Republicans are never going to control Congress, with the South having so many uncontested seats. And why should I go down there? We'd have to move. We'd have to leave our wonderful home here. We'd have to do all those things."

But then, when it got right down to it, Conable realized if he didn't take on the challenge he would always wonder if he had made a mistake. Besides, how often had someone from Alexander, New York, been asked to run for Congress, especially with nearly unanimous party support? So, with Charlotte's support, they decided to do it.[18]

The next day, Harold Ostertag announced his decision to retire from Congress at a press conference in Washington. Moments later, from his law office in Batavia, Barber Conable released a statement to the press announcing his candidacy for Ostertag's position. "With a feeling I can only describe as one of surprise," Conable said in his prepared statement, "I must report that the five Republican county chairmen of the 37th Congressional District have asked me to seek the Republican nomination for Congress to succeed Harold C. Ostertag. I did not expect to be called on to serve in this position. The decision to run involves a major commitment, particularly when considered in the light of loyalty, devotion and excellence that Harold Ostertag has brought to the office. . . ."[19]

News of Conable's decision to run for Congress was particularly well received throughout the rural counties of his district. *The* [Batavia] *Daily News* noted, however, that "there was some eyebrow raising in political circles [due] to the fact that Monroe County, which has 60 percent of the population of the 37th District, agreed to back the Genesee senator." With the satisfaction of seeing their own tapped for the nomination, the *Daily News* added that "Monroe leaders were very impressed by Mr. Conable's showing at the polls two years ago and were agreed that they could not come up with as strong a candidate."[20]

On hearing of Conable's decision to run for Congress, Robert H. Manley, an old Conable friend from Warsaw, who had previously announced that he would challenge Ostertag for the Republican nomination, told the press, "Senator Conable, a long-standing friend, is extremely well qualified for this position due to his years of community service, his record with the Marines and his work as a state senator. I regard him as an ideal candidate and feel he will make an outstanding congressman. I support him 100 percent in this campaign as I did when he ran for the state Senate."[21]

Conable's old friend, Al Walkley, the Batavia insurance agent, congratulated Conable from his winter home in Zephyrhills, Florida.

> In rapid succession we have received *Daily News* that there is a possibility of your running for congressman and then that you definitely are! We think that is wonderful and certainly wish you our best in this effort. To have the backing of all the county committees is something too. That means you are a shoo-in. I know you won't take it that way and that you will be making about four speeches every day and traveling all over the territory and deserting your family for days and nights. I feel sorry for them

but after it is all over—the election—the glory of it all and
the opportunity will make it all very worthwhile.

But "what I want to know," Walkley jested, "is will you still
whistle up my stairway when you get to be a congressman?"[22]—
recalling how Conable used to whistle at the bottom of Walkley's
stairway in Batavia when he was ready to go out for afternoon coffee
with Walkley and Karl Buchholtz.

Election to Congress

Conable formally opened his campaign for Congress the day after
the New York Senate adjourned on March 25. Appearing with other
Republican candidates at the Chili Women's Republican Club in
suburban Monroe County, Conable answered a series of questions
on some of the issues emerging in the campaign.

On the question of civil rights, which was the burning issue of
the day, with civil rights leaders and liberal Democrats pressing for
federal laws to end racial discrimination, Conable said "there's no
justification for discrimination. But to solve civil rights problems,
economic and housing problems must come first. Until we get the
Negroes out of the ghettos, we will have civil rights problems." On
affirmative action policies favored by liberal Democrats to end racial
discrimination, Conable "warned against giving a man a job just
because he is a Negro, because that's a form of discrimination too."

He saw President Johnson's War on Poverty, a large federal
government program Johnson had announced to eliminate poverty,
as "largely a publicity gimmick which I don't take very seriously.
The best source of jobs is private industry. The president has used a
great deal of fanfare for his program because that's where he thinks
the voters are."

On taxes, he argued that "the real estate tax is one of the poor-
est taxes we've got, one of the most regressive. The income tax," on
the other hand, he believed, making a point he would often make
later in Congress on the Ways and Means Committee, "is fairer even
though it might be considered incentive stifling. It is less likely to
create hardship than real estate taxes which are based on a particular piece of property regardless of the owner's ability to pay."

And on President Johnson's federal tax cut to stimulate the
economy, which he had successfully steered through Congress
after Kennedy's assassination in 1963, Conable said he thought it
was "an interesting experiment." But he said, as an old fashioned,

fiscal conservative, he believed in "pay as you go. A person ought to pay for the things he wants to buy. I believe in a balanced budget."[23]

Conable's biggest problem in his campaign was the deep ideological division within the National Republican Party that threatened to undermine his own race for Congress in western New York. For well over a year, Republicans had been battling nationally about who would lead the party in the 1964 presidential election. The conservative Republican senator from Arizona, Barry Goldwater, was locked in a bitter struggle with the liberal governor of New York, Nelson Rockefeller, for the Republican presidential nomination. Conable favored Rockefeller for the Republican presidential nomination, believing that he offered a more moderate, centrist approach to American politics with the broadest appeal to the Republican Party and the country at large.

Despite a well financed and articulate campaign, Rockefeller was not able to dislodge the strong support for Goldwater in the state party organizations across the country. With his narrow defeat to Goldwater in the crucial June 2 California primary, Rockefeller effectively withdrew from the race.

Republican liberals and moderates remained convinced a Goldwater nomination would be disastrous for the party in the fall general election. And so, in a last ditch effort to stop it, another northeastern Republican governor, William Scranton of Pennsylvania, entered the race on June 12. With the apparent support of former President Dwight D. Eisenhower, who reportedly was also quietly working behind the scenes to block the Goldwater nomination, Scranton, a thoughtful and well-respected liberal within the party, hoped to offer a more acceptable alternative than Goldwater when the Republicans met in July at their national convention in San Francisco.[24]

Increasingly anxious about the negative effect a Goldwater candidacy would have on his own congressional campaign and Republican prospects nationally, Conable quickly fell in line behind Scranton's last-minute effort to stop Goldwater. "I organized all of western New Yorkers for Scranton out of my little law office in Batavia," Conable recalled. "But before the convention, I never could get through to Scranton. If he had a campaign, it was totally abysmal. I could see that Goldwater had it won.

"And so I refused to go to the convention, even though I was a candidate for Congress, and instead went off to the National War College in Washington DC [for two weeks training with the Marine Corps Reserve], and my family and I sat in horrid fascination and watched that frightful convention when the Republican Party went down the drain."[25]

As a pragmatist, Barber Conable never accepted Goldwater's brand of ideological partisan politics in the United States. Speaking to the Onondaga County Young Republican Club in Syracuse in August 1963, Conable had warned his young friends against the danger of the Goldwater movement that even then was sweeping the Republican Party. It would be a great mistake, "simply and bluntly political suicide," he warned them, for either of the two major political parties of the country "to rework themselves into a radical movement to the left or right. . . . The great mass of our voting population prefer the center, be it the Republican center or the Democratic center. This center likes to consider itself uncommitted, free to swing either way with the current of popular thought, but resentful and suspicious of extremes and partisanship." The inclusiveness of the American two-party system, where each of the two major political parties "seems to have room in it for a wide spectrum of economic and social thought," Conable said, sounding as much like a political scientist as a politician, "was the country's unique and accidental contribution to the science of politics."[26]

With Barry Goldwater's nomination, Conable saw his worst fears come true. Conable and other moderate, mainstream politicians within the Republican Party watched helplessly as the Goldwater movement turned the party into a "radical movement of the right." There was much about Goldwater conservatism with which Conable could agree—Goldwater's call for a greater decentralization of power at the state and local levels of government, long one of the most defining principles of Conable's own political philosophy, and his strong opposition to the spread of international communism around the world, a natural for Conable as an ex-Marine and veteran of World War II. But Goldwater and his band of crusading followers, who opposed the federal income tax, civil rights legislation, Social Security, and much of the social-welfare system most Americans had come to accept as a necessity, and who talked recklessly about the use of nuclear weapons, had gone too far for Conable and other more moderate Republicans.

The question for many disgruntled Republican politicians immediately after the Republican convention was whether or not, in good conscience, and for the sake of their own political survival, they could endorse Barry Goldwater's nomination for president. The liberal Republican senator from New York and a native Rochesterian, Kenneth Keating, who was up for reelection, and the other liberal New York Republican senator, Jacob Javits, both announced shortly after the Republican convention that they could not support their party's presidential nominee.

Conable, too, had to decide if he would support Goldwater's nomination. "I waited about two weeks," Conable recalled, "fussed and fumed and finally said that Goldwater had won the nomination fair and square. He was the Republican candidate. I was running on the Republican ticket for the first time, and I felt that it would be inappropriate for me as a Republican not to support the head of the ticket. And so I publicly endorsed Goldwater."[27]

As expected, on August 26, in Atlantic City, New Jersey, the Democrats nominated Lyndon Johnson to be president. Johnson had chosen one of the most liberal Democrats in the United States Senate, Hubert Humphrey of Minnesota, to be his vice presidential running mate, a decision that seemed to underscore the sharp ideological contrast the Democrats planned to make in the November election with the ultraconservative Barry Goldwater and his equally conservative running mate, Congressman William Miller from the small town of Lockport near Buffalo.

The following evening, Lyndon Johnson outlined his vision for America for the next four years in his acceptance speech. Emphasizing the accomplishments of the Kennedy and Johnson administrations for the past four years—primarily the tax cut, Civil Rights Act, and the War on Poverty that Johnson had successfully steered through Congress after Kennedy's assassination—the president promised to create a "Great Society" for the country if elected.[28]

Thus, with the conclusion of the political conventions in the summer of 1964, the stage was set for one of the most ideologically polarized and significant presidential elections in American history. Most of the public opinion polls indicated that Goldwater was failing to convince the American public and that Johnson and Humphrey, with their activist, reform agenda were being more successful in capturing the central concerns of American voters, and would in all likelihood win the general election in November by a landslide. One national public opinion poll, released shortly after the Democratic Convention, showed Johnson with a commanding 65 percent to 29 percent lead over Goldwater.[29]

Against the backdrop of almost sure defeat for the Republican presidential ticket in the fall, Conable concentrated most of his own congressional campaigning in the suburbs of Monroe County and the western half of the city of Rochester, where two-thirds of the voters in his congressional district lived. Conable could be fairly certain of strong support from the four traditionally Republican, rural counties in his district that had given him large majorities in his earlier state Senate race. But he was less confident of electoral support in Monroe County, where he was not as well known.

The Democrats nominated Neil F. Bubel, a forty-two-year-old town attorney of the Monroe County suburb of Gates, to run against Conable. A native Rochesterian and Syracuse University Law School graduate, Bubel had originally wanted to run for the New York Senate. But he was persuaded by the party to challenge Conable for the House seat. "With Goldwater in the race," Bubel recalled, he thought he had a "good chance of beating Conable."[30]

The Liberal Party, a separate party in New York, also chose a resident of Monroe County, David L. MacAdam from the large suburb of Greece and a research physicist at Eastman Kodak, as a candidate for Congress. Fortunately though for Conable, MacAdam's political agenda—which included such popular liberal causes as strengthening the United Nations, passing more congressional legislation to protect blacks and civil rights workers in the South, and providing federal governmental assistance to retain workers laid-off through automation—threatened to detract more voters from the Democratic Neil Bubel's efforts than from the more traditionally Republican campaign Barber Conable was waging.[31]

While his wife, Charlotte, clipped newspaper articles and made phone calls, when she was not herself on the campaign trail or tending to their children, Conable drove back and forth between his rural Genesee County home and Rochester and the western Monroe County suburbs.[32] Assisted by his old friend and legislative aide Tom Benton, Conable placed newspaper ads and billboards throughout Monroe County to improve his name recognition in that crucial part of the district. To assist him in making personal contacts and speaking arrangements with Monroe County groups, Conable designated Michael Telesca, a popular GOP leader and attorney, as his official campaign manager. Telesca was particularly influential among the large Italian population in Monroe County. Speaking to civic and party groups throughout the county—where Telesca noted Conable was especially appealing to women voters with "his innocent, yet masculine, very gentlemanly way"—campaigning door-to-door, greeting workers at factory gates, and meeting voters at shopping malls, Conable pressed his case to the voters of Monroe County.[33]

"He was a tireless campaigner," added John Riedman, another suburban Republican leader and prominent Rochester businessman who assisted Conable in the campaign. "You could see he was an intellectual who understood the complexity of things, but he wasn't afraid to go campaigning with people. He had a very easy and likable way of talking to people and explaining things to them."[34]

Throughout the campaign, though, Conable walked a tight-rope between endorsing Goldwater and asserting his own political independence in his congressional district. When Goldwater's running-mate, William Miller, from nearby Lockport, made a campaign swing through western New York in October, Conable was asked by the party to introduce Miller at a political rally at the Batavia train station. "For fourteen years Bill Miller has led the fight for good government in Congress," Conable told the crowd in a few carefully chosen words for the occasion, "and for the last two months he has been the peerless partner of Barry Goldwater. We are pleased that destiny has placed its hand on western New York once again." But generally throughout the campaign, Conable tried as much as possible to distance himself from the Goldwater-Miller ticket and played to his own independence and strength as a western New Yorker.[35]

This proved to be a wise decision, as Goldwater politics was not well received by western New York voters. "We just could not get rid of Goldwater stickers," Conable's campaign manager, Michael Telesca, noted. "And quite frankly, I didn't push [them] on anybody.

"Goldwater had passed himself off as a war monger who wanted to escalate the Vietnam War, and he was very, very unpopular. With the speeches he made, he alienated himself from the mainstream. And there was nothing we could do retroactively to counter-act that. I personally liked the man," Telesca added. "I liked him for his stand, for his political philosophy. I appreciated him, but on the Vietnam issue, he came across as being a real hawk. It became very obvious to us, very early on that we had to run our own campaign. We would do nothing to hurt the presidential campaign. We felt the die was cast there. We couldn't change that at all. But we had to run our own campaign."[36]

Conable also had to walk a tightrope in his association with Kenneth Keating, the incumbent liberal Republican senator running against Robert F. Kennedy, who had refused to endorse Goldwater. "I liked Ken," Conable recalled, "but I was scared to death about how any association with him would play in the rural Republican counties of my district. Ken wanted to go with me to a county fair down in Warsaw, and I remember I asked Harold Ostertag to come and sit in between us in the car so people wouldn't associate me with Keating."[37]

For his part, the Democratic candidate, Neil Bubel, enthusiastically embraced Lyndon Johnson's presidential campaign, having his picture taken with the president in the Oval Office and then appearing on the platform with Johnson in October when he visited

Rochester. "I loved LBJ," Bubel said. "Whatever Lyndon Johnson said, I was for it."

Bubel tried to link Barber Conable with Barry Goldwater as the centerpiece of his campaign, especially trying to associate Conable with the controversial comments Goldwater had made about Social Security. During the New Hampshire primary, Goldwater had suggested that Social Security should be turned into a voluntary program. "This statement was widely interpreted by the press and the Democrats as Goldwater being against Social Security," Bubel recalled. "So everywhere I talked during the campaign, I always said you are going to lose your Social Security if Goldwater is elected president. I will protect your Social Security. If you elect Conable, of course he will agree with Goldwater, and you will lose a lot of your Social Security. Conable tried to refute the charge by saying he would be independent and vote his conscience.

"That was the big thing," Bubel said, as he recalled the campaign. "To me, Social Security was the whole issue—Social Security and Monroe County."

During the early stages of the campaign, Bubel had spent some time in the district's heavily Republican rural counties. He quickly discovered that he could make little headway in Conable's rural stronghold. Local merchants refused to put his campaign posters in their store windows and publishers were reluctant to sell him advertising space. "Those folks out there in the rural areas are nice people," Bubel found, "the kind of people you'd want to have as friends, but then they turn around and vote for a Republican every four years. That's just the way it is out there. It's that simple."

Bubel also discovered that Conable, with his roots in the rural parts of his district, "knew how to talk to those people out there. He lived in Genesee County, and he had those buddies he talked to all the time. He could really talk to those people out there, just as though they were brothers or close friends, because he was a country boy, a very smart, brilliant man, but a country boy."

Bubel clearly saw that if he had any chance of beating Conable, he would have to carry Monroe County by at least twenty thousand votes to offset Conable's huge advantage in the rural parts of the district. So, like Conable, Bubel spent most of his time campaigning in his own backyard of suburban Monroe County and Rochester.[38]

Neither Conable nor Bubel spent very much money on the campaign by today's standards. Conable spent about $10,000, mostly on advertising.[39] Bubel spent even less, feeling financially strapped throughout the campaign by the Democratic Party's decision to devote most of their resources to the defeat of the freshman

Republican Congressman Frank Horton, who represented the eastern half of Rochester and Monroe County and all of rural Wayne County in the adjacent Thirty-sixth Congressional District. Horton, a transplanted Louisianian, who was a classmate of Conable's in law school and a former Rochester city councilman, was locked in a close contest with the assistant Rochester city manager, John C. Williams, who, like Bubel, was trying to link his Republican opponent to the unpopular Barry Goldwater.[40]

A week before the election, Conable's prospects in Monroe County received a boost with his endorsement by the *Rochester Democrat and Chronicle*. Citing his New York Senate experience, his ties to the retiring Congressman Harold Ostertag, and his demonstrated abilities, the Rochester newspaper urged their Monroe County readers to vote for the state senator from Genesee County as their new congressman. Indicating that Conable had already made an impression on the press about the type of nationally oriented congressman he wanted to become, the *Democrat and Chronicle* wrote in their editorial:

> Conable bluntly plumps for the Ostertag type of lawmaking, one of broad outlook, one with a steady influence on national policies. Young, a lawyer, and most recently a state senator, Conable already has won the respect of his more seasoned colleagues. A loyal Republican, he wasted no time showing he has the quality of spunky independence which leads him to kick over the traces. He has personality and competence; his election assures continuity of the sort of 5-county western New York representation that should be in Washington.[41]

On Tuesday, November 3, Barber Conable scored an impressive victory over Neil Bubel to win his first congressional seat. Bucking the year's Democratic landslide, Conable defeated his Democratic opponent by a margin of 54 percent to 45 percent (97,242 votes to 80,502), with the third-party Liberal candidate, David MacAdam receiving 2 percent (2,904) of the votes cast. Conable lost Monroe County, receiving only 47 percent of the vote in that part of the district. This was offset by his strong showing in the four rural counties, where he racked up huge majorities as expected.

"I am very pleased that my own people in the rural areas carried the day for me," a grateful and relieved Barber Conable told the Batavia newspaper the day after the election.[42]

With the exception of Conable's victory, and the reelection of the freshman Republican Congressman Frank Horton in the Thirty-sixth

Congressional District, where Horton had used his liberal voting record in Congress in support of the Civil Rights Act and the War on Poverty to discredit Democratic attempts to brand him as a Goldwaterite, the election results were grim for Rochester-area Republicans.[43] The Democrats won three of four New York Assembly seats in Rochester. Statewide, the Democrats also won control of both houses of the state legislature for the first time since 1935, with the powerful Senate Republican Majority Leader Walter Mahoney, who had played such a large role in Conable's days in the New York Senate, being one of the many Republican lawmakers defeated for reelection. And the Rochesterian and incumbent Republican Senator Kenneth Keating, despite his efforts to distance himself from Barry Goldwater, was soundly defeated by Bobby Kennedy. "It was an Avalanche with Debris Everywhere," the headline of a Rochester editorial proclaimed the next day.[44]

At the national level, where the avalanche began, Lyndon Johnson defeated Barry Goldwater by the largest popular vote margin in American presidential history since George Washington's two uncontested presidential elections. With his 61.1 percent to 38.5 percent victory over Goldwater in the popular vote, Johnson had surpassed even Franklin Roosevelt's historic, landslide defeat of Alfred Landon in 1936. And in the electoral college, Johnson defeated Goldwater by the huge margin of 486 to 52.

Johnson's victory was impressive throughout most of the country, including Conable's congressional district. All five counties in Conable's district voted for Johnson, with three of the rural counties (Wyoming, Genesee, and Livingston) voting for a Democratic candidate for president for the first time in their long histories.[45]

In the Congress, the news was also bleak for the Republicans. The Democrats picked up one seat in the Senate for a 68 to 32 majority in the new Eighty-ninth Congress. And in the House of Representatives, where Conable would spend his time, the Democrats gained 37 seats for a 295 to 140 majority, the largest Democratic majority in the House since the Roosevelt landslide of 1936.

Thus, the Goldwater experiment on how to elect a conservative president, as Conable and other Republican skeptics had feared, cost the party not only a devastating defeat in the presidential election, but also a landslide defeat of historic proportions in the Congress. Conable had managed to survive the landslide by relying on his strengths in the rural counties of his district and minimizing his losses in Monroe County. But he would enter Congress as part of a greatly diminished and demoralized Republican minority, at the mercy of Lyndon Johnson and the victorious Democrats.

"What kind of congressman will he be?" the press wondered about Conable the day after the election. "Conable believes in a dialogue between a representative and his constituents," noted a Rochester reporter who had observed Conable as a state senator and congressional candidate. Conable told him, "It's my job to interpret government to my voters—and sometimes shield them from it," emphasizing the educational orientation he had taken on his job as a state senator and which he would now take on his job as a congressman.[46]

Conable's dialogue with his constituents, indeed, began immediately after the election, as he tried to interpret the Goldwater defeat and spell out his own plans for the future. While remaining committed to his own moderate, pragmatic brand of western New York conservatism, Conable candidly described Barry Goldwater's campaign as "a disaster." He said that his own sampling of public opinion during the campaign had convinced him "that most voters disliked President Johnson but feared Barry Goldwater."

"Any conservative," he said, "who puts his head in the sand and says there are no problems, will be destroyed by the inevitability of change."

As their new congressman and a more positive conservative, Conable promised his constituents that he would not bury his head in the sand, but seek "to channel change into constructive courses" of action, those which he believed were "close to the people. Mainly, these involve private business and local government. In this respect," Conable added, he was a Jeffersonian "decentralist, preferring to see accomplishments undertaken by sectors other than the federal government."[47]

Conable's formal dialogue with his constituents would not fully begin until he was officially sworn into the new Eighty-ninth Congress on January 3, 1965. In the meantime, he and Charlotte, who had been his indispensable partner now for more than a decade in helping him organize his political life as well as domestic affairs, had more pressing business to attend. They had to close Conable's law practice in Batavia, decide what to do with their home in Alexander, find a new home for themselves and their four young children in Washington, and organize a congressional office for the start of the new Congress—a lot to do with less than two months before Congress convened.[48]

Chapter 5

A Freshman in the Eighty-Ninth Congress

On January 4, 1965, with Charlotte looking on from the House gallery, Barber Conable was sworn into the Eighty-ninth Congress, along with 434 other members of the House of Representatives, 295 Democrats and 140 Republicans. Constitutionally, Conable's first term in Congress had actually begun at noon on January 3. But since the third fell on Sunday, Conable and the other members were not formally sworn into office until the next day, following the election of the Speaker, John W. McCormack of Massachusetts, who defeated the newly elected Republican leader, Gerald R. Ford of Michigan.[1]

Conable's efforts during his first term in Congress focused on the twin responsibilities of learning how to be a congressman in Washington and learning how to cultivate relations with his constituents back in his district. By focusing on how Conable carried out these two interrelated responsibilities, which are the primary necessities of any new member of Congress, we can get a good sense of what it was like for him to be a freshman congressman and how he methodically laid the foundations for his subsequent twenty-year congressional career.

In Washington: Three Lessons for a Freshman

Richard F. Fenno Jr., a political scientist at the University of Rochester noted for his participant-observation studies of Congress, and also one of Conable's new constituents, had been very impressed with Conable during his congressional campaign. Shortly after the election was over, Fenno asked Conable if he could follow him around during his early days in the new Congress to study how a new member is inducted.

Fenno was most interested in "how the education process works in the House"—how a new member learns to be a congressman. Quoting an early twentieth-century Speaker, Champ Clark, Fenno noted: "A man has to learn to be a representative just as he must learn to be a blacksmith, a carpenter, a farmer, an engineer, a lawyer or a doctor." By following around Conable and another newly elected New York congressman, James S. Scheuer, a Democrat from the Bronx, during the early days of their freshman year, Fenno hoped to "discover how Speaker Clark's education process works and, at the same time, get a revealing perspective on one of our most important political institutions."[2]

Conable quickly accepted Fenno's invitation, and for the next several weeks he let Fenno follow him in Washington, observing what it was like to be a new member of Congress.

In the course of his study, Fenno observed that new members of Congress must learn three important lessons if they are to be effective members of the House of Representatives, lessons which Conable had already begun to learn in the New York Senate, but which would now be pressed on him on a larger scale as a new member of the Congress. From Fenno's three lessons, plus additional observations and insights Conable provided in later interviews, we can get a glimpse of what it was like for him to be a freshman member of the Eighty-ninth Congress.

First Lesson: "The House is a Hierarchy"

"A perceptive freshman" like Barber Conable, Fenno noted in his study, "realizes almost immediately that a vast gap in experience, information and influence separates him from those senior members who effectively run the House. 'I know I've got a great deal to learn,'" Fenno overheard Conable telling Speaker McCormack, when the two first met at a picture-taking ceremony following the formal swearing in of the new Congress on January 4. The Speaker, who began his rise up the House hierarchy as a freshman congressman from Boston in 1929, responded, "I'm still learning too," noting the difficulty and continuing importance he attached to mastering the complexities of the House of Representatives.

"One factor which gives a hierarchical cast to life in the chamber," Fenno observed, "is the pervasiveness of seniority rules in filling such powerful positions as committee chairmen and in distributing such perquisites as office space, Capitol Hill patronage and seating arrangements on social occasions."

The first important decision, therefore, in every freshman's career, "involves his assignment to one of the House's 20 standing committees. . . . No decision is better calculated to impress the idea of hierarchy upon him. He can campaign for the assignment he wants, and usually does, but his fate rests almost entirely in the hands of a few senior congressmen."

In making his committee requests, Conable tried not to repeat the mistake he had made two years earlier in the New York Senate. "When I first went to the Senate," he told Fenno,

> I was the victim of some bad advice. I went around to see Walter Mahoney, the Republican leader, and he asked me what committees I wanted. Following my advice, I named the three most important ones—Finance, Judiciary, and Codes. Mahoney's eyes popped out, then they rolled around in his head for a whole minute and he finally said, "Well!"—and he changed the subject. Needless to say, the conversation didn't help my committee assignments. This time I'm not going whistling up a rain spout after top committees like Appropriations. The main thing I've told [our leader] is that I want to go on a working committee where I can learn the business of legislation.

Thus Conable went to Washington without any particular committee preference. "I talked to a lot of people about it and decided that Science and Astronautics was a good one that I might have a chance to get," he told Fenno. "I put that first on my list, but I told Howie Robison [the senior Republican in the New York delegation, responsible for representing New York on the Republican Committee on Committees] I would trust his judgment."[3]

As it turned out, Conable's freshman committee assignment in the Eighty-ninth Congress was caught up in the House politics of the moment and was ultimately dependent on the outcome of a hotly contested Republican leadership race between the incumbent minority leader, Charles Halleck of Indiana, and the challenger, Gerald Ford from Michigan. Following the disastrous Republican defeat in the November elections of 1964, Ford, representing the younger, more pragmatic wing of the Republican Party in the House, had been persuaded by some of the "Young Turks" in the House (notably Charles Goodell, 39, from New York, Robert Griffin, 42, from Michigan, and Donald Rumsfeld, 33, from Illinois) to challenge Halleck and the old guard for the party leadership of the House. This important 1965 contest, at least on the surface, as the political scientist Robert L. Peabody noted, was not a dispute over ideologies.

> Both candidates had equally conservative voting records, but these records masked rather sharp differences in age, image, and the kind of strategy that the minority party should adopt in the months ahead. Ford, at 51, sandy-haired with the athlete's trim build, the symbol of a new generation of young, articulate, executive type politicians, urged the promotion of a "fighting, forward-looking party seeking responsible and constructive solutions to national problems." Halleck, at 64 [and party leader since 1959], the old pro of 30 years of service in the House, red-faced and heavy jowled, campaigned on a "record of solidarity in support of party principles," and near-unanimous opposition to the "costly, unwise and unnecessary proposals" put forward by Democratic administrations.[4]

Conable could not at first make up his mind about which of these two candidates to support for his party's leadership position, knowing full well that whichever choice he made could have ramifications for his own career in the House. "I didn't know either Charlie Halleck or Jerry Ford when I went to Washington," Conable recounted. "I didn't know which one I wanted to support, and I kind of vacillated between the two. I tended to be fairly conservative, and Jerry was somewhat inarticulate. So I had the impression that maybe I should support Halleck."

To complicate Conable's life further and to give him even more reason to support Halleck for the party leadership position, "the Republican Committee on Committees that assigned people to committees was dominated by [the long-time assistant party leader since 1943, the seventy-year-old] Les Arends, the whip, who was very strongly for Halleck and against Jerry Ford. He was an old line, really conservative Illinois representative and a close friend of Halleck's," Conable recalled.

Arends came up to Conable shortly after he arrived in Washington and said, "Barber, I have a lot of friends, and I can see that you're a comer here, and I want to make a contribution to your campaign fund." Arends pulled out five $100 bills and said, "These are from some friends of mine who are interested in Republican politics."

"I don't accept cash money," Conable told Arends.

"Oh, come on, this is all right," Arends said.

"I don't know who your friends are," Conable replied.

"Well, I'm not going to tell you," Arends said.

"Well, then, I don't want it," Conable said.

"So Les was really down on me, and he was for all practical purposes the chairman of the Committee on Committees since Halleck, technically the chairman, delegated most of the committee's responsibilities to Arends."

As the larger drama of the Halleck-Ford leadership contest unfolded, Conable continued to move back and forth between Halleck and Ford. "As I vacillated between the two," Conable said,

> I started reading the *Washington Post*. You know, everyone gets the *Washington Post* if you're inside the beltway. And William S. White, who was a great friend of Lyndon Johnson, was writing columns that Jerry Ford couldn't chew gum and walk at the same time.
>
> That's the way it started, and it was all quoting Lyndon—all from Lyndon. Lyndon started intervening on behalf of his great poker playing and whisky drinking buddy Charlie Halleck.
>
> Well, I discovered that Lyndon Johnson just couldn't keep his hands off Republican politics, much less Democratic politics, and he was intervening on behalf of Charlie Halleck. And to me, because I could see Lyndon as a dealer, that meant Charlie Halleck was a dealer.
>
> So I went to Jerry Ford and said, "I'll support you and what can I do." I had him come and meet with the

freshman class of Republicans of which I was a member. There were 20 of us, and something like nine of them were from the deep South and had come in on Barry Goldwater's coattails. They were very conservative, very strongly for Halleck. And I got into some fights in my own class on behalf of Jerry.

"Well, the result was that Jerry decided that I was a decent guy, and I was his friend," Conable recalled. "And it was all because of these columns by William S. White, saying Jerry played too much football without a helmet. It was all Lyndon Johnson trying to influence the outcome of this tough leadership fight."[5]

The fight between Halleck and Ford for the Republican leadership position, on which much depended, not only for Barber Conable, but also, many believed, for the future of the Republican Party, was not finally decided until the morning of January 4 when Ford narrowly defeated Halleck in the Republican Conference by a vote of 73 to 67.[6]

Years later, Conable remembered sitting in the Republican Conference that morning just before the secret vote on the minority leader. "I was sitting there next to Bob McEwen [his friend and colleague from the New York Senate who had also been elected as a Republican representative from New York], and I said how many people in the room do you think will acknowledge voting for whoever loses this election? I said to avoid any confusion on how we voted, why don't we show each other our ballots. So I held up my ballot and Bob held up his, and they both said 'Ford.'

"I told Jerry about that later," Conable remembered, and he said, "You know, I haven't found anybody yet who voted against me."

Later that same day, Conable also recalled, as the House convened for the first session of the Eighty-ninth Congress, the newly-elected minority leader came up to him on the House floor and asked him what committee assignment he had gotten.

Conable told Ford he had not received a committee assignment yet.

"You haven't!" Ford exclaimed.

"No," Conable said. "I put in for several. I put in for the Energy and Commerce Committee, and I put in for the Banking Committee," though he knew he wouldn't get any of the prestigious committees because he was a freshman. "And I put in for the Science and Astronautics Committee," he told Ford.

Ford said, "You ought to be on Science and Astronautics. Every Rotary Club in your area will want you to talk to them."

"Well, Jerry, it's all full," Conable said. "All the Republicans have been appointed."

"I'll go see John McCormack to see if I can add another Republican to the committee," Ford told Conable.

The next day, as promised, Ford went to see McCormack, and "before you knew it, I had been appointed to the Science and Astronautics Committee. And Jerry was right. All the Rotarians wanted me to come and talk about the space program. And I realized also that being on the Science and Astronautics Committee gave me something to bargain with, if I wanted to move up [to another committee] after two years, because there were a lot of guys who wanted to get on the space committee by then."[7]

Thus, Conable began his climb up the hierarchy of the House of Representatives, but not without first also getting a simultaneous lesson in the oligarchical ways of the House.

Second Lesson: "The House is an Oligarchy"

The second lesson a freshman must learn, Fenno noted, is that "the House is an oligarchy," where most of the important decisions are made by a few leaders at the top of the committee and party hierarchies in the House. As Fenno explained in his study of Conable's freshman year:

> Though the principle of hierarchy pervades the relationship between the senior old-timer and the junior newcomer, a closer inspection of the House reveals not one monolithic pyramid but many smaller pyramids. A few weeks of experience make it clear to the freshman that each of these lesser hierarchies bestows influence on its leaders and that it is these leaders—40 or 50 of them—who manage the affairs of the chamber. In practice, then, the House of Representatives is an oligarchy; and the committee chairmen, the subcommittee chairmen and the party leaders are its oligarchs. The ambitious freshman must still climb to a position of influence. But the oligarchical structure of the House means that he will be climbing several medium-sized ladders instead of a single ladder 435 rungs high.

"Since most of the day to day legislative work of the House is done in its committees, it is here, more than any place else," Fenno added, "that the freshman will make or break his House career. Influence inside the chamber rests heavily on expertise, and expertise rests in turn on specialization in the field of one's committee or sub-committee."

Once Conable was assigned to the Science and Astronautics Committee, he immediately began his search for knowledge on space problems and the kind of expertise that would enable him to distinguish himself on the committee and in the House. "The committee chairman [George P. Miller from California] called the nine new members together the other day," Conable explained to Fenno.

> He told us, "you fellows will be helping to decide on a five billion dollar budget for NASA, and the hearings begin in two weeks. I want you at least to have seen the installations where the bulk of the money is spent. You can't visualize what's going on in the field unless you've had some experience. I'm going to ask you to make yourselves available to go south this week to Huntsville, Cape Kennedy and the Mississippi Test Facility." He ordered us to go—well you don't order a congressman—but he put it in strong terms that we should go.

On the second ladder, the party ladder that freshmen must also learn to climb, Fenno noted:

> Nearly all decision-making in the House is organized, if not actually conducted, by the two parties. Every freshman, therefore, stands on a party as well as a committee ladder. He will not of course be admitted to the councils of his party leaders; but he will talk constantly with other members of his party about the business of the House and the issues of the day. Much of this intra-party communication is *ad hoc* and fragmentary, but some of it is organized. And it is through the lesser party organizations that cluster beneath the top leadership that a freshman gets his best opportunity to participate in party activity and pursue a party career.

Conable was already a couple rungs up on the party ladder through his endorsement of the winning candidate for the minority leadership position, which would pay him even bigger dividends in the years ahead. But it was primarily through "the lesser party organizations that cluster beneath the top leadership," as Fenno indicated, that provided Conable his "best opportunity to participate in party activity and pursue a party career."

Conable was active, for example, in helping to start the Eighty-Ninth Club, an organization comprised of all the new Republican members of the House. "Communication is obviously a problem around here," Conable reported to Fenno. "So we meet every Monday in the office of one of the members to swap experiences, discuss evolving legislative issues and make common cause if we can. Usually we have a guest speaker too—last week it was Senator Thruston Morton, Senate Campaign Committee chairman."[8]

Particularly important to Conable's rise up the party hierarchy was an invitation he received his freshman year to join the informal SOS Club—an in-group of eighteen Republicans, including such party leaders as Melvin Laird from Wisconsin, the newly elected chairman of the Republican Conference, and Bob Wilson from California, who was chairman of the Republican Campaign Committee in the House, which met regularly to exchange information and discuss policy.

The circumstances surrounding his invitation to join the SOS Club Conable found particularly amusing, as he reflected back on his membership in this important group after his retirement from Congress. "The big issues in the new Congress were replenishing Egypt with PL 480 [Food for Peace] funds and the seating of the [five-man] Mississippi delegation," whose election had been challenged by the Mississippi Freedom Democratic Party on grounds that eligible blacks had been excluded from voting, Conable recalled.

As he watched the voting on these issues with Bob Wilson the first day on the floor of the House, Conable commented that, "as the party of Abraham Lincoln, the Republicans should vote the pro civil rights position on the Mississippi issue." But, as they watched, the Republicans voted against the civil rights position on the Mississippi issue and also against replenishing Egypt with 480 funds. Many of the Jewish congressmen in the House supported the Republican amendment on Egypt, and it immediately passed.

After the vote, Conable commented to Wilson that "the Republican Party may no longer be the party of Abraham Lincoln, but it had shown through its vote that it was the party of Abraham."

"Wilson laughed and laughed at that and spread what I had said around the House," Conable recalled. "It's funny what things affect other things. As it turned out, that exchange with Bob Wilson on the floor was important, because he spread this story around the House, and it became a way for others to know me. It sounded as if I had a sense of humor."

Shortly after that, Conable and one other freshman, Howard Callaway from Georgia, were asked to join the SOS Club. "They met for breakfast Wednesday morning to discuss policy and party affairs in the House. Mel Laird was chairman of the group," Conable recalled, "but there was no program chairman. One day I asked Mel if I could serve as program chairman to liven up things a bit.

He agreed and I arranged for a lot of interesting speakers to come in and discuss things with us. It showed I was a man willing to take responsibility and was a real boost to my career in the House."[9]

Third Lesson: "The House is a Community"

The third lesson impressed on Conable as a new member of Congress—a lesson to which Conable, with his small-town, rural values, particularly related—was the fundamental point that, despite its hierarchical and oligarchical structure, "the House is a community."

"A great deal of what the freshman learns sums up to this," Fenno said: "The House is a little world of its own and . . . legislative careers are shaped primarily by what happens in that world. The House has its own traditions, customs and rules. It has its own formulas for success, its standards of judgment and its ways of punishing nonconformity."

For four days in early January, as Congress was beginning its work, Fenno observed eight senior, experienced members, in collaboration with the American Political Science Association, conduct a series of freshman orientation seminars for the Class of 1965 on how to become a successful member of the House of Representatives. Speaker McCormack set the tone of the sessions by advising the new members to "learn the rules of the House" and "work hard in committee" so "you will enlist and secure the confidence of your colleagues."

Repeatedly, Fenno observed the senior members telling the freshmen that "the House is the best judge of its members;" "we measure each other;" "the House is the greatest jury in the world," and "we spend a lot of time sizing each other up."

To get ahead in the House, the seminar leaders advised the new members, "work hard," "specialize," "do your homework," "be in attendance on the floor," "don't speak till you know what you are talking about," "follow your committees," "if you want to get along, go along," "learn parliamentary procedure," and "be courteous to your colleagues."

"The member who follows these canons of behavior," Fenno concluded from the orientation sessions, "stands the best chance of being judged favorably. And with favorable judgment comes the most enduring basis for influence in the House"—that is, the confidence, respect, and trust of one's peers.

There was little doubt in Fenno's mind from following Conable around during the early days of his freshman year that he very quickly came to see himself as a "member of a little community," not unlike the small communities where he had grown up and practiced law in western New York. "I haven't made any speeches," Conable reported to Fenno. "I know a man's effectiveness is not measured by the amount of his palaver on the floor. I'm still studying my manual," he said, knowing personal relations are important in all small communities, "trying to match up the different members' pictures, faces, and names. That's important. You can't do anything all by yourself around here. It's a collective operation."

Conable was learning, as members before him had learned, that success in the House of Representatives depended on learning the rules of the game and working effectively with others in the common support of mutual goals. "By the time of the 96th [1979–80] or 97th Congress [1981–82]," Fenno conjectured, Conable himself "may well be among the oligarchs of the House. Before [his] ultimate ambition [is] satisfied, however, [he] must solve for himself the greatest of all problems facing a first-term congressman—how to become a second-term congressman."[10]

At Home: Developing Relations with Constituents

As an astute politician, Conable knew from the beginning of his career that his chances of becoming a second-term congressman depended much more on the relationships he developed with his constituents back in his western New York district than with the relations he developed with his colleagues in Washington. He was from the outset most interested in the legislative aspect of his job in Washington. He wanted to make a legislative contribution to solving the public problems of the country. But he knew he could not successfully focus on legislation unless he also forged good relationships with his constituents in his district. Therefore, Conable acted from his first day in Washington to develop the kind of supportive relationships with his constituents which he needed to sustain his legislative career in Washington.

To understand how Conable developed his relationships with his constituents, we use another useful concept developed by Richard F. Fenno Jr. In the 1970s, Fenno followed around eighteen congressmen from various parts of the country in their districts to observe how they developed their "home styles"—by which Fenno simply meant how they "cultivate relations with their constituents." Fenno discovered that congressmen have many different ways of developing home styles in their districts. Some focus on constituent services, emphasizing the services they can provide individual constituents, as a way of building trust and support in their districts. Some members emphasize their role as political leaders in their communities. Others concentrate on articulating their views on controversial legislative issues as a way of building support at home.[11]

In cultivating his relationship with his constituents, Conable developed essentially the same pedagogical home style he had begun to develop so successfully two years earlier as a state senator. As he had done when he was in Albany, Conable wrote a newspaper column, now entitled the "Washington Report," for the newspapers in his district, generally explaining to his constituents some of the issues with which he was dealing in Washington.

As a congressman Conable supplemented his newspaper columns, which were published two or three times a month in district newspapers, with a longer newsletter, also called the "Washington Report," which he sent monthly to the most public-spirited constituents in his district. "I was interested in Washington," Conable later explained, "and I wanted to link myself to others in the district who were interested in Congress. So I decided I'd write a newsletter and try to sort out for them some of the issues we were dealing with in Congress in an objective way. The newsletter," he said, "gave me a devoted group who knew what was going on and to whom I would be tied."[12]

Writing his newsletter also enabled Conable to distinguish himself from the other popular Republican congressman in the Rochester area, Frank Horton, who in two short years since his first election to Congress in 1962, had already developed a reputation for the individual attention and constituent services he provided to the people in his district. Horton excelled in assisting constituents with their veterans benefits, Social Security checks, immigration proceedings, and in any other way he could be of service. Horton was, in the words of a Democrat who unsuccessfully ran against him, "the best constituent-services congressman in the country."[13] Conable was interested in being responsive to the individual needs of constituents, but he believed most of that type of work should be done by his staff. His newsletters provided him with a good opportunity to focus on the legislative aspect of his job in Washington, but also stay connected to the folks back home.[14]

Using the newsletter distribution list of his predecessor, Harold Ostertag, and adding some of his own names from the campaign, Conable sent out his first congressional newsletter on February 3, 1965 to three thousand of the most publically involved and interested constituents in his district. "You were placed on this list," he wrote in his first newsletter, "because your community activity and your hard work for me or the other political party told us that you were interested in what goes on and are concerned for your fellow man. Doubtless, we've missed many people who would like to receive such a report regularly, and we hope you'll help us by sending their names and addresses to me at the House of Representatives."[15]

For the next twenty years, Conable used the newsletters to regularly report to his constituents about what was going on in Washington. The newsletters were an important part of what he later called "the dialogue of representation"—by which he meant the "two-way communication" or "exchange of ideas" between a representative and his constituents—which he often described as the "lifeline of the representative process."[16] Though these newsletters, all of which Conable personally wrote himself, were intended primarily for his constituents, they quickly drew the attention of journalists and academicians who valued Conable's informative reports on the inner workings of Congress.[17]

One of the first things Conable communicated in his newsletter was what kind of congressman he wanted to be. "For the next two years, barring personal calamity," Conable wrote in his first newsletter, which could be described as a kind of course syllabus for his career, "I am going to serve as your congressman. It is a complex job, and will require much hard work. As a citizen, you are entitled to a periodic accounting of my conduct in office, and this is the main reason for starting this newsletter."

"What is my mission?" Conable asked. "As I see it, there are three important aspects of my job":

> 1.   Legislative—This is our real reason for being. These newsletters will report this aspect of the job more than the others, because you will want to know how I am exercising the vote you gave me and what the issues are. With the Senate, we in the House of Representatives constitute the legislative branch of the government, and one of our constant struggles for the next two years will be to keep it a proud, independent and creative branch, rather than just another White House annex.
>
> 2.   Representative—All too often, constituents need help with some governmental program which has become impersonal and unfair through bigness. Part of my job is to help if I can, and to explain or to consider legislative changes if the rules make help impossible. I am your agent in Washington. It is surprising to me how much respect an elected official gets from

those who are not elected—no matter how big government gets, a bureaucrat still knows that the ultimate
power rests with the people.

3.   Political—Political activity is the vehicle of democracy. I believe in the two-party system, and I expect to
be a participating member of the team which supports
me politically. Nevertheless, my representative responsibilities will bear no relation to politics, since I represent everybody in the 37th District, regardless of party.
Although I want to strengthen my party, I will not vote
against my better judgment on important legislation
just for party unity.[18]

Conable used this framework throughout his career to order his
own priorities in Washington and to explain his job to his constituents. By following Conable through some of his newsletter-
reporting in his freshman term and listening to the dialogue he had
with his constituents about representative government, we can get
a good sense not only about some of the important events of the
Eighty-ninth Congress, but also how Conable used these newsletters to develop his impressive pedagogical home style that was
so appealing to his constituents and others who observed his
congressional career.

Legislative Aspect

The legislative life of the Eighty-ninth Congress was dominated
from the start by the strong presidential leadership of Lyndon
Johnson as he sought to steer his ambitious Great Society Program
through Congress. Anxious to get off to a good start with the members of Congress, Johnson began to invite small groups of congressmen and their wives for "informal briefings" at the White
House almost immediately after the new Congress convened.
Conable and his wife visited with the president at the White House
on March 7, and a few days later Conable wrote his constituents a
vivid description of his visit with the president and other leaders at
the White House, giving his constituents the feeling that they could
have been there with him.

This was a pleasant and instructive event. For the bulk of
the evening the congressmen discussed matters of
national concern with the president, vice president, secretary of defense and secretary of state in the Blue Room.
While this was on, our wives were shown a film on the
White House, then taken on a tour of the living quarters

by Mrs. Johnson. An informal buffet followed, and we were home by 10:30. I came away with a number of conclusions, some of which surprised me [and] may be of interest to you.

1. The White House is a great national museum, filled with historic, artistic and cultural treasures, and is not primarily a house.
2. I had expected the president to be easy-going in a social situation, because of his slow, soft speech. He wasn't. He was constantly on the move, whispering in people's ears, consulting with aides, interrupting the secretary of state to emphasize a point, leaping from his chair to pump a hand, twisting this way and that to identify a questioner or get a better view, pounding his hand on the podium to drive home the point, and so forth. Repose is not in him, and every second with him is an expression of the most remarkable kinetic energy.
3. Secretary of State Dean Rusk has the facility of the true intellectual to express himself lucidly in simple terms. Thus his remarks inspire confidence that he knows what he is talking about.
4. Secretary of Defense McNamara lives up to his reputation of being a living computer. He spews out a torrent of facts with apparent total recall. He probably knows more about Vietnam than Ho Chi Minh and Nguyen Khanh put together.
5. Him Johnson is an ordinary but very friendly beagle.[19]

Four weeks later Conable offered his newsletter readers a lengthy description of one of his typical, legislative days in Washington, reminiscent of the kind of reporting he had done earlier in his "Albany Report" when he was a state senator in New York. "The pattern of my day is affected by many things, including the state of traffic in suburban Washington," Conable wrote home in his informal, conversational style.

A TYPICAL DAY—I usually leave my house about 7:15 A.M. to avoid the rush which comes later, and so I am in my office before 8:00, reading our newspapers and checking the first of our four mail deliveries. Two or three times a week I must skip breakfast at home to go to some sort of legislative breakfast. I dictate some answers to mail or do other writing before the committee or subcommittee hearing or meeting, which normally comes at either 9:00 or 10:00 and takes the rest of the morning.

The House of Representatives convenes at noon; sometimes it meets for only an hour or two, sometimes well into the evening. Chances are that I don't attend the entire session, unless an important vote is pending or I need to inform myself about issues that are being discussed. I return to my office through the long subterranean tunnels connecting the Capitol and the House Office Building to deal with inquiries of constituents, meet with callers, study and confer on legislative proposals, and respond to more correspondence.

At 5:00, if Congress has adjourned, various study groups to which I belong meet in the office of some member, comparing committee reports, pooling information, discussing issues and so forth until 6:30. Following this I sign the mail and leave either for home or for dinner with some organization having its Washington meeting at which constituents are in attendance. The social life here is extensive, and congressmen are fair game, with the result that I do not go to parties or dinners unless someone from back home provides good reason for going.

On top of this schedule for weekdays, I have found myself back home in the district four out of five weekends since the beginning of the year. It is a privilege to be busy in an interesting pursuit, and I have described my day not to complain but to give you some idea of how I spend my time representing you in Washington.[20]

Much of Conable's own legislative life in the Eighty-ninth Congress, of course, centered on his responsibilities as a new member of the Science and Astronautics Committee. So he devoted several early newsletters to explaining his various activities, including visiting space centers in the South,[21] attending subcommittee budgeting hearings on the National Science Foundation,[22] and observing a Rose Garden ceremony at the White House for two astronauts who had recently returned from space.[23] A knowledgeable and enthusiastic supporter of the space program, Conable offered to make "a 30-minute sound and color film" on the American astronauts' first walk in space available to service clubs, churches, schools, and other organizations in his district, an offer that was quickly accepted as Gerald Ford had predicted when he appointed Conable to the Science and Astronautics Committee.[24] Conable traveled to California to be on hand at the Jet Propulsion Laboratory in Pasadena "when the fabulous Surveyor I landed on the moon," sending back thousands of pictures, which he reported would be a "great source of information" for future missions.[25]

More generally, Conable spent much of his time in the Congress responding to Lyndon Johnson's Great Society initiatives. Capturing the essence of his dilemma as a freshman member of a small

Republican minority, badly outvoted in the previous November elections, Conable wrote his constituents in his fifth congressional newsletter on March 31, 1965:

> The president is a consummate politician, and his success in this field is transforming the country. His legislative program is skillfully constructed of the most appealing labels. Opposition is fraught with peril. In his political strategy, if you think the "War on Poverty" is duplicative and wasteful, you're in favor of poverty; if you question the school bill, you're against education; if you don't approve of the medicare approach, you're against the aged and the infirm; if you don't favor deficit financing, you're necessarily for higher taxes . . .; if you question the way he has constructed the voting rights bill, you're an obstructionist on racial matters; and so it goes. By saying, "Take it this way or not at all," he leaves the representative the unhappy alternative of having to vote for what he feels is bad legislation, or appearing heartless.

"Does a good end justify bad means?" Conable asked. "This is one of the problems I find myself struggling with constantly here in the 'Great Society.' "[26]

As a fiscal conservative, Conable was skeptical of Johnson's Great Society program from the beginning. "We were pleased to learn from the president's budget that he has projected expenditures of less than $100 billion for the Fiscal Year 1966, which begins July 1," Conable reported to his constituents in his first newsletter on February 3. But he said he was concerned about a "deficit of $5.3 billion," which Johnson had "budgeted for the most prosperous times this country has ever known, despite the fact that we are already paying $11.3 billion this year on our $318 billion national debt." On top of this, Conable said, "the president's budget calls for embarkation on numerous new programs, the future cost of which is a 'riddle wrapped in a mystery inside an enigma' to borrow Mr. Churchill's phrase."[27]

As a decentralist, Conable also opposed much of Johnson's Great Society on the grounds that many of the new programs he advocated, despite their "appealing labels," would concentrate too much power in the hands of the federal government at the expense of the state and local governments. He opposed, for example, one of the first and most popular of Johnson's Great Society programs, the Elementary and Secondary Education Act of 1965, which provided federal aid to elementary and secondary schools in the United States for the first time in the nation's history. President Johnson sold the bill to Congress primarily as a way for the federal government to provide financial aid to children from low-income families. But Conable and other conservative Republicans saw the bill as a more general effort by the federal government to unnecessarily involve itself in the affairs of local school districts around the country. "I do not oppose education; indeed I have said many times that I consider it the key to the future," Conable wrote his constituents on March 31, 1965. "The decision to vote against the bill was not an easy one, because it is always politically safer and more comfortable to be in favor of legislation passionately desired by some, not understood by many and promising relief in an area of national need. This is deceptive, even dishonest legislation. . . . In the guise of aiding children from poorer families we are changing the basic character of our educational system and its emphasis on independence, diversity and freedom."[28]

Congressional Quarterly noted that in addition to voting against the Elementary and Secondary Education Act of 1965, Conable also voted against six other key Great Society measures proposed by President Johnson in the first seven months of 1965. He voted against the repeal of Section 14(b) of the Taft-Hartley Act which permitted states to adopt so called "right-to-work" laws to prevent union shops in their states. He voted against the Appalachian Regional Development Act. He voted against the creation of the Federal Department of Housing and Urban Development. He voted against federal rent subsidies for low-income families. He voted against successful efforts by the Democrats to add a number of supplemental benefits to the Medicare program. And he voted against a presidential proposal to allow federal officials to override a state governor's veto of certain federal anti-poverty activities in their states.[29]

Conable was particularly disturbed by the Johnson administration's attempt to eliminate the power state governors had been given in the original legislation to veto federal anti-poverty programs in their respective states if they did not approve the type or location of the project. "Very few governors exercised this power," Conable wrote his constituents in his September 22 newsletter, "but some, Governor Rockefeller included, used the threat of vetoes effectively to ensure that no federal poverty program conflicted with existing state or municipal programs in the fields of education, job training or welfare. Sargent Shriver, director of the Poverty Program, considered this veto power to be an interference with his freedom of action. . . .

"As far as I am concerned," an irate Barber Conable wrote home, "a pretty basic principle is involved here. Labels aside, we all want a great society for our country. We're more likely to achieve it if we don't make it the exclusive province of the federal government, but employ the energies and talents at all levels."[30]

But seeking to balance his own conservatism with the changing needs of the country, Conable ended up supporting five of the twelve most important Great Society measures on which *Congressional Quarterly* evaluated freshmen for the first seven months of the Johnson presidency. He voted for the Medicare program, which established a health care system for the elderly. He voted for the Voting Rights Act of 1965, the most comprehensive voting rights legislation to pass Congress in almost a century, to ensure the registration of black voters in the South. He voted for the Twenty-fifth Amendment, which permitted the vice president to become acting president in case of presidential disability and provided for the filling of a vacancy in the office of vice president. He voted for the Excise Tax Reduction Act, which reduced federal excise taxes by $1.8 billion over a five-year period. And on the one foreign policy issue on which *Congressional Quarterly* evaluated freshmen, Conable also voted in support of President Johnson's recommended funding of the Foreign Assistance Act of 1965.[31]

Conable knew, of course, that the people in his district were concerned not only about domestic politics, but also about the growing war in Vietnam, the issue that would cause Conable so much grief over the next few years and end up destroying Lyndon Johnson's presidency. "Judging from my mail," he wrote in his March 3, 1965, newsletter, "one of the most disturbing problems to the people of our district is our position in Vietnam. We all wish there was a simple, honorable solution. We cannot afford to pull out and yet we cannot afford to stay indefinitely. We give the appearance of being without hope and without plan. One of the military maxims I remember from my days in the Marine Corps is that you cannot win unless you can isolate the battlefield, so that enemy reinforcements cannot be brought in against you. The infiltration of men and supplies from North Vietnam is the life blood of the Viet Cong, and we need not risk striking the heart if we can just somehow tie off the arteries."

As a veteran of World War II, Conable was inclined to support his commander-in-chief on Vietnam. "Our position in Vietnam is so inextricably tied to the military situation that I am astounded by the public debate within the government about the basic military decisions made by the president as commander-in-chief. Americans of high office who call for withdrawal persuade the little Vietnamese villager in the rice paddies that we cannot be trusted to continue our support, and that his long term best chance for survival lies on the side of the Communists. Rather than signaling retreat," Conable believed, "we should leave no doubt that we remain committed to the protection of the interests of freedom in Southeast Asia."[32]

"Inexorably, by painful degrees, the country drifts deeper into war in Southeast Asia," Conable reported to his constituents a few months later on July 28, 1965. "Wherever congressmen gather to talk, the subject of Vietnam soon joins the group like a brooding presence. What is the right course militarily, morally, politically?" Conable wondered as he surveyed the options and reported to his constituents on the most recent developments.

> As I write this newsletter, it is apparent that the president will soon ask Congress for some sort of emergency powers including the power to call up at least some of the military reserves. For two weeks he has been sending up trial balloons, as if he were reluctant to move without warning the American people again and again to expect the worst. His poker game in Vietnam has not forced the enemy to withdraw, and something government leaders (and almost everyone else) have been saying for years, that we must not allow ourselves to get into a land war in Asia, is coming to pass.
>
> With human lives in increasing number at stake, we must continue to consider the alternatives: (1) Pull out. (2) Fight a war of containment within South Vietnam with enough troops to handle both the native Viet Cong and infiltrators from the north. (3) Impose a naval quarantine and extend the bombing of major targets in North Vietnam, including the port of Haiphong, industrial sites, and the Russian missile sites in and around Hanoi, with attendant risk of further escalation.[33]

A year later, with conditions continuing to deteriorate in Vietnam and public protest against administration policies mounting at home, Conable offered his constituents a frank assessment of where he and other politicians stood on Vietnam, writing in his May 18, 1966, newsletter:

> The Republican politicians are biting their tongues at this point, assuming that anything they may say involves them in dispute and identifies them with an issue fraught with political peril. The Democratic politicians are also biting their tongues with a few exceptions, lest they contribute to their deep and anguished decision over Vietnam which is tearing at the serenity of their national

majority. The country needs to be united, but not at any cost. Can we constructively criticize the commander-in-chief in an undeclared war? Can we legitimately draw a distinction between support of our fighting men on the battlefield and approval of our military strategy in Southeast Asia? Are disclosures of "shocking misman-agement" giving comfort to the enemy in the same sense that charges that the war is "illegal" do?

After a good deal of reluctance, I have come to the conclusion that we should talk about these things. Notwithstanding the perils, a free society is going to be neither understood nor free in an atmosphere which rejects discussion. If doubts exist, they should be expressed and confronted, rather than squelched. . . .

"At this time, based on my understanding, this is where I stand," Conable wrote.

I do not think we can pull out without taking a big step towards World War III. We cannot let the Chinese communist "hard line" succeed without inviting "wars of liberation" everywhere. I disagree with many aspects of the military conduct of the war. I do not want to see us bomb civilian populations of Hanoi-Haiphong or China, but I cannot understand why the harbor at Haiphong has not been sealed. This could be done with mines, rather than an active blockade, and would not involve a moral confrontation with the Russians. Most of the war material coming into North Vietnam comes this way. A passive blockade is far more humane, and probably more effec-tive, than trying to bomb trucks on the way to the front. If we must bomb to protect our troops from the infiltrat-ing North Vietnamese, I would like to see the emphasis on bombing North Vietnam rather than South Vietnam. I think we should avoid putting more American troops in South Vietnam, or taking other steps toward a massive land war in Asia, primarily because this is not consistent with our world-wide responsibilities nor is it likely to be a successful military tactic. Our boys ought to get as much language training as they can absorb, to maximize contact with the people and improve our communication with them, but we ought to stay out of Saigon politics. We shouldn't commit ourselves to an election until we know it will be an honest one.

I know there are many who will disagree with me about one or more of the attitudes I have expressed above. These attitudes are not fixed, and changing circumstances will change them. Like others in government, I would like to hide from this issue, if I could, in the hope it will go away, but it's just too important.[34]

Representative Aspect

Though Conable was most interested in the legislative aspect of his job, he also used his newsletters to talk about the representative aspect of his job, by which he meant the traditional constituent services that representatives are expected to provide their constituents. From the beginning of his career, Conable was responsive to the individual needs of his constituents, but most of the help given to individual constituents with the complexity of federal governmental programs was done by his staff. For his part, as his freshman newsletters clearly indicate, Conable preferred to focus his energies on the larger educational responsibilities of his job.

As an enthusiastic and natural born teacher, Conable took special delight in sharing his Washington experiences with the hundreds of school children who visited Washington in the spring to see the cherry blossoms and national monuments. "The school groups visiting Washington at this time of year are a particular satisfaction to one who believes that the government should have a real meaning to our citizens, rather than being that impersonal force off in the distance," he wrote in his newsletter of May 12, 1965.

> Many of the young people who visit Washington with their classes are seeing it for the first and last time before the routine of daily life anchors them to their desks or their lathes or their butcher stores. To have seen that it really exists, that it is peopled with human beings trying to represent their hopes for our society and to grapple with their problems, will give the federal government meaning to them which it never would achieve on the pages of a textbook.
>
> I have been grateful for the opportunity to talk with a number of school and other groups during the past weeks, telling them how the government works or doesn't work, urging them to maintain their interest as they grow older and to be participating, rather than spectating citizens.[35]

Indeed, one of Conable's favorite activities, his long-time personal secretary and office manager, Linda McLaughlin, remembered, was to have his picture taken with school children on the Capitol steps. "He liked doing that and telling them all about the Library of Congress across the street and Thomas Jefferson, who was one of his heroes. If he had time and the House was in session, he would take them over to the House floor. He had a way of communicating with students and not talking down to them," McLaughlin said. "This is why he was a successful congressman. He did that with people generally."[36]

Interested in providing all Capitol visitors the same kind of educational opportunities he tried to provide his own constituents, Conable proposed his freshman year "to glass in the galleries of the House of Representatives and . . . provide visitors with earphones for a running commentary explaining proceedings on the floor. . . . I have noticed that when I am able to sit with visiting constituents in the galleries and explain to them what is going on, they seem to get a great deal more out of a visit to Congress than they would otherwise."[37]

Though Congress never did adopt Conable's proposal for glassing in the galleries of the House, they did eventually approve the live gavel-to-gavel televised coverage of the House and Senate floor proceedings, now broadcast on C-SPAN, and they approved plans to construct a Capitol Visitors' Center to advance the educational opportunities for visiting constituents, which was always a prime concern of Conable from his first days in Congress.[38]

The specific constituent services Conable mentioned in his newsletters also had a distinctive educational tone. When a fire damaged the community library in the village of Hilton in northern Monroe County, for example, destroying 1,440 of the library's books, Conable arranged through a federal program for the Library of Congress to send Hilton five hundred of its surplus books to help restore the losses.[39] Mindful of the agricultural nature of his district, he made copies of the federal government's annual *Yearbook of Agriculture* available to his constituents free of charge.[40] At tax time, he advised his constituents on the most common errors in filing their tax returns.[41] He reported on visiting the young men from his district who were attending the U.S. Naval Academy in Annapolis, Maryland, and encouraged other outstanding young men from the district to apply for appointment to all four of the nation's service academies through his congressional office.[42] He announced the creation of a summer internship for college students in his office.[43]

Though Conable relished the educational opportunities the representative aspect of his job provided him, he quickly tired of some of the more extreme requests for constituent services. "A congressman soon learns not to be surprised by any inquiry or request from a constituent. But a recent one came close," he wrote in his newsletter in the summer of 1966.

A woman called my Rochester office recently to complain that there was a bat in her garage. She expressed fear it might attack her children.

Mrs. Ringwood, my Rochester secretary, properly concluded there wasn't much I could do about it in Washington, so she called the Monroe County Sheriff's Office. With their usual efficiency, the Sheriff's men promptly removed the invader.

Why did the woman call her congressman about this?

"He helped my mother with a Social Security problem," the woman explained, "and so . . ."[44]

Then again, in a humorous but educationally effective newsletter a month later, Conable asked his constituents to "please" not ask him to do the following things because, as he said, "experience has shown me that I'm not able to be of much assistance":

1. Bring the president or Senator Dirksen to speak at the local clambake.
2. Get a son out of the service when he doesn't want to get out.
3. Get a private White House tour for five people tomorrow morning.
4. Get you a ride on a rocket.
5. Ask me to find you a good, reasonable hotel room during Inauguration week.
6. Make an ironclad one hour appointment with Senator Kennedy for three weeks from today.
7. Get somebody a Small Business loan after the funds for the year have all been used up.
8. Get somebody of the minority party a post office appointment.
9. Tell you over the phone how to get to my office from your motel in Alexandria, Virginia during the rush hour, or ask me to reserve a parking space for you on Capitol Hill.
10. Get you an invitation to *the* wedding [of President Johnson's daughter, Luci Bains Johnson, to Patrick Nugent in August 1966].[45]

Conable's attitude toward the representative aspect of his job was also reflected in the manner in which he conducted his first constituent questionnaire in early 1966. "In the near future," Conable wrote in his first newsletter of 1966, "I am sending out to all the postal patrons of the 37th Congressional District a brief questionnaire, asking opinions about some for the pressing issues of the session. I do this with some trepidation," Conable confessed, echoing a view of representation first expressed by the English parliamentarian and founder of British conservatism, Edmund Burke, in the eighteenth century, whose views Conable was often fond of citing. "I realize that it is my job to use my judgment about these issues, and I do not believe in substituting a popular poll of this sort for my own responsibility as a representative, but I do think such a tool can be a helpful guide in a system like ours."[46]

Conable used the results of the opinion poll not only as a guide to what his constituents were thinking on some of the legislative issues of the day, but also as an occasion to educate them about the legislative complexity of his job. "Several people have written how difficult it is to answer some of these questions with a single yes or no. I can sympathize with this complaint. This is what I do almost every day here in Washington—try to respond to complex legislation presented for a vote in the Congress with a single yes or no. We have not yet devised a means of voting in the Congress equivalent to 'Yes, but . . .' or 'Perhaps.' "[47]

The final results of the district opinion poll indicated that there was not much disagreement between Conable's general views on the issues and those of his constituents. Like Conable, most of his constituents, 72 percent, for example, favored a constitutional amendment, proposed by the Senate Republican Minority Leader Everett Dirksen, to overturn a recent Supreme Court decision (*Reynolds v. Sims* in 1964) mandating that both houses of state legislatures be apportioned on the basis of population. A large majority of Conable's constituents (65 percent) were also against the repeal of Section 14(b) of the Taft-Hartley Act permitting states to enact "right-to-work" laws. An even larger majority (85 percent) supported Conable's opposition to federal rent subsidies for low income families. Sixty percent of the respondents favored taking "whatever military action is necessary to achieve decisive victory," and 64 percent believed "if the Vietnam War continues . . ., 'Great Society' programs should be reduced."

"I want to repeat" though, Conable said in announcing the final results of the opinion poll, "what I said at the time I mailed these questionnaires out, that I do not expect to conduct this office by polling my neighbors about issues which it is my responsibility to decide. The questions asked were very simplified because the pertinent legislation is frequently extremely complex. Nevertheless, the conclusions will be helpful to me as a representative and I am grateful for the assistance you all gave. Knowing that this is what you expect of me, I shall continue to use my best judgment about any given issue, based on all the facts available to me."[48]

The Political Aspect

Conable also used his newsletters to discuss the political aspect of his job, by which he meant the traditionally partisan activities which organize and control so much of the work of Congress. As a freshman member of a small Republican minority in the Eighty-ninth Congress, Conable was at a distinct disadvantage in affecting the legislative process.

The immediate task for the Republican Party in the new Congress was to regroup from the party's disastrous defeat in the 1964 elections and present a more positive image to the country about the party's future. Conable, therefore, spent some time in his second newsletter on March 17, 1965, describing the party's efforts in this regard.

> Despite the fact that not all who read this letter are Republicans, I believe all of us agree that the country is better off with a flourishing two-party system. For this reason, I would like to tell you what the Republicans in Congress are trying to do to re-establish their influence in national affairs, after last fall's election disaster. First, we selected new leadership, and now there is an effort to create the "positive image." Under this concept, our role as an opposition party must not be solely negative, but must concentrate on the constructive alternative.
>
> The new Republican leadership of the House has wisely created two committees to shepherd us through our doctrinal difficulties and help us establish sound political positions and develop intelligent programs. The first, the Research and Planning Committee, headed by Charles Goodell of Jamestown, will try to advise about long-term party positions. It will function not only as an overall coordinating committee, but also through a number of special task forces addressed to matters of current interest. For instance, I am a member of the Republican Task Force on Economic Opportunity, surveying the field of anti-poverty legislation. The second committee, the Policy Committee, headed by John Rhodes of Arizona, advises appropriate party positions on specific legislation coming before the Congress, after consultation with the minority members of the standing committee responsible for the legislation.
>
> If these two committees do their job well, and we heed their advice, the Republican image should be improved by 1966, at least as far as the Congress is concerned.[49]

Three months later, in a June 23 newsletter, Conable reported to his constituents in more detail about his activities on the

Republican Task Force on Economic Opportunity. "I have been spending quite a bit of my time during the past week attending hearings on the Economic Opportunity Act [Johnson's War on Poverty legislation] as a member of the Republican Task Force on Economic Opportunity. These hearings result from a curious situation." This was one of his more partisan newsletters.

> Last year the War on Poverty was initiated with an appropriation in excess of $800 million in a great blast of publicity and concern. The fact that somebody *cared* and that poverty was at last going to be eliminated (despite the fact that myriad social welfare programs costing more than $30 billion had long been addressed to the problems of the poor) was mentioned frequently during the election campaign. . . .
>
> The bill to extend the program, on which Congress will soon be asked to act, bears a magical price tag of $1.9 billion, more than twice the first year's cost. Let me say at this point that I think there are many worthwhile parts of this program. A billion, or two billion, or three billion dollars applied to the problem of poverty, is going to have some impact somewhere. If the program is well designed to strike at root causes, it may have a lasting value far beyond initial expense. But what we sometimes forget is that the taking of the billion, or two billion, or three billion dollars from the taxpayers so that it can be applied to a social or economic problem, is also going to have another impact everywhere on every taxpayer. What we have to do is to strike a balance—do the probable social benefits match or exceed the cost to the public?
>
> I have heard the government approach, which refuses to strike this balance, referred to as "undifferentiated goodness," and I commend this term to your consideration. Are people poor? Give them money. Do they need shelter? Build them houses. Are they unhappy? Buy them a ticket to the circus. This approach assumes unlimited resources and a beneficence unencumbered by priorities. Unfortunately, social wisdom cannot ignore priorities because no society can ignore costs, human or economic.

"So how do we stand on the poverty program?" Conable asked. "Who knows. The press across the country rumbles with local discontent about high salaries, patronage fights, lack of coordination, minimal involvement of the poor on the planning level, the undercutting of existing local programs, assaults by federally financed projects on city hall, etc. etc.

"The point is," Conable said, as he summarized his Republican perspective on the bill, "we are now asked to double the size of the program without any assurances that it is accomplishing what it was supposed to do, ignoring the rumblings of discontent noticeable around the country. I am glad my party has established a Task Force on this matter to look for further facts, and I shall do what I can as a member of this Task Force to keep it moving constructively."[50]

A month later, however, bowing to pressure from his district, Conable reported to his constituents that he had voted for continued funding for the anti-poverty program at the $1.9 billion level requested by the administration, despite some serious reservations about the program. "Many responsible community leaders in the Rochester area let me know of the educational needs this program is fulfilling following last year's [race] riots, and on the strength of their advice, I voted for final passage of the bill after first supporting a number of Republican limiting and modifying amendments that were beaten back by party-line votes." But he added: "My tolerance of programs conceptually and administratively as weak as this, no matter how appealing the slogans or valuable the local assistance, is pretty limited."[51]

Although Conable disagreed with the Democratic approach for eliminating poverty in the United States and much of Johnson's Great Society program in general, he found himself in agreement with President Johnson's efforts to control campaign expenses for federal elections, reflecting the independent, bipartisan spirit that would characterize much of Conable's congressional career. "One of my concerns about representative government is based on the cost of running for office," Conable wrote in his "Washington Report" five months after assuming office. "Campaign times are times of mass mailings, TV spot commercials, newspaper advertisements, billboards, slick handouts, and saturation radio coverage. It is not unusual for a congressional candidate in an urban area to spend as much as $250,000 in an election campaign. In addition to direct costs, a candidate probably will have to leave his business or employment during the campaign period, and his income shrinks to zero. The ordinary young man thinks twice about these expenditures and risks.

"Who makes the better office holder in a representative democracy," Conable asked,

> the neighbor who knows your problems because he has shared them, or the man with unlimited amounts of public relations money (his own, or somebody else's) to spend? A man is not to be condemned because of his

wealth or the support of wealthy friends or organizations, but I worry about an election system which does not insist that all candidates come before the people on an equal footing, to be judged for their intrinsic qualities.

The problem is to find a way effectively to limit campaign expenditures. How can you deny a man's friends the right to put together a committee to work for or share the cost of his election? How can you tell a labor union or a group of business men that they can't buy a billboard for the candidate of their choice? How can we effectively stop what in some cases amounts to the buying of high office?

I consider this a real danger to representative government, and I would appreciate receiving suggestions and comments from readers of this *Report* who share my concern about this.[52]

Conable's own solution to the growing problem of campaign expenses in federal elections came a year later, in June 1966, when he submitted a campaign finance reform bill to the House of Representatives. The Conable bill, which was similar to a bill President Johnson also submitted to Congress, would have placed a $5,000 limit on campaign contributions to House and Senate candidates and a $10,000 limit to presidential candidates. The Conable bill, unlike the Johnson bill, would also have limited total campaign expenses in a federal election to ten cents per person in the area represented, which would have been $45,000 for a congressional district of 450,000 people, about the average size of a congressional district in those days. In addition, both the Conable and Johnson bills would have required public disclosure of all campaign contributions and expenditures and stiff penalties for violators.

Though neither the Conable nor the Johnson bills passed the Eighty-ninth Congress, their submissions reflected how two men of two very different political philosophies and backgrounds converged on seeing the high cost of running for public office as one of the most serious dangers facing representative government, a danger that has become even more acute since these reforms were first proposed in 1966.[53]

As the midterm 1966 congressional elections approached, Conable's newsletters turned philosophical as he reflected on the upcoming elections. "One in my position has an interesting perspective on the election process," he wrote his constituents on May 18, 1966.

For two years, I have served in a group of 435 people as diverse as any group in the nation and yet having one thing in common: they all have to be elected every two years, or they leave the group. In this period of time, I have come to know most of these men and women— some as friends, some antagonists, some relaxed and jovial, some intense and demanding. But however they appear to their colleagues, their image at home controls their membership in the group. Already, via the primary, some have been tried by their neighbors and found wanting. Some, for various reasons of their own, have announced their retirement. This fall's election will take out even more, insuring that the 90th Congress will have a new and different group personality, although enough will remain to provide a strong similarity to the 89th Congress. In 1962, the last off-year congressional election, 68 seats changed hands, moving in both directions politically and demonstrating dramatically the desire of the people to review their representation in Washington every two years.

As one of the grizzled veterans of many a congressional campaign told me, "Persons come and go in this group, but the People are always with you. You get to be philosophical about changes."[54]

President Johnson kept the Eighty-ninth Congress in session until October 22, allowing members only two weeks to campaign before the congressional elections on November 8. "We would have liked more than two weeks to campaign, and we could have had it if the strategy of the administration had been different," Conable wrote his constituents in the last newsletter before the election.

The president apparently felt that the longest possible session would favor the incumbents, and he wants the 90th Congress to be as much like the 89th Congress (where his party held a 2 to 1 majority) as his efforts can make it.

The last three weeks were typically hectic, with feverish activity, long hours, and the usual irksome delays while the two Houses of Congress negotiated the final versions of bills which had taken unexpected turns in one House or the other. We passed some major legislation and had some bitter exchanges, but now that it's over, it all seems to have merged in one great effort to adjourn. Whether we come back before the convening of the 90th Congress depends on the president: we don't have to come back to finish our regular work in any event. I suspect the outcome of the elections will finally answer this question. In the meantime, we have adjourned "sine die"—without a date for reconvening.

Conable ended his last newsletter of the Eighty-ninth Congress with a "valedictory" to his constituents—a revealing choice of words for this educationally minded congressman—indicating just how important he thought these newsletters had been in establishing his home style. "With this letter," he wrote, "I close this series of regular communications to some 15,000 residents of the 37th Congressional District." The newsletter had more than tripled in circulation since the first newsletter two years earlier. "If I am a member of the 90th Congress," he said, "I hope to continue and to extend my effort, grateful for the kind comments so many of you have sent, even when you disagreed with an expressed viewpoint. It has been good for me to have to report regularly as I committed myself to do. I hope you have benefitted also. I know election day will see you casting your vote intelligently for the kind of government you want our country to have."[55]

Conclusion: Foundation Laid

With his last newsletter of the Eighty-ninth Congress, Barber Conable completed laying the foundation of his congressional career. He had gotten off to a bumpy start in Washington two years earlier as he got caught up in the intense leadership struggle between Charles Halleck and Gerald Ford for control of the Republican Party in the House. But in the end, as luck and circumstances would have it, Conable's decision to back Ford proved advantageous in his own rise up the party and committee hierarchies of the House. Ford's influence helped Conable obtain a position on the popular Science and Astronautics Committee, where he quickly demonstrated his skills as a legislator. The favorable impression Conable made on other Republican leaders of the House, most notably the Republican Campaign Chairman Bob Wilson of California who helped him obtain membership in the influential SOS Club, also paved the way for Conable's rise up the party hierarchy of the House. "Somehow, I had a feeling right from the start," Gerald Ford recalled later, "that Barber was going to be a very able, effective, and constructive member of the House."[56]

From the beginning of his career, though, Conable knew that his image at home would control his membership in Congress more than any friends or positions of power he might obtain in Washington. So he acted from day one in Congress to cultivate an image with his constituents that would allow him to be the kind of legislatively oriented congressman he wanted to be. By linking his constituents so knowledgeably and intimately to his work in Washington through his newsletters and newspaper columns, Conable successfully cultivated an image as a teacher, as a thoughtful and articulate congressman who wanted to inform and educate his constituents about what went on in Congress. Indeed, it was Conable's impressive ability to explain how the system works that became the distinctive feature of his home style.

As one of Conable's admiring constituents, an art professor at a local university, recalled later,

> I used to look forward to the heart-to-heart discussions Conable had in his newsletters. It was almost like having a one-on-one conversation with your congressman where he sat down in the living room with you and tried to explain to you in a fireside chat what was going on in Congress. Whatever he wrote seemed to come from such deeply felt views which went beyond partisanship and external views to get to the heart of the matter. He didn't just present the facts, but he tried to explain and interpret the facts in the broader context of things. He was a great educator. Reading his newsletters made you feel more connected to Congress and more connected to your congressman.[57]

The end result of the hard work at constituent building was that Barber Conable was overwhelmingly reelected to a second term in the United States Congress on November 8, 1966. Retaining the large majorities he had won in the four rural counties of his district two years earlier, he also won Monroe County for the first time to defeat his Democratic opponent, Kenneth Hed, a thirty-five-year-old vocational teacher from Brockport, with an impressive 68 percent of the vote.[58]

The election results also brought good news to other Republicans in Congress and around the country. Rebounding from their devastating defeat in 1964, the Republicans won an additional 47 seats in the House of Representatives to reduce the Democratic majority in the new House to 61 (248 to 187). The Republicans also gained three seats in the Senate to lessen the Democratic majority in that chamber to 28 (64 to 36). At the national level the Republicans also won 23 of the 35 gubernatorial contests to give them control of twenty-five states.

The election results were widely interpreted to have important policy implications for the continuation of President Johnson's Great Society program and for the war in Vietnam. "Continued funding of the new programs enacted by the Eighty-ninth Congress promised to be an especially difficult problem for the administration in 1967–68," *Congressional Quarterly* reported. "On the other hand, the basic broad base of support registered in the past Congress for President Johnson's Vietnam policies was confirmed by election results. Rather than sending opponents of the Vietnam War to Congress, the voters elected new representatives who seemed more in favor of stepped-up miliary effort in Vietnam than their predecessors."[59]

Thus, Barber Conable's sophomore term in Congress promised to be substantially different from his freshman term, not only because of his added experience, but also because of the changed political and legislative realities, more to his liking, that would characterize the new Ninetieth Congress.

Chapter 6

Appointment to the Ways and Means Committee

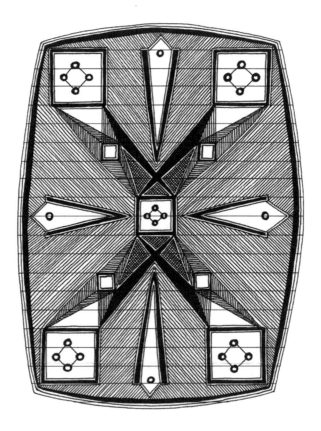

With his freshman term behind him, Conable began his second term in January 1967. The Ninetieth Congress was an important time for Conable, as his appointment to the influential Ways and Means Committee would significantly shape the duration of his congressional career. The Ninetieth Congress would also be an important time in the nation's history, with the growing war in Vietnam and domestic conflict that would force Lyndon Johnson not to seek reelection to the presidency in 1968.

"The first few weeks of any new Congress are almost totally given up to the rather occult process of organizing the committees which are such an important part of the legislative process," Conable wrote his constituents in his first newsletter of his second term. "Four hundred and thirty-five men and women cannot arrive as a group of unrelated representatives and start passing laws without first going through a great deal of sorting and arranging. From an individual congressman's point of view, nothing more important happens all year long, because his committee assignment determines in large part what specialty he will study, with what group he will associate, and what will be the scope of his primary legislative responsibility."

Responding to reports in his district that he might be appointed to the Ways and Means Committee in the new Congress,[1] Conable cautioned his constituents that such an appointment was "still indefinite . . . and might not happen. . . . The filling of vacancies by the congressional Committee on Committees is a notoriously uncertain and unsentimental process. In matters of this sort, one of my colleagues told me, it is wise to remember the words of Max Ehrmann: 'Whether or not it is clear to you, no doubt, the universe is unfolding as it should.' "[2]

But Barber Conable, never one to leave his fate entirely to chance, had helped the unfolding of his own political universe a few weeks earlier when he paid a visit to his political mentor and Republican minority leader, Gerald Ford, to see if he should consider changing his committee assignments in the new Congress. Conable had liked his membership in the Science and Astronautics Committee and House Administration Committee in the previous Congress, but he aspired to be on one of the important legislative committees of the House. Since the Republicans picked up forty-seven additional seats in the Ninetieth Congress, causing the expansion of Republican representation on all the House committees, Conable approached Ford after the November elections about the possibility of improving his committee assignments.

"Do you want to go to Ways and Means?" Ford asked Conable at their meeting. "There was no New Yorker on Ways and Means," Conable explained later, "and there had not been a Republican from the state on Ways and Means since Steven Derounian from Long Island was defeated for reelection in the Goldwater landslide of 1964. The same people who had kept me from getting a committee assignment my freshman year had denied Charles Goodell [a liberal Republican from Jamestown, New York] a seat when he put in for Ways and Means in 1965. New York did not have a seat on Ways and Means and that was very offensive to the financial section in New York City. They wanted to have a New Yorker on there from the Republican Party, and they raised hell with the leadership."

"No, I don't want to go on Ways and Means," Conable remembered telling Ford when they met to discuss his committee assignments. "I don't know anything about tax law. I always refused to practice tax law as a lawyer. I don't like it."

As alternative committee assignments, Conable suggested that Ford consider him for either the Foreign Affairs Committee, where he could become more involved in some of the issues of the world about which he was developing an increasing interest, or the Appropriations Committee, where his predecessor, Harold Ostertag, had served. The final choice, of course, would have to be made by the twenty-nine-member Republican Committee on Committees of which Ford was only one member, but an important member.

"New York already has a member [Howard W. Robinson from Oswego in Tioga County] on the Appropriations Committee," Ford replied.

"As for Foreign Affairs," Ford counseled his friend, "it doesn't amount to anything in the House. You could be distinguished being on the Foreign Affairs Committee, but you have no power. It's politically insignificant."

"Do you want to get somewhere where you've got some power?" Ford asked Conable, encouraging him to accept an opening on one of the oldest, most powerful committees in Congress. "Ways and Means has a constitutional role. All money bills originate from the House. All tax bills have to come from the Ways and Means Committee. You're not a guy who came down here to hide, Barber. So you go there and start fighting for what's right in the tax law."

"I'll think about it, "Conable told Ford as he left the meeting.

On the way back to his office after his meeting with Ford, Conable ran into Melvin Laird from Wisconsin, one of his prominent friends from the SOS Club and also a member of the Republican Campaign Committee in the House, and told him about his meeting with Ford. Laird also urged Conable to go on the Ways and Means Committee. "You'll never have to worry about raising money again," Laird told Conable, mindful of the success Ways and Means members had in attracting campaign contributions from interest groups affected by Ways and Means legislation.

"Well, that's nothing that I'm very worried about," Conable retorted.

"But you ought to be," Laird replied.

"Well, I don't think I'll get Ways and Means anyway," an incredulous Conable responded, still not fully understanding the process of organizing committees in the House, and remembering too the disappointment Charlie Goodell had experienced when he tried to get the Ways and Means Committee two years earlier.

"You'll get it," said Laird, who was known for his inside knowledge of the House.

Afterwards, Conable, anxious to touch base with the other principal leaders of his party, also conferred with Howard Robison, who, in addition to being on the Appropriations Committee, was the New York representative on the Committee on Committees, and Leslie Arends, the long-time Republican whip from Illinois and an important member of the Committee on Committees. Conable also contacted Charlie Goodell to assure himself that Goodell did not want to try for the Ways and Means position again in the Ninetieth Congress. All three men urged Conable to seek a seat on the Ways and Means Committee in the new Congress.

Later that day, Conable went back to his office and said to his administrative assistant, Harry Nicholas, "You know, I left here this morning thinking I wanted to be on Foreign Affairs or Appropriations, and let me tell you what happened. . . ."

And Nicholas sat there and held his head and said, "Oh God, I gotta learn the tax law."

He said, "Barber, you're being told something. If all the leaders of the party told you that they wanted you to go on Ways and Means, there's been a decision made about this."[3]

And thus, with a little nudging of his own and with a little help from his friends, the political universe was unfolding as it should for Barber Conable. On January 26, 1967, the day after Conable sent out his newsletter alerting his constituents to a possible committee change, the official word came from Washington that Conable had been selected as a new Republican member of the Committee on Ways and Means.

The newspapers in Conable's home district were full of praise and pride for their congressman. "Conable Named to Ways and Means," the front page of the *Rochester Democrat and Chronicle* hailed, as it announced that House Republicans had named Conable to one of two openings on the committee. The paper noted that Conable was the fourth congressman from western New York to serve on the committee in the twentieth century. One of them, Daniel Reed, a Republican from Chautaugua County, who served in Congress for forty years from 1919 to 1959, eventually became chairman of the committee during one of the rare periods after World War II when the Republicans had a majority in the House in 1953 and 1954. The other Republican opening on the committee, the paper also reported in a matter of some future historical importance, would be filled by freshman Representative George Bush of Texas, who would remain in the House only four years before running unsuccessfully for the Senate in 1970.[4]

Publicly, Conable told the press he thought there were two major reasons for his appointment to the Ways and Means Committee. The first, he said, was "the strong claim New York state has to a Republican seat on the committee, since we are the greatest taxpaying and importing state" in the country. The second reason was "the assistance of good friends from New York and outside the state . . . in Congress who worked to support my appointment."[5]

Privately, Conable also thought that "the growth of my election plurality from 52 percent to 68 percent in two years also persuaded my political leaders that I would be a survivor, able to make tough decisions and thus suitable for a hot seat on the Ways and Means Committee."[6]

It was particularly important to Conable that the congressmen who supported his appointment did not hold him to any specific positions on committee issues. Thus, he entered the Ways and Means Committee with the same open-mindedness and independence that had been important to him since the beginning of his political career. He would be a good party man. He had to be to get the assignment on the Ways and Means from his party. But operating within the framework of his party, which after all he saw as a rather large umbrella, tolerating many points of view, he would try to exercise the same open-mindedness and independence that had been a hallmark of his political career.

The next week Conable reflected on his committee assignment and conveyed to his constituents the excitement with which he accepted his new responsibility. "The assignment will change my work in the House of Representatives in many ways, not all of them good," he reported to his constituents in his February 8 newsletter.

> I have had to give up my other committees and curtail less important activities. The Ways and Means Committee is so demanding that I will not be able to get back to the district so often or do as much outside political work as previously. After one week on the committee,

my staff already is looking startled every time I return to the office during the day.

Why would I give up relative tranquillity in this way to go on a tax-writing committee? I can just hear some of my friends back home ask in consternation, "Why should you want to involve yourself in controversial issues like taxes and Social Security, Barber, when you had such interesting work before?" The answer, I suppose, lies in the excitement of participation [of making of public policy]. On the Space Committee . . . I was essentially an observer of the space program.

But "there is something much more central about Ways and Means," he explained, indicating that he had fully recovered from his reservations about serving on the committee.

These 25 men and women [15 Democrats and 10 Republicans] actually establish the tax structure for the country, and decide what the Social Security benefits and payroll taxes shall be. Every cent the government raises is their responsibility. The Constitution assigns to the House the initiation of all revenue bills. The traditions of Congress are such that the House Ways and Means Committee has a unique initiating role: rarely can its bills be amended on the floor, but the rest of the House has to accept or reject its suggested legislation as the committee has drawn it. This sort of responsibility is a magnet, and most congressmen are drawn by it if they get the chance.

By its nature much of the work of the committee is technical, requiring the mastery of a volume of exasperating detail. What makes it interesting is its impact on the lives of all those who pay, directly or indirectly, for the operation of our federal government. I assumed, in grasping this opportunity, that you would want me to grapple with these central issues rather than seeking a more comfortable, less controversial assignment. I trust that's a correct judgment.[7]

Conable's joy at being selected to the Ways and Means Committee was tempered a few months later, however, when his eighty-six-year-old father, the man who had the greatest influence on his young life growing up in western New York, died on June 20, 1967. Barber Conable Sr. had not been happy about his youngest son and namesake's running for the New York Senate in 1962, Conable later recalled. "He said the only public job that's worth having is a judgeship. He said you'll just be an 'errand boy' if you go to the state Senate." But the senior Mr. Conable had grown increasingly proud of his son's legislative career and was especially pleased when he was appointed to the Ways and Means Committee, universally recognized as one of the most important committees in Congress, and a committee that had been chaired by Mr. Conable's Cornell classmate, Daniel Reed, in the early 1950s. "My mother told [Dad about the appointment] in the hospital," Conable recalled. "He repeated, 'Ways and Means, Ways and Means.' And he acted pleased."[8]

Impressions of Wilbur Mills and John Byrnes

A big part of being a new member of the Ways and Means Committee was working with the legendary Chairman Wilbur Mills, and the ranking Republican member, John Byrnes, both of whom Conable came to greatly admire.

Wilbur Mills was born in 1909 in the small town of Kensett, Arkansas. His father was a prominent businessman in town. After attending nearby Hendrix College, he went on to Harvard Law School. "Despite his Cambridge training and his obvious skill in tax law," Conable recalled in a book he wrote on the Ways and Means Committee after he left Congress, "he appeared to relish the deceptive role of country lawyer, a position he actually held for a very few years in Searcy, Arkansas, between his graduation from Harvard in 1933 and his election to Congress in 1938." After serving two terms on the Banking and Currency Committee, Mills was appointed to the Ways and Means Committee in 1943 and served as chairman from 1958 to 1974.

Mills was Conable's legislative hero because he practiced the kind of bipartisan, consensus politics that appealed to Conable. Mills made Conable feel like he was an important member of the committee from the start. Conable wanted to make a significant contribution to the deliberations of the Ways and Means Committee, and Wilbur Mills gave him the chance. Mills worried as much about the votes of Republican newcomers, Barber Conable and George Bush, as he did about the votes of senior Democrats on the committee. As chairman, Mills "wanted to stretch the tent so that everybody could get in it," Conable recalled. "He wanted to bring his bills to the floor with consensus support. At that time, the committee had 25 members and he preferred a vote of at least 23 to 2 to show clearly that the committee strongly supported whatever measure was brought forth.

"Mills was a legislative leader in the old-fashioned sense of the word; he gave his entire attention to the process. He was a psychologist, too," Conable added, "who knew what we thought before we knew it ourselves—a brilliant man, and quite devious."

In his heyday, Wilbur Mills had a remarkable record of success on the House floor. "His bills almost always passed," Conable explained.

> They passed, not because he was authoritarian . . . but because he worried about winning—always. He would disappear from our view for two or three days before we were about to disgorge a bill from the Ways and Means Committee. He would be out on the floor of the House talking and listening, holding an envelope, on the back of which he had written names of key Democrats. He would go around making sure that these influential members were able to accept this or that provision of the bill. He might come back the day before we were to vote it out of committee and say: "Fellows, we have to change the bill. We are going to have trouble." And he would suggest this or that potential change. In other words, he went through an informal democratic process to be sure that he was not going to be defeated on the floor with respect to any detail.[9]

As the Democratic leader of the Ways and Means Committee, Mills also presided over a political function of considerable importance during this period. Since 1911—in the aftermath of the revolt against Speaker Joe Cannon who up to that point had held the power to appoint all congressional committees—the Democratic members of the Ways and Means Committee, who themselves were elected by the Democratic Caucus, had served as the Democratic Committee on Committees, with the power to appoint all their Democratic colleagues to committees. So, in addition to being chairman of the Committee on Ways and Means, Mills was also chairman of the Democratic Committee on Committees and an important part of the power structure of the Democratic Party in the House.[10]

John Byrnes, the Republican leader on the Ways and Means Committee, was not as well known as Wilbur Mills, "but his contributions to the legislative process and to the achievements of the Committee on Ways and Means were well known by close observers," Conable noted.

Four years younger than Mills, John Byrnes was born in Green Bay, Wisconsin, in 1913. He received a law degree from the University of Wisconsin in 1938. Two years later he was elected to the Wisconsin Senate, and in 1944 he was elected to Congress. He became a member of the Committee on Ways and Means in 1947, and he and Mills served together on that committee for a quarter of a century, until Byrnes's resignation from Congress in 1973. Mills and Byrnes "often disagreed," Conable noted, "but when they were united on a measure, it usually carried both House and Senate by large majorities."

Conable was particularly impressed by the working relationship between Byrnes and Mills.

> John Byrnes was as direct and intellectually honest as Wilbur was elusive. John was, in a way, the first sergeant of the Ways and Means company. An issue would come up, and John would plunge head on into the heart of it with both arms flailing. Not a bit politic, but very direct and forceful, he would get the committee formed in line and marching off down the road. When he saw that the committee had decided what it wanted to do, thanks to John Byrnes' honest and persuasive ministrations, the company commander—Wilbur Mills—would appear out of the bushes, position himself at the head of the column, and the committee consensus would become the Mills bill.
>
> An effective military organization needs both a company commander and a first sergeant, and in the Ways and Means Committee this also constituted very effective leadership.[11]

The cooperative relationship between Mills and Byrnes that produced the bipartisanship Conable so admired had "an interesting side effect. Since Wilbur wanted a consensus, since John Byrnes provided a lot of the momentum within the committee, and since Wilbur was a legislative psychologist who waited for the committee to make up its mind and then positioned himself at the head of the column, the result was that the Ways and Means Committee came to have a consensus that was much more conservative than was the case with the majority of the Democratic Party in the House. The committee was viewed as having a life of its own, to the dismay of liberal Democrats."[12]

The liberal Democrats in the House would eventually rein in the Ways and Means Committee in the mid-1970s, stripping Wilbur Mills of his committee chairmanship, removing the committee's power to make committee assignments, and finding other ways to make the committee more responsive to the larger Democratic membership of the House. But during the six years in which Conable served under the Mills–Byrnes consensus model of bipartisan, committee leadership from 1967 to 1973, he would have more influence as a minority member in shaping committee action than minority members would come to expect in the more partisan atmosphere of the future. The Mills–Byrnes years were, therefore, always a model for Conable on how the two political parties could constructively work together in committee to forge legislation, the likes of which would not be duplicated in the latter stages of Conable's career, particularly after Dan Rostenkowski, the more partisan-minded, liberal Democrat from Chicago, became chairman of the Ways and Means Committee in 1981.[13]

Learning to be a Member of the Ways and Means Committee

One of the first things Conable learned about being on the Ways and Means Committee had nothing to do with tax law, but everything to do with the politics of the committee and the financial pressures brought to bear on committee members by interest groups. Shortly after Conable got on the committee, a lobbyist for a major shoe manufacturer in Binghamton, New York, approached Conable with an offer that had a profound effect on the kind of Ways and Means member he became.

The Ways and Means Committee was about to consider a free trade bill with obvious implications for the shoe industry in the United States. Anxious to gain favorable legislation from the Ways and Means Committee, the shoe lobbyist, who was a former staff member of the committee and a friend of Wilbur Mills, visited with Conable in his Washington office.

"A man from Endicott Johnson would like to make a large contribution to your reelection campaign," the lobbyist told Conable.

"I got nervous knowing the way money flows in the Ways and Means Committee," Conable recalled, "and I told the lobbyist I only accept fifty-dollar campaign contributions."

The lobbyist said, "This man is not going to come down from New York to give you fifty dollars."

"That's up to him," Conable said. "That's his choice. I'll only accept fifty dollars."

"The lobbyist didn't believe me," Conable said. "He thought I was just playing games with him."

After the lobbyist left, Conable talked to his staff about the strange conversation he had just had and told them he wanted to place a fifty-dollar limit on campaign contributions.

The staff said, "It won't work."

Conable said, "Let's try it and see how it works. If necessary, we can always change it later."

But it did work. And for the rest of his career, Conable never accepted campaign contributions of more than fifty dollars, from which he was able to raise all the money he needed in his comparatively safe reelection campaigns, which typically cost around $30,000, half of which usually came from his newsletter readers and the other half from the Republican Party.[14]

Conable's fifty-dollar campaign limit was widely reported in newspapers in and out of his congressional district and contributed significantly to his reputation as an honest and independent-minded member of the Ways and Means Committee.[15]

Free of any special financial or political interest, Conable could concentrate more generally on learning the tax law and legislate for the country's broader national interest. Though he never much liked tax law, he quickly threw himself into learning the tax legislation of the Ways and Means Committee, much as he had thrown himself into learning about science and astronautic issues in his previous committee assignment.

The two most important issues coming before the Ways and Means Committee in Conable's first year were President Johnson's request for an increase in Social Security benefits to help retired Americans keep pace with inflation and his request for a temporary increase in income taxes to help finance the growing war in Vietnam. In both cases, Conable got an early lesson in the leadership styles of Wilbur Mills and John Byrnes.

In January 1967 President Johnson proposed a 15 percent across-the-board increase in Social Security benefits to be financed by higher payroll taxes and an increase in the amount of earnings subject to the tax. Following the constitutional requirement that revenue measures originate in the House of Representatives, Wilbur Mills arranged for the Ways and Means Committee to conduct extensive hearings on Johnson's proposal in March and April of 1967. On August 7, after five months of committee deliberations, Mills got the committee, with only one dissenting vote, to report a scaled down version of the administration's bill, which lowered the Social Security increase to 12.5 percent and, most importantly and controversially, attached a mandatory work-training program for welfare recipients. Under the more conservative Mills bill, all welfare recipients, including mothers, would be required to participate in work training programs as a condition for receiving welfare benefits.

Liberals in the House angrily criticized the bill as a return to "the poor laws of centuries gone by." The secretary of Health, Education and Welfare, John Gardner, for example, opposed "any atmosphere of coercion about training," because, he said, "the great bulk of the people we're concerned with here are mothers, and there is a real question as to whether society gains if a mother leaves four children to go to work."

However, "the passage of the Ways and Means bill exactly as reported by the committee was a foregone conclusion," *Congressional Quarterly* observed, "because the bill was brought to the House floor under a closed rule which prohibited any amendments from the floor," as was the case with most Ways and Means bills Mills reported.

Echoing the conservative views of the Ways and Means Committee, Mills was particularly adamant about defending the welfare reform portions of the revised Social Security bill on the floor of the House. "Is it in the public interest for welfare to become a way of life?" Mills asked. "We want the states to see to it that those who are drawing [welfare checks] as unemployed fathers or . . . as [single, unemployed] mothers . . . take training and then work. Is there anything wrong with that? What in the world is wrong with requiring these people to submit themselves, if they are to draw public funds, to a test of their ability to learn a job? Is that not the way we should go? Is that not the thing we should do?"

Despite liberal objections, the full House of Representatives passed the Mills-backed Social Security bill with the welfare reforms intact, with only three dissenting votes, on August 17.

The Senate, in a more liberal fashion, approved the full 15 percent increase in Social Security benefits requested by President Johnson, without the strict limits on welfare recipients contained in the House bill.

But the conference committee, called to resolve the differences between the House and Senate versions of the Social Security legislation, sided more with the House bill and on December 15 approved a 13 percent across-the-board increase in Social Security benefits and most of the mandatory work requirements for welfare recipients contained in the bill Mills had steered through the House of Representatives. As Barber Conable and other newcomers to the Ways and Means Committee could see, Wilbur Mills usually got most of what he wanted.[16]

In January 1967, President Johnson also requested a temporary, two-year, 6 percent "surcharge" on personal and corporate income taxes to help finance the war in Vietnam, a war that was rapidly draining the treasury and costing the country in excess of $22 billion a year. By the time Johnson made his formal request for the surcharge to Congress on August 3, however, the economic conditions of the country had worsened, with a budget deficit approaching $30 billion projected for 1968, and the president was forced to increase his surcharge tax proposal to 10 percent.

Once again, Wilbur Mills held extensive hearings on the president's request for a tax increase in August and September of 1967. But Mills and John Byrnes were opposed to the surcharge without the president also making major cuts in domestic spending. In checking with other House members and leaders outside the Ways and Means Committee, Mills confirmed that there was little support for Johnson's surcharge without also making substantial cuts in the budget. So on October 3, with help from John Byrnes, Mills got 20 out of the 25 members of the Ways and Means Committee—10 of the 15 Democrats and all 10 Republicans—to agree on a motion to set aside the Johnson's surcharge proposal until the president and Congress could agree on a means for reducing expenditures.[17]

Publicly, Lyndon Johnson blasted Mills for not supporting his surcharge proposal. In an unusually strong statement on November 17, President Johnson told reporters that Mills and Minority Leader Gerald Ford, who supported Mills's position, would "live to rue the day" when they decided to oppose the surcharge proposal. Without a tax increase, Johnson warned, the economy would be threatened with a budget deficit as high as $30 to $35 billion, which could be translated, he said, into an inflation rate of between 5 and 6 percent.[18]

Privately, though, as Conable learned in a conversation he and George Bush had with Mills a few months later, Johnson and Mills worked quietly behind the scenes to assure the adoption of a surcharge that would also include the budget cuts Mills and the Ways and Means Committee wanted. In an interesting entry in a personal journal Conable began to keep in March 1968, he revealed much about Mills's low-key, behind-the-scenes leadership style, as well as his own efforts and those of his friend, George Bush, to learn about the politics and substance of matters before the Ways and Means Committee.

"George Bush and I decided after our committee adjournment this morning to follow the chairman into his office and ask what was going on with respect to the surtax," Conable wrote on March 27, 1968.

> The chairman, as usual, was very frank and appeared to be quite open with us in the discussion of what he was thinking of doing. We spent half an hour with him as he

described his conversation with the president and the concerns he had about the Senate maneuvering which was going on.

The chairman told us that last Sunday night the president called him at his home and talked with him for over an hour on the phone. The gist of the president's conversation was that he would accept any decision on cutbacks on which Chairman [George] Mahon of Appropriations and Frank Bow, the ranking Republican [on the Appropriations Committee], Wilbur Mills and John Byrnes could agree, but that he was not in a position to take the initiative with respect to cutbacks, feeling that any significant cutbacks would have to be at the expense of programs addressed to our urban problems, and this would put him politically in a bad position relative to the mayors of our northern cities to whom he had made so many promises. In other words [Johnson told Mills], whatever you want to do is all right, but don't make me take the initiative on it.

Though the public relationship between Johnson and Mills continued to be tense on the surcharge issue, Conable reported from his private conversation with Mills that "the chairman seemed surprisingly sanguine that the president and the Ways and Means Committee will be able to agree on the conditions of a tax increase coupled with a spending cutback."[19]

Six days later, as Mills predicted in his private conversation with Conable and Bush, the Senate passed a 10 percent surcharge tax as an amendment to a fairly noncontroversial House-passed, excise tax bill, which also included significant reductions in spending. Mills and Byrnes then successfully negotiated with Senate conferees for the final passage of the bill. As President Johnson wanted, the new legislation included a temporary, one-year, 10 percent surcharge tax on personal and corporate income taxes. It did not fill the original two-year request Johnson had made, but it was estimated that it would produce an additional $15.5 billion of income for the coming year. As the Ways and Means Committee members and other fiscal conservatives in the House and Senate wanted, the new law also called for major cuts in federal spending—a $6 billion reduction in spending for the fiscal year 1969, an $8 billion recision of unspent appropriations for 1968, and a 245,000-man reduction in the number of civilian employees in the executive branch.

Once again, the Ways and Means Committee, under the combined leadership of Wilbur Mills and John Byrnes, proved to be a major force in the writing of the country's tax laws. President

Johnson quietly signed the new Revenue and Expenditure Control Act into law, without the customary bill-signing ceremonies, at the White House on June 28, 1968.[20]

As someone without much interest or background in tax law, Conable struggled during his first term on the Ways and Means Committee to understand the immense complexity of tax legislation. "This past week has found me struggling with a committee responsibility of great importance but only modest drama," he wrote his constituents in a February 1967 newsletter. "As a matter of fact, it's been hard to stay alert as we pondered the intricacies of international credit flows, comparative interest ceilings and balance of payments deficits during the hearings the Ways and Means Committee has been holding on the Interest Equalization Tax. This sort of thing, complex in every way and of little interest outside the realm of the professional economist, sometimes has a greater impact on our lives than the political controversy about which everyone has an opinion. So we struggle to understand and make the right decision."[21]

To help him stay awake during the many hours of complicated hearings, Conable would eventually take up the art of doodling during committee meetings. "It's a concentration aid," he liked to tell the press. "And it keeps me from chatting with the boys (staffers and committee members)."[22] It also made him "appear industrious in meetings [and] speakers always assumed he was making notes." These intricate doodles, which Conable did both in Ways and Means hearings and later at meetings at the White House, World Bank, and other high places where concentration aids are needed, were very popular with constituents back home and helped establish his reputation in Washington as a "world-class doodler" (samples of which have been reproduced on the dust jacket and at the start of each chapter).[23]

The doodles aside, Wilbur Mills's open leadership style encouraged Conable's active participation in all the committee deliberations. He never missed a committee meeting or an opportunity to learn about tax law. His diligent administrative assistant, Harry Nicholas, also began to pay more attention to taxes. And Conable's personal journal helped him retain and reflect on the details of Ways and Means legislation and politics.

But Conable quickly found that his congressional newsletters were the most help to him in learning the tax law. "To understand the tax law," he said,

> I had to reduce it to simple terms so I could explain it to my constituents. That was one of the advantages of the

newsletters. They helped me think about things more clearly.

As it turned out, the fact that I had not been a tax lawyer was a big help, because I didn't know anything about the intricacies of the tax law. I had to reduce all the decisions to the lowest, simple denominator. I didn't think in terms of tax loopholes, and I didn't think in terms of tax preferences of one sort or another. I didn't think in terms of the administration of tax law. I thought of it as a theoretical problem. But in communicating with my constituency, of course, I was talking to them as a citizen, not as a tax specialist. So it was good that I was not a tax lawyer. It worked out much better that way.[24]

By the end of the Ninetieth Congress in October 1968, Conable had already begun to distinguish himself as a junior member of the Ways and Means Committee. Not only had he worked well with the ranking minority member, John Byrnes, and the other Republicans on the committee, but he had also made a very favorable impression on the Democratic chairman, Wilbur Mills, whose respect and support Conable had assiduously courted from the beginning. Similar in many ways—both from small towns, both country lawyers, both fiscal conservatives, both serious, courteous, smart, pragmatic men—Conable and Mills developed a close, working relationship during Conable's first term on the committee. In recognition of his support and service, Mills wrote Conable a very complimentary letter of appreciation at the end of the Ninetieth Congress in October 1968, praising Conable for his "conscientious and able service" to the Ways and Means Committee. "It is always a source of satisfaction for the chairman of any committee," Mills wrote his protégé, "to receive the type of cooperation which you have extended to me, although we're in different political parties, through your conscientious attendance at our many sessions and your diligence in attending to your duties and work in connection with the complex subjects presented to us. Your membership in the Committee on Ways and Means has indeed been an asset to the committee, and you can rest secure in the knowledge that your contributions in the development of legislation have been significant and important."[25]

1968 Election

Beyond his committee responsibilities on the Ways and Means Committee, Conable's own congressional career was also caught up in the turbulent presidential election of 1968. In a surprise decision on March 31, Lyndon Johnson announced that he would not seek reelection as president. With the war in Vietnam not going well and demonstrations against the war mounting at home, President Johnson told the nation in a dramatic television address from the Oval Office that he would "not seek . . . [or] accept the nomination of [his] party for another term as . . . president."[26]

With Lyndon Johnson out of the presidential race, the competition for the Democratic presidential nomination heated up between Senator Eugene McCarthy, the antiwar critic from Minnesota, who had entered the race back in November of the previous year, and another war critic, Robert Kennedy, the junior senator from New York and brother of the late president, who had entered the race a few days before Johnson's surprise announcement. As expected, Johnson's vice president, Hubert H. Humphrey, also announced that he would be a candidate in late April.

Then, tragically, on June 5, Robert Kennedy was assassinated in Los Angeles, just after winning the California presidential primary. Though he differed with Kennedy on many of the policy operations of the day, Conable, like the rest of the country, was profoundly affected by the second Kennedy assassination within five years. "Everyone in the country is upset when a central public figure is struck down by an assassin," Conable wrote his constituents in a newspaper column shortly after Kennedy's death. "Anyone who has lost a loved one knows that each person is unique. We grasp this truth only in personal terms. We in government love to say that no man is indispensable, and in the sense that the world goes on and history continues to unfold no one can deny the obviousness of this saying. But in government, as in everything else, the human factor looms largest, and the unexpected loss of a commanding figure leaves an aftermath of painful readjustment."[27]

On the Republican side, former Vice President Richard M. Nixon easily won the Republican nomination for president on the first ballot at the Republican National Convention in Miami Beach on August 8. On Nixon's recommendation, the next day the Republican Convention unanimously nominated Spiro T. Agnew, the little-known Republican governor of Maryland, to be his vice presidential running mate. Seeking to avoid the party's mistakes of 1964, the Republican platform of 1968 struck a middle ground on nearly all of the issues, calling for a reduction of American troops in Vietnam, a negotiated settlement to the war, and a series of domestic reforms at home.[28]

Two weeks later on August 28, amid much violence and protest against the war in Vietnam on the streets of Chicago, the Democratic

National Convention nominated Vice President Humphrey as the party's nominee for president and Senator Edmund S. Muskie of Maine as his running mate. The Democratic platform, strongly influenced by Lyndon Johnson, was generally more hawkish on the Vietnam War and more liberal on domestic issues than the platform adopted by the Republicans. The strong domestic program in the Democratic platform, calling for an expansion of Johnson's Great Society program, drew the united support of the party, but the Vietnam plank, which called for a continued strong American war effort, threatened to divide the party in the general election.

The electoral prospects of both parties were also threatened by the third-party movement of the former Democratic governor of Alabama, George C. Wallace. A leader in the South's fight against desegregation and the general liberal direction of the country in the 1960s, Wallace was not happy with either of the two main political parties, and formed a third party, the American Independent Party, in which to run for president in 1968. With a tough, conservative platform, balanced by a call for an immediate increase in Social Security benefits and federal subsidies for agriculture, Wallace hoped to win enough southern and border states to deny either of the major party candidates a majority victory in the electoral college.[29]

"At this point," Conable observed in his journal on September 20, "it looks like a runaway for Richard Nixon. The polls each day indicate him widening the gap between himself and Humphrey. . . . The whole thing has an unreal ring to it, and I keep suspecting that there is a conspiracy afoot to make the Republicans over-confident. Be that as it may, Nixon is being active, and yesterday I heard a very fine talk by him over the radio, striking just what I thought was a sound and constructive note in what has otherwise been a comparatively disruptive and noisy political campaign."

In this heightened political context of the election, Conable also recorded in his journal a conversation he had on the floor of the House with his legislative mentor and chairman of the Ways and Means Committee, Wilbur Mills.

> Yesterday morning Humphrey announced himself as favoring a 50 percent increase in Social Security benefits to be partially financed out of the general treasury. This appears to be the same proposal made by Bobby Kennedy during consideration of the Social Security bill last year. Although the vice president did not spell out in detail what his plan would be, he's simply dangling the bait before our older citizens.

I couldn't resist the temptation to go over to the chairman on the floor yesterday afternoon to say, "Mr. Chairman, I was curious to know if the vice president cleared with you the statement that Social Security benefits will be increased by 50 percent."

"Well, no," the chairman replied, "I can't say that he did discuss it with me."

He looked so embarrassed that I didn't feel I should press it any further. It was obvious that Humphrey would not talk over such a scheme with Mills in the first place. Therein lies the fallacy of making such promises during presidential elections.[30]

Though Conable did not face a serious challenge to his own reelection, Gerald Ford continued to promote Conable's career and made a campaign appearance for him in his district on October 3, 1968. Attempting to link a vote for the popular Barber Conable with a vote for Richard Nixon, Ford urged his partisan crowd to give their "support to Dick Nixon and Barber Conable and we'll change America for the better."[31]

Back in Washington, the Ninetieth Congress finally adjourned to make way for the fall election. Generally disappointed with the unproductive results of the Ninetieth Congress, Conable wrote his constituents shortly after adjournment that the "pertinent question at the close of the Ninetieth Congress is not so much, 'What have we done in the past two years,' as 'Where do we go from here?'

"Fortunately," he said, "the people have it within their power to answer that question. We in government shall have to abide by their decision, but I for one hope the decision will result in a united government with one party or the other having a clear opportunity to rule. Our problems are too pressing and too dangerous to relish the thought of another two years in the hands of caretakers."[32]

With no question about his own reelection, and as an indication of his growing reputation within the Republican Party, Conable was asked to campaign for the Republican presidential ticket during the fall campaign. On the recommendation of his congressional colleague, Donald Rumsfeld from Illinois, the Republican National Committee asked Conable to join prominent Republicans in leading the party's criticism against the Democratic presidential ticket in the fall general election. Known as the Republican Truth Squad, this group of Republican leaders was responsible for following the Democratic presidential candidate, Hubert Humphrey, around the country and challenging his political assertions during the campaign. The Republicans had been using this campaign technique more or less successfully to force a dialogue with Democratic presidential candidates since Dwight Eisenhower first ran against Adlai Stevenson for the presidency in 1952.

Conable joined the Republican Truth Squad in Chicago on the afternoon of Wednesday, October 17. At the time, Representative Peter Frelinghuysen of New Jersey, with Senators Jack Miller of Iowa and Clifford Hansen of Wyoming, plus Conable made up the entire squad. They went to Rockford, Illinois, that night, and the next day to Muskegon, Lansing, Saginaw, and Flint, Michigan. On Friday, they traveled to Detroit, and on to Green Bay, Eau Plaine, and Milwaukee, Wisconsin, and then back to Chicago, following and rebutting Humphrey at each campaign stop.

"We were on a hostile mission," Conable, the ex-Marine, now deep in a political battle, recorded in his journal, "because our instructions were not to advance the cause of Nixon or even to waste much time in his defense, but to attempt to engage Humphrey in dialogue by pointing out his inconsistencies or his downright prevarications.

"It usually worked," Conable noted "at least to the extent that it prevented a news blackout by Humphrey in the local area of his speech. We made most 11:00 o'clock news summaries in the area and were almost always reported, though not always in complimentary fashion, in the local paper. The total cost to the Republican Party was less than $100,000 or less than the cost of a half an hour of national TV, and the effort demonstrated a team support the Democrats were not able to match, since their congressmen thought they were each fighting for their own lives."

The week before the election, Conable was not scheduled to travel with the Truth Squad, whose membership changed off and on during the campaign. Five days before the election, after midnight on November 1, Conable was called by Bob Kunzig, the staff director of the Truth Squad, and asked to come to Texas. Conable wrote in his journal that Kunzig told him "LBJ and Humphrey were going to hold a rally in the Astrodome in Houston on Sunday and that Texas was so close the Republican State Committee was unwilling to let the president and vice-president have the final word. They had bought a half an hour of TV time and wanted a panel discussion by the Truth Squad to fill it. The only trouble was, the Truth Squad was supposedly finished the day before," hence the frantic calls to anyone who might be available.

"I went," Conable wrote in his journal. "I was by then convinced [with Humphrey rapidly rising in the polls] we were in danger of losing the election. It was a good thing I did. The other three on the panel—Senator John Tower and Congressman George Bush of Texas and Bud Wilkinson of Oklahoma [the popular University of Oklahoma football coach]—had not done Truth Squad work, and were all from the area. Because I was from New York, I gave a legitimacy to the effort and made it appear like a more broadly based answer" to the Humphrey rally than it might have looked otherwise.[33]

Despite the last-minute efforts by the Republican Truth Squad to rescue Texas for Richard Nixon, Nixon ended up narrowly losing Texas to Humphrey in the presidential election by less than 50,000 votes.

Elsewhere in the country, Nixon managed to defeat Humphrey in one of the closest elections—43.4 percent to 42.7 percent—in American presidential history to become the thirty-seventh president of the United States. But in the all-important electoral college, where a majority of 270 votes was needed for victory, Nixon decisively defeated his Democratic opponent 301 to 191. George Wallace did well as a third-party candidate, receiving 13.5 percent of the popular vote and carrying five states in the South for 46 electoral votes, but failed in his bid to deny one of the two major parties a majority in the electoral college.

The Republicans, however, were unable to regain control of Congress, making Richard Nixon the first president since Zachary Taylor in 1848 to be elected without carrying a majority for his party in either the House or the Senate. The Republicans picked up five additional seats in the Senate, but they would still be in a 58 to 42 minority in the new Congress. And in the House of Representatives, the Republicans gained only four seats, twenty-six seats short of what they needed for a majority. The new House would have 243 Democrats and 192 Republicans.

As expected, Barber Conable easily won reelection to his own seat in Congress, defeating his Democratic opponent, Norman Gerhard, a Bausch and Lomb accountant from the Rochester suburb of Greece, by a margin of 72 to 28 percent.[34]

Thus, the November elections did not produce the united government Conable had hoped for. For the next two years, the national government would be divided between a Republican president and a Democratic Congress, a division which, as Conable anticipated, would have a profound affect on the partisan politics of the country.

The relationship between the Republican minority in Congress and the president would now clearly change with a Republican in the White House. Rather than opposing the president, as the Republican congressional minority had been inclined to do for the previous eight years of Democratic presidents, they would now be more inclined to cooperate with a member of their own party. And in this changed institutional context, Barber Conable would end up being one of the strongest congressional supporters of Nixon administration policies.

Chapter 7

Support for Richard Nixon

At his inauguration on January 20, 1969, Richard Milhous Nixon set the stage for the first four years of his presidency. As a long-time, conservative critic of big government, Nixon warned that the country was fast "approaching the limits on what government alone could do" and he promised to "reach beyond government" for private and local solutions to public problems. On the international stage, Nixon cast himself as a "peace-maker," and pledged "to help lead the world . . . out of the valley of turmoil [in Vietnam and elsewhere] and onto [the] high ground of peace."[1]

Six weeks later Barber Conable offered his newsletter readers an early and sympathetic assessment of the new president. "Richard Nixon has now been in office more than a month. The temptation to judge his performance at a time like this is more than any politician, myself included, can resist."

> We Americans tend to personalize our government—to expect the white knight to sweep up from nowhere and set the ills of our country aright with one sweep of the sword of justice. When it doesn't happen, and it never does, we retreat into the thicket of political disillusionment, muttering imprecations and immediately assuming we have chosen the wrong white knight. It is a medieval reaction and a medieval view of the complexities of our modern problems.
>
> As a white knight, Richard Nixon has some advantages over his predecessors. He didn't sweep up from nowhere; his personality and abilities have been debated for two decades now; his actions and reactions have been soberly assessed in every conceivable circumstance. From looking at the cartoons on the editorial pages he has known for years that his public image does not glow with the romance of a Sir Galahad. No one has better reason than he to know that his touch does not automatically dissipate evil or turn opportunity to gold. In short, he is a realist in the realm of government, living in and identifying with the real world, distrustful of panaceas and working for slow and steady progress rather than the wizard's magic moment.
>
> Politically, as well, he lives in the real world. He controls only half the government with both houses of Congress firmly in the hands of the other party. The programs the executive branch must administer were created by the same congressional majority with whom he must work if he is eventually to impart his own direction to government. His is the initiative now, but that initiative must be delicately exercised if it is to have any long term significance. . . .

"Foreign affairs are a different matter," Conable also observed. "The Constitution says the president, not Congress, is the director of our foreign affairs. Here he can make a clean slate on which to write a policy of his own. The world seems to be falling apart. Traditional American interests and historical alliances dictate American response to a certain extent, but at least the management of that response clearly rests in the hands of the man who is president."[2]

As Conable indicated in this optimistic assessment of the new president, he was generally inclined, as a good Republican, to support Nixon's policies at home and abroad.

Support for Nixon's Domestic Reforms

President Nixon was slow in presenting his legislative program to the Congress. But gradually, piece by piece, Nixon laid before the Congress an ambitious reform agenda for the country, which Conable, as a reformer himself, strongly supported.

A month after his inauguration, Nixon asked Congress to reform the electoral college. In April, he requested a major revision of the federal income tax laws of the country, removing more than two million low income families from the federal tax rolls and eliminating a variety of tax loopholes for wealthy Americans. President Nixon also proposed a major reorganization of the government of the District of Columbia to give citizens of the district more control over their own affairs. In May, in an effort to defuse some of the domestic controversy on the military draft, Nixon asked Congress to give him the executive authority to institute the nation's first draft lottery system for military service since World War II. Later in May, the president also asked Congress to reform the postal service by turning one of the most partisan and inefficient of the cabinet-level departments into an independent, government-owned corporation.

Then in August President Nixon proposed a set of additional reforms, which together he called his program of "New Federalism." With this program, the president hoped to more clearly define the policy responsibilities of the various levels of government within the American federal system. Under Nixon's New Federalism, Washington would assume responsibility for solving problems that were truly national in scope, but states and localities would be given more responsibility for solving the problems of their own regions.

The heart of Nixon's New Federalism program called for the federal government to take over and manage the nation's welfare system from the financially strapped state governments in exchange for allocating a certain portion of federal income taxes to state and local governments to help them better manage problems in their own regions. Many observers were surprised that Nixon, a long-time conservative, was prepared to federalize welfare policy. But public welfare, President Nixon reasoned, was a national problem, requiring a national solution. At the urging of his domestic policy adviser,

Daniel Patrick Moynihan, the president called for completely scrapping the state-run welfare system and replacing it with a federal income maintenance or negative income tax program, which Nixon called a "family assistance system." Under the controversial Nixon proposal, the federal government would "build a foundation under the income of every American family with dependent children that cannot care for itself." For a family of four on welfare, with no outside income, Nixon and his advisers estimated, the basic federal payment would be about $1,600 a year.

To offset the increase of federal power in the area of welfare reform, President Nixon proposed an innovative revenue-sharing program with state and local governments. Nixon was prepared to increase national responsibilities in the area of welfare reform, but in other areas, he wanted to distribute more power to the state and local levels. Specifically, Nixon proposed setting aside a small portion of federal income taxes each year for state and local governments to use as they saw fit. "The funds provided under this program will not be great the first year [about $500 million]," the president said. "But the principle will have been established and the amounts will increase [to a projected $5 billion within five years] as our budgetary situation improves."

With the reforms Nixon presented to Congress in the first nine months of his presidency, he clearly indicated that he wanted to be regarded as one of the most reform-oriented presidents of the twentieth century.[3]

A supportive Barber Conable wrote his constituents a few weeks later, "President Nixon has made a thoughtful appeal to the conservatives, regardless of party, who are alleged to represent a majority in Congress. . . . What does the conservative conserve?" Conable asked, as he rationalized his conservative support for Nixon's reforms. "In my view, the only legitimate goal of the true conservative is the conserving of a system, in our case a system designed to facilitate the closing of class barriers."

Paraphrasing the eighteenth-century British conservative, Edmund Burke, to support his own brand of conservatism, Conable warned: "If the system isn't working well (or if those who live under the system think it isn't working), the conservative had better consider Edmund Burke's view that an early reform is an accommodation made with a friend, while a late reform is capitulation to an enemy." Conable added:

> I am aware of my reputation for conservatism among the people interested in my record here in Congress. Some of

my friends profess to be confused by my interest in tax
reform, election reform, welfare reform, draft reform, and
congressional reorganization. I see nothing inconsistent
with my reputation in my desire to make these central
institutions in our American system of government function better. To me the president struck a responsive chord
when he pointed out that the obligation for those who
believe in our American system of government is to work
to improve our willingness to accommodate the system
to new hopes, new needs and new opportunities.[4]

Of course not all members of Congress shared Conable's
enthusiasm for Nixon's reforms. Congress did give Nixon executive
authority to institute a national lottery system for the military draft,
relieving some of the domestic, political pressure on this controversial issue. Congress also passed a major tax reform bill, exceeding
even the reforms the president recommended to tighten loopholes
on the wealthy and lessen the tax burden for the poor. Included
within the tax reform legislation, Congress also provided for a 15
percent increase in Social Security benefits (exceeding here too
Nixon's original proposal for a 10 percent increase), but Congress
did not approve the president's request for future automatic
cost-of-living increases for Social Security recipients. Congress
also refused to adopt the other reforms Nixon advocated: welfare
reform, revenue sharing, postal reform, District of Columbia
reform, and the reform of the electoral college.[5]

Support for Nixon's Vietnam Policy

Conable was also a strong supporter of President Nixon's plan to
end the Vietnam War. Nixon had campaigned on a pledge to bring
this costly, unpopular war to a conclusion. Soon after becoming
president in January 1969, Nixon began to put into place a plan to
achieve this objective.

Working closely with his newly appointed national security
advisor, Henry Kissinger, Nixon rejected the demand of the North
Vietnamese that he immediately withdraw all American troops from
South Vietnam. Instead, the president pursued a two-pronged strategy for achieving a "peace with justice" on the diplomatic front and
on the battlefield.

On the diplomatic front, President Nixon pushed for a negotiated settlement to the war. At the Paris peace talks, Nixon proposed
an immediate cease-fire, the complete withdrawal of all outside

forces from South Vietnam within a year, and free elections under international supervision with the Communist Party fully participating in the organization and execution of the elections. On the battlefield, Nixon called for a Vietnamization plan involving greater support and training of the South Vietnamese forces to enable the American troops to gradually withdraw, even if the Paris peace talks were unsuccessful.

President Nixon's dual strategy for ending the war worked well in quieting domestic critics for most of 1969. Though the Paris peace talks did not go well, with the North Vietnamese refusing to discuss Nixon's proposal and insisting on the unilateral withdrawal of all American troops from South Vietnam, the Vietnamization plan worked well enough for the president to announce the withdrawal of 25,000 of the 540,000 American troops from South Vietnam on June 8.[6]

Conable praised President Nixon's decision to begin withdrawing American troops from South Vietnam. But, as a congressman who had brooded about the war for over four years, Conable warned his constituents in his "Washington Report" that "the politics of withdrawal is every bit as complicated as the politics of escalation, and the stakes are no less high when fine American boys and billions in American resources have already been sacrificed every day."

Some of Nixon's opponents, Conable observed, had "participated in what our hindsight tells us was the disastrous policy of the past four years, and they realize if Nixon succeeds with his new tack where they failed, unfortunate political inferences will be drawn for years to come."

On the other hand, Nixon's opponents "can hold their tongues if they think he will not succeed, or they can hedge their bets (and grab for history's olive branch) by saying conditions have changed and the president is moving too slowly—that they would take out 100,000 troops where he had taken out 25,000, that they would call an immediate cease fire, that they would now call on the Russians for disarmament negotiations where they did not do so before, that they would reduce the Pentagon budget, etc."[7]

As Conable foresaw, the politics of withdrawal from Vietnam indeed turned out to be as complicated as those of escalation. President Nixon announced the withdrawal of another 35,000 troops from Vietnam on September 16. But that was not enough to satisfy the more ardent opponents of the war, who demanded an immediate withdrawal of all American troops from Vietnam.

On October 15, the Vietnam Moratorium Committee, which favored the unconditional and immediate withdrawal of all American troops from Vietnam, organized a national day of protest against the war. Although not everyone who participated in the protest supported the demand for the immediate pull-out of all American troops from Vietnam, practically all of the participants favored a more rapid conclusion to the war.[8]

Observing the Washington moratorium from a distance, Conable was impressed by the peaceful nature of the demonstration, but he was perplexed by some of the protesters' demand for the immediate, unconditional withdrawal of all American troops. "In view of the effort the president seems to be making to transfer the burden of the reduced fighting to the South Vietnamese by withdrawing troops, and in view also of the increasing flexibility of our position at the Paris peace talks," Conable wrote his constituents a few days after the moratorium, "I am unsure about the purpose of the demonstrations. Surely few people in government today harbor the illusion that this is a popular war or that the people do not want it ended in the quickest and best way possible. It is still hard for me to believe that thoughtful people feel that world peace would be advanced by an American withdrawal without some sort of stabilizing agreement, settlement or circumstance."[9]

President Nixon answered the war protesters in a television speech to the nation on November 3 with words that agreed with Conable's thoughts. "We really only have two choices open to us if we want to end this war," Nixon said. "I can order an immediate, precipitate withdrawal of all Americans from Vietnam without regard to the effects of that action. Or we can persist in our search for a just peace through a negotiated settlement if possible, or through continued implementation of our plan for Vietnamization if necessary. I have chosen the second course. It is not the easy way, but it is the right way. It is a plan which will end the war and secure the cause of peace." Convinced that most Americans supported his plan for peace, and not the more radical demands of the students and other street demonstrators, Nixon appealed to the "great silent majority" of Americans for support.[10]

Nixon's speech, as most observers predicted, failed to placate the antiwar demonstrators. In mid-November, another 250,000 demonstrators descended on the nation's capital to participate in a forty-hour "march against death" in Vietnam.

Nixon, however, had more success in getting Congress to accept his policy for ending the war in South Vietnam. On December 2, with Barber Conable voting in the affirmative, the House of Representatives passed a resolution in support of President Nixon's efforts to achieve "peace with justice" in Vietnam by the overwhelming majority of 334 to 55.[11]

A Leader in Congressional Reforms

Though there was little action on President Nixon's reform agenda or movement toward peace in Vietnam in 1969, Conable's own congressional career continued to soar. Early in 1970, at the beginning of the second session of the Ninety-first Congress, Gerald Ford appointed Conable to another important leadership position within the Republican Party. On March 17, 1970 Ford asked Conable to head a nineteen-member Republican task force to study alternatives to the seniority system as the means for selecting House committee leaders.[12]

For more than fifty years both political parties had used the seniority system as the method for choosing committee leaders —a system that automatically promoted the member of the majority party with the longest service on the committee to the chairmanship of the committee and designated the senior minority member to the ranking minority position on the committee. In recent years the seniority system had become controversial within both political parties as some chairmen arbitrarily used their power to block the will of committees.

"The seniority system does stabilize committee politics, since everyone knows exactly where he stands at all times," Conable said as he succinctly explained the problem to his constituents. "The harm comes when the rules permit a capricious or obstructionist chairman to frustrate a majority of the committee by his abuse of power."[13]

Conable accepted the chairmanship of the Task Force on Seniority on the condition that Ford also appoint John Byrnes, the ranking Republican minority member on the Ways and Means Committee, to the task force. "I didn't want any implication that I was upset about the leadership on the Ways and Means Committee," a cautious Conable recalled later. "I greatly admired John Byrnes, and I didn't want it to appear that my working on the Seniority Task Force was a reaction to my own committee leadership. That was the smartest thing I ever did," Conable said, referring to the influential role Byrnes played in getting the task force's recommendations adopted by the party.

For the next seven months, Conable and Byrnes and the other seventeen members of the Task Force on Seniority studied the alternatives for picking Republican committee leaders in the House. The majority Democrats also created a task force, under the leadership of Julia Hansen from Washington, to study alternatives to the Democratic seniority system in the House. In October, the Republican Task Force on Seniority issued its recommendations.

In its report, the Republican Task Force recommended that all Republican members of the House vote on committee leaders. The recommendations called for the Republican Committee on Committees, which consisted of one Republican representative from each state with Republican members in Congress, to submit nominations for committee leadership positions to the Republican Conference, where all Republican members of the House would vote by secret ballot. If the Republican Conference rejected a nomination for a leadership position, then the Committee on Committees would be required to submit another nomination.[14]

The full Republican Party accepted the task force's recommendations for modifying the seniority system when the party met to organize the Ninety-second Congress three months later. "I got the recommendation adopted," Conable recalled later "by having John Byrnes, our leader on the Ways and Means Committee, speak at the Republican Conference when the issue came up. John got up and made an emotional speech about how he wanted to be able to go home to his people and say he was the Republican leader of the Ways and Means Committee because he was chosen leader, not just because he'd survived longer than anybody else. And it shamed some of the old guys who opposed electing the leaders into voting for the change."[15]

The Democrats also slightly modified their use of the seniority system in the Ninety-second Congress. Like the Republicans, the Democratic Committee on Committees, which consisted of all the Democratic members of the Ways and Means Committee, made nominations for committee leadership positions to the full party assembled in the party caucus. But unlike the Republicans, the Democrats required that at least ten Democrats demand a debate and vote on a committee leader before a caucus vote could be taken on the nomination.[16]

Although these organizational changes in the seniority rule which Conable and others pushed through the Ninety-second Congress did not result in any immediate committee leadership changes in either party in 1971, they laid the foundations for the development of a more democratic and responsive committee system in the years ahead. "Anybody who got a big no vote in the conference almost invariably retired in the next Congress," Conable recalled, recounting the long-range impact of the revisions.[17]

As Conable was leading the Republican attempt to reform the seniority system in the House, he was also involved in a broader, bipartisan effort to democratize the House's rules and procedures. Donald Rumsfeld, Conable's ambitious young colleague from Illinois (and future secretary of defense under both Gerald Ford and George W. Bush), had left Congress in 1969 to become President Nixon's director of the Office of Economic Opportunity. Conable succeeded Rumsfeld as the leader of this small group of Republican reformers, known as Rumsfeld's Raiders, who wanted to reform the rules of the House.[18]

Conable and his colleagues were particularly critical of the long-standing House practice of allowing unrecorded teller votes in the Committee of the Whole, the smaller group of at least one hundred members into which the full House resolves itself in order to debate the details of legislation. According to this procedure, as Conable explained:

> Members would march down the aisle in the Committee of the Whole, and tellers [House clerks assigned to count the votes] would count them, but nobody recorded who was marching down the aisle. It became a leadership device where John McCormack [the Speaker] or Carl Albert [majority leader] would get Democrats who opposed a bill to vote for it on an unrecorded teller vote in the Committee of the Whole in the hope that they would get the thing through. They understood that if a majority of the full House later insisted on a recorded vote, the same guys that had voted the other way on the teller vote would vote on the record to protect themselves at home.
>
> The result was that it was a crooked kind of deal where the press would see guys walking down the aisle voting the opposite way they voted on the record in an effort to help the leadership get something passed without it ever being recorded. It was a hypocritical device. It gave guys a chance to support the leadership as long as their name wasn't on the record.

"I decided there were a lot of liberal Democrats who might be able to help us," Conable recalled. "So I went to the liberal Democratic Study Group [an informal group of liberal Democrats in the House] and I said, 'I'm now running Rumsfeld's Raiders. Would you guys be interested in helping?' And they immediately decided they would, even Tip O'Neill [the popular liberal Democrat from Massachusetts and future Speaker], joined the group."[19]

With Sam Gibbons, Conable's Democratic colleague on the Ways and Means Committee, and some of the reform-minded members of the Democratic Study Group, Conable and his colleagues proposed a series of amendments to a modest reorganization bill that had worked its way through the Rules Committee. In addition to calling for elimination of teller voting in the Committee of the Whole, the coalition moved to open all committee meetings and hearings to the public, unless a majority of the committee voted to close a particular session, and to make the public aware how each member voted on committee roll call votes. To more fairly distribute committee resources to the minority party, the reform coalition rules guaranteed that at least one-third of committee staff funds be allocated to the minority members of committees and that both majority and minority members had the right to choose their own staff without a veto from the other party. To ensure more discussion of legislative proposals on the floor of the House, the reformers introduced rules providing for at least ten minutes of debates on amendments and motions to recommit bills to committees. To prevent hasty agreement on negotiated legislative compromises with the Senate, the reformers submitted a rule prohibiting House action on any House-Senate conference report until at least three days after the report had been printed in the *Congressional Record*. To give the Congress more time to prepare the federal budget, the bipartisan reform coalition recommended changing the beginning of the fiscal year from July 1 to January 1 to coincide with the calendar year.[20]

With the exception of the proposal to synchronize the fiscal year with the calendar year, all of the proposed amendments were eventually accepted by the House of Representatives in the Legislative Reorganization Act of 1970. They became part of the most significant set of changes in the rules and procedures of the House of Representatives since 1946 and helped to establish Conable's reputation as an influential congressional reformer.[21]

Congress Adjourns

Despite the bickering between a Republican president and a Democratic Congress, Richard Nixon's Ninety-first Congress in 1969–70 actually tied with Lyndon Johnson's Great Society Eighty-ninth Congress in 1965–66 in David Mayhew's study of the most legislatively significant Congresses in the four and a half decades after World War II. Each Congress enacted twenty-two major pieces of legislation, indicating that under the right conditions, significant legislation is as likely to be enacted during periods of divided party government as during periods when the Congress and presidency are controlled by the same political party.[22]

In addition to the important laws enacted by Congress in 1969, the second session of the Ninety-first Congress in 1970 enacted major legislation in the areas of crime control, drug abuse, the environment, voting rights, occupational safety, postal reform, urban mass transportation, food stamps, unemployment compensation, agricultural production, airport and airway development, rail passenger service, economic stabilization, and a ban on cigarette advertising on radio and television.

Barber Conable voted for most of the major legislation enacted by the Ninety-first Congress. The only exceptions were in the areas of voting rights, federal subsidies for agricultural production, and the expansion of the food stamp program. Conable favored lowering the voting age to eighteen, but as a lawyer sensitive to the constitutional dimensions of the issue, Conable did not believe Congress had the authority to change the voting age by statute as was proposed by the 1970 extension of the Voting Rights Act. Lowering the voting age required a formal amendment to the Constitution, he said in explaining his negative vote to his constituents. President Nixon also took this position, but nevertheless felt politically compelled to sign the bill into law when it was passed by Congress in 1970.[23]

Both houses of Congress recessed on October 14 to prepare for the midterm congressional elections, with a strong hint from President Nixon that he would call Congress back into a special lame-duck session after the election to complete work on his legislative agenda.

Conable easily won reelection for a third congressional term, defeating his Democratic opponent, a teacher from Spencerport, by a 66 percent to 30 percent margin, with the Conservative Party candidate receiving 5 percent of the vote.[24]

Nationally, however, the Republicans did not fare as well. They lost nine seats in the House of Representatives to give the Democrats a 255 to 180 advantage in the new Ninety-second Congress. In the Senate, the Republicans did better, picking up two additional seats, but they still fell five seats short of what they needed to take numerical control of the upper chamber. The Senate would have 55 Democrats and 45 Republicans. With "less than two percent turnover in Congress in the 1968 election," Conable wrote his constituents, "the 92nd Congress will be almost a carbon copy of the 91st."[25]

As expected, President Nixon, much to Conable's disapproval, called Congress back into a special lame-duck session after the elections. "Although I have not participated in such a session previously," Conable wrote his constituents in unhappy anticipation of a lame-duck session a few weeks earlier,

> I can well imagine how inglorious it is likely to be. A lame-duck session, of course, is one conducted after elections

but before the expiring terms of office have expired. It is a
time of minimum responsiveness and minimum responsibility. Even assuming that the character of the body and its
politics have not been changed radically by the election,
and assuming the large majority of the incumbents have
been reelected, the prevailing mood is not one encouraging
serious work. The congressmen have been away from their
families for close to a month, campaigning at the outer limits of physical exhaustion. They want either to celebrate or
to seek new jobs. Those who have been reelected know
that the first week in January they will have to start organizing a new Congress, one that will probably meet almost
continuously for the next 22 months; they know they will
be plunged back into the familiar turmoil which normally
achieves surcease only briefly after elections.

"I'm sorry to sound so sour," a grumpy Barber Conable added,
"but I simply can't see how any real good can possibly come from
a lame-duck session. And I'm angry that the leadership's poor planning [made] one necessary."[26]

As Conable feared, the lame-duck session of Congress proved
to be a fairly unpleasant experience both for the Congress and the
president. "Marked by intense controversy, filibusters and unfin-
ished business," the lame-duck session finally ended on January 2,
1971, with no final action on the president's request for trade restric-
tions or welfare reform.[27]

President Nixon was particularly unhappy with the Senate's
refusal to pass his welfare reform proposal. The House Ways and
Means Committee, with Conable's support, had favorably reported
a slightly modified version of Nixon's family assistance plan in March
and the full House had adopted the bill in April 1970. However, the
Senate Finance Committee, under the leadership of Russell B. Long
of Louisiana, refused to bring Nixon's welfare reform plan to a vote
on the floor of the Senate.[28]

Unhappy with the performance of the lame-duck session,
President Nixon issued a statement on January 5 that was especially
critical of the Senate where he had the most difficulty in getting his
legislative program adopted. "In the final months and weeks of
1970," he observed, "the nation was presented with the spectacle of
a legislative body that had seemingly lost the capacity to decide
and the will to act. In probably no month in recent memory did the
reputation of the whole Congress suffer more in the eyes of the
American people."[29]

The legislative productivity of the lame-duck session, as with
the whole Ninety-first Congress itself, seems more impressive now

in hindsight than it apparently did to Nixon and others at the time. Four of the most important laws enacted by this Congress—the Clean Air Act, the Occupational Safety and Health Act, the Omnibus Crime Control Act, and expansion of the food stamp program—were all passed during the lame-duck session.[30] Conable voted for all these measures except for the expansion of the food stamp program.

A New Beginning

The Ninety-second Congress convened three weeks later on January 21, 1971. Happy for an opportunity for a new beginning on the legislative work of Congress, Conable wrote his constituents a very up-beat newsletter a few days later, in praise of the constitutional system that made such a new legislative beginning possible.

> In this frequently tiresome and tiring world new beginnings are good and I hope we'll make the most of this one. We know the 92nd Congress will move haltingly at first, that it will be a partisan matter, disorderly and inefficient and mirroring the nation's frailties as much as its excellences; that it will record disappointments more than triumphs and that it will be the apt target for the assaults of criticism; but nevertheless it's a new beginning and that's enough reason for hope.
>
> How sad it would be to live under a system that didn't give this hope! There are such systems and the human spirit sags to contemplate them. Maybe there are only 51 new members of the House—a little more than 10 percent—but who is to say that some great new leader is not among them, cutting his legislative teeth and waiting for his moment in history? If I sound too lyrical about the possibilities for congressional renewal, I hope you will ascribe it not to my own complacency, but to the wisdom of the Founding Fathers in giving us the opportunity to correct our past mistakes so quickly by dismissing every Congress after only two years.[31]

To begin the Ninety-second Congress, the Democratic majority in the House made some important changes in party leadership. The Democratic majority leader for the previous nine years, Carl Albert of Oklahoma, was elected with only token opposition to succeed the retiring John McCormack of Massachusetts as the new Speaker of the House. In his twenty-four years in the House, the diminutive 5-foot-4-inch former Rhodes Scholar had gained the approval of practically all factions within the Democratic Party in the House.

There was a more heated contest in the Democratic Caucus to select Albert's successor as majority leader. In the end, the assistant majority leader or whip, Hale Boggs of Louisiana, defeated the more liberal and reform-minded Morris K. Udall and three other candidates to become the Democrats' new majority leader. To placate the liberal wing of the party, the liberal Democratic Congressman Thomas P. "Tip" O'Neill, who held the seat from Boston once occupied by John F. Kennedy, was appointed whip in the new Congress.

The Republican minority in the House continued with the same leadership it had in the previous Congress. Gerald Ford was reelected minority leader and Leslie Arends was reelected whip without opposition.[32]

In his State of the Union address to Congress on January 22, President Nixon proposed "six great goals" for the Ninety-second Congress. First, as his top priority, the president urged Congress to complete passage of his welfare reform bill establishing a minimum level of income for all American families which he had first proposed in 1969. Second, on the economy, President Nixon said he would submit to the Congress "an expansionary budget . . . to help stimulate the economy and . . . open up new job opportunities for millions of Americans." Third, building on the environmental record of the previous Congress, Nixon announced he would propose "a strong set of initiatives to clean up our air and water, to combat noise, and to preserve and restore our surroundings." Fourth, the president said he would offer "a far-reaching set of proposals for improving America's health care and making it available more fairly to more people." Fifth—a goal that was particularly important to Conable—Nixon said he would ask Congress to pass an expanded version of the revenue-sharing program with state and local governments he had first proposed to Congress, along with his welfare reform bill, in 1969. And sixth, President Nixon stated he would propose a complete reform of the federal government, reducing the existing twelve cabinet departments to eight.

With these changes, Nixon said, he hoped to help create a "New American Revolution"—a phrase which the president hoped would replace the phrase, "New Federalism," which he had used sparingly and without much success to capture the essential themes of his administration—"in which power was turned back to the people, in which government at all levels was refreshed and renewed, and made truly responsive."[33]

Conable Elected to Republican Leadership

By the beginning of the Ninety-second Congress in 1971, Conable was widely regarded as one of the "up and coming" members of Congress.[34] Capitalizing on his growing reputation, Conable sought and was unanimously elected as chairman of the Republican Committee on Research and Planning, a position that was part of the formal Republican leadership in the House. Created by Gerald Ford when he became minority leader in 1965, the Research and Planning Committee was responsible for studying broad policy areas in the House of Representatives and recommending party positions for House Republicans. With the assistance of a small staff, the chairman of the Research and Planning Committee presided over a dozen or so Republican task forces that sought policy alternatives to the Democratic majority.[35]

Sensitive to the reaction of folks back home to his new party leadership position in Washington, Conable wrote his constituents in his February 3, 1971, newsletter:

> I have explained so often in these letters that Congress is run by the political parties that I must almost sound defensive about it. I'm not, and I don't apologize for the two-party system despite the bad name that politicians seem to have in some circles. Congressmen are much more pragmatic and relaxed about politics than the public would think possible, sharing a camaraderie with the political figures of other parties, and advocacy or partisan function does not estrange us from each other so much as do personality differences or bad social relationships.
>
> These preliminaries refer to my having been elected to the position of chairman of Research for the Republican Party in the House. As such I will be coordinating the task forces studying possible party issues during the 92nd Congress. Some readers, of both political parties, may feel that I should abhor this kind of political function, but I view it as a further expression of my responsibility to be as effective and as influential as I can in representing the 37th District. I did not come to Washington to hide or to avoid controversy, but to participate in the business of government. I have been known to criticize my party's positions, and I'd better be prepared to work positively for their improvement, given the opportunity, if my criticisms are going to have any substance.
>
> Since the job is filled by vote of all Republican members of the House, it is considered part of the minority's leadership and so involves me in weekly leadership

meetings at the White House. Later, after I have had the
chance to attend several of these meetings, I'll describe a
typical one in some detail, since I assume you will want
to peer through any new windows in the government
that I can open to you.[36]

True to form, and to the maximum educational benefit of his
constituents, Conable wrote his constituents a long newsletter three
months later describing what it was like to be part of GOP leadership meetings with President Nixon at the White House.

The Cabinet Room in the West Wing of the White House
looks out on the Rose Garden. It is a long room with a
big oval table in the middle. At one end is a fireplace,
usually burning, over which is a portrait showing the
famous Eisenhower smile. At the other end is the door
leading to the Oval Office, through which the president
always comes at 8 o'clock sharp each meeting morning.
He exchanges pleasantries on the way in, but quickly
seats himself in the middle of the long side of the oval
table with his back to the Rose Garden. Directly across
from him sits the vice president. Most of the senators are
to his right, most of the representatives to his left. I sit to
his left, diagonally across the table, with Senator
[Robert] Griffin of Michigan between me and the vice
president.
   The White House staff present changes from meeting
to meeting, depending upon what the president wants to
talk about. The same consideration determines the
Cabinet officials who attend. The president controls the
discussion, opening with items of current topical interest.
Anyone can interrupt, but at this point it rarely happens
since he is only setting the agenda for the meeting.
   During the meetings earlier this year the usual major
topics consisted of two or three of the items of the president's program as outlined in the State of the Union
message. A Cabinet official or staff members would give
a quick but detailed briefing on each idea and then the
president would turn to us and say, "How about it? Do
you see any problems here? Can we get support for such
a proposal? We'll have a message (for the Congress) on
this item next week, so we're almost ready to go." He
turns first to the minority leaders. Senator [Hugh] Scott
[of Pennsylvania, the Republican minority leader in the
Senate] and Congressman Ford, who sit on either side
of him, before opening it up for general discussion. We
normally take an hour or less on an item, and then repeat
the procedure for a second or third item.

Lately he has asked us to report to him on what Congress is doing with his proposals, asking what he can do to help. On several occasions he has asked for brief special reports of current interest from Dr. Kissinger (his foreign policy adviser), George Shultz (his management and budget man), and Secretary [John] Connally of Treasury.

The White House is about as establishment as you can get, and it is difficult not to be over-awed by the experience. I think most of us try very hard to participate fully, and the president helps us in this respect with an informal manner, frequent refillings of coffee cups and occasional digressions in the form of anecdotes. There is a pad at each place; he, himself, frequently writes notes in a quick hand and puts them in his pocket. No news embargo is placed on anything said.

"The president knows my name as a result of these meetings and listens to my opinion," Conable added, "but I would not want to pretend that such attendance makes me an insider at the White House. I do not meet him as an individual, but as one of a group. This group represents a minority in the Congress, which can advise but cannot deliver. The meeting is an opportunity to participate, however, not just an act of deference."[37]

"Nixon was good at these meetings," Conable recalled years later.

I never saw the side of him that emerged in the [Watergate] tapes. He was not crude. He didn't use four-letter words, didn't talk about getting people, didn't talk about his enemies. He was an active part of the dialogue, unlike Ronald Reagan, who would come in and have a three-by-five card and give a little graceful welcoming statement and then turn it over to the House and Senate leadership members who would talk about what was going on with his programs and so forth. Occasionally he'd have a story and tell a little joke and everybody would laugh and we'd go out of there not being aware of whether we really had gotten through to him or not. But Nixon was always engaged in active dialogue.[38]

Unbeknownst to Conable and the other participants, Nixon began secretly taping these White House Republican leadership meetings from the very first meeting Conable attended on March 9, 1971. For the next two and a half years, Nixon secretly recorded twenty-six meetings until his recording system was revealed by his assistant, Alexander Butterfield, at the 1973 Senate Watergate

Hearings. The last taped leadership meeting at the White House was on July 10, 1973. The National Archives log of these meetings shows that Conable was an active participant, attending all twenty-six meetings from March 9, 1971, to July 10, 1973. He was particularly vocal in informing the president and others on the legislative matters that came before the Ways and Means Committee, where he was rapidly becoming one of the committee's most influential members.[39]

Conable Leads Fight for Revenue Sharing

As President Nixon had indicated in his 1971 State of the Union address, he reintroduced his revenue-sharing proposal in the Ninety-second Congress. During his first year as president, Nixon proposed a modest revenue-sharing plan to designate a small percentage of federal personal income tax revenues for state-local government use. One-third of one percent or $500 million was to be allotted in the first year, increasing to one percent of total personal income taxes or a projected $5 billion by 1976. Nixon envisioned this type of general revenue-sharing program as a major Republican alternative to the well-established categorical grant programs that mandated state and local government expenditure of federal funds.

Conable was a strong supporter of President Nixon's revenue-sharing proposal when it was first introduced in 1969. "I remember when Nixon first became president," he recalled. "I was talking to one of my Democratic friends one day and told him one of the big reasons I support Nixon so strongly is because he's a decentralist and believes the most important aspects of democracy occur at the local level. And this Democratic friend said, 'Come on, Dick Nixon is a power man. When he gets control of the federal government, he'll be for federal power. He'll change his role.' Well that wasn't true at all. Nixon continued to be a decentralist and the most important element in his decentralist reform effort was the revenue-sharing bill.

"The major thing about revenue sharing as far as I was concerned," Conable said, "was that it was a way of getting progressive tax money into an area that was previously nourished entirely by regressive taxes—sales taxes and real estate taxes. And the important thing about revenue sharing was that they tied no strings to it. The localities got the money, a significant amount, without any mandates as to how it would be spent. That's what revenue sharing was all about, and I felt very strongly about it."

The Nixon revenue-sharing program, for obvious reasons, was strongly supported by the financially strapped state and local governments, but it ran into heavy opposition from the Democratically controlled Congress, particularly from the powerful chairman of the Ways and Means Committee, Wilbur Mills, and the ranking Republican member on the committee, John Byrnes. "Neither Wilbur nor John would touch revenue sharing with a ten-foot pole," Conable explained. "They felt very strongly they shouldn't be expected to raise taxes for the spending of money over which they had no say. In other words, why should they tax people to benefit local politicians?"[40]

With John Byrnes and other senior Republicans on the Ways and Means Committee opposing revenue sharing, it was Barber Conable, the sixth ranking out of ten Republicans on the Ways and Means Committee in the previous Congress, who led the Nixon charge for revenue sharing in 1969 and 1970. Despite their best efforts, however, Conable and the five other members of the Ways and Means Committee, who supported revenue sharing during the Ninety-first Congress, were not able to persuade Mills to conduct hearings on the subject.

Nixon, though, did not give up. Encouraged by the national support he had received for revenue sharing from state and local officials, he introduced an even larger, more ambitious plan in the Ninety-second Congress. In his 1971 State of the Union message Nixon proposed giving state and local governments 1.3 percent of the revenues the federal government collected each year from personal income taxes, estimated to be $5 billion in 1972, and rising automatically to about $10 billion by 1980, with funds divided evenly between state and local governments.

Three days after the president's message, Wilbur Mills announced that he would conduct Ways and Means Committee hearings on the new proposal. Still strongly opposed to revenue sharing, Mills candidly told a press conference on January 23 that the primary purpose of the hearings would be "to expose the dangers and weaknesses of the revenue-sharing concept and to kill the bill."

But midway through the hearings in June 1971, Mills, feeling the political pressure from state and local governments and also considering a presidential bid himself, had a change of heart and announced that he would support a revenue-sharing plan that gave most of its benefits to the financially troubled and heavily populated urban areas of the country. For the next five months, Mills worked closely with the Nixon administration to hammer out a compromise bill that would be acceptable to both President Nixon and the Democratic Ways and Means Committee.

Finally, on November 30, 1971, Mills introduced his compromise revenue-sharing bill in the House. Building substantially on the Nixon bill, Mills proposed a limited five-year $30 billion plan that would allocate two-thirds of the $5.3 billion the first year to local governments and the other one-third to the states. On April 17, 1972, following the leadership of their chairman, the full Ways and Means Committee voted eighteen to seven to report the new bill to the House.[41]

"Barber didn't get a lot of credit," recalled Murray Weidenbaum, the assistant secretary of the Department of Treasury who was responsible for developing the administration's plan, "but there's no doubt he was the prime mover for revenue sharing inside the committee."[42]

"We were able to keep revenue sharing alive in the committee, not because I was such a fierce advocate, but because the Democrats were afraid to kill it," Conable recalled.

> There was very strong support for it from all the local governments. Of course, you can just imagine, Rocky [Governor Nelson Rockefeller of New York] was just beside himself. He had budgeted a $500 million empty sack in the state budget on the hope that he would get revenue sharing. And at that point Rocky found new virtues in me. Rocky and I had had a lot of problems when I was in the state Senate, but he became a very fast friend of mine on the Ways and Means Committee, particularly when revenue sharing was pending in the committee. Mayor Daley [Richard Daley, the powerful Democratic mayor of Chicago] was also very strongly for it. And the result was Danny [Rostenkowski, the Democratic congressman from Chicago and protégé of Mayor Daley, who later became chairman of the Ways and Means Committee] was for it, even though he didn't know what it was.[43]

Opponents of revenue sharing continued to oppose Mills's bill after it left the Ways and Means Committee. First, they tried to deny Mills's request for a closed rule from the Rules Committee to prohibit amendments to the bill on the floor of the House, as was the tradition for Ways and Means bills. Failing in this effort by a narrow eight to seven vote in the Rules Committee, the opponents proceeded to try to block the acceptance of the closed rule on the floor of the House. Failing here, too, in an important 223 to 185 test vote of the bill's strength, the revenue-sharing opponents then focused their attack on the substance of the legislation in the floor debate. John Byrnes, critical of Wilbur Mills's last minute conversion to revenue sharing, launched a vigorous attack on the bill in the House floor debate. Quoting extensively from two speeches Mills had made against revenue sharing before his sudden endorsement of the idea in the summer of 1971, Byrnes warned that "a vote for revenue sharing [would] be a vote for a tax increase" and ultimately lead the Congress "into a dark tunnel of fiscal chaos with no light at the end."

But Conable, working closely with Mills, and disagreeing with his own Republican leader, made a strong speech for the revenue-sharing legislation on the floor of the House. Describing himself as a "Jeffersonian Republican, a man who believes in keeping government as close to the people as possible," Conable disagreed with critics of the legislation who feared local governments would misspend the money without greater accountability. "That is a possibility," Conable conceded. "There is nothing magic about local government. There is nothing magic about federal government either." But, he added, "I personally think there is a much closer degree of accountability held on the local government by our constituents out there than is held on us here in this remote and distant seat of government on the Potomac. Frankly, I have more confidence in accountability on the local level than I do on the federal level. Distance and activity insulates us. We do not live directly with our neighbors, subject to their direct control."[44]

In the end, the House sided with Mills and Conable and overwhelmingly approved the revenue-sharing legislation by a large bipartisan majority of 275 to 122 on June 22, 1972. The Senate passed a slightly different version of the bill by the lopsided majority of 64 to 20 on September 12. A conference committee of House and Senate members then successfully negotiated the differences between the House and Senate versions of the bill and President Nixon signed the State and Local Fiscal Assistance Act into law, eighteen days before the presidential election, on October 20, 1972. Signing the bill into law before a large crowd of state and local officials outside Independence Hall in Philadelphia, Nixon attempted to make the symbolic point that the revenue-sharing law moved toward a greater system of decentralized power, much as the creators of the Constitution had envisioned.[45]

Retroactive to January 1, 1972, the new law allocated about $30 billion to state and local governments through December 31, 1976. As proposed by Mills, two-thirds of the money set aside for revenue sharing the first year was allocated to local governments and the other one-third went to the states. Described by political scientist David Mayhew as one of the most significant laws enacted by

Congress since World War II, Congress renewed the State and Local Fiscal Assistance Act when it expired during the Ford presidency in 1976.[46] Ironically, and quite unhappily for Barber Conable, the revenue-sharing law did not survive the budget cuts of the conservative Reagan presidency in the early 1980s.

Thus, throughout both the Ninety-first and the Ninety-second Congress, Conable was a strong supporter of Nixon administration programs, not just on revenue sharing, which was the most appealing part of the Nixon program to him, but on a whole host of domestic and foreign issues. In fact, with each passing year, as the *Congressional Quarterly* annual survey of congressional voting behavior indicated, Conable became a stronger Nixon supporter. His support for Nixon's program in Congress increased from 66 percent in 1969 to 78 percent in 1970, and increased again from 82 percent in 1971 to 89 percent in 1972.[47]

Conable's strong support for Nixon's legislative agenda, however, did not hamper the good reputation he had also managed to develop among liberals in the political community. The liberal Ralph Nader organization, for example, conducted an extensive investigation of Conable's congressional career in 1972 as part of their overall evaluation of Congress. The Nader group noted Conable's quick rise up the party and committee ladders of the House and praised him for his leadership in the recent party and institutional reforms of the House. Quoting a journalist who had closely followed Conable's career, the liberal-oriented Nader group concluded that Conable was "the best kind of conservative there is" and "one of the most respected members of Congress," noted for his "friendliness, fairness, and hard work."[48]

The Nader report also recognized Conable's strong support for the Equal Rights Amendment. In the same traditions as his grandmother and mother, Conable was particularly vocal in support of women's rights. "This amendment shouldn't be necessary, but it is," he wrote his constituents in a 1971 newsletter. "Persons are assured the equal protection of the law, but for many purposes the courts have interpreted the constitutional mandate not to apply with the same force to women as to men." To correct this situation, Conable argued, as a liberal on this social and constitutional question, that a formal amendment should be added to the Constitution granting women "equality of rights under the law."[49]

Conable was skeptical of the Nader investigation when it was first announced, complaining to his constituents in a newspaper column that "nobody appointed [Nader] to be a 'public citizen,' as he likes to call himself."[50] But he was naturally pleased with the final results of the investigation in October, telling a Rochester newspaper that he was "amazed at the amount of information collected and its even-handed presentation. The Nader organization has not approved of everything I have done in the past, just as I don't agree with everything they've done. But I am glad the report finds that on balance my efforts in Congress are constructive and effective."[51]

1972 Elections Continue Divided Government

The national elections in November 1972 continued the divided government between the Congress and the president which had begun four years earlier. Nixon, who had barely lost the 1960 election and barely won the 1968 election for president, scored a massive landslide victory over his Democratic challenger, Senator George McGovern from South Dakota. Receiving 60.8 percent of the popular vote, only slightly below Lyndon Johnson's defeat of Barry Goldwater in 1964, Nixon won even more impressively in the electoral college, where he carried forty-nine out of fifty states with a total of 521 electoral votes. McGovern won only Massachusetts and the District of Columbia with a meager seventeen electoral votes.

Nixon did not do much personal campaigning during the election. Instead, he relied on Vice President Spiro Agnew, cabinet officers, and other prominent Republicans to take his case to the American people. The Nixon campaign, though, was very well organized and funded, with the Committee to Reelect the President reportedly spending a record $50 million on the president's reelection.

By contrast, the Democratic presidential nominee, George McGovern, and his running mate, Sargent Shriver, the first director of the Peace Corps and then of the Office of Economic Opportunity, were on the road campaigning almost constantly from Labor Day to Election Day. But the McGovern campaign, poorly organized and underfunded from the beginning, was never able to draw Nixon into a debate on the issues. The McGovern campaign also suffered a serious setback shortly after the Democratic convention in the summer, when McGovern was forced to replace his original running mate, Senator Thomas F. Eagleton of Missouri with Shriver, after it was revealed that Eagleton had suffered from a history of psychiatric problems.

McGovern's chief issue, the Nixon administration's handling of the war in Vietnam, was seriously undermined in the closing days of the campaign with reports that a Nixon negotiated peace with Vietnam was close at hand. McGovern tried to discount these reports as a "cynical effort" to win the election. "Peace is not at hand," McGovern said on November 5. "It is not even in sight." Despite his best efforts, McGovern was never able to cut into the comfortable lead Nixon enjoyed throughout the campaign.

One potentially damaging issue to Nixon were widely published reports that Nixon administration officials had been involved in a June break-in of the Democratic Party headquarters in Washington, D.C., in an illegal and covert attempt to sabotage the McGovern campaign. McGovern tried to link this issue with other charges of Republican favoritism toward big business, calling it "the most corrupt administration in history." But this charge failed to excite many voters.[52]

Despite his landslide victory in the presidential election, Nixon was not able to carry a Republican Congress with him. Once again, Barber Conable easily won reelection to his own House seat, in a slightly reapportioned but still predominantly Republican district, with a 71 percent majority vote.[53] The Republicans also picked up twelve seats in the House, but fell far short of the thirty-nine additional seats they needed to capture a majority in the House, leaving them at a 244 to 191 seat disadvantage in the new House. In the Senate, the Republicans lost two seats, giving the Democrats a 57 to 43 seat majority. Even worse for the Republicans, eight new senators were Democrats, half of whom were more liberal than the Republican incumbents they replaced, giving the Senate a decidedly more liberal ideological orientation in the new Congress.

Thus divided government between the Congress and the president would continue in the new Ninety-third Congress, prompting many, including Barber Conable, to speculate on the consequences. "Are we in for four more years of the same divisions of government, the same domestic paralysis, the same buck-passing, the same institutional unresponsiveness which gave a national feeling of uneasiness to the last four years?" Conable asked in a thoughtful newsletter he wrote his constituents after the election. "Nobody really can tell until we see what history deposits on our doorstep during the next four years."

> Although the political outlines of the government have not changed in any reassuring way, frequently events have more to do with the impetus of government than do the forces at work within the institution itself. Certainly the president is anxious to translate his electoral mandate (or was it a McGovern un-mandate?) into domestic leadership as well as leadership abroad. Certainly the majority party Democrats in Congress are anxious to develop

effective initiatives and a unity which have eluded them during recent years. Certainly the people, however they split their tickets, want a government that functions and deals with their problems or at least decides what its role is going to be. We know from history that the system is capable of working, given an appropriate interaction of its elements.

The difficulties facing us are obvious. The Senate, with a 57-43 majority of Democrats, and more ideologically polarized than before, is less susceptible to presidential leadership. The House (244 to 191) is about the same in ideological makeup, but the president's own party begins four years of declining presidential influence with widespread resentment over the failure to proffer coattails as he coasted to victory. The fiscal legacy of the last four years is ominous, with probably more than $100 billion of additional national debt and an economy that is not likely to continue its remarkable improvement indefinitely. We have prices to pay for a volunteer army, for stimulative government spending, for more jobs and a higher level of affluence with a livable environment.

"So what else is new?" Conable concluded. "Troubles, opportunities, struggles, and occasionally a little progress. Let us all put on a hopeful face."[54]

Chapter 8

The Watergate Betrayal

As President Nixon became more and more embroiled in the Watergate scandal, Conable's support for Nixon began to fade and he tried to distance himself and the Republican Party from Nixon. "The whole issue," Conable recalled after his retirement from Congress, "was the survival of the Republican Party and how to disengage Nixon from the image of the Republican Party, because we were all tied to him. This is why it was such a terrible experience, because you didn't have any control over it."[1]

Conable did not know Nixon well personally, but for four years he had agreed with him on most of the important policy questions of the day. In 1972, *Congressional Quarterly* identified Conable, along with his fellow Republican Clifford Carlson from Illinois, as "the two most loyal Nixon supporters in the House." Of all the members of Congress, only the archconservative Republican Senator Roman L. Hruska from Nebraska, who agreed with the president 91 percent of the time, had supported Nixon more than Conable and Carlson in 1972.[2]

This close public association with Nixon, increasingly linked to the Watergate scandal, began to bother Conable in 1973 as he searched for ways to explain his general policy agreement with the president without simultaneously endorsing Nixon's handling of Watergate, which Conable regarded as an "incredibly stupid affair right from the start. The idea that you could learn any secrets by looking in the Democratic National Headquarters is a crazy idea," Conable recalled. "Their documents are as public as any documents that you'll find anywhere. I don't really believe that Nixon had anything to do with planning the break-in, but he created the environment in which that kind of petty stuff occurred. The G. Gordon Liddys of this world are not sensible people."[3]

Publicly, Conable was quite restrained in his judgment about Nixon's involvement in Watergate, preferring to give the president the benefit of the doubt, right up to the revelation on August 5, 1974, of the White House tape—"the smoking gun" that implicated Nixon in the Watergate cover-up and forced his resignation from office four days later. Privately Conable was deeply troubled by allegations of Nixon's involvement in Watergate. Conable's journal shows that he went through five fairly distinct stages in his reactions to Watergate and in his efforts to cope with the most significant political crisis of his career.

Disbelief

Conable's first reaction to Watergate, like that of most Americans, was one of disbelief. "Frankly," Conable said, "we thought the whole thing was a put-up job at the time. Watergate wasn't anything that we were all that excited about. It seemed like a grubby little affair, and everybody thought Dick Nixon was too smart to get into something like that."[4]

Conable's first journal entry on Watergate, in fact, was not until almost three months after the break-in of the Democratic Party headquarters on the evening of June 17, 1972. That night five men, with ties to the Committee to Reelect the President, were caught planting electronic surveillance devices in the Democratic National Committee Headquarters in the Watergate office building in Washington, D.C. In an off-hand comment in his journal on September 7, 1972, Conable noted, "The Watergate bugging affair is on the television and in the press almost daily. It seems from comments I've heard back home, it is beginning to impinge on the consciousness of the American voter to a slight degree." But Conable discounted any major effect the break-in would have on the presidential campaign, since most voters already believed that "both political parties are dirty, and can't be trusted. It is about the only issue the Democrats seem to be enjoying and so they are pressing it hard." Conable privately conceded though that "if there are further revelations of high level involvement," the scandal could "perhaps eventually be damaging to the Republicans."[5]

Conable's next entry in his journal on Watergate was not written until six months later—after Richard Nixon's reelection—on March 26, 1973. Conable still found the "whole business hard to believe." But with the conviction of the Watergate break-in defendants in January and the establishment of the Senate Watergate Committee to investigate the break-in in February, Conable, like many others, particularly in the Republican party, became increasingly alarmed about the implications of the scandal. "It now seems apparent," Conable wrote in his journal,

> that there were incredible stupidities in this affair going either to the top or very close to the top in the Republican Party. I do not find grave moral turpitude in the bugging of the Democrats, but I do find incredible stupidity and serious reflection on the judgment of those who thought this was the way to political success. The other day one of the figures [G. Gordon Liddy] was given 6 to 20 years in jail and a $40,000 fine as his penalty for participating in this comic opera caper. Why Nixon does not put an end to this mess by meeting it head-on makes it apparent that he finds it considerably more embarrassing than anything which has currently come to light would indicate. As a result, I can only assume the worst.[6]

The Watergate scandal came at a particularly bad time in Conable's own congressional career. With a growing national reputation, Conable was expected to play a leading role in the enactment of the Nixon agenda in his second term. In a cover story on January 15, 1973, on "Congress in Crisis," *Time* magazine had listed Conable as one of the twenty most important leaders in the Ninety-third

Congress, who would "face not only the usual legislative tasks but also the enormous job of revitalizing the Congress itself."

> Representative Barber Conable, 50, is one of those congressmen little known to the public but highly regarded by colleagues in the House. A moderate from upstate New York, he is one of the ablest Republicans on the Ways and Means Committee and has fought hard for legislation requiring complete campaign-funding disclosures. He was the leading Republican backing the Legislative Reorganization Act of 1970. His ties to the White House are strong; Conable is an important Nixonian voice in the ranks of Ways and Means.[7]

Several months later, the *Wall Street Journal* also ran a long, very complimentary article on Conable's rising influence in the House. "Barber Conable is not a household word, but his views seem likely to have an increasing effect on not only households but businesses across the country," Albert R. Hunt wrote, "for Mr. Conable . . . is rapidly emerging as one of the key GOP operatives in the House. Indeed, he's rated a good bet to fill the void created by the retirement of Wisconsin Republican John Byrnes as House Republicans' chief economic expert."[8]

But Watergate seriously threatened Conable's leadership and legislative ambitions, as it cast a growing cloud over Nixon's presidency and the Republican members of Congress as they fought to ward off the negative and destructive consequences of Watergate on their party.

Anger

By early May, with growing evidence of criminal involvement by the White House in the Watergate scandal and the resignation of Nixon's chief of staff, H. R. Haldeman, and his chief domestic adviser, John D. Ehrlichman, Conable's disbelief had turned to anger—"anger that the president has been so stupid as to create an environment in which petty criminality could become the norm in high places," he wrote in his journal on May 8, 1973.[9]

Conable was particularly angry at the way President Nixon had ignored the Republican Party in his handling of Watergate. He described the mood among rank and file Republicans as "desperate, with absolute conviction that the president is not going to change his approach" to Watergate and other matters of mutual concern to his Republican colleagues in Congress. Conable began to urge other members of the Republican leadership to "take the president on, head on," if they were to "express any legitimacy" and save the party. "The whole thing is very depressing," Conable wrote in his journal on May 21, five days after the Senate opened its hearings on Watergate and four days after Attorney General Elliot Richardson appointed Harvard Law School professor Archibald Cox as the special prosecutor for the Watergate case. "It seems that the only way to possibly salvage anything is by joint action on the part of the leadership: something that is difficult at best and particularly difficult when Jerry [Ford] has his head in the sand and is convinced the president is doing all that is necessary and desirable to alleviate the situation, making his tenure in office increasingly difficult. I see this thing as badly hurting Jerry's leadership, and I don't want to have him that badly hurt, because the alternatives are all less desirable than he."[10]

On June 5 Conable joined Ford and the other Republican leaders of Congress for a joint leadership meeting with Nixon at the White House to discuss how to improve presidential–congressional relations. "The questions did not have any relevance to Watergate, but had considerable relevance to the relationship between the White House and the Republicans in Congress. It was interesting to see how closely we watch the president now that we assume he is under great pressure on account of Watergate," Conable observed in his journal.

> He came into the room with his head down and his face red and a rather grim look on his face. Realizing that he was in the company of friends, he began to open up and act more relaxed after he had been in the room a little while. He fidgeted with his watch for the first half hour or so and acted distracted throughout, although he was pleasant and attempted to be anxious to please us with concessions he was willing to make about the manner of operating on such items as the development of administrative positions, patronage and the consultation necessary before any compromise on a legislative confrontation with the Democrats. Watergate was not mentioned except to the extent he talked about the show going on in town and how it was distracting people from their work.
>
> None of the boys took him on directly, but there was considerable firmness in the position expressed about defects in the White House standard operation. I am sure he has the best of intentions with respect to possible

improvements in the relations between the two institutions. Whether or not they come to fruition depends on a follow through which has heretofore been entirely lacking. . . .

All in all I expected more of the meeting than ultimately emerged, a not infrequent condition. I got quite tense about it, feeling it was terribly important to us to get through to the president the extent of the difficulty in which he now finds himself. But looking at him and sensing the tension of the group as we met with him, we all found it difficult to believe that he was not firmly aware of the extent to which his triumphs have turned to ashes in the squalid little affair known as Watergate.[11]

Over the summer the Watergate conditions worsened. In June, Nixon's former legal counsel, John Dean, told the Senate Watergate Committee that he had been part of an organized White House effort to cover up the Watergate scandal, and he also indicated, even more devastatingly to Nixon, that he thought the president himself had known about the cover-up as early as September 1972. Citing a specific conversation he had with Nixon about Watergate on April 15, 1973, in which he told Nixon he was cooperating with the special prosecutor about his own personal involvement in the Watergate cover-up, Dean testified that Nixon then began asking "leading questions which made me think that the conversation was being taped."

On July 16 Alexander Butterfield, a former aide to the president's chief of staff, H. R. Haldeman, indicated in a surprise testimony before the committee that, in fact, President Nixon had secretly tape-recorded all conversations in the Oval Office since the spring of 1971, thus providing possible evidence to confirm or refute Dean's accusations that the president had known about, and perhaps even been a party to, the Watergate cover-up. Later in the afternoon, the White House acknowledged that all of Nixon's conversations in the Oval Office and in his office in the Executive Office Building had been taped since early 1971.

The Senate Watergate Committee immediately asked Nixon to provide them the records and tapes of White House conversations that were relevant to the Watergate investigation. Nixon refused to allow either the Senate Watergate Committee or the special prosecutor access to the White House tapes, citing his constitutional right of executive privilege to protect private conversations within the White House. The Senate Watergate Committee and the Special Prosecutor Archibald Cox, in turn, subpoenaed the White House for

the tapes and documents relevant to their Watergate investigation.
The president rejected the subpoenas. U. S. District Court Judge
John J. Sirica then ordered Nixon to turn the tape recordings subpoenaed by the Watergate special prosecutor over to him for use
before the federal grand jury hearing the Watergate case. President
Nixon and his lawyers then appealed Judge Sirica's decision to the
U. S. Circuit Court of Appeals, arguing that Sirica's decision was
inconsistent with the principle of separation of powers and the
president's need to preserve the confidentiality of private presidential conversations.[12]

Conable returned after the August recess to his district "deeply
depressed and unrefreshed by the amount of time spent at home."
With Watergate "casting its shadow over all the conversations I had
with my constituents, I found very little pleasure in my work," he
wrote in his journal.

Conable became so despondent that when he was back home in
his district during the August recess he seriously considered resigning from Congress to accept the presidency of the Security Trust
Company of Rochester. He would make a salary more than twice
what he was making in Congress and have the opportunity of
serving on a number of boards of directors for corporations in the
Rochester area.

> I personally considered this much more seriously than
> the rest of my family did, feeling that it was an opportu-
> nity for a new start or offered a different lifestyle than I
> had been able to achieve as a congressman. The ultimate
> decision to reject the offer was based on the strange feel-
> ing that I would be doing something quite inappropriate
> for a person of my background and values and that the
> offer was doubtless based on misinformation and lack
> of knowledge about my true qualifications. Nevertheless,
> it was good to find at the time when my morale was so
> low at least one group of businessmen who felt I was
> employable despite my eight years in the Congress.[13]

On returning to Washington in September Conable had an
added reason for despondency. A *Congressional Quarterly* study,
released on September 1, showed that for the first seven months of
1973, Conable again led all of his colleagues in his support, at 84
percent, for Nixon's policies in Congress. At a time when congressional support for Nixon policies was sharply declining, Conable's
support for the president's policies remained high.[14]

"I'm increasingly distressed and depressed with the necessity of dealing with and following the presidential leadership of

Richard Nixon," Conable wrote in his journal after the *Congressional Quarterly* study was widely publicized in his district.[15] Pondering his political choices, Conable wrote:

> I do not feel that I am in fact making any effort to respond to any such leadership and have to conclude that my support is based generally on agreement with his policies, but I'm sorely tempted to vote against some things the president wants just to try to draw a different picture not only for my constituency but also for myself. A year ago those who were highest in support of the president were mostly liberal or moderate. This year they were mostly conservative. In both cases I am number one, thus eliminating any possible excuse that my support was based on ideological convictions.
>
> Drawing such a picture of myself as a rubber stamp is very bad for my self respect. I am puzzling about what to do about it short of attacking the president or varying my voting pattern.
>
> It is difficult to have very much respect for him as a man, and I muse a good deal about the dilemma of how we live in the same government: how Congress and the president can work together for the next three and a half years, taking advantage of the constructive opportunities ahead of us rather than bogging down and continuing destructive confrontation. The whole business is pretty depressing.[16]

During the fall Conable's discomfort with Nixon as president increased as the political conditions continued to deteriorate. On October 12, the U. S. Circuit Court of Appeals for the District of Columbia upheld Judge Sirica's August ruling that President Nixon should surrender the court subpoenaed tape recordings relevant to the Watergate case. A week later, in what became known as the "Saturday Night Massacre," Nixon's attorney general, Elliot Richardson, and his deputy attorney general, William Ruckelshaus, both resigned, rather than carrying out Nixon's order to dismiss the Watergate Special Prosecutor Archibald Cox. Nixon had been in a dispute with Cox over the Watergate tapes. In an effort to reach a compromise, Nixon promised to provide a written summary of the subpoenaed tapes that would be verified for accuracy by Democratic Senator John C. Stennis from Mississippi. In return, Nixon asked Archibald Cox to agree to make "no further attempt . . . to subpoena still more tapes." The special prosecutor rejected this offer.

Ten days later, on October 22, the House Democratic leader tentatively agreed to instruct the House Judiciary Committee to begin an inquiry into the impeachment of President Nixon. The following day, Nixon's attorney announced that the president would abide by the Court of Appeals decision that he should turn over the subpoenaed tapes and documents to the court. In November, Acting Attorney General Robert Bork, who had finally carried out Nixon's order to fire Archibald Cox, appointed Houston attorney Leon Jaworski as the new Watergate special prosecutor. On November 26, Nixon turned over the subpoenaed tapes to the court, noting an eighteen-minute gap in a conversation between President Nixon and H. R. Haldeman on a June 20, 1972, tape, which Nixon's secretary, Rose Mary Woods, explained she had accidentally erased in transcribing the tape for the president.[17]

Conable's own political career took an unexpected turn upward in December when his friend and political mentor, Gerald Ford, became Nixon's new vice president. Spiro Agnew had resigned from the vice presidency on October 10, pleading no contest to a charge of income tax evasion unrelated to Watergate. Using the recently ratified Twenty-fifth Amendment, Nixon nominated Gerald Ford, the House Republican leader, to be his new vice president. Ford was confirmed by majority vote of the House and Senate and sworn in as vice president two months later on December 7, 1973.

Ford's elevation to the vice presidency created a vacancy in the top Republican leadership position in the House. On December 13, the House Republican Conference chose John Rhodes of Arizona, who had served for eight years as chairman of the Republican Policy Committee, to be the new Republican minority leader of the House of Representatives.

The same day, the House Republican Conference chose Conable to replace Rhodes as the chairman of the Policy Committee. Conable, the candidate of the younger, more moderate wing of the House Republican Party, defeated the conservative Del Clawson of California in a spirited contest by a vote of 88 to 77. Conable's election as Policy Committee chairman—a job that focused on generating and coordinating Republican policy positions in the House—made Conable the fourth ranking Republican leader in the House, just behind the new minority leader, John Rhodes, the whip, Leslie Arends (who as an old-time Nixon loyalist was by-passed for the top leadership position), and the liberal, urbane John Anderson of Illinois, who was chairman of the House Republican Conference.[18]

Conable, who always saw himself as more of a legislative leader than a partisan leader, now found himself in the personally uncomfortable position of quickly advancing up the party ladder, putting him in line to become leader of the Republican Party in the House and perhaps even Speaker, if his party were ever so fortunate as to capture majority control. Realizing that he was now on a different track than the one on which he had set out when he began his career, Conable wrote his constituents explaining, almost apologetically, his ascent up the party ladder. "I have said many times in this newsletter that Congress is run by the political parties, and that some acceptance of political responsibility is necessary for a representative to be fully effective," he wrote in a January 1974 newsletter. But he said frankly to his constituents:

> I do not view myself as a potential top political leader in the House, and I hope you will not expect me to try to struggle further up the political ladder. My interests and expertise are primarily legislative, not partisan. The Ways and Means Committee takes more and more of my time, and under the rules of my party I cannot have both committee leadership and a party leadership role.
>
> I want to be as effective as I can; but while I can accept secondary roles in both committee and party, the necessity of eventually choosing a top role in one or the other would find me prejudiced in favor of the committee where I already put the great bulk of my time.[19]

So Conable, who saw himself as temporarily on leave from his primary legislative interests to carry out his partisan responsibilities, embarked on an even greater effort to save the Republican Party from Richard Nixon and the debacle of Watergate. Conable was more bitter than ever toward Nixon as he concluded in a December 1973 journal entry. "I find it hard to think about him or to look at him without revulsion at this point, not because I consider him loathsome, but because I consider him incredibly stupid as a leader. I doubt that he is much worse than any other president in historic terms, and I doubt that he is even more amoral, but he is insensitive to a degree that makes everyone, who has by force of circumstances been identified with him, a potential political victim."[20]

Disassociation

By early 1974, Conable's anger at Richard Nixon led to a more purposeful effort to disassociate himself and the Republican Party from Nixon and the destructive consequences of Watergate. The scandal was now a matter of individual and collective political survival. Ever since September 1973, when *Congressional Quarterly* reported that Conable led his congressional colleagues in his support of Nixon programs in the House for the second year, Conable had searched for ways to disassociate himself from Nixon. Now, on February 6, 1974—the day the House of Representatives voted 410 to 4 to authorize the Judiciary Committee to begin a formal inquiry into the impeachment of President Nixon—Conable felt more compelled than ever to explain to his constituents that his support for Nixon programs in Congress had been based totally on his philosophical agreement with the Nixon's policies and not on any agreement with his conduct of the Watergate affair.

"Since I have been widely reported as supporting Nixon administration program measures last year as much as anyone in Congress," Conable wrote, "I have been doing some analysis to understand why it has worked out that way. Aspects of Nixon administration doctrine which appeal to me as a western New Yorker are not hard to find in such an analysis, and here are some of the major elements."

First, Conable said, as a western New Yorker, he agreed with Nixon's policies of "decentralization," where he was trying to distribute more power to state and local governments. "We like strong local institutions in western New York, and prefer the pluralism of the total federal system to the centralized problem solving which the Washington bureaucracy and the majority in Congress seem hung up on."

Second, as a long-time fiscal conservative, like most of his neighbors, he liked the "fiscal reality" of the Nixon administration. "To many people, the fiscal policy of the Nixon administration has not been conservative enough." But frankly, he believed "it has been realistic compared to the major alternatives bludgeoning it. Posturing is easy in this field, and it has taken some courage for the administration to try to hold to a realistic line in the face of short-term political opportunism from both ends of the congressional spectrum."

Third, he supported the "institutional reforms" initiated by Nixon. "In light of its scandals it may seem odd to talk of the Nixon administration as reform oriented, and yet it really has tried to change the way the government functions. . . . Administrative proposals only partially adopted and then only partially successful, have at least tried to change the massive status quo through such maneuvers as restructuring of the departments, welfare reform, tax reform, fiscal reform and even postal reform. We can't get more responsive government without this kind of effort."

Fourth, Conable liked the combination of "strength and negotiation" he found in the Nixon foreign policy. "In foreign policy, strength is dangerous without an open mind and an open mind is wasted without strength. . . . I don't like communism, but I don't consider war inevitable if we remain strong and constantly seek ways to try to reduce tensions. Most of the initiatives for peace in the world today [are] traceable directly to the remarkable Nixon–Kissinger alliance.

"I feel I would be advocating [these] principles . . . no matter who occupied the White House," Conable wrote in what he considered to be his most important newsletter in his congressional career. "I certainly will not reject implementation of these principles legislatively simply to demonstrate an independence which my friends in western New York know is bred in the bone."[21]

With this newsletter—which Conable entitled "A Declaration About Independence"—he began the delicate public process of distinguishing between his support for Nixon policies in Congress and his attitude toward Nixon's handling of Watergate. He would not vote against the president's policies just to demonstrate his independence, but he left little doubt with his constituents and colleagues in the coming weeks and months that he wanted to be completely free and independent to judge Nixon's guilt or innocence on Watergate on the basis of the evidence and not on the basis of his policy agreement with the president.

From February to May the House Judiciary Committee worked to gather information for the possible impeachment of President Nixon. Much of this work centered on obtaining access to the presidential tapes. In early March, President Nixon, speaking through his lawyer, James D. St. Clair, a prominent Boston trial attorney, agreed to provide the Judiciary Committee the same nineteen taped conversations and documents he had given the grand jury through the special prosecutor in 1973, but he refused to turn over additional tapes requested by the committee. "The granting of a request for virtually unlimited access to presidential documents, conversations and other materials would, in the president's judgment, completely destroy the presidency as an equal coordinate branch to our government," St. Clair explained.[22]

Far from absolving the president from involvement in Watergate, the released tapes raised even more questions about Nixon's role in the Watergate cover-up. Perhaps even more damaging to the president, the tapes also revealed a dark side of Richard Nixon not seen before, a man who had created an atmosphere of deep hostility and suspicion within the White House, with many "expletives deleted" directed toward his political enemies, both real and imagined, outside the White House. Reflecting the general negative reaction to the White House transcripts, the *Chicago Tribune* noted in an editorial, "We saw the public man in [Nixon's] first administration and we were impressed. Now in about 300,000 words we have seen the private man and we are appalled."[23]

Dissatisfied with the president's response, the Judiciary Committee voted on April 11 to subpoena the president for the additional tapes and records, consisting of more than forty Watergate-related conversations between Nixon and his aides in February, March, and April 1973, and set April 25—later extended to April 30—for the president to comply.

In a dramatic televised response on April 30, President Nixon released more than 1,300 pages of transcripts of some, but not all, of the additional taped presidential conversations subpoenaed by the Judiciary Committee. In releasing the transcripts, the president expressed the view that they would make "the record of my actions [on Watergate] . . . totally clear now, and I still believe it was totally correct then."[24]

Not satisfied with the White House transcripts, a day later the Judiciary Committee voted twenty to eighteen, dividing generally along party lines, to inform the president that the transcripts were not an adequate response to their subpoena. They wanted all of the subpoenaed transcripts of the White House tapes submitted to the committee at once.

At the White House, the president's chief of staff, Army General Alexander M. Haig Jr., who had replaced H. R. Haldeman, coordinated the White House's response to the Judiciary Committee's request for more tapes. After consulting with Nixon's lawyer, St. Clair, William Timmons, head of the White House congressional-relations office, and Ron Ziegler, the president's press secretary, "they all agreed," according to Bob Woodward and Carl Bernstein's account of Richard Nixon's final days, "that it was essential now to place the impeachment issue in as partisan a light as possible. The Republicans on the Judiciary Committee had to be held. The president's decision to resist the subpoena would need the support of other influential politicians in the House, especially those who weren't regarded as down-the-line Nixon supporters." Two such men, they believed, were Barber Conable and John N. Erlenborn of Illinois. "Conable's influence in the House, where he was the fourth-ranking Republican, was enormous," Woodward and Bernstein noted. "Nervous, vocal, intellectual, he was regarded by his colleagues as almost puritanical in his standards of personal and political conduct, a man of unquestioned integrity. Erlenborn, though a party man and a conservative, had a reputation for independence and was generally opposed to broad claims of executive privilege. He was highly regarded in the Illinois Republican delegation; two of its members, Thomas F. Railsback and Robert McClory, were members of the Judiciary Committee."[25]

On Tuesday, May 7, Haig and St. Clair invited Conable and Erlenborn for breakfast at the White House. They wanted their personal advice on how to respond to the Judiciary Committee's request for more White House tapes. "In addition to the tapes under subpoena, the committee had informally requested another 141 presidential tapes," which Haig and St. Clair thought would also be subpoenaed. Haig complained that it would take six months or more to transcribe the other tapes and result in further delay of the impeachment proceedings. He explained that "the president wanted to cooperate" with the impeachment inquiry, but thought the demands of the committee for additional tapes were "unreasonable".

Conable was impressed with the White House's efforts to cooperate with the Judiciary Committee. "Now that the president has been forced to take off his clothes and expose himself in public," Conable suggested that the request for additional tapes could be handled "like a game of Russian roulette." He proposed as a last-ditch effort to resolve the matter that the White House tell the Judiciary Committee that they would not turn over all of the requested tapes, but that they would let the committee select the five or ten tapes they most wanted to hear. These tapes, not the transcripts, would then be turned over to the committee, making it clear to the committee that the president had "nothing to hide." Conable believed this solution would preserve the principle of executive privilege, but also show Nixon's willingness to cooperate with the Judiciary Committee.

"St. Clair showed a good deal of interest in my proposal," Conable wrote in his journal, "and said it was an intelligent suggestion, that he would consider it seriously."[26]

At four o'clock that afternoon St. Clair announced that Nixon had rejected the Judiciary Committee's requests for more tapes. As far as Nixon was concerned, the full story of Watergate was contained in the tapes he had already released. "The only basis for further requests would be a desire by some to erode the presidency, and the president is not going to stand for it," St. Clair said. If the Judiciary Committee persisted in their request, "then we are going to have a confrontation, because the president is firm in his resolve that he has done more than is necessary."[27]

On Capitol Hill, Conable was incensed at the swift, outright rejection of his compromise proposal by the White House, "thus preparing the whole matter for confrontation and in no way indicating the president's willingness to be forthcoming in other ways."

> Sometime next week I'm very likely to suggest [to the House Republican leadership] that I think the time is right for us to try to put together a high level group of Republicans to discuss the possibility of going to the president and telling him that we were in a position where we have to withdraw any support we were capable of giving him. . . . I do not know if John Rhodes is at all receptive to the idea of trying to put together such a group, but I'm beginning to feel that it is very necessary for us to avoid outright revolt among the Republicans in the House of Representatives, mass defection on an individual basis, and mass retribution by the Republican loyalists out there who somehow identify loyalty to the presidency with party loyalty. We need to make some disassociation from the president respectable.

But finding a way to disassociate the party from Nixon was not an easy matter. During the Republican leadership meeting at the White House two days later Conable found great despondency among other Republican leaders. After the meeting—a routine one on the economy—Conable pulled aside his old friend George Bush, whom Nixon had appointed to head the Republican National Committee in 1973, and told him he thought "it was awfully important for the party to assert its corporate identity." Bush said he was "extremely uptight, didn't know what the right thing to do was," and indicated to Conable that he was "considering resigning." Conable told Bush he thought that would be a "serious mistake because of the necessity of the party having a clear identity in the event the president as leader of the party was further pulled down."

When Conable returned to his office, he discovered that the House minority leader, John Rhodes, who had not attended the White House leadership meeting, had suggested at breakfast with a group of reporters that morning that the "president should consider resignation among the various options open to him." Later that same morning, Conable recorded in his journal, the even more vocal John Anderson, the third ranking Republican leader, "actually called for the president's resignation."

Concerned with this "new trend" of the Republican leaders "going over the side one by one," Conable went to see John Rhodes that afternoon and suggested that he call a meeting of the Republican Conference to give all the Republicans in the House an opportunity to discuss how they thought the party should handle its relations with the president and the growing Watergate crisis. Rhodes said he "doubted if a conference meeting was the thing to do," but he agreed to call a leadership meeting the following week to discuss the party's options and strategy.[28]

At the Republican leadership meeting the following week, the leaders discussed "what should be done to buck up the morale of the Republicans in the House." They decided that rather than calling a conference meeting to discuss their situation—which would be too public and potentially divisive to the party—they would use a lower key approach and have each member of the Republican leadership interview twenty-five or so of the rank and file members and ask for their advice on the "appropriate party posture, not only for the collective group, but also for the leadership itself."

The strong consensus that emerged from the interviews with the Republican members, Conable recorded in his journal, was that the leadership should downplay any talk of a presidential resignation and instead focus on their constitutional responsibilities in the impeachment proceedings. Most of the members said they "expected, however they voted, to lose a substantial part of their support at home. But if they indicated an unwillingness to prejudge the president, and instead base their decisions on impeachment on the evidence produced by the Judiciary Committee, they would at least have some basis for discussion with those disappointed with the final result of their vote on impeachment."

"It appeared to us in the leadership, on reconsideration," Conable wrote, "this was the best posture for the leadership also to take . . . in order to avoid the polarization and politicization of the issue, [although] some members still seem to want to play impeachment politics in one way or another."

Realizing that Conable's support was crucial to an impeachment vote in the House, President Nixon invited Conable and ten other congressmen, five Republicans and five Democrats, for dinner on the presidential yacht on May 29. "We went aboard the *Sequoia* about 6:30 and were back at 8:30," Conable recorded in his journal, "having simply steamed out onto the Potomac and then made a quick circle rather than going upstream or down stream in any way."[29]

All eleven congressmen invited to dinner—seven of whom were from the South—were conservatives, with records of supporting Nixon policies in Congress, and presumably inclined to be sympathetic with him on impeachment. Also joining the president and congressmen for dinner were the president's chief of staff, Al Haig, and William Timmons, the head of the White House congressional liaison office.

"Ninety-five percent of the time was spent talking about foreign policy," Conable told a reporter the next day. "The president told us about the difficulties of Henry Kissinger's negotiations in the Middle East and the problem of dealing with the Russians."

But the talk did turn to politics and impeachment at dinner. "When we were sitting around the dinner table, some of the southerners asked what they could do to help him. The president didn't discuss guilt, innocence or strategy, but he said there was absolute need for someone to speak for the country.

"He talked about the length of an impeachment trial and the effect it might have on foreign policy. That was the one and only comment he made all night that sounded like a plea for help."[30]

"It was a substantial mistake for me politically to have accepted the invitation to have gone out on the yacht," Conable later reflected with some discomfort in his journal, "since it has been reported a great deal in the press and on the radio since that time, the impression being that this identifies me clearly as a man willing to engage in opulent support of the president at the taxpayer's expense, when I shouldn't be a party to jury tampering."

As impeachment pressures mounted in June—with an increasing likelihood that the House Judiciary Committee would vote to impeach the president—Conable detected a "good deal of grumbling among the rank and file Republican members of the House about the lack of leadership that has been demonstrated in our leadership group." Conable attributed the "increasingly rank and file disenchantment with the Republican leadership" to the "comparatively low key, low silhouette and indecisive type leadership that [John] Rhodes has been giving. There is little doubt," Conable wrote in his journal, "that Rhodes is a less outgoing leader than Jerry Ford. He seems to expect us to follow him without making any clear effort to indicate to us in which direction he himself is moving.

"To the extent there's been leadership that is flashed from the sky in recognizable form," Conable added, "it is John Anderson's leadership [which was much more liberal and openly critical of Nixon] with which most of the boys do not agree. John continues to summon with thunderbolts in ways that are not traditional among conservative loyalists. He now seems not to be doing it as a matter of absentmindedness but as a deliberate matter, reflecting an increasing liberalism on his part rather than just the insensitivity of the past."

Conable, in his own distress, was also having growing doubts about his own commitment and willingness to continue as chairman of the Republican Policy Committee in the House. He "did not feel committed to a political function in the House" and thought his "time would be better spent in Ways and Means where the committee appears to be falling apart before our very eyes," with the departure of the Republican leader, John Byrnes, in 1973 and the declining leadership of Wilbur Mills, who would be forced to relinquish his chairmanship later in the year.

So, frustrated with his new political responsibilities, made worse by Watergate, Conable sought the opportunity to talk with John Rhodes in late June and told him that he "did not expect to run for Policy chairman again." Rhodes' response, Conable wrote in his journal, "was unequivocal in that he wanted me to stay in the leadership." Conable told Rhodes he "was doing a lousy job as Policy chairman," to which Rhodes replied "that he had spent eight years in that frustrating job and he was well aware that it was not the most satisfying opportunity in the world." Rhodes told Conable that he "didn't care what [he] did about the Policy job, but that he wanted [his] brain and judgment at leadership meetings.

"It was a flattering response, whether sincere or not," Conable reflected later, and he "agreed to put off any decision about a leadership role until after the election."

Conable's private criticism of Rhodes's leadership notwithstanding, he wrote in his journal that he "felt sorry for Rhodes," who had to walk "a desperate tightrope between the Nixon loyalists on the one hand and the inveterate haters on the other. . . . I feel badly about the pressures that are on Rhodes, and have talked with him privately and pledged my continuing help in any individual way I can do it."[31]

The Smoking Gun

On Monday, July 24, in a crushing blow to President Nixon's claims of executive privilege, the Supreme Court ruled unanimously that President Nixon did not have an absolute right to withhold subpoenaed tapes and ordered him to turn over sixty-four tapes of White House conversations subpoenaed by Special Watergate Prosecutor Leon Jaworski for use as evidence in the Watergate cover-up trial.

Also, on the evening of July 24—after two months of investigation—the House Judiciary Committee began five days of dramatically televised debates on the three articles of impeachment filed against President Nixon. Meeting in a Saturday session on July 27, the Judiciary Committee approved in a twenty-seven to eleven vote, with the eleven opposition votes coming from Republican members of the committee, the first article of impeachment charging Nixon with obstruction of justice in the Watergate cover-up.[32]

With the impeachment of the president a virtual certainty, speculation now shifted to the size of the vote in the House. The size of the impeachment vote, wrote Albert R. Hunt of the *Wall Street Journal*, depended on the votes of eight key individual members of the House, who "have great collective influence on other House members." How these members—a diverse group of Democrats and Republicans—voted would "sway a lot of votes" and influence the margin and the composition of the House vote, where a simple 51 percent majority was required, which, in turn, would have an important bearing on the outcome of the eventual Senate trial of the president, which required a larger two-thirds majority for conviction.

One of the most important of the eight members to watch on the impeachment vote, Hunt said, was Barber Conable. He was "the first person mentioned by numerous GOP House members when asked who will be a crucial figure in impeachment voting. . . . A wide variety of Republicans regard him as having a keen analytical mind and astute political perspectives," Hunt observed.[33]

Meanwhile the situation worsened for the president as the House Judiciary Committee voted twenty-eight to ten on July 29 to recommend a second article of impeachment against Nixon, charging him with misuse of his presidential powers in violation of his oath of office. And on July 30, by a twenty to seventeen vote, the committee approved the third article of impeachment, charging Nixon with contempt of Congress for refusing to comply with the committee's subpoenas.

As the case mounted against the president, reports began to circulate in the media that Conable was "leaning toward impeachment." Still adamant about maintaining his independence on impeachment until he had read all the Judiciary Committee's evidence, Conable took to the House floor on the morning of Thursday, August 1 to deny reports in the media that he had already made up his mind to vote for impeachment. "I am told that the New York *Daily News* and several TV network news shows have reported during the past 24 hours that I am 'leaning toward impeachment,' " Conable told the House. "I am at a loss to know how that conclusion has been reached since I have not read the evidence yet, do not consider newspaper and television reports to be evidence, and have every intention of basing my decision only on the evidence. In short, since I take seriously my constitutional responsibility in this matter, I have no intention to lean for or against impeachment until I can do so on a fully informed basis."[34]

The next day Conable informed Wilbur Mills he would not be available for committee work the following week because he wanted to read the evidence that was being distributed in printed form by the Judiciary Committee. "Mr. Mills looked completely blank," Conable reported in his journal. "Apparently it had not occurred to most of the Democrats present [at the Ways and Means Committee meeting] that they should read the evidence about Mr. Nixon."

On the same day, Conable instructed his staff to pull out the evidence from the Judiciary Committee that related to the abuse of power charges against the president, "feeling that was probably the most serious charge against Mr. Nixon." He reported being "deeply troubled by allegations the president used IRS, FBI and others to harass citizens who he considered to be political enemies of his."

He was shocked when Harry Nicholas, his administrative assistant, offered him six of the thirty-six books of evidence from the Judiciary Committee, saying "these all relate to presidential abuses of power." He took the books home with him to New York and managed to read one of the books over the weekend. He had heard the transcripts of Nixon's conversations in the Oval Office were bad, he recalled, but he was not prepared even then for the tone of them, describing them in his journal as "comparatively low grade and immature, consisting of a number of conversations between President Nixon and H. R. Haldeman and John Dean about how they were going to get this or that political enemy. It seemed like the sort of thing that would go on in a college fraternity."

On Sunday several Washington reporters called Conable at home in Alexander and asked him if he knew anything about what was going on at Camp David. He said he did not, but it appeared that Nixon had summoned his speech writers to his presidential retreat to prepare for a major statement on Watergate. He also learned from the reporters John Rhodes had called off his press conference scheduled for Monday, where he was expected to announce his decision on impeachment, claiming he had laryngitis.

When Conable returned to Washington on Monday, he reported in his journal:

> The day was normal up to about quarter to four when John Rhodes called and told me the president was ready to drop another shoe and that it consisted of a tape showing his involvement from the start and substantial misleading of Republican members of the Judiciary Committee who had stood up for him and voted against impeachment in the committee. . . . He said at that very moment St. Clair was meeting with the 10 Judiciary members who had supported the president and that the statement would be available over on the floor in a little while with the president expected to release the tape at 4:15.[35]

Conable rushed over to the House floor and found Joe Bartlett, the minority clerk in the House, who got him a copy of the president's statement. Nixon admitted that on June 23, 1972, six days after the Watergate break-in, in three separate conversations with his chief of staff, H. R. Haldeman, he had attempted to halt the investigation of the break-in for political as well as national security reasons and he had withheld evidence of his role in this cover-up from his lawyer and supporters on the House Judiciary Committee. Calling his impeachment in the House "virtually a foregone conclusion," Nixon nevertheless said he hoped that the Senate would see the evidence in perspective and vote to acquit him.[36]

As Conable was reading Nixon's statement, he saw the Republican members of the Judiciary Committee filing into the back of the House chamber with St. Clair "looking gray and unhappy." At that moment, he recalled in his journal,

> Sam Donaldson of ABC rapped on the door of the lobby and asked me if I knew anything that I could make a statement about. I said I did and followed him into the House television studio, where I said before all three network television cameras that as far as I was concerned I had found the "smoking gun" where the president had lied to us, and that I felt sad and angry that I had put my trust in a man who is not worthy of that trust. I said as far as I was concerned the only issue remaining was the orderly transition of power from Richard Nixon to Gerald Ford.

"I reacted with such anger before the television cameras that I could not remember exactly what I had said," Conable recalled.

"I was somewhat chagrined that I had not been more artful in my denunciation of the president. I received quite a bit of hate mail about this later on by people who had not yet absorbed the extent of the president's confession." [37]

Since Conable was the first congressman to react publicly to the presidential release—before the statement was completely out—his comments describing the June 23 tape as "the smoking gun," implicating the president in the Watergate cover-up, were widely quoted throughout the country.[38] William Safire would later credit Conable with helping to add the phrase "smoking gun" to the American political vocabulary. Henceforth, Safire said, after Conable's description of the June 23 tape as the "smoking gun" that should force the president from office, the term would be used in American politics to describe "the inconvertible evidence, the proof of guilt that precipitates resignation."[39]

An hour and a half after Conable appeared on television denouncing the president, Charles Wiggins of California, Nixon's articulate Republican defender on the Judiciary Committee, put out a statement, agreeing that the June 23 transcript was a "smoking gun," and announcing that he was changing his vote for impeachment on the obstruction of justice charge.

The following day, support for the president collapsed in the House, when the other Republican members of the Judiciary Committee who had stood by the president announced that they were also changing their votes for impeachment, and the minority leader, John Rhodes, said that he too would vote to impeach the president on obstruction of justice charges.

On Thursday evening, August 8, Nixon announced in a televised address that he would resign the presidency, effective at noon on the following day, because "it has become evident to me that I no longer have a strong enough political base in the Congress to justify continuing. . . ." He ended the speech with no mention of Watergate.[40]

The next day, at 12:03 P.M. in the East Room of the White House, with Conable sitting in the audience, Vice President Gerald R. Ford was sworn in as the Thirty-eighth president of the United States.

Total Alienation

Barber Conable would never speak to Richard Nixon again, so complete was his alienation from Nixon as a result of the Watergate scandal. "No man did more to damage my enjoyment of public service than Richard Nixon," he would later say. "He was a very badly flawed personality. I hate the bastard. I just hate him. . . . I don't know how many times I'd heard him say, 'Never underestimate the power of this office.' Well, he overestimated it until he was out on his ear."[41]

After he left the presidency, Nixon wrote Conable two personal hand-written letters hoping to renew contact with his old congressional ally, as he had with many of his former colleagues over the years, trying to rehabilitate his reputation and continue to be an off-stage influence in American politics. In 1980 after Nixon had seen Conable on television talking about Social Security, Nixon wrote Conable a letter, praising his ability to explain complex issues and advising him on what he thought should be done to save Social Security. In 1986, after Conable's appointment to the presidency of the World Bank, Nixon wrote him another letter, telling him what he thought the World Bank should be doing and offering to talk to him about such matters. Conable did not respond to either letter.

Not even after Nixon's death in April 1994—twenty years after his resignation from the presidency—did Conable soften his reaction to the former president's betrayal. While some of Nixon's old partisan adversaries, such as George McGovern, offered conciliatory comments on Nixon's death, and even attended his funeral, Barber Conable offered a terse, "No comment," when asked by the media for his reaction to Nixon's death. Even Conable's wife gave him a hard time about it. "Barber, you're not a vindictive person," she said. "But he lied to me," Conable replied.

"We had a lot of frank talks with him [about Watergate]. We'd say to him at the leadership meetings, 'Mr. President, you've got to get it all out on the table.' And he'd say, 'It's all there.' And two weeks later there'd be another downward spiral of disclosure that left you feeling queasy. He lied to us. We were the people he needed, and he didn't care about us. . . . The whole thing was a crummy affair. It didn't have anything to do with his getting elected. He didn't need to do it. It was so incredibly inept and stupid that we couldn't believe that a bright guy like Nixon would do it."[42]

Chapter 9

Toughest Reelection

Richard Nixon's resignation on August 9, 1974 did not end the nightmare of Watergate for Barber Conable. His public identification with Nixon would continue to hound him in his reelection campaign in the fall. After surviving the Johnson landslide in 1964, there had been four easy reelections. Now with the Watergate scandal casting a cloud over all Republican candidates, particularly those with any identification with Nixon, Conable faced the toughest reelection campaign of his career.

Defeat in the Conservative Primary

"It's going to be a rough year for all incumbents, especially Republicans," Conable told the annual meeting of the Rochester Jaycees in May 1974, "and we'll probably have further polarizing events before the election." But, still confident of his own reelection, he said he did not plan on putting any additional time or money into the campaign. "I have been coming home about 40 times a year," he said. "I make an average of four speeches a weekend. I don't see how I could put in more time."

Conable told the Jaycees that he planned to keep his campaign budget under $30,000 and continue his policy of not accepting more than $50 from any contributor. "But in this business," he added, anticipating how the unpredictable political circumstances of 1974 might cause him to change his plans, "you have to do what's necessary."[1]

One thing that Conable concluded early in 1974 that was necessary, or at least desirable to maximize his own reelection prospects, was to enter the Conservative Party's primary for the first time in his congressional career. He had avoided the Conservative primary in his five previous elections, preferring to distance himself from the more ideologically right-wing extremes of his district. He particularly objected to the Conservative Party's adamant stand against abortion, and he was also generally opposed to third parties, believing that the traditional two-party system in the United States provided the moderating influences necessary in American politics.

But, now, facing a strong challenge from the left and others disillusioned by Richard Nixon, Conable reached out to the district's Conservative Party hoping to attract the four thousand votes that usually went to the Conservative candidate. In a close election, that could spell the difference between victory and defeat.

However, Conable was strongly challenged in the Conservative primary by Clarence E. Carman Jr., a forty-two-year-old Rochester art designer and steel engraver and "dyed-in-the-wood conservative," who had moved to Rochester from New York City in 1956. "At the very best, Conable is a 50-50 conservative," Carman said. "That's not good enough. I will get the nomination because I am the conservative. I feel I represent 90 percent of the membership of the Conservative Party."[2]

Carman, who had been active in the Conservative Party since its founding in New York in 1960, was particularly irked that the leaders of the Monroe County Conservative Party had endorsed

Conable in the primary. "We had little use for each other until now, and Conable once said that third parties were a nuisance," Carman remembered. "Now that he's in trouble, he comes to us on his knees. I feel that the party leadership has broken faith with the rank and file, and that's why I'm running."

Leo Kesselring, chairman of the Monroe County Conservative Party, responded it was "not completely true" that Conable "came running" to the Conservatives. "There was no overt pitch," Kesselring said. "There were people on both sides that suggested we get together and talk." Kesselring said Conable had made "injudicious remarks" about Conservatives and third-party movements in the past. "But he's apparently decided that we have a function to serve."

Kesselring explained that the Conservative Party leadership had decided to endorse Conable because of its concern that organized labor had "singled him out for extinction" in an attempt to elect a "veto-proof Congress" in the fall. The Democratic candidate, who had the backing of Rochester labor groups, "would be the local component of that veto-proof Congress," which would give the Democrats enough votes to override any presidential veto of Congress. "I would feel comfortable with Carman," Kesselring explained, "but Conable is the more viable candidate and fits well within the parameters of conservative dogma."[3]

Despite Kesselring's endorsement and the support of Conservative Senator James L. Buckley and to the surprise of most local analysts, Conable lost the Conservative primary for the first and only electoral defeat of his career. With fewer than 300 of the registered 2,900 Conservatives voting in the primary, Carman defeated Conable by a vote of 148 to 103. Carman won all five counties in the congressional district except Conable's native Wyoming County. With so few voting in the primary, it was difficult to interpret the ultimate meaning of the vote, but its immediate impact was apparent. Conable could not count on the extra four thousand votes that normally went to the Conservative Party candidate on the congressional ballot. His effort to move right to shore up his base for a strong challenge from the left had backfired.[4]

Conable attributed his defeat to President Ford's appointment of Nelson Rockefeller as vice president and the news that Ford might grant a blanket pardon for Watergate defendants. "I'm sure there is some disenchantment with the Republican Party because of the appointment of Nelson Rockefeller," Conable said. While the rumored blanket pardon for the Watergate defendants never materialized, Conable felt it added to the deepening public cynicism and distrust of incumbents. "Disappointed" by his defeat, Conable hoped nevertheless that since he had "a reputation of being a conservative," he would not need the Conservative Party label to win the bulk of the conservative vote in November.[5]

A Strong Democratic Challenger

As Conable worked subtly and indirectly to disassociate himself and the Republican Party from Richard Nixon, Democratic opponents from his district were interested in keeping the public's association between Barber Conable and the unpopular president alive. Not many of Conable's constituents had much sympathy for the leadership dilemma he faced as one of the elected Republican leaders of the House, that is, of having to work with President Nixon while at the same time remaining detached from him and hopefully unaffected by his Watergate problems. Many of Conable's constituents would have preferred that he follow the leadership example of the liberal Republican John Anderson and publicly call for Nixon's resignation or impeachment. They saw Conable's cautious and restrained public reaction to Watergate as one of indecision and vacillation in the face of obvious guilt on the part of the president.

Capitalizing on the growing public mood against Nixon and anyone associated with him, three Democrats in Conable's district—Margaret "Midge" Costanza, the vice mayor of Rochester, Michael Macaluso, a conservative Rochester businessman and local anti-pornography crusader, and Terrence Spencer, a political newcomer from rural Ontario County—announced in the spring of 1974 that they would seek the Democratic nomination to challenge Conable for his congressional seat in the fall general elections. David L. MacAdam, a research scientist at Eastman Kodak, announced he would again challenge Conable as the congressional candidate for the Liberal Party, and then there was the Conservative Party nominee, Clarence Carman.

From the outset, Midge Costanza, the Rochester city councilwoman and vice mayor, was by far the most serious contender. The vivacious forty-year-old Costanza, known for her candor and liberal views and intense dislike of Richard Nixon, posed a serious threat to Conable's reelection. Although Costanza had been on the city council less than a year, she had already proven to be one of the most popular and effective vote-getters in Rochester history. With the strong encouragement of organized labor, Costanza saw in Conable an opportunity to defeat an incumbent Republican congressman closely identified with Richard Nixon and at the same time advance the liberal Democratic agenda to which she and her enthusiastic supporters adhered.

In September Costanza scored an impressive victory over her two primary challengers, winning 52 percent of the vote, to earn the right to challenge Conable as the Democratic candidate. She told her excited followers on primary election night that she planned on "running hard against Conable's record" and showing that he had been a consistent supporter of the deposed and disgraced Richard Nixon and therefore should not be returned to Congress.[6]

Costanza knew from the beginning that she could not match Conable's economic expertise, where she acknowledged that he was "one of the most able and brilliant men in Congress." But she thought she "had a better communication style and more personality" than Conable, and hoped as much as possible to maximize her own personality advantage in the campaign, as she sought simultaneously to link Conable to the disgraced Richard Nixon.[7]

Costanza was able to enlist the services of two young political science professors at the University of Rochester, Peter Regenstreif and Gordon Black, to her cause. Regenstreif, a Canadian scholar with a doctorate from Cornell and practical experience in elective politics, agreed to manage Costanza's campaign. And Black, who had a Ph.D. from Stanford and professional interest in polling, agreed to serve as Costanza's pollster. With these two ambitious assistants and a large number of devoted followers, Costanza embarked on an aggressive campaign to defeat Barber Conable in the November congressional elections.

"Mr. Regenstreif proved to be a virtual Pygmalion, polishing Midge, filling her head full of slogans, running issue polls and adapting her debating techniques to my weak spots," Conable wrote in his journal afterwards. "During the campaign she wrapped President Nixon around my neck so frequently that I rarely got the leisure of a substantive discussion."[8]

Regenstreif had been drawn to the Costanza campaign by his strong dislike of Richard Nixon and his disapproval of Conable's continued association with Nixon. He was particularly critical of Conable's acceptance of Nixon's invitation in May to have dinner with Nixon and ten other congressmen on the presidential yacht. "I only got into the Costanza campaign," Regenstreif said, "because of Conable's connection with Nixon. He would send back newsletters about how he was riding on the presidential yacht with Nixon down the Potomac."

The issue for Costanza, Regenstreif, and Black was: "How close was Conable to the Trick?" They were banking on this association as the means to wining the election. Conable's strong voting record in support of Nixon's programs in Congress, his membership in the House Republican leadership, and his refusal to publicly condemn Nixon and call for his resignation or impeachment made him vulnerable to the opposition's charge that he was too close to the "Trick."[9]

On August 6, 1974, the day after Nixon revealed that he had been part of the Watergate cover-up and the day after Conable publicly stated he would vote for impeachment, Midge Costanza held a press conference in Rochester to criticize Conable for his slow response to the Watergate affair. "Mr. Nixon's confession added nothing," she said. "Still, Mr. Conable refused to speak out until yesterday afternoon, when he was slapped in the face by the man he was so stubbornly and blindly supporting." She said she did not believe Nixon should resign, but that the "due process of law [should] be carried out and the president . . . be brought to trial."[10]

Nixon's resignation was the major event that could, and did, in the end, deal a severe blow to Midge Costanza's campaign. Regenstreif concluded years later that "Conable only won because Nixon resigned. He never would have won if Nixon had stayed in there."[11]

Even after Nixon's resignation on August 9, 1974, however, Conable's association with Nixon still posed a serious threat to his reelection, though he did not fully realize the magnitude of the threat until he received a phone call from his friend, political science professor Dick Fenno, a man whose judgment Conable greatly respected. Returning to Rochester from his summer vacation in late August, Fenno was surprised to learn that two of his University of Rochester colleagues, Regenstreif and Black, were actively working to defeat Conable's reelection to Congress. "As soon as they saw me," Fenno recalled later, "they reported excitedly that their polls indicated that Barber Conable was in trouble. Since his election in 1964, he had had four sleepy reelections without serious opposition; he had no organization left; his supporters were not energized; and his challenger was scoring points by portraying him as someone who was addicted to Washington and had lost touch with the folks back home."

Alarmed that two of his own colleagues were actually working against a man who had become his close personal friend as well as a valuable source of his own scholarly research on Congress, Fenno placed a phone call to Conable's old friend Tom Benton in Genesee County, who was coordinating the campaign. Benton told Fenno, "I can't get Barber to come home and campaign. You had better call him yourself." So Fenno called Conable's home in Washington, related the poll results to him, and told him, "You're in trouble, you get your ass up here and start campaigning now." When Conable protested that he had legislative work to tend to in Washington, Fenno said, "I mean now, Barber, now!"[12]

Thus, heeding Fenno's advice, and the advice of others with similar concerns (notably Jack Germond of the *Washington Star*, who had also seen some inside polling data from Conable's district and called to warn him of the dangers), Conable dropped everything in Washington and returned to his district in early October, a week and a half before Congress finally adjourned. "This had never been my custom in the past," he wrote in his journal, "but my attendance record was already badly marred by attendance at the inflation pre-summit and summit meetings [to which President Ford had summoned congressional leaders], and since survival was the issue, I felt entirely justified in neglecting my legislative job." It was "also a fact that very little work was done during the last week and a half of Congress since Democrats in the House seemed more inclined to continue wheel spinning in session rather than returning home to a boring campaign against an already defeated Republican Party."[13]

Jimmy Carter Tries to Link Conable to Watergate

When Conable returned to his district in early October, he found out quickly just how determined the Democrats were to defeat him. He had been targeted for defeat not only by the AFL-CIO's Committee on Political Education, but also by the Democratic National Committee.

On Tuesday, October 8—the same day President Ford pardoned Richard Nixon for any crimes he may have committed in the Watergate affair—the former governor of Georgia, Jimmy Carter, arrived in Rochester to begin two days of campaigning for Midge Costanza. Carter was the chairman of the national Democratic Campaign Committee in 1974 and also himself exploring a bid for the presidency in 1976.

Carter was in Rochester not just to campaign for Midge Costanza and boost his own political visibility, but also to campaign specifically against Barber Conable. "We had Carter come in and attack Conable," Regenstreif recalled.

Regenstreif told Carter, "We can't get one person in the whole Goddamn Congress to attack Conable. You know how it works. It's the old boy system. You aren't part of the old boy system, so you have to do it. I want you to crack him in the nuts."

"You shouldn't use language like that," Carter told Regenstreif.

"I know," Regenstreif responded, "but we want you to do it anyway."[14]

For the next two days, campaigning with Costanza in the district, Carter pressed the Democratic case against Conable. "This is one of the very few congressional districts I've visited this year," Carter told an enthusiastic group of Costanza supporters at a reception on Tuesday evening. "This is one district that's very important to me, because you have a congressman who deserves to be defeated." Besides, he added, "Conable is very vulnerable."[15]

"There's a massive hunger that exists among people in this nation for a new kind of office holder," Carter said at a press conference the next morning. "We're interested in this race, because we feel the Republican incumbent represents an attitude toward government—a withdrawal from his constituents—that is no longer acceptable to the American people." By contrast, he said, "Midge Costanza would represent the district in a way that is responsive to people."[16]

In a joint luncheon appearance before the Avon Rotary Club in the rural part of the district, Costanza launched a fiery attack on Conable's voting record, which she said showed "a disregard for the elderly, the handicapped, the environment, and consumers."

"The political leaders of the nation are watching this district to see what happens to a new type of politician like Midge Costanza," Carter told the Rotarians. "This is a special district that exemplifies the kind of hopes and dreams the American people are trying to reinstitute in government."[17]

Carter's sharpest attack against Conable—the kind Regenstreif was hoping for—came in a local Rochester television show when Carter tried to link Conable to the Watergate cover-up. Working with material provided to him by Regenstreif, Carter raised the issue of why Conable had not reported an important Watergate conversation he had had with the former attorney for the Committee to Reelect the President, Paul A. O'Brien, about "hush money" that was being paid by the Committee to Reelect and the White House to silence Watergate defendants.

To substantiate his charge, and to draw Conable into the Watergate cover-up, Carter and Regenstreif provided the press the transcript of an exchange between O'Brien, an unindicted co-conspirator in the Watergate cover-up trial, and William Cohen (R-Maine) in closed hearings before the House Judiciary Committee investigating President Nixon's impeachment in July 1974, in which O'Brien talked about a meeting he had had with Barber Conable in March 1973.

> *Cohen*: Going back to the question I originally asked you about political funds used for legal fees and sustenance, you indicated you had concern over this and that you expressed that concern to other people. Would you tell us what other people and what times, under what circumstances?
>
> *O'Brien*: My concern led me to seek an audience with Congressman Barber Conable, among others. And I did eventually have such an audience. . . .
>
> *Cohen*: And who were the others?
>
> *O'Brien*: There was one other congressman from Illinois who was present with Congressman Conable, whose name, I am sorry to state, I forget at the moment.
>
> *Cohen*: What was the general condition you were talking about?
>
> *O'Brien*: Well, you mean what areas did I cover?
>
> *Cohen*: That's right.
>
> *O'Brien*: Well, I expressed to Congressman Conable the difficulty that I was placed in because of attorney-client privilege, and that I had to be very careful as to any disclosures, but I indicated to him that there had been money passed in this case. He asked me if I had. I said, "No, I had not. . . ."
>
> *Cohen*: What were your general concerns that you were expressing?
>
> *O'Brien*: My general concern that I was expressing is that, among others, there were people who had [made] inconsistent statements that I thought probably were false. I felt that there were serious consequences potentially in these areas for the president of the United States. I raised the issue with Congressman Conable about this. These were the general areas. . . .[18]

Barber Conable's failure to reveal the information he had obtained from his meeting with O'Brien, Carter and the Costanza campaign suggested, indicated that Conable had known more about the Watergate cover-up than he had indicated.

Conable immediately responded to this accusation by saying that it was a "non-issue" and "an effort to involve me in Watergate." He said there was "nothing to it" and that he did "not intend to wallow" in the Watergate issue.

But Conable was forced to spend the next few days explaining to the press why his meeting with O'Brien about Watergate was a "non-issue." Meeting with reporters, Conable acknowledged that he had seen O'Brien for about an hour on March 28, 1973, at the request of a mutual friend—a Washington, D.C. lawyer named Richard Bishop, who had served in the Marine Corps with Conable. Concerned about the purpose of the requested meeting from the outset, Conable had asked his House colleague, John Erlenborn, a Republican congressman from Illinois, to sit in on the meeting with him.

Conable told reporters that O'Brien "thought maybe we could get him to the president. He was convinced the president was innocent and the White House should not be involved." O'Brien thought "I could pick up the phone and talk with Dick Nixon. . . . I never had a personal conversation with Nixon in my life," Conable said.

Conable said O'Brien told him "there was a mess down there at the Committee to Reelect, there was a lot of chaos, people were making inconsistent statements. They were raising money for attorneys' fees. He heard it was even being done in the White House and he thought it was a mistake."

Conable said he asked O'Brien "if he had handled any money himself." O'Brien told him "No. He just heard about it."

Asked why he never informed anybody about what O'Brien told him, Conable explained, "There wasn't anything he told us that wasn't in the papers at the time. The Washington papers headlined it every day."

Conable said O'Brien told him and Erlenborn that if he learned anything else, he'd come back and talk to them, but he never contacted either of them again.

The reported meeting with O'Brien was a "non-issue" and an effort to involve him in Watergate, Conable reiterated. "This is happening all over the country. People are trying to imply the whole Republican Party is tainted" by Watergate, he said.

Costanza responded that Conable is "making an issue out of it, not I. The only thing I charge Barber Conable with," she said, "is the lack of courage to speak out on an issue he should have definitely talked out on."[19]

After the local press had thrashed the matter around for a few days, they generally agreed with Conable that he had been unfairly "splashed by Watergate." But Conable did not emerge unscathed from the adverse publicity. He had been "wise enough to protect himself at the time by calling in another congressman, John N. Erlenborn of Illinois, as a witness to the meeting with O'Brien," a local newspaper editorial commented. "Given the benefit of hindsight, he would have been even wiser to at least have telephoned the special prosecutor, Archibald Cox, to tell him O'Brien had been in to see him. Too many people in Washington waited too long before taking action on Watergate.

"Overall, though," the editorial concluded, "Conable has established a reputation for honesty and forthrightness. The O'Brien incident seems to be a case of undeserved trouble knocking at his door."[20]

A Tough Campaign

Though Conable was able to successfully refute the specific charges of Jimmy Carter and the Costanza campaign efforts to involve him in the Watergate cover-up, he continued to have a tough time in his reelection bid against his Democratic opponent. Public opinion polls in early October showed that Costanza was running even with Conable in the district and ten percentage points ahead of him in the suburbs of Rochester.[21] Commenting on the general difficulty Republicans were having throughout the country in the aftermath of Watergate, R. W. Apple Jr. noted in the Sunday *New York Times* the weekend after Carter's visit to Rochester that even "Representative Barber Conable, one of the most respected and influential Republicans in the House [is] hard-pressed" in his campaign for reelection.[22]

Faced with a serious financial challenge from Midge Costanza, who had generated important union and party support, Conable was forced to revise his original plans, announced earlier in the year, to hold his campaign expenditures to $30,000. On Friday, October 12, in the midst of the Watergate flap, two days after Jimmy Carter had leveled his Watergate charges against him, Conable held the first public fund-raiser of his career. Campaign aides told reporters that about five hundred $35 tickets were sold for the reception, netting the campaign about $17,500.

"I've never had a fund-raiser before, and I don't like them," Conable told his supporters crowded into a reception room at the Rochester Downtown Holiday Inn. In previous campaigns, Conable explained, he had raised funds for his campaign by asking recipients of his congressional newsletters, his most devoted supporters, to make campaign contributions of $10 or less. And since 1967, he said, he had limited campaign contributions to

$50 per person. But, this year, he said, it appeared he was in for a "tight race" against his Democratic challenger, who was financially supported by organized labor. "I feel I've really got to protect myself. I don't want to take a chance of a media advertising blitz by my opponent.

"We had two choices: we could raise the ante for contributions from $50, or we could have a fund-raiser. We decided on the fund-raiser," he told his supporters. The fund-raiser was limited to $35 per person to allow the newsletter recipients to make their normal $10 contribution and stay within the $50 limit.[23]

The contest between Conable and Costanza, one reporter observed, was a "choice between images."

> It is a bubbling pot of spaghetti sauce vs. pate de fois gras.
> It is heart vs. head, personality vs. intellect, Kiss Me, I'm Italian vs. Shake My Hand, I'm Your U. S. Representative.
> It is love vs. respect; woman vs. man.
> The issues—inflation, tax reform, energy crisis, Middle East, health care, Social Security, aid to Turkey—all float out there in the background, but they don't seem to make that much difference.
> The choice is between images.[24]

"The personalities and styles are polls apart," another reporter noted in a similar vein.

> Miss Costanza comes out in a fighter's stance—vocal and aggressive.
> Her speeches, even serious ones, are laced with wit and humor.
> She also seems to relish meeting voters, and even while fighting fatigue, appears genuinely warm and friendly. . . .
> He, on the other hand, appears the reserved, quiet statesman, while visiting with a small group of friends in his hometown, or passing out literature at a shopping center.
> Involved in a discussion about an issue with a small group of voters, Conable appears relaxed. But in the shopping center-church social-handshake route, he looks stiff and ill-at-ease.[25]

When a woman at a Rochester suburban shopping center complained about how slowly government acts, Conable explained,

"It's almost inevitable because you have such a cumbersome procedure to protect the process."

"Why are we trying to feed the world?" a man at the same shopping center asked. "Because we grow more than we need," Conable answered. Then he proceeded to try to explain how private industry sells food and government only regulates the sales.

"I'm too damn professorial," Conable said with exasperation one day on the campaign trail as he tried to explain himself to a reporter. Like all incumbents, he said he was encumbered by the "burden of explanation" and the frustration of trying to explain complex problems. "These things are all so complicated. It's virtually impossible to talk to people out there."

He complained to the reporter that the "people in his district did not realize all he had done for them." Asked why he didn't publicize it more, he explained, "I haven't been blowing my own horn. I don't like that kind of operation, and now that I have to do it, I resent it. I rarely put out press releases. Publicity seeking detracts from some of the things I'm doing."

"There are no easy answers," to inflation and other complicated governmental problems, Conable repeatedly emphasized in his communications with constituents.

Meanwhile, a more aggressive and combative Midge Costanza, with less experience and patience with the complexity of governmental problems, pressed her case against Barber Conable throughout the district. She marched in volunteer fire department parades in small towns in the district. She campaigned door to door, attended coffee hours, greeted spectators at football games, appeared at shopping centers, factory gates, schools, and senior citizen events. "Her billboards seem to pop up everywhere," one local reporter noted, "and she has gone for broke in her television and radio commercials." Her message was the same everywhere: "Government doesn't feel any more, government doesn't have a heart." She promised to "put the heart back in" government.

It takes "courage and guts" to be a "congressperson," she said, "and Barber Conable doesn't have it." "Courage," she said, meant "being able to speak out when you hear or see evil," referring to Conable's meeting with Paul O'Brien, the former lawyer for the Committee to Reelect the President. "Guts," she said, meant "being able to speak out" against President Ford's pardon of Richard Nixon, which Conable condoned, "when you know" a pardon does not "exemplify equal justice under the law."

Costanza hammered away at Conable's approval of Nixon's legislative program in Congress and his votes against "human needs" legislation. "He voted against the Older Americans Act, against Social Security, against health care plans, against help to the handicapped, against aid to education," she said.

She continually described Conable as "cold and arrogant" and charged that he had acted more like a "staff member" to former President Nixon than a representative of his constituents.

"The Costanza camp," a reporter noted, "acts as if it were on a crusade. It views Conable as Public Enemy Number One, as being uncaring. Her supporters swear they are out to save the 35th District from another two years of his disdain."[26]

"While Miss Costanza was busy passing out literature that states issues and attacks Conable's record," a reporter observed during the campaign, "Conable was passing out 'Barber Conable's Congressional Cook Book.' The cookbook, a Conable tradition, says almost nothing about the congressman or the race," the reporter noted, "although it has an interesting recipe for 'Barber's Super Special.' But Conable says the cookbook is popular and that there are always requests for it after the campaign ends."

Two of the issues raised wherever the two candidates went were campaign reform and the economy. Conable pointed to his $50-limit on contributions and then to Costanza's large financial backing from organized labor. Costanza responded that she had received only about $11,000 from labor and said she had projected a $60,000 debt by the end of the campaign.[27]

Conable down played his role in the Nixon administration, but emphasized his position and respect in Washington. He said "congressmen don't have power, but they can develop influence. They develop it not by pulling strings, but by hard work, and gaining the respect of their colleagues."[28]

Conable admitted that Watergate had hurt him and that "the race would be much easier if there wasn't a resistance to incumbents in general." He said he also had to fight voter apathy. "Republicans," he said, "feel robbed of their self-respect."

"But Conable isn't running around tooting the party's horn or even his own record in much detail," a reporter who followed Conable on the campaign trail wrote. "He urged a small group of hometown supporters to ask people to vote for him, and not his party. Even before a group of Republican men," the reporter noted, "he seemed hesitant to speak of his record." Later he told the reporter that "a record drew attention to incumbency and it's a bad year for incumbents."[29]

"He's scared, there's no doubt about it, he's scared," a feisty Midge Costanza boasted.[30]

The thoughtful and pedagogical style that Conable had employed so successfully throughout his career—through his newsletters, newspaper columns, speeches, and personal contact with constituents—now seemed strangely out of place in the rough and tumble of a political campaign where he was being portrayed, in the aftermath of Watergate, as the villain, not the hero of representative government he had aspired to be. His gentlemanly ways and his refusal to attack Costanza personally put Conable on the defensive for the first time in his career.

Aware of Conable's political difficulty, one of his friends, Fred Eckert, an advertising executive and Republican state senator living in Conable's district, offered him some important campaign assistance as the campaign ended. Eckert had tried to warn Conable much earlier that he needed more aggressive advertising for such a tough race. With eight days left until the election, a public opinion poll showed Costanza slightly ahead of Conable in Monroe County, with a large number of voters still undecided. Finally, Conable agreed to let Eckert revise his media campaign. Adopting a more combative stance, Eckert redid Conable's radio and television ads to more forcefully state his record and defend him against Costanza's charges that he was an uncaring congressman, aloof from the human needs of his constituents.

On Thursday, October 31, six days before the election, Costanza came out with an ad criticizing Conable's voting record and saying that, unlike Barber Conable, "I understand, I care." Eckert, whose own election to the state Senate was not in jeopardy, stayed up all night writing two rebuttals to Costanza's ad. The new Eckert-produced Conable ads charged that Midge Costanza "doesn't seem to understand the issues and apparently she doesn't care if she distorts Barber Conable's voting record," specifically on the eighteen-year old vote and the Older Americans Act. "Conable understands the issues, and he cares about the truth."

"We turned her slogan around against her," Eckert said, reflecting on the campaign. A second ad further explained Conable's votes, again rebutting Costanza's claims. "So what happened was, it was impossible for a Costanza ad to be on any of the four stations without Conable's rebuttal of those coming on in a matter of minutes."

On Election Day, when Eckert discovered that Costanza was using a last-minute newspaper story about Conable to her favor, he wrote his own last-minute rebuttal while getting a hair cut. He dictated the ad over the barbershop telephone in time for it to get on the air by 3:00 P.M., only six hours before the polls closed, but in time for the rush-hour listeners driving home.

Among the dozen advertisements that Eckert wrote the last eight days of the campaign, one had Conable saying: "If you're not satisfied with how Congress is being run, how do you think I feel? For the past ten years, I have been struggling against the tide. . . . I'm not happy I was right." Another said, "When Wilbur Mills was fighting against revenue sharing, I was for it. . . ." The purpose of these ads, Eckert explained, was to "identify Conable as someone who has been consistently right on a number of things."

Another ad Eckert wrote in the closing days of the campaign stressed Conable's national reputation and cited all the good things that had been said about Conable in such publications as *Time*, *Newsweek*, and the *Washington Post*.[31]

The Rochester elite also came to Conable's rescue in the closing days of the campaign. Increasingly concerned that Midge Costanza might defeat Conable, three hundred of the most prominent business, civic, and educational leaders of Rochester took out a half-page ad in the *Democrat and Chronicle* five days before the election urging the voters of the Thirty-fifth Congressional District to return Barber Conable to Congress.[32]

Victory in the End

With a media blitz by both candidates in the waning days of the campaign, the results of the election were uncertain right up to the end. Despite a 58 percent to 30 percent Republican registration advantage in the district, the *Democrat and Chronicle* speculated the Sunday before the election that "Rochester Vice Mayor Margaret Costanza, the self-proclaimed 'loud-mouth broad,' may edge 10-year incumbent Barber B. Conable, Jr."[33]

"Midge was quite confident at the end that she had won," Conable also wrote in his journal, "and I was by no means confident that she had not."[34]

Indeed, Costanza was so confident of victory on election night, she said, "Winning tonight will be anti-climatic to bringing Barber Conable to his knees." She said she thought she would win because of "my warmth versus his aloofness [and] the kind of campaign I ran on issues versus his constant personal attacks on me."[35]

But within two hours of the polls closing on Tuesday, November 5, it became apparent that Midge Costanza would not win. "Son of a gun, I lost," she told her disappointed followers in an 11:00 P.M. concession statement from her election night headquarters at the Flagship Rochester Hotel. "If you run a good race, you can still function in the community. You will just have a whisper in Washington instead of a big voice," she said.

At 11:05 P.M., a few blocks away at the Holiday Inn, Conable accepted his opponent's concession. "This whisper in Washington can go back and speak with a strong voice," he told several hundred cheering supporters gathered to celebrate his victory. "I haven't felt so good in three weeks. When I came back three weeks ago from Congress, things were not good."[36]

But through hard work and the support of friends, he said, they had prevailed. He conceded he had been in a tough race, fighting off not only an aggressive Democratic challenger but also the effects of Watergate, which "cast a pall over the election."[37]

In the end, when all the votes were counted, Conable defeated Costanza 57 percent to 40 percent, 90,269 to 63,012, with the Conservative candidate, Clarence Carman, receiving a bare 3 percent (4,667) of the votes. Though this was an impressive victory, given the heated nature of the campaign and the uncertainty of the results, Conable's winning percentage fell considerably below what he had customarily been receiving in his reelection bids.

Midge Costanza had spent nearly twice as much as Conable ($125,000 to $76,000), and she had given him the toughest reelection campaign of his career.[38]

Conable publicly and privately acknowledged the importance of the media assistance Fred Eckert had provided toward the end of the campaign. "It was incredible, the speed with which Fred moved," Conable told a reporter after the election. "It was extremely helpful to me."[39] The "counter-punching campaign ads" which Eckert produced in the last week of the campaign, Conable also later reflected in his journal, resulted in "a considerable improvement in the morale of my troops. Fred Eckert's help was quite decisive."[40]

Conable's victory turned out to be one of the few bright spots for Republicans that evening. Elsewhere, across the country, Republican candidates for Congress, particularly those who had been identified with Richard Nixon, were going down in massive defeat. From Nixon's staunchest supporter, Representative Earl Landgrebe from Indiana—who, even after the disclosure of the June 23 "smoking gun" tape that had implicated Nixon in the Watergate cover-up, had said, "I'm sticking by my president even if he and I have to be carried out of this building and shot"—to the four Republicans who had most consistently supported Nixon during the House Judiciary Committee impeachment inquiry, all were soundly defeated in the election.[41] The Republicans lost a total of forty-three seats in the new House of Representatives—their worst defeat since the 1958 midterm elections. The new House would have 291 Democrats and 144 Republicans. In the Senate the Democrats also gained three seats to give them a 61 to 39 majority in the new Congress.[42]

Chapter 10

A Friend in the White House

At the same time Conable was fighting his most difficult campaign battle, he was being summoned to the White House to help his old friend and new president, Gerald Ford, in his selection of a vice president. Under the Twenty-fifth Amendment, ratified in 1967, Ford had the responsibility to nominate a new vice president to the Congress, just as Nixon had invoked the amendment to nominate Ford for the vice presidency after the resignation of Spiro T. Agnew in 1973.

After attending the Ford presidential swearing-in ceremony in the East Room of the White House on Friday, August 9, Conable drove home to spend the weekend with his constituents. Unexpectedly, on Saturday afternoon he received a phone call at his Alexander home from the White House, asking him to return to Washington the next day for a 2:30 meeting with President Ford to confer on his choice for vice president. Rising early Sunday morning, August 11, Conable drove the nine hours back to Washington for his appointment with the president.

Arriving at the White House a half hour before his old friend George Bush, chairman of the Republican National Committee, who was scheduled to see President Ford at 3 P.M., Conable was taken into the Oval Office, where he found himself alone with the president.

"I like where you work," Conable said to Ford as he walked into the Oval Office.

"Well, you've been in here before, haven't you?" Ford asked Conable.

"No, I haven't," Conable replied.

"You've been in the leadership for four years and you mean you've never been here before?" Ford asked.

"No, Nixon and I never knew each other. He never was at all interested in me," Conable said.

"Oh, I can't believe that, Barber. You must have been in here," Ford said.

"No, I haven't," Conable replied. "This is the first time."[1]

After having his photograph taken with the new president, Conable asked him why he was meeting individually with congressional leaders instead of having a group meeting. President Ford replied that he didn't want the legislators to exert too much influence on each other and wanted their frank appraisals of the various people involved, something he knew would not be forthcoming if others were there.[2]

Conable asked Ford what kind of vice president he wanted to have, to which the president responded, "That's what I brought you in to tell me. You know me better than I know myself. I want you to be completely open about who would be the best addition to my administration."[3]

Ford and Conable, who inadvertently kept calling the president Jerry, talked primarily about Nelson Rockefeller and George Bush. "If you want to legitimize your administration," Conable advised Ford, "you should appoint somebody who has been elected to high office many times and who is an accepted public figure, like Nelson Rockefeller. On the other hand, if you want to start rebuilding the Republican Party, you should get somebody who is part of the future and George is that. You've got to make up your mind which is more important, legitimizing an unelected presidency or trying to save the two party system."[4]

"It was a relaxed and direct conversation and I look back on it with pleasure," Conable later reflected in his journal. "Leaving the West Wing of the White House, a whole mob of television and radio reporters taped my comments in detail. Subsequently, I had an unhappy time about the recommendation for vice president. . . . I was interviewed a great deal and talked indiscriminately about both George Bush and Nelson Rockefeller."[5]

On the following day, Conable was called by Dick Rosenbaum, the Republican chairman in New York state, and told that "George Hinman, a Rockefeller confidant, was very upset that I was pushing George Bush so hard. I, of course, denied that I was pushing George any harder than Rockefeller, saying that either one would be an acceptable vice president, but they would reflect quite different wishes on the part of the president for his administration. It wasn't an hour later," Conable noted in his journal, "that Jerry Pettis [Conable's Republican colleague on the Ways and Means Committee from California, who was trying to organize support for George Bush], said to me that George was personally hurt, after having sat next to me for four years on the Ways and Means Committee, that I was pushing Nelson Rockefeller so hard. I appeared to have offended both sides and convinced them that I was for the other . . ., the worst of all possible worlds," a distressed Conable wrote in his journal.

"When Rockefeller was announced as the new vice president," Conable recorded, "I was perfectly well satisfied, although the reaction in my district was bad, and I took it as evidence that Ford wanted strong people rather than sycophants around him. Two days later, Rocky called on me at my office as a courtesy call. We had a polite conversation in which I stated that I thought he would have good credibility as a budget cutter, expressing comments that he would be tough enough to do what was expected of him in this regard, as compared to someone like Ronald Reagan who had not had the opportunity to demonstrate the human concerns Rockefeller had shown as governor of New York. He seemed to think that this analysis was good and probably it had a great deal to do with his appointment by Gerald Ford. He seemed well informed," Conable observed, "and obviously knows we are headed into very serious trouble as we try to cut back on the budget and government borrowing in order to get inflation under control."[6]

Rockefeller was confirmed as vice president on December 19, 1974, after the House confirmed his nomination by a vote of 287 to 128. The Senate had approved Rockefeller's nomination a week earlier by a margin of 90 to 7. Thus, for the first time in the nation's history, both the president and vice president were chosen under the Twenty-fifth Amendment to the Constitution, rather than by a national election, setting up the unusual circumstances that would prevail in Washington for the next two and a half years.[7]

A Presidential Pardon

Eager to heal the wounds of Watergate within weeks of becoming president, Ford dismantled many of "the trappings of the so-called imperial presidency." The White House staff was reduced by 10 percent, from 540 to 485. The Marine Corps band was ordered to replace "Hail to the Chief" with the fight song of the new president's alma mater, the University of Michigan, for certain events. The living quarters in the White House were now called "the residence" instead of "the mansion."[8]

These symbolic gestures by President Ford were supplemented by new policies and a different style of presidential leadership. The first week in office, Ford accepted a Senate recommendation that he call a White House "summit" on the economy. The Conference on Inflation, which Conable and other congressional leaders helped organize, included meetings with economists, business and labor leaders, governors, mayors, and county officials, and was part of Ford's effort to create a more open and responsive presidency.

One of the most dramatic attempts by President Ford to heal the wounds of the nation came in a speech he gave to the annual convention of the Veterans of Foreign Wars in Chicago on August 19. In that speech, Ford offered an amnesty plan for the fifty thousand draft evaders and deserters from the Vietnam War to win back their citizenship.

Ford's innovative style and policy initiatives won him considerable praise during the early days of his administration. To capture Ford's relaxed, easy-going style, the press ran favorable stories of the new president toasting his own English muffins in the morning and taking a swim in the evening. In his first week in office, a Gallup poll showed that 71 percent of the public approved of Ford's performance in office.

Almost immediately, however, the high approval rating Ford enjoyed with the public and the press collapsed. On September 8, 1974, after being in office only a month, Ford granted Richard Nixon "a full, free and absolute pardon." As he had tried to do with the Vietnam amnesty program, Ford hoped to use the Nixon pardon to heal the wounds of the nation's recent past. Instead, the pardon backfired and Ford himself seemed to become a casualty of the Watergate scandal.

For many Americans, Ford's pardon of Nixon overwhelmed the atmosphere of openness and good will he had begun to establish in the country. Within days, Ford's approval rating in the national public opinion polls dropped to 50 percent. "The early press celebration of [Ford's] unpretentious personal style," two presidential scholars have written, "was transformed into an attitude of scorn and ridicule," from which the new president never totally recovered. Ford "now was caricatured as a clumsy, slow-witted bumbler."[9]

Unlike many others in Congress and in the country, Barber Conable was supportive of his old friend's pardon of Richard Nixon. Although Conable personally felt totally betrayed by Nixon, he felt Ford "did the right thing" by pardoning Nixon, though he conceded the pardon, so unpopular at the time, probably cost Ford the presidential election two years later. "It would have been terrible for our country's image of itself to have sixteen months of Nixon on the front pages of the nation's papers saying 'I am not a crook,'" Conable recalled, offering essentially the same rationale Ford had given in pardoning Nixon. "It would also have been very bad for our relations with other countries, because most other countries couldn't understand why we had done what we had done with Nixon. They thought he was a great president in most cases, because he was so active and generally quite coherent as a foreign affairs man. . . . So I thought at the time Jerry did the right thing by pardoning Nixon."[10]

Though Ford's Nixon pardon continues to be controversial, the historical verdict seems to be running in Ford's favor and in agreement with Conable's assessment of the situation at the time. The Kennedy Foundation, for example, presented Ford with a Profile in Courage Award in 2001 for the political courage he showed in making this difficult decision in 1974. "Ford's ambition for the country was larger than his own ambition. Restored confidence was more important than his reelection. That's courage," Bob Woodward wrote.[11]

Sea Change in Congress

The Democratic landslide in the midterm congressional elections in November made life even more difficult for Ford and the

Republicans in Congress. The Democrats scored a sweeping victory in the House of Representatives, making Conable's successful fight against Midge Costanza even more significant. Most of the 37 incumbent Republicans who were defeated had been strong, conservative supporters of Richard Nixon. They were replaced in many cases by liberal Democrats, thus swelling the ranks of liberals in the new Congress. The new House would be more liberal than at any time since Lyndon Johnson's Eighty-ninth Congress in 1965–66.[12]

Determined to push a more liberal, reform agenda in the Ninety-fourth Congress, the victorious House Democrats met in early December 1974 to elect their leaders for the new Congress and adopt a series of major institutional changes that would have a significant effect on Ford's ability to get his legislative program through Congress and on Conable's own work on the Ways and Means Committee. They unanimously renominated Carl Albert for Speaker and reelected the liberal Tip O'Neill as majority leader. In an important victory for the increased number of liberals in the House, the Democrats also elected Phillip Burton, a forty-eight-year-old veteran reformer from California and one of the most liberal members of the House, as the new chairman of the Democratic Caucus.

The Democrats also adopted a number of institutional changes to increase the collective power of the caucus and party leadership over committee chairmen. They voted, for example, to require that all committee chairmen be elected by a majority vote of the caucus. The seventy-five new Democrats in the House, anxious to reform the committee system, then used their collective power to force the removal of several committee chairmen they considered to be either too autocratic or too conservative.

The Democrats also required, for the first time, that all chairmen of Appropriations subcommittees, considered to be major sources of power in their own right, be elected by the caucus. In addition, they increased the power of the Speaker by giving him the power to nominate all members of the Rules Committee, subject to ratification by the caucus.[13]

The most important changes, however, took place in the Ways and Means Committee. For some time, the committee, under the leadership of Wilbur Mills, had been seen as more conservative than the larger body of Democrats in the House. Now, with the help of the large bloc of liberal freshmen in the House, the Democratic Caucus moved to adopt a series of major reforms to reduce the power of the Ways and Means Committee and make it more subservient to the caucus and elected party leadership.

Long in the making, these reforms in the Ways and Means Committee were precipitated by a series of bizarre events involving Wilbur Mills, the focal point of much of the liberal criticism. In the early morning hours of October 9, Washington D.C. police stopped Mills's car along the Potomac River tidal basin after noticing it was speeding. A young woman, identified later as an Argentine strip-tease dancer, named Fanne Fox, jumped from the car into the tidal basin, but was rescued by police. Press reports indicated that Mills's face was scratched and bleeding and he appeared to be intoxicated. Many observers thought this incident might threaten Mills's chances of reelection to Congress. But Mills's Arkansas constituents were more forgiving. "Some of us think it's pretty good for a man of 65 with a bad back to be out with a go-go dancer," a veteran Arkansas politician told a reporter shortly before the election.[14] Mills went on to easily win his twelfth reelection to Congress on November 5, capturing over 57 percent of his district's votes.

Mills's congressional relations slowly improved after the elections, but then were seriously damaged on November 30, when quite remarkably, on national television, he appeared on a Boston stage with Fox to congratulate her on a striptease performance. Three days later, as the Democratic Caucus was meeting to organize for the Ninety-fourth Congress, Mills entered Bethesda Naval Hospital, reportedly suffering from exhaustion. "He was one of the greatest congressmen of my generation," Speaker Albert said at the time, "but he is a sick man." Mills resigned his chairmanship of the Ways and Means Committee a few days later and issued a statement that he was being treated for alcoholism.[15]

With Mills discredited as a leader and unable to resist a challenge to his authority, the Democratic Caucus proceeded to adopt a series of significant reforms of the Ways and Means Committee to make the committee more subservient to the larger liberal Democratic majority in the House. In the most significant of these changes, the caucus voted 146 to 122 to strip committee members of their power to make Democratic committee assignments for other committees of the House. Democrats on Ways and Means had exercised this committee appointment power since the party gained control of the House of Representatives in 1911, following the bipartisan revolt against the dictatorial Republican Speaker Joe Cannon the previous year. Now, by virtue of the caucus's decision, the power to make Democratic committee appointments would be placed in the hands of a twenty-four-member Policy and Steering Committee, headed by the Speaker, giving the Speaker once again centralizing power over committee assignments.[16]

In a related move, the Democratic Caucus also decided to increase the size and party ratio of the Ways and Means Committee from 25 (15 Democrats and 10 Republicans) to 37 members (25 Democrats and 12 Republicans), "thereby enabling party leaders to pack the committee with liberal Democrats," *Congressional Quarterly* explained. "Liberals had complained for years that the committee was dominated by a coalition of conservative Democrats and Republicans who voted together to block liberal legislation supported by most Democrats."[17]

In an effort to further weaken the power of the committee chairman, the Democratic Caucus instructed the Ways and Means Committee to create subcommittees in the new Congress. Mills had abolished subcommittees when he became chairman in 1958, preferring instead to have the full membership collectively consider all legislative matters that came before the Ways and Means Committee. The new Ways and Means Committee, however, would be broken into six subcommittees: one oversight committee and five substantive committees on health, public assistance, unemployment compensation, trade (with Barber Conable as the senior Republican member), and Social Security (where Conable was the second-ranking Republican, just behind Bill Archer of Houston, Texas).

In a final effort to control the Ways and Means Committee, the Democratic Caucus also indicated that it would require the new Ways and Means Committee to seek open, not closed, rules from the Rules Committee to allow members, especially liberal Democrats, to amend Ways and Means bills on the floor of the House.[18]

Always the teacher, anxious to report to the folks back home on what was going on in Washington, Conable wrote his constituents an informative newsletter on December 12, 1974, explaining to them the significance of the recent organizational changes in Congress.

> Those who are confused about what has been happening in Washington this past week probably have only forgotten that Congress is run by political parties.
>
> People who think politics is dirty resist this idea, feeling that the process of organizing a Congress should be sanitized by individual decisions (didn't they vote for the person, not the party?) and that the rules of the House should be much more important than the rules of the party. But the rules of the House are designed only to protect the rights of minorities and individuals. The processes of control and accountability, the structure of decision, the vesting of leadership, even the assignment

and diffusion of committee membership—all these are party decisions. . . .

The Democrats, the majority party by more than two to one in the House next year, have been making major changes this past week. Whether or not it constitutes reform depends upon your point of view. Expressed in feudal terms, the power of the barons (committee and subcommittee chairmen) has been reduced relative to both the king (the Speaker) and the serfs (caucus).

Conable's own attention, he wrote his constituents, had been focused on the changes the Democrats were making in the Ways and Means Committee.

Although it affects me only indirectly, I thoroughly approve of one of the changes. The Democratic side of the Ways and Means Committee has served as the Democrats' Committee on Committees, the group that assigns members to committees. To some majority members, this political function was more important than the legislative work of the committee. They served on the committee, not because of their interests or abilities, but because some powerful politician back home wanted to project his power into Congress through control of the committee assignments of the congressmen from his area. Some of these political appointments were also good legislators, but in the long run, the decision . . . to vest the Committee on Committees responsibility elsewhere will improve the attentiveness of the Democrats on the Ways and Means Committee to their legislative responsibilities.

As for the other changes the Democrats planned to make in the Ways and Means Committee, Conable was more skeptical. He believed the reason for increasing the size of the Ways and Means Committee from 25 to 37 was "plainly to enhance party control and to change ideological bias toward liberalism."

In addition, Conable noted that the "closed rule," which Wilbur Mills had traditionally received from the Rules Committee to limit amendments to Ways and Means bills on the floor of the House, would now, on instructions from the Democratic Caucus, "become a thing of the past, and we can expect a new practice of extensive efforts to amend Ways and Means bills on the floor of the House." The Ways and Means Committee has "historically disparaged floor amendments made by the Senate because they have so frequently been misinformed and occasionally even the direct result of special interest lobbying. The closed rule in the House has many times protected the members from their admitted inability to resist undisciplined 'motherhood' type amendments. The effects of the demise of the closed rule will have to be closely watched."

The new requirement by the Democratic Caucus for the Ways and Means Committee to create subcommittees, Conable believed, was related to the increase in the size of the committee.

> The myth about Ways and Means' refusal to have subcommittees in the past is that it was Chairman Mills' decision to enhance his control. While he may have believed this, the more basic reasons were the members' desires to participate fully in the development of each sensitive bill, and our feelings that the nation's interests were all served by a diffusion of special interest lobbying pressure among all the members of the committee rather than concentrating it at a few subcommittee focal points. These theories can now be tested. The Democrats' rule changes will spread subcommittee assignments broadly among the new members as well as the old. Certainly it will be a whole new ball game for the lobbyists.
>
> While changes in Ways and Means are going to affect the way it functions and make service there difficult in terms of the recent past, I don't believe anybody will want to leave the committee. Our committee has always been the goal of congressmen who want to improve their committee assignments, and so it likely will remain. The assignment is controversial and the work burdensome, but there is no better way to get astride the big issues between government and the American people than to serve on the Ways and Means Committee. Because its jurisdiction is not changed, the central role is not changed either.

Conable also noted, in explaining the Ways and Means changes to his constituents, that his "own personal relationship to the changed process [had] been upgraded by [his] increasing seniority," from the fourth-ranking Republican position on the Ways and Means Committee in the previous Congress to the second-ranking Republican position in the new Congress. For the first time, he would be participating in the conferences between the House and Senate on Ways and Means bills, where he observed "much of the real work of legislating takes place."

> One is usually tempted to interpret change in personal terms. However, these changes are not the result of the sad condition of Wilbur Mills. His inability effectively to

resist may have hurried the process, but the inevitable forces at work were not to be denied. The committee system has been frustrating to those who view government as the prime problem-solver because it can interrupt the smooth flow of political power. It is part of a larger system of checks and balances, but apparently checks and balances are not as popular as they used to be. Abuses of power will change that, whether that abuse is practiced by king, the barons, or the mob of serfs.

"It appears that the Democratic Party in the House may have decided to depose Wilbur Mills as chairman of Ways and Means," Conable concluded, which they did a few days later, replacing him as chairman with the second-ranking Democrat on the committee, Al Ullman of Oregon. "I do not tell shabby jokes about Wilbur Mills," Conable said of his friend and legislative mentor of eight years.

> For 35 years he served the country with great skill in a comparatively anonymous central role, and when he tried to run for president in 1972 he discovered that he had two percentage points less name recognition than Bella Abzug, then a freshman congressperson from New York City. That he is now a household word says something about the values of our media and our political system. I am sad about my friend, who has been stable and decent in his relationship with the members of his committee, whose mind is much admired, whose personal life until recently was completely submerged in his work, and for whose family recent events must be personal tragedy. Beyond that, I simply do not understand what has happened to him.[19]

Much speculation at the time centered on how the Ways and Means Committee would change under the leadership of Al Ullman. An eighteen-year veteran of the House from eastern Oregon, Ullman differed little with Mills on the major policy issues that came before the Ways and Means Committee. But lacking Mills's thorough knowledge of the tax laws, most inside observers predicted that the "cautious, deliberate Al Ullman" would run the committee in a more open fashion and allow individual members more influence on legislation. Also importantly, with the Democratic Caucus exerting more authority over the Ways and Means Committee, the new chairman would be expected to act more as an agent of the larger Democratic majority in the House than had been the case during the leadership of Wilbur Mills.[20]

Though most of the news coverage in early December centered on the changes the Democrats were making in the new Congress, the House Republicans also met on December 2 to select their leaders for the Ninety-fourth Congress. As expected, the conservative John Rhodes of Arizona was unanimously reelected as minority leader. Bob Michel, a fifty-one-year-old conservative from Illinois and an eighteen-year veteran of the House, defeated two candidates, Jerry Pettis of California and John Erlenborn of Illinois, to succeed the retiring Leslie Arends as the minority whip. The moderate John Anderson from Illinois easily defeated three conservatives and the leading Nixon supporter on the House Judiciary Committee, Charles Wiggins of California, to retain his chairmanship of the Republican Conference. And Barber Conable was reelected, without opposition this time, as chairman of the House Republican Policy Committee.[21]

Helping Gerald Ford in Congress

In his State of the Union address to Congress on January 15, 1975, President Ford indicated that his two most important legislative priorities for the Ninety-fourth Congress would focus on the ailing economy and national energy crisis. With the country mired in a deep recession and the annual inflation rate running at over 12 percent, Ford proposed a one-year $16 billion tax cut to stimulate the economy, with three-quarters of the reduction going to individuals and one-quarter designed to promote business investment.

In response to the Arab oil embargo of 1973, which had quadrupled oil prices, Ford also proposed a comprehensive energy policy to make the country self-sufficient in energy production and consumption by 1985. Ford proposed a set of specific policies both to reduce the consumption of energy at home and lift the cap on oil and petroleum prices which had been put in place by Nixon's wage- and price-control policies of 1971. By relying on the free enterprise system, Ford hoped primarily to use the forces of competition and the marketplace to increase the supply of domestic oil and thereby lower the dependency on foreign sources.[22]

With a Democratically controlled Congress, determined to be more assertive in the policy-making process in the post-Watergate era, Ford had only limited success in getting his legislative agenda through the Ninety-fourth Congress. But throughout Ford's legislative efforts, Conable continually assisted and advised his friend. Conable's journal during this period shows the intensity of his political efforts to advance Ford's legislative agenda and interests in Congress.

A week after the president's State of the Union message, Conable recorded that he and other congressional Republican leaders met with the president at the White House to devise a strategy for getting the Ford's legislative agenda through Congress. "The president expressed his determination in respect to the economic and energy policy, and he gave us a very earnest talk about his need for our support as well as his plans for trying to enlist public support. There was no dearth of suggestions from those present. And once again, I marvel that the atmosphere in the Ford presidency is so open and so forthcoming in contrast to the Nixon administration where people tended to hang back when the president asked for comments and suggestions."[23]

At the end of March, presidential leadership did succeed in producing tax cut legislation to stimulate the economy, but the liberal Democratic Congress exceeded the size of the tax cut requested by the president. Instead of the $16 billion tax cut Ford had requested in his State of the Union address, the Democratic Congress enacted a $22.8 billion tax cut, which included the elimination of oil and gas depletion allowances for corporations as advocated by the newly empowered Democratic Caucus and liberal Democrats on the Ways and Means Committee.

Barber Conable, as well as Treasury Secretary Bill Simon, fearing the increase in the national debt that would result from such a large tax cut, urged the president to veto the Democratic bill. "Conable was chairman of the House Republican Policy Committee and a personal friend whose political judgment was very astute," Ford wrote in his autobiography, "so I listened to him carefully." But, in the end, Ford sided with Alan Greenspan, chairman of the Council of Economic Advisors, and Arthur Burns, chairman of the Federal Reserve Board, who thought this tax cut, though exorbitant, was better than no tax cut at all, and signed the largest tax cut in American history into law on March 31.[24]

But the Democrats continued to delay the enactment of the president's energy proposal. Seeking a Democratic alternative to Ford's plan to decontrol domestic oil prices, the new chairman of the Ways and Means Committee, Al Ullman, proposed a forty-cents-a-gallon increase in gasoline taxes, to be phased in over five years, as a way of limiting the demand for gasoline in the United States.[25]

During a Republican leadership meeting at the White House at the end of April, Conable expressed considerable irritation at Ford's apparent willingness to cooperate with Ullman on his gasoline tax alternative. "I found the president generally more complimentary to the cooperation of Al Ullman than I felt was justified," Conable wrote in his journal.

> As he continued to talk about what a good job Al was doing and trying to bring the members of his caucus into line with his own program, I interrupted at one point and said, "Wait a minute, Mr. President. Let me understand. Are you urging us to support this Mickey Mouse proposal my committee is coming up with?" The president flushed, put his head down, and said no, he wasn't necessarily asking us to vote for anything that wasn't acceptable. I then pressed him as to what was acceptable in his view, saying that many of us in the House were concerned about his possibly accepting a gasoline tax as the central idea of this program, repeating to him, as I had before, that his own program is far preferable to the Democratic program and that he mustn't allow Al Ullman or anyone else to force him into pushing a compromise on which they couldn't deliver.

Continuing to reflect on Ford's leadership, Conable wrote, "I find myself to be embarrassed to be one of the few people in the leadership group who concerns himself about the president's image as a man who is weak and unable to take a strong position relative to a Congress that is carving out his gizzard constantly. I seem to be emerging as a hard-liner, a man who's constantly advising the president to go beyond what he himself is willing to do. It seems to me that the president's legislative background and training are constantly pushing him toward compromise, when his image would be much better enhanced by the appearance of willingness to stand up and fight for what he believes in."

Conable expressed similar, and even sharper, concerns about Ford's leadership following a meeting by the president with members of the SOS and other Republican study groups in the House in April. "We went down to the Blue Room [in the White House] and sat like a lodge meeting in old oak chairs with the president at one end fielding questions," Conable wrote in his journal.

> Once again I sat very near the president as he turned to me several times to check on things going on in Ways and Means which were inevitably the subject of discussion. I saw to it to interpret to him the concerns of the members of the group about his relationship to the gas tax and concerns about a leadership which might in effect pull the rug

out from under a number of staunch Republicans . . . who would get out on a limb, only to find him compromising with the Democratic alternative which we had been fighting. It seems as though on almost every issue, this is the posture we find ourselves in. So when people press the president to what his position is going to be, he sounds squishy about it. I become increasingly pessimistic as to whether it is worthwhile for us to fight for what we otherwise would consider to be worthwhile positions in the political process in which we serve. I don't think there is any doubt that the members of Congress still admire and like this man, but we increasingly lose confidence in his ability to be a strong leader. That is what we want more than anything else, since our destinies are so closely tied to him. We are not in any way advanced by identifying ourselves with a man who winds up looking like a eunuch on every issue.[26]

Ford, of course, wound up being far from a eunuch in his dealings with Congress, as Conable later acknowledged. Outnumbered by the liberal Democrats in Congress, Ford aggressively used his presidential veto of congressional legislation sixty-six times during his brief twenty-nine-month presidency. With significant help from the thirty conservative Democrats in the House, who generally sided more with Ford than their own liberal Democratic leadership, fifty-four of those Ford vetoes were sustained, giving Ford an important and effective weapon in his legislative dealings with Congress during these years. But at the time, Conable, anxious for Ford to be more aggressive in his relations with Congress, failed to see just how aggressive Ford was prepared to be.[27]

Despite his private concerns and criticisms of Ford's presidential leadership, Conable remained fiercely loyal and protective of the president and pinned most of his own hope for the future on Ford's victory in the 1976 election, though Ford had not yet officially announced he would run. "I continue to be very discouraged about my role in the Congress," Conable lamented in his journal in April.

The Republicans are such a small group that I have very little opportunity to affect the course of events. . . . It's tough to be irrelevant and to be excluded from the moment of decision. I would find consolation in the hope that some day the Republicans will be in the majority in the House. That goal seems to be receding farther and farther, thanks to the splendid leadership of Richard Nixon and the increasing minority of our congressional Republicans. . . .

> If I thought Gerald Ford was not going to run for the presidency in 1976, or if it was beyond the realm of possibility for him to be elected, I think I would seriously question whether I should try to stay another two years. As it is, I shall conduct myself with the expectations that he is going to be a candidate and that thus there is some chance of having a modest relation to the uncertain process of a democracy in our declining country.

In the midst of dealing with economic and energy matters, Ford was also faced with the military and political collapse of South Vietnam in the spring of 1975. Disregarding the 1973 peace accord, the North Vietnamese forces launched a major attack on the Central Highlands of South Vietnam in early March. With the Congress refusing President Ford's request for emergency financial aid to South Vietnam, and North Vietnamese troops rapidly advancing on South Vietnam, the American military forces were forced to completely withdraw from South Vietnam by the end of April. The White House leadership meeting on April 22, Conable reported in his journal, "centered mostly on the means of getting evacuation without untold anti-American incidents and possible chaos resulting in American loss of life as the South Vietnamese realized that we are completing our pull out. Also, it is clear that the president would like to bring out as many South Vietnamese with the Americans as possible, thus minimizing the loss of life for Vietnamese who identified themselves with the American effort in South Vietnam. It is difficult not to feel some grim satisfaction that however unsuccessful our effort there has been, nevertheless it will not continue."[28]

When the end finally came, with the frantic withdrawal of the last American troops and as many of their South Vietnamese friends as they could take with them on April 29, Conable reported to his constituents.

> After all I have written about the Vietnam War since I came to Congress some six months after passage of the Tonkin Gulf Resolution, the South Vietnamese government and military collapsed so quickly and so completely that the end was almost as unreal as the beginning had been imperceptible. The refugees are still uncounted and their resettlement uncertain, although I hope America will do its part. . . .
>
> The first war to be fought in our living rooms [which had cost Americans over 46,000 deaths, 300,000 wounded, and $140 billion since 1965], has now left our

living rooms, and we will no longer worry about what we
cannot see. We have lost, if you can lose what you are not
trying to win, and history will decide what that means in
our view of ourselves. The length of the war and the
unfairness of its burdens affected a whole generation.
If our national life is the sum of our national experiences, Vietnam has made us a much more complicated
people. . . .

I frequently retreat into poetry to find the right word
for the moment of truth, but in this case I don't know
whether it would be more appropriate to say, "What
I aspired to be and was not comforts me," or "All looks
yellow to the jaundic'd eye." I guess the right word is
"period." The Vietnam War has ended, period.[29]

In May Conable continued "to worry about the Ford presidency,
as any normal Republican would. It is apparent that the strong
people in the administration are rapidly becoming targets as issues
like Vietnam and Watergate fade into the background and the sharks
in the press yearn for more blood in the water." Identifying Treasury
Secretary William Simon and Secretary of State Henry Kissinger as
primary targets of the press, Conable believed Simon was "attacked
usually because of his outspoken conservatism" and Kissinger
because "he is so generally assumed to dominate the president in
foreign policy matters." As a show of support for both men, Conable
reported sending Simon and Kissinger each a half-gallon of maple
syrup, with an accompanying letter indicating that "I hoped they
would stay in government despite the barbs of late, telling each that
I thought it was a compliment to him that he was considered such an
appropriate target."[30]

Meanwhile, back in Congress the Democrats continued to look
for an alternative to President Ford's energy proposal. Excluding the
Republicans from committee deliberations, much unlike Wilbur
Mills had done earlier, Al Ullman worked with Democratic task
forces he appointed to draft an energy bill. An angry Barber
Conable, anxious to explain the situation to the press, told reporters
in March that Ullman "can't afford to deal with the Republicans" on
the energy bill, because of pressures from the liberal Democrats on
the Ways and Means Committee and the constant threat to his leadership from the newly influential House Democratic Caucus. In
Conable's view, now that the Democratic Caucus was asserting its
authority to remove committee chairmen, bipartisan consensus was
no longer possible, as the chairman's position depended on his
party.[31]

By the time Ullman brought the Democratic energy proposal for a vote in the Ways and Means Committee on May 12, his original forty-cents-a-gallon gasoline tax had been scaled back to a twenty-cent tax to be gradually phased in by 1979. But the modified Ullman bill, that also included the reimposition of a direct quota system on oil imports and a tax on gas guzzling automobiles, was still unacceptable to Conable and the other Republicans on the Ways and Means Committee. Like President Ford, they were more interested in finding ways to increase the domestic production of energy than in forcing the conservation of energy through higher taxes. Acting as the primary Republican spokesman on the committee, since the ranking Republican, Herman Schneebeli of Pennsylvania, had for all practical purposes relinquished that responsibility to his more forceful and articulate colleague, Conable was able to unite all twelve Republicans and win over four Democratic members in opposition to the Ullman bill, which barely passed the Ways and Means Committee by a vote of nineteen to sixteen.[32]

Anticipating what would happen when the bill reached the House floor, Conable was not surprised when the full House handily defeated the Ullman gasoline tax proposal, which was the central feature of the Democratic alternative, on June 11. By a stunning vote of 345 to 72, the House stripped the twenty-cent gasoline tax from the Ways and Means bill.[33] In the final analysis, as one congressional scholar noted, while the Democrats preferred to deal with the energy shortage "through conservation rather than by giving the oil companies economic incentives to increase production, they shrank from imposing the added costs on consumers that most conservation measures necessarily entailed."[34]

The final energy bill which the House passed, largely on a partisan vote, on June 19 was at best only the beginning of a national energy policy. The watered-down House bill, which focused on reestablishing oil import quotas and providing various tax incentives for oil and gas conservation, was subsequently referred to the Senate where it died of inaction in the Senate Finance Committee.[35]

The Democratic Congress, however, did eventually pass an energy bill at the end of the year, but a bill that was much more to the liking of the Democrats in Congress than to President Ford. The legislation the Democrats passed in December gave President Ford energy emergency authority and established a national strategic oil reserve, which he had requested. But much to the distaste of President Ford and his Republican allies in Congress, including Conable, the Democratic bill required that the federal controls on the price of oil be continued until 1979. Despite intensive lobbying against the bill by the oil industry, Ford signed the energy bill into law on December 22, 1975, believing that the bill, though "by no means perfect," would provide "a foundation upon which we can build a more comprehensive program" in the future.[36]

This legislation reflected the growing sense of partisanship in the Congress that Conable also perceived to be a problem in the Ways and Means Committee since the departure of Wilbur Mills. In July 1975 Conable jumped at the opportunity to have a heart-to-heart talk with his former chairman and the man who had done more than any other to provide him a bipartisan model of the way he thought the Ways and Means Committee should work. As he was leaving the floor of the House, Conable spotted Mills sitting in the lobby, and Mills asked him to sit down next to him and talk for a few minutes. "I, of course, launched into a lively discussion with him right away," Conable wrote in his journal the next day, "saying that I had heard he was not feeling well again and that I was sorry to hear it and hoped he would be able to return to full activity soon."

Mills told Conable that he felt pretty well physically, but emotionally, he said, he wasn't as well as he had been. He said he had seen a new doctor who advised him not to return to full duty for at least another six months.

"Mr. Chairman," Conable said, "we need you. We need a constructive force on the committee again such as you can offer. We need you on tax reform in particular."

"Barber, I have every intention of sitting with the committee and actively participating in any mark-up of the tax-reform bill," Mills replied. "But I guess I'll have to take it easy until then."

Mills then confided in Conable that he was concerned about "Al Ullman's bitterness toward Gerald Ford." He said Ullman felt that "Ford was playing politics with him constantly. He was not being supportive and was pulling the rug out from under him whenever he got a chance."

Conable told Mills "how silly" he thought this was, reminding the chairman that only twelve of the thirty-seven members on the new Ways and Means Committee were Republicans, and explaining to him that "during the energy proposal Ullman had not consulted with us at all, and yet considered us partisan when we didn't give him support when he needed it." Conable also told Mills that he had "actively participated in the meeting at the White House in which the president had offered to try to help work out a compromise on energy, which was rejected by the Democrats, including Ullman."

At the end of the conversation, Mills indicated to Conable that he was "awfully disappointed with the way things were going and didn't like to see so much politics in the committee." He also expressed "dismay in how little the new members [on the committee] knew about anything and how assertive they are." But, he told Conable, "I have to be awfully careful not to appear to undercut Al Ullman myself," indicating that he had been invited to the White House a couple of times to talk to the president and felt each time he should not go, "in view of the delicacy of his relationship to Al."

> I have no idea why Wilbur Mills would have had a conversation like this with me, but I suspect that it does not relate to his intentions on the committee, but simply to an effort to recapture some of his old friendships. It may be that he's planning to leave the House, because of the impossibility of his position on a committee which has been taken over by someone else and by changed circumstances. Certainly, I do not take his report of another doctor telling him that he could not be active for another six months very seriously, although that might be the sort of thing he would hold out as a reason for resigning from the House. I suspect he's beginning to realize that he made a mistake in not making a clear break at the time of his greatest embarrassment and that he is at this stage not inclined to want to reassert any degree of authority on the committee, since it's evidently beyond his control. I may be wrong. He may in fact start taking a strong line on the committee when tax reform comes up, but the conversation I had with him seemed more like a cover-up or further withdrawal . . . from the constructive work of the committee.[37]

As Conable suspected, Mills took no active role in drafting the tax reform legislation which the House enacted later that year. The former chairman quietly served out his eighteenth term in Congress, but did not seek reelection to the House in 1976. He joined a prestigious Washington, D.C. law firm where he practiced until his death in 1992.

By this stage of his career, Conable was also growing increasingly weary of his own life in Congress, particularly with his role as a member of the minority party. Early in 1976, he indicated he would seek a seventh congressional term, but at the time of his announcement, he bluntly told the press: "Sometime before I die I want to do something else. I'm clear I don't want to make Congress a career."[38]

1976 Election

Conable tried very hard to help Jerry Ford, not only in getting his legislative program through Congress, but also in gaining his party's nomination and winning the 1976 presidential election. Much of Conable's journal from mid-1975 through the presidential election in November 1976 is devoted to the politics and intrigue of the upcoming presidential election.

Although Ford did not officially announce his candidacy for the 1976 presidential election until July 8, 1975, Conable and other Ford administration insiders had already begun to devise a strategy for the Ford presidential campaign in the spring. Much of Conable's concern for the campaign centered on New York state where Senator James Buckley had refused to support Ford's candidacy and was widely seen as sympathetic to the presidential aspirations of Ronald Reagan, the conservative Republican governor of California. Buckley had been elected as the third-party Conservative candidate to the Senate from New York in 1970, but he had aligned himself with Republicans in the Senate. "I have been deeply concerned about the probability of trouble with the president in James Buckley's continued reluctance to support him," Conable wrote in his journal on June 9, 1975.

> I talked to the president at a supper party several weeks ago, urging him to have an accommodation with Buckley through some sort of personal conference as quickly as possible, fearing that if the Republican Party did not work out its problems with Buckley, the result would be a series of primary contests affecting the president's candidacy in New York state, as the capital 'C' Conservatives [the Conservative Party in New York state] through their conservative Republican friends, react against Ford's identification with Rockefeller. . . . I do not think Buckley can be reelected in any event, unless the Democrats really blow it in their nominee, but I'm concerned about the impact on Ford with continued Buckley defection.[39]

Seeing no indication that Ford was moving to head off a confrontation with Buckley and the right-wing element of the Republican Party in New York and elsewhere in the country, Conable made an appointment to see the president at the White House on July 8, the day Ford announced he would seek the Republican presidential nomination. "When I arrived," Conable recalled in his journal,

I was taken quickly to the Oval Office where the president
and Don Rumsfeld [Conable's former congressional
colleague and now Ford's chief of staff] sat and talked
with me, Rummy apparently taking notes, but saying very
little. I went over the whole ground again and the president made some exploratory and exclamatory remarks of
one sort or another.

Subsequently, he asked Rummy to tell me what had
been going on since I had first raised the issue. He's had
several meetings with Jim Buckley that have been incon-
clusive. Rumsfeld has also talked to Clifton White,
Buckley's campaign manager. The upshot is that the president is not seriously alarmed at this point, still does
not have a handle to take hold of, and needs additional
suggestions beyond the suggestion that he have the
personal consultations with Buckley that he's already had.

I told him about the president of Rochester Gas and
Electric, Francis Drake, calling me during the past week
to ask what his attitude should be toward raising money
for Buckley. The president immediately decided this was
a possibility for pressuring Buckley and suggested that
I mention to my friends in Rochester the reservations
they should . . . express about money raising for Buckley
until Buckley agrees to support the president [which,
Conable reported in his journal, he did at a breakfast with
Rochester business leaders on July 12].

My conclusion about the meeting on Tuesday afternoon with the president was that he was interested, active,
and as yet unresolved about how to handle the New York
situation and how to prevent Buckley-initiated problems
there, as a result of Buckley's almost religious ministry to
the conservatives of New York State.[40]

Two and a half months later, on October 28, in his weekly meeting with the president, Nelson Rockefeller offered to withdraw as
Ford's vice presidential running mate in the 1976 elections. Though
Ford had consistently stated publicly that Rockefeller would be his
vice presidential running mate, both he and Rockefeller were aware
that Rockefeller's presence on the ticket continued to pose a problem for Ford among the ultraconservatives in the Republican Party,
not only in New York but elsewhere in the country as well. Gerald
Ford reluctantly accepted Rockefeller's offer to withdraw, hoping to
increase his conservative support.[41]

Conable thought Rockefeller's withdrawal from the ticket
"would be useful in some ways," as he had suggested to Ford in
private conversations, but he remembered being "surprised" at the
time when the announcement was finally made. "But by then," he

recalled, "Rockefeller had been virtually shut out of contact with Ford by Rummy. Rummy hated him." It was partly an ideological disagreement, with Rockefeller being far too liberal for the conservative Rumsfeld. "But it was also a clash of two strong personalities," Conable recalled. "Rummy wanted to control access to the president, because he was personally ambitious. He wanted to be secretary of defense," a position he got in November 1975, when Ford made his forty-three-year-old chief of staff the youngest secretary of defense in history.[42]

With Rockefeller off the ticket, Ford and his advisers hoped they had placated the right-wing of the Republican Party and maybe even dissuaded their leader, Ronald Reagan, from entering the presidential race. But Reagan was not to be discouraged. On the afternoon of November 19, as Ford was conferring with Rockefeller and some of his aides in the Oval Office, he received a phone call from Reagan, telling him of his intentions to run for president.

Ford now knew the challenge from Reagan was serious and would be divisive for the Republican Party. "I thought ruefully about all the time we had frittered away trying to convince ourselves that Reagan wouldn't enter the race," Ford wrote in his autobiography.

> My supporters had been crisscrossing America lining up endorsements from prominent Republicans. We had most of the generals on our side. But Reagan had many of the troops. His volunteers were already out ringing doorbells. The first test would come in New Hampshire on February 24. Reagan had recruited former Governor Hugh Gregg, a moderate Republican, to head his efforts there, and he had secured the only computerized list of registered voters in the state. His people were holding meetings, mapping strategy. By contrast, my own efforts seemed in disarray. A defeat in New Hampshire, I knew, would render a crippling blow to my entire campaign.[43]

With a renewed sense of urgency and a stepped-up campaign over the next three months, Ford was able to squeak out a narrow 51 percent victory over Reagan in the New Hampshire primary.

Though Ford "won by the narrowest of margins," Conable wrote in his journal after the election, "the general feeling in the House following his win was that it was psychologically a big boost to his campaign and that Reagan is definitely going to be on the defensive in Florida [the next primary scheduled for March 9], and virtually out of the race if he does not win there.

"Ford's campaign," though, Conable noted,

> appears to be badly organized and there's little doubt that if he gets the nomination, it will be the result of muddling through rather than demonstrating high political confidence as a national campaigner. [But] the economy has been cooperating very well, and if he muddles through to the nomination, I persistently feel he has a good chance of beating whatever emerges from the pack of Democratic candidates.
>
> I hope so. I'm convinced the Republicans will not survive as a national party if it is led into this election by a candidate who appeals to a very narrow ideological segment. The American democracy will not continue as we have known it, if we do not have two inclusive national parties with at least the potential of majority control, rather than the ideological fragments characteristic of some of the other developing nations of the world. Thus, I see Ford's leadership not only as vitally necessary to my own survival as an effective member of the House, but a necessary ingredient in the continuance of the two party system as we have known it.[44]

Two weeks later on March 9, as Conable hoped, Ford defeated Reagan in the Florida primary with 53 percent of the vote. But, contrary to the expectations of Ford and others, Ford's defeat of Reagan in the Florida primary did not knock Reagan out of the race.

Reagan intensified his efforts and with the help of the North Carolina Senator Jesse Helms, scored a stunning victory over Ford in the North Carolina primary on March 23. Capitalizing on conservative opposition to a treaty Ford was negotiating to return the ownership of the Panama Canal to Panama, Reagan received 52 percent of the primary vote and won twenty-eight of the available fifty-four convention delegates from North Carolina.

Buoyed by his unexpected victory in North Carolina, Reagan withdrew from the Wisconsin primary, where he was never a serious challenger, and bought television time for an address to the nation on March 31. In his television address, Reagan stressed the outsider theme which had been central to his campaign from the beginning. "For most of his adult life," Reagan told his audience, Ford "has been part of the Washington establishment." By contrast, "most of my adult life has been spent outside government." Reagan went on to sharply criticize Ford's conduct of the presidency, particularly Ford's policy of détente with the Soviet Union. As a result of Reagan's television address, money poured into the Reagan campaign, several congressmen who had previously been uncommitted announced their support for Reagan, and Reagan won all ninety-six convention delegates in the Texas primary on May 1.[45]

Discouraged by the Ford campaign, Conable wrote in his journal on May 4:

> During the spring, we have seen the apparent momentum of Gerald Ford gradually slow. His victories have been thin at best. . . . While the public is giving him some presumptions on account of incumbency, that presumption is not an enthusiastic one, nor is it one which attracts one to him personally, beyond a generally pleasant feeling people have about his character and his motivations. . . . Ronald Reagan, on the other hand, whom I do not find to be an attractive man in almost any sense, has superficial glitter and a sense of timing combined with considerable oratorical credibility which has an appeal beyond the simplicity and shallowness of his views.

Written on the day of the Indiana primary, Conable thought the results there would be critical to the outcome of the national convention. "If Ford wins comfortably," Conable believed, "Reagan will look like a southern and western phenomenon, while if Reagan does well in Indiana, Ford will look like a faltering candidacy."[46]

As it turned out on May 4, Reagan did well in Indiana, winning a narrow victory over Ford in that state's primary, and he also won substantial victories over Ford the same day in Alabama and Georgia, thus further jeopardizing Ford's nomination. Ford had very badly underestimated Reagan and now he was in the political fight of his life.

The next morning Conable attended the regularly scheduled Republican leadership meeting at the White House. Although the leadership meeting had not been called to discuss the presidential primaries, "political discussion was the main order of business," Conable reported in his journal.

> John Rhodes at one point indicated that he wanted to talk about political matters, and the president, in his usual open manner, accepted and permitted 45 minutes of gratuitous advice from the many politicians present.
>
> I did not have much to say, because the very things that were being suggested at the visit were things I had urged on the president three months ago in the personal interview I had with him at my request to talk about political

matters in New York state. He continues not to use his many allies on Capitol Hill to speak for him and to supplement his virtually one-man campaign organization.

Clearly the so-called professionals of [Stuart] Spencer and [Bill] Roberts [two highly respected campaign managers] on the staff do not either have adequate control to do what's necessary or do not know what to do. . . .

Meanwhile, Conable also reported,

the congressional scene is gloomy . . . with the Republicans terrified at the prospect of a possible campaign headed by Ronald Reagan appealing to a very narrow segment of the public. The Democrats are terrified also by their lack of relationship to Jimmy Carter [who apparently had the Democratic nomination locked up] and their lack of personal ties to him or an understanding of what he stands for or where he is headed. I would judge the Democrats are going through a difficult period of adjustment. The American people may want a new face, but the old pros want to have a face they can be comfortable with. They have nothing with which to come to grips.

On Friday, May 7, Conable went to West Virginia to campaign for Ford. "It was interesting to see how his campaign committee there worked," Conable wrote in his journal, as he discovered firsthand just how disorganized Ford's campaign was. "I was called by Bill Steiger [a young Republican congressman from Wisconsin who was helping with the Ford campaign] late Thursday afternoon and asked if I could possibly go to West Virginia with Caldwell Butler, the congressman from Roanoke, Virginia, to campaign on Ford's behalf. . . . I was pleased to be asked to do something for Ford, having volunteered on many occasions and never have been taken up. And despite this casual arrangement, I canceled a number of appointments to go up early in the morning with Butler in a small plane," Conable recounted.

We went to Charleston, West Virginia, the capital, only to find that we had arrived too late for the press conference scheduled for us early that morning, due to a scheduling error on the itinerary that had been handed to us. We met the Ford chairman from West Virginia, an attractive state legislator, who then journeyed with us to three successive county seats in southern West Virginia where press conferences had been set up. For each of these, we attested to our great affection and respect for President Ford and the type of leadership he represented, then submitting to questions from a ho hum press, usually one newspaper reporter and one radio station operator with a tape recorder, then answering questions from a ho hum audience of old biddies who had been brought out on the party's behest to fill out the small room in which our press conferences were scheduled. We stayed nowhere longer than half an hour and I was satisfied when we completed the work. But we probably had not made six votes for Ford, even though each of us had missed six votes on the floor of the House. Thus, except for the inner satisfaction of having at least done something for President Ford in the campaign, nothing was accomplished, and one could only conclude that the probable cost of $1,000 on our project was largely wasted by the President Ford committee.[47]

Despite not doing much personal campaigning in West Virginia, Ford easily won the West Virginia primary on May 11. On the same day, however, Reagan scored an impressive victory in Nebraska, as the primary results continued in see-saw between the two candidates.

Then, a week later, on May 18, Ford won much needed victories in his home state of Michigan and Maryland. Victories in these two states, Conable reported in his journal, "greatly improved the mood of congressional Republicans [and] provided considerable reassurance to Ford supporters that the Reagan momentum was not going to build in a straight line," though Conable predicted Ford would have "a very difficult time over the next couple weeks."[48]

To counter the slight lead that Reagan had in the delegate count at this point, the influential chairman of the New York Republican Party, Richard Rosenbaum, announced on May 20 that he was throwing the support of most of New York state's 154 delegates, which was formally decided at the state convention level, to Ford. Two days later, Pennsylvania's delegates also decided at their state convention to give Ford 88 of their 103 convention votes.

On May 25, Reagan and Ford split six primaries. Reagan won Arkansas, Nevada, and Idaho. Ford won in Oregon, where he was expected to win, and also in Tennessee and Kentucky, where he was not expected to win.

The big concluding primaries were held in California, Ohio, and New Jersey on June 8. As expected, Reagan won all 167 delegates in the winner-take-all California primary. But Ford won most of the delegates in Ohio, and the delegates in New Jersey where Reagan had not campaigned.

At the end of the primary elections, Ford reported in his autobiography, he had won 992 delegates, 138 short of the 1,130 delegates needed to win the nomination, and Reagan had 886 delegates, or 244 short of the nomination.[49]

With the primaries concluded and neither candidate having enough delegate support to claim the nomination, the crucial stage of the campaign turned to the eleven states that chose the remaining 267 delegates through state conventions. Here, Ford had a decided advantage. Though the Ford organization was not well prepared for the state conventions, never imagining at the outset of the campaign that they would need them to win the nomination, Ford now used the power of presidential incumbency to court the few remaining delegates he needed. "Special phone calls, White House visits and fulfillment of other political favors," *Congressional Quarterly* reported, "were all included in the package used by Ford" to win the support of the state conventions.[50]

By the last of the state conventions on July 18, Ford had closed the gap and was reported to have 1,109 first-ballot delegates—twenty-eight short of what he needed for the nomination. Reagan had 1,063 delegates, sixty-seven short. Ninety-four delegates were still uncommitted.

On July 26, in a last-ditch effort, Reagan announced that, if nominated, he would select the liberal Republican Senator Richard Schweicker from Pennsylvania as his vice presidential running mate. Never before in American history had a presidential nominee announced his vice presidential choice prior to his own nomination. By taking this unprecedented gamble, urged on him by his campaign manager John Sears, as his only remaining chance to win the nomination, Reagan hoped to win over enough of the Pennsylvania delegation to edge out Ford. But the Reagan strategy backfired. The Pennsylvania delegates held firm and even increased their support for Ford (ninety-three to ten), and in the process Reagan alienated his own conservative base with his announced intention to choose one of the most liberal members of the Senate as his running mate.[51]

A few days later Conable commented in his journal on the glee and astonishment with which the Ford camp greeted the Schweicker announcement:

> This affair is one that defies comprehension. It is apparent that Reagan had not checked Schweicker out. . . . Schweicker has very little respect in either the conservative or the liberal camp. The conservatives hate him

because he is the most liberal Republican Senator, far surpassing Clifford Case [New Jersey], Edward Brooke [Massachusetts] and Jacob Javits [New York] in opposition to his own party position. . . . The liberals consider him a formula politician, a man who shops around for support and does not truly believe in the positions he espouses and votes on in the Senate. . . .

Schweicker appears even to have eroded Reagan's position with the Pennsylvania delegation where it was not strong to begin with. And certainly the alienation of the true believers in the South with the Reagan ticket is likely to reach nearly stampede proportions. Clarke Reed of Mississippi [the conservative leader there] has already announced his disenchantment of Ronald Reagan and his intention to support Ford, and he is, of course, one of the hardest-line conservatives among the Republican southern leaders.

When the announcement came, it was confirmed by a Schweicker press conference. . . . Many of our true believers in the House of Representatives were slinking around with their tails between their legs, caught completely off guard because they had not been consulted at all before the announcement, and were completely shaking their heads in disbelief.

"We Ford supporters," on the other hand, "held virtually a full day of celebration in the lounge off the floor of the House, savoring the dimensions of the Reagan disaster, marveling that the press was underplaying it as much as it was, and speculating about the motivation. That night, I went to a state dinner at the White House with the Australian Ambassador and found that the president was feeling pretty cocky. He told me he had written the scenario for the campaign so far, including the Reagan announcement [and] that I should have more faith that things were going to turn out all right. I suspect though, he was just as surprised and delighted as I was by this turn of events.[52]

With most observers now believing that Ford probably had enough delegates to win the nomination on the first ballot, the Republican National Convention convened in Kansas City on August 16. In a final attempt to deny Ford the nomination, Reagan's campaign manager, John Sears, had appeared before the Rules Committee of the Republican National Convention on August 9 and proposed that all presidential candidates, including Ford, be required to disclose the name of their vice presidential running mate before the presidential balloting began. Under the Sears proposal, failure of a candidate to comply with this rule would free all delegates from any commitment to vote for him. The Sears proposal was handily defeated in the preconvention Rules Committee, where Ford supporters predominated. But confident he could win on this issue on the convention floor, Sears arranged for this amendment to be presented to the full convention just before the presidential balloting on August 17, believing that the passage of this amendment would be the stepping stone for Reagan's nomination. The Reagan forces came very close indeed to getting this amendment adopted on the convention floor. But, in the end, the convention rejected the Reagan-backed amendment by a small margin. Ford went on to win a first-ballot nomination by a vote of 1187 to 1070. Thus by a margin of only 117 votes, Gerald Ford squeaked out a victory against his arch-rival to win the Republican presidential nomination.[53]

Though Reagan did not win the nomination, he was able to get his man—Senator Robert Dole from Kansas—chosen as Ford's vice presidential running mate. The day after his nomination, Ford had boiled down his choices for a running mate to four names: Anne Armstrong, former co-chairwoman of the Republican National Committee and ambassador to England, Assistant Attorney General William Ruckelshaus, Senator Howard Baker of Tennessee, and Dole. According to Ford's press secretary, Ron Nessen, Ford was leaning toward Ruckelshaus, but some last minute pressure from the Reagan camp persuaded him to choose Dole.[54]

As for the convention itself, "it was not an intellectual exercise," Conable wrote in his journal. "Once Ford demonstrated in the rules fight that he had the votes to win the nomination," Conable wrote,

> I lost interest in participation and spent much of the time in the gallery with my wife, marveling at the hubbub below. I had the worst seat in the House, two seats directly behind the vice president. Rocky appeared relaxed and outgoing, so the aisle was constantly clogged with newsmen and others interviewing him, drowning the speeches, clawing at those of us who sat near Rockefeller in order to get closer to the great man . . .
>
> At the end of the convention, the president gave an acceptance speech which was as good as any speech I have heard him give and generally accepted as such. We left there dispirited by all that had transpired up until the acceptance speech, but feeling a thrill of hope as the din died down that the president had given us the necessary upbeat for an end of an exhausting and not very satisfying political exercise.[55]

Ford left the Republican Convention in August, still badly trailing Jimmy Carter in the public opinion polls, by as much as twenty-three percentage points in the latest Gallup poll, and by an even larger margin in the Harris survey.[56] But with some very personable and effective television advertising over the next few weeks, Ford quickly narrowed the gap with Carter.

Ford's cause was further helped in early September as a result of a controversial interview Carter did with *Playboy* magazine. In an effort to show his human side, "born-again" Jimmy Carter admitted that he had "looked on a lot of women with lust" and "committed adultery in my heart many times." Ford narrowed the gap with Carter to twelve points. On September 26 in Philadelphia, in the first of three scheduled debates, Ford did very well in his confrontation with Carter, further closing the Carter lead to eight percentage points.

But then came the second presidential debate in San Francisco on October 6, where Ford committed his famous Iron Curtain gaffe, raising doubts once again about his competence to be president. In response to a reporter's question, Ford boldly declared that "there is no Soviet domination of Eastern Europe, and there never will be under a Ford administration."[57]

"Ford meant to say," according to his biographer James Cannon, "that the United States did not *accept* Soviet control of Eastern Europe, and thought he had said that. When [Brent] Scowcroft [head of the National Security Council], [Dick] Cheney [Ford's new chief of staff], and [Stuart] Spencer [Ford's campaign adviser] tried to get him to clarify his statement, Ford—in a display of the stubbornness he sometimes inflicted on himself—flatly refused to listen. Some three days later, when Ford finally did admit publicly that he had made a mistake, the damage was done. Ford had planned that this debate would show Carter's inexperience in foreign policy; instead, the news stories were about his own inexplicable blunder."[58]

Four days after the disastrous second presidential debate, with Ford dropping fast in the polls once again, a despondent Barber Conable wrote in his journal.

> The presidential campaign goes badly. I have uneasy feelings about the final outcome. Gerald Ford, a man whom I have been forced to place my confidence in because there is no one else available, is proving to have the feet of clay that we always acknowledged him to have, but hoped they would not show. He is a decent, earnest, well-intentioned man in deep water and swimming in a school

of sharks who seem increasingly lethal as he thrashes
around in the water.

Jimmy Carter himself is a shark with the sharpest teeth
and the most insatiable appetite. My misgivings about him
are not in any way diminished by his conduct in the
campaign to date. One yearns for him to overstep the
bounds of decency in some illuminating way that will suddenly give the turn to the campaign in favor of Ford. One
fears that Carter is too smart and managed by too many
intelligent people to permit that illuminating moment.

"If Carter is elected and the Republicans do not pick up
substantial strength in the House," Conable also wrote, "I can see
circumstances combining during the next two years in such a way
that I would not want to stay to face the electorate once more in
1978. I feel jaded and ineffective, and the toll of the life I lead on
my personal values and my family's peace of mind is beginning to
tell. I have not made a decision to retire [after the next Congress],
but I've certainly not made a decision not to retire either, and the
next two years will have to see some earnest soul searching about
the probability of continued effectiveness, since it is difficult in a
minority role."[59]

Ford did better in the third presidential debate in Williamsburg
on October 21. With Carter holding onto a slim six-point lead in the
polls, neither candidate made any major mistake to affect the outcome of the election.

Determined to close the gap with Carter and move ahead at the
finish line, Ford crisscrossed the country during the final days of
the campaign, promising to cut taxes if elected. Ford's promise of a
tax cut was offset, though, by bad economic news on October 28
when the Commerce Department reported that the index of leading
economic indicators had declined for the second straight month.[60]

"I leaned on [Ford's] staff very hard to get him to Rochester,"
Conable reported in his journal, "feeling that it would be a considerable boost for us in our area if he would come through. He came
in a drenching rain to the Rochester airport a few days before the
election, acting like a man possessed, performing a presidential
candidate's role to the hilt, evoking a crowd response of warmth
and support that would have gotten any politician's heart."[61]

"Barb, I'm coming up in the polls," Conable remembered Ford
telling him as they shook hands quickly at the Rochester airport.
"We can't stay here any length of time. I've got to get on to some other
bigger populations because the rallies will help. We're narrowing
Carter's lead."[62]

Ford did indeed move up in the polls in the final days of the campaign, but not enough to overtake the Carter lead. In an extremely close election, Jimmy Carter defeated Gerald Ford on November 2 by a vote of 49.7 percent to 47.7 percent. Carter's margin in the electoral college was even closer—the closest since 1916—edging Ford out 297 to 241. "If only 8,000 voters in Hawaii and Ohio had gone for Ford," one observer noted, "he would have won."[63]

"Election night," Conable wrote in his journal, "was a strange combination of personal sadness that my friend had come so close and yet had lost, and anxiety as to the uncertainty of the Carter administration . . ., and relief that I would no longer have to struggle in the mixed role of supporting a minority president in a hostile congressional atmosphere. It really has not been a very happy or comfortable time, even after the demise of Richard Nixon, for Republicans in Congress."[64]

The Democrats also held onto their two-to-one margin in the House of Representatives, winning one additional seat to give them a 292 to 143 majority in the Ninety-fifth Congress. Most of the liberal Democratic freshmen elected in 1974 were reelected, making the new House about as liberal as the old House. With eighteen new members, the Senate had its largest turnover since 1958, but the partisan composition of the new Senate would remain the same as the old Senate—62 Democrats and 38 Republicans.[65]

Conable was easily reelected, defeating his Democratic challenger, Michael Macaluso, who, much to Conable's annoyance, had been cross-endorsed by the Conservative Party, by a margin of 66 percent to 34 percent.[66] Reflecting on his campaign against Macaluso, a Rochester businessman and antipornography crusader who had lost to Midge Costanza for the Democratic nomination two years earlier, Conable wrote in his journal:

> The campaign period, the election, and the post-election period have not been times to gladden one's heart. The campaign itself was drudgery and my opponent, Mike Macaluso, was an earnest and committed ideologue, more Conservative than Democrat, who believed sincerely that I am a dangerous and fuzzy-minded liberal. If he could defeat me by any means, [he thought it] would be a service to the country, and if people simply understood me better, I would be turned out of office. I debated him several times and three themes emerged: that I have persistently voted for high deficits, thus robbing the American people of their savings by inflation; second, that for some reason probably related to my lack of

patriotism and understanding, I am anxious to turn the Panama Canal over to a Marxist government; and third, that I have been persistent in efforts to give special concessions to the Soviet Union so that American technology and research could be diverted into aiding them in their destructive military buildup.

As I said at one point during the campaign, I am used to having my judgment questioned, but not my honesty and my patriotism. I thought he was simply mistaken about me early in the campaign and tried to explain my record in the earlier debates. In the debate on public television he zapped me in a way which led me to believe that he was not amenable to reason or explanation, and so in subsequent appearances, limited in number, I took him on more directly and more rigorously. The Democratic officials in our area all told me they were voting for me and described him as a fascist, who had received the Democratic nomination by default and in some cases with their active opposition.

The success in receiving the Conservative endorsement, as well as the Democratic, led me to believe that the Conservative Party really wants to beat me and has made me feel somewhat bitter about their use of the word "conservative."

In the New York Senate race, Daniel Patrick Moynihan, the Harvard intellectual and presidential adviser, whom Conable had gotten to know during the Nixon administration, defeated the incumbent conservative Republican senator, James Buckley, to win his first term in the United States Senate. "My relations with Buckley during the campaign were tense," Conable wrote in his journal after the election.

I was, of course, angry the Conservative Party endorsed my Democratic opponent, so I was determined not to be active in Buckley's support in any avail. He asked me when he announced his candidacy for reelection to stand on the platform with him in New York City at the time of his announcement. I refused to do so, saying that I would agree to only if he would agree to back President Ford. Since he was not prepared to do this, I therefore did not stand up with him. Subsequently he was asked if he was going to endorse me. He replied that the way such things work, that I must ask for his endorsement and he would doubtless confer it. I did not ask him. Some of my Republican county chairmen told him when he came through that I was a popular politician in the area and that he needed me a good deal more than I needed him. Thus, when reporters in Rochester asked him if he would support the Conservative-endorsed Macaluso or the Republican-endorsed Conable, he did not hesitate and said he considered me to be a national asset and he would support me. Although there was no quid pro quo for this statement on his part, I decided that it would be expedient for me to at least appear with him on the platform and so I introduced him from the rear of the train when he whistle-stopped through Batavia. The burden of my remarks in introducing him was that he was a man of sufficient personal integrity not to have been corrupted by the Washington scene and that he was the same low key, unassuming fellow he had been when we sent him to Washington six years before. I declined, however, to introduce him from the rear of the train when he went through Rochester. . . .

I must say that he did well in the debates with Moynihan, who always created a lively spirit. . . . On the basis of the debates, I would have voted for Buckley, but knowing the two men and their potential from other parts of their records, I finally, quietly, and without telling anyone, voted for Moynihan, as did most of the members of my family. I look forward to working with him, having some confidence that he will be the same creative type of person in the difficult environment of the Senate that he was in some of his earlier incarnations.[67]

Preparing for the New Congress

Following the elections, as is customary, House Democrats and Republicans met in their respective party caucuses to elect their leaders and organize for the new Ninety-fifth Congress. The Democrats chose the Majority Leader Thomas P. "Tip" O'Neill of Massachusetts to replace the retiring Carl Albert of Oklahoma as Speaker. Then in a heated four-way contest to succeed O'Neill, the moderate-conservative Jim Wright of Texas defeated Phillip Burton of California, the liberal chairman of the Democratic Caucus, Richard Bolling of Missouri, another prominent liberal reformer, and John J. McFall of California, the Democratic whip, to become the new Democratic majority leader.

On the Republican side, the House Republicans reelected John Rhodes of Arizona as minority leader, Bob Michel of Illinois as whip, and John Anderson of Illinois as chairman of the Republican Conference. They also chose Del Clawson from California, who had narrowly lost to Conable two years earlier, to be the new chairman of the Policy Committee.[68]

Herman Schneebeli of Pennsylvania, who had been the ranking member on the Ways and Means Committee in the two previous Congresses, had retired at the end of the Ninety-fourth Congress, elevating Conable to the top Republican position on the committee in the new Congress. According to the rules of the party, Conable could not continue to chair the Republican Policy Committee and also serve as the Republican leader of Ways and Means. Thus, he had to decide at the beginning of the new Congress whether he wanted to seek the chairmanship of the Policy Committee again or become the Republican leader of the Ways and Means Committee.

Without hesitation, Conable chose the Ways and Means position, which, he explained to his constituents, "will give me access to a highly skilled minority staff, with the opportunity for creative work in the tax, trade and health areas. As one who has heretofore majored in extracurricular activities, I welcome the chance to devote myself to interesting studies with which I am already more than a little familiar. I have long felt that my temperament is not as partisan as the past role in which my colleagues have cast me for the past six years, and I go to this new legislative appointment with a quiet sense of relief."[69]

Though Conable would not be an elected party leader in the new Congress, he would continue to be part of the Republican leadership in the House. Since his election to the leadership in 1969, other leaders of the party had come to depend on Conable for his economic expertise and political judgment. To retain his counsel, Minority Leader Rhodes asked Conable to continue to serve in the Republican leadership group in the House, a political appointment which Conable held for the duration of his service, meeting regularly with other party leaders and presidents at the White House to discuss legislative and political matters before the Congress.

Relieved of an elected party leadership position in the new Congress, Conable hoped for a "somewhat less partisan role" in the Ways and Means Committee. But the early signs from Al Ullman were not encouraging. "Ullman is already saying that he will have a much happier time with his chairmanship of Ways and Means next year, because I will no longer have a friend in the White House," Conable wrote in his journal early in December 1976. "He doesn't seem to understand that our partisanship in the 94th Congress related to his unwillingness to consult with us to make us part of a committee consensus [as Wilbur Mills had done earlier]. I think he may have a rude awakening if he feels that unified Republican response to his partisan initiatives was simply a matter of personal embarrassment on my part. I am determined to have the Republicans get as much input into the decision of the committee as our abilities and our willingness to participate will permit. And if this requires bloc voting, he'll find us as capable of doing that during the 95th Congress as we were during the 94th."[70]

In December Conable attended a meeting with President-elect Carter and some of the other leaders of Congress. After the meeting, Conable introduced himself to Carter, who immediately recognized him. "Oh, yes," Carter said, "I campaigned against you a couple years ago. That Midge is a wonderful girl." In a few weeks, Carter would appoint Conable's 1974 congressional opponent, Midge Costanza, as his special assistant for public affairs.[71]

"My general impression of Carter," Conable wrote afterwards in his journal, "was that he was an attractive and articulate man, very self-confident about his abilities and his capacity to control the events affecting the presidency, but with comparatively modest understanding of the complexity of the goals he has set for himself.

"This view of Jimmy Carter was confirmed by [the Federal Reserve Chairman] Arthur Burns' view of him when I had a private breakfast with Arthur at the Federal Reserve Building a few days later. Arthur described Governor Carter as very inexperienced. He said he was persuaded that he would need a great deal of help in Congress, if Carter's inexperience was not to do some damage to the country, and said that he was deeply concerned that the right kind of input into the Carter administration be organized in some way."[72]

Thus, Barber Conable, now in the thirteenth year of his congressional career, prepared for a new Congress and a new president.

Chapter 11

Republican Leader of
Ways and Means

Like most Americans, Conable was impressed with the early days of the Carter presidency. "After three weeks in office, one thing is apparent about Jimmy Carter," Conable wrote his constituents on February 17, 1977.

He understands the public relations potential of the presidency as no other president since Franklin Roosevelt. He started with the walk up Pennsylvania Avenue [on Inauguration Day], a refreshing glimpse after years of an embattled presidency. He proceeded through a conscious and deliberate series of symbolically informed gestures—the sending of his daughter to public school, the fireside chat in a sweater, the visits to the government agencies where in his shirtsleeves he told the bureaucrats that they were no better than the people they serve, the "open line" to the White House, the virtuoso performance in the first press conference—to impart a style to his presidency which is neither a simple expression of his personality nor the creature of casual coincidence.

While the traditions of American democracy work against a personality cult appropriate to monarchs or dictators, we do yearn for the chance to identify with our government and to think of government as a process in which one man can make a difference. President Carter apparently understands this, and has gone out of his way to make the obvious gestures that will quickly identify him as a man leading rather than a leader. That he has done this helps confirm his image as an outsider, a man who didn't come up through the same old establishment chains; and of course that's why he was elected in the first place. It also confirms that as a politician he is no amateur.

Conable warned his constituents, however, that they could not assume that President Carter would have an easy time with Congress just because it was run by his political party. "In early maneuvers between the two institutions," he observed, "there has already been evidence that congressional leaders will not accept his leadership automatically; and he is not about to stand hat in hand, politely waiting until they make up their minds about him. By the emphasis he has put on direct communication with their constituents, he is saying to congressmen, 'I don't need you to talk to the public. I just may talk to you through the public, since I know that will get your attention.'

"Theodore Roosevelt called the presidency a 'bully pulpit.' In the hands of someone like Jimmy Carter that's true, but of course the presidency is more than that," Conable noted. "Whether or not he's a great president will depend on how he organizes the government to meet the people's needs and how he and his team respond to the inevitable crises of the modern world. He will have to be in the kitchen longer before we will know if he can bake that kind of cake. Nobody wants only frosting for a meal, but if the ingredients for a cake are there, this man has shown he will know how to frost it."[1]

As Conable was sizing up Jimmy Carter and the new Congress, he was also busy adjusting to his own new job as the ranking minority member of the Ways and Means Committee. Though Conable had served as the defacto Republican leader of the Ways and Means Committee for the previous two Congresses, he now had the formal responsibility for leading the twelve Republican minority members on the Ways and Means Committee in the Ninety-fifth Congress. To assist him in his administrative duties on the committee, Conable brought with him his long-time assistant, Martha Phillips, who had ably assisted him first on the Republican Research Committee from 1971 to 1973 and then on the Policy Committee from 1973 to 1976. He also retained John Meagher, who had been his predecessor's chief assistant, as his minority chief of staff on the Ways and Means Committee.

From the beginning, Conable recorded in his journal, he had a difficult time with Meagher. "I'm finding it a little nerve wracking to have to administer the minority staff, since John Meagher is an extremely lively person," he wrote in his journal on February 16, 1977.[2] "John was an idea man. I had to tell him about seven times a day to shut up and sit down, we're not going to do that. But every now and then, I'd get a good idea from him. So I kept him on."[3]

Conable also had trouble with the Democrats' decision that no member could serve on more than two subcommittees in the new Congress. This decision resulted in a cutback in committee membership and some tense conflict among the Republican members for the reduced subcommittee slots. This "subcommittee consolidation," for example, Conable reported in his journal, "resulted in a confrontation between Bill Steiger [the fifth ranking Republican on the committee from Wisconsin and one of the rising stars on the committee] and Bill Frenzel [the seventh ranking Republican from Minnesota and one of Conable's closest friends on the committee], an unhappy fact for me since I depend on both of them and their communication is important to the health of the committee. Steiger wound up claiming seniority and bumping Frenzel out of the ranking minority membership on the Trade Subcommittee, a post he dearly coveted and would have been good at. He squirmed a good deal in the process. Both John Duncan [from Tennessee] and Phil Crane [from Illinois] had to give up their ambitions for the Trade Subcommittee in order to even keep Frenzel on it. There was a lot of bruised feeling," Conable noted. "So I sat down and wrote letters to all concerned, thanking them for their cooperation when everything was over."[4]

More generally, Conable continued to be bothered by the Democrats' decision two years earlier to force the Ways and Means Committee into a subcommittee structure. "I've been having a difficult time personally," Conable confided in his journal in October 1977, "because of the subcommittee structure and the expectancy people have that I will stay on top of whatever is happening in subcommittees. I have spread myself so thin trying to do this that I have very little understanding of what's happening in any subcommittee much less all of them. . . . While I regret this, I suppose it's fruitless to complain about it, since this type of development follows the pattern of the Congress generally, since members seem to know less and less about more and more, rather than dealing with issues with improved understanding and over-all perspective."[5]

Outnumbered twenty-five to twelve by the Democrats on Ways and Means, and with a Democrat in the White House anxious to push his legislative agenda through Congress, Conable would not have an easy time as the new minority leader of the Ways and Means Committee. But he quickly threw himself into his new leadership responsibilities with the same gusto he had exhibited throughout his life and congressional career.

A brief look at how Conable and his Republican colleagues responded to three of the most important legislative proposals President Carter presented to the Ways and Means Committee during the first two years of his presidency will provide a glimpse into the complicated politics and personalities of the Ways and Means Committee during this phase of Conable's career. Unfortunately for Conable, with the deck stacked against him, the first two examples—President Carter's comprehensive energy proposal and his request for a Social Security tax increase—illustrate the deep partisan divisions that had characterized the Ways and Means Committee since the departure of Wilbur Mills in 1974 and to which Conable so strongly objected. In the third example, the Tax Act of 1978, however, Conable and his Republican colleagues were able to approximate the bipartisan model of committee cooperation that had existed during the heyday of Wilbur Mills and John Byrnes a decade earlier.

Energy Plan

President Carter's top legislative priority in his first year of office was to develop a comprehensive energy plan for the country. Conable had already been around the track several times on energy legislation, as both the Nixon and Ford administrations had grappled unsuccessfully with the energy problems of the country, and he and other congressional leaders in both parties knew first-hand how difficult it would be to pass legislation in this area.

On April 18, in a television address to the nation, President Carter outlined the broad dimensions of the energy problem facing the country. With the United States now importing almost half of its oil supply, an increase of 30 percent since 1972, and in continual danger of another Arab oil embargo, Carter warned that "with the exception of preventing war, this is the greatest challenge our country will face during our lifetime. The energy crisis has not yet overwhelmed us," he said, "but it will if we do not act quickly."[6]

Two days later, in a nationally televised address to a joint session of Congress, President Carter spelled out the details of his elaborate and comprehensive energy program. "The heart of our energy problem is that our demand for fuel keeps rising more quickly than our production and our primary means of solving this problem is to reduce waste and inefficiency." To this end, Carter proposed a complex set of tax and regulatory policies to reduce the country's dependence on oil and natural gas, which constituted 75 percent of the nation's energy consumption, and to encourage conservation and the development of alternative energy sources.[7]

President Carter's "reliance on the tax system to accomplish his energy goals is so complete . . . that it boggles the mind," a skeptical Barber Conable wrote his constituents in a May 5, 1977, newsletter.[8]

Specifically, Carter proposed to raise the cost of domestic oil to the world market price over the next three years. He proposed new taxes on industries using oil and natural gas and tax credits for industries converting to coal. He proposed a standby five-cents-a-gallon gasoline tax if national consumption exceeded targets set by the federal government and a "gas guzzler" tax on inefficient automobiles. In addition, he proposed a variety of tax incentives to promote conservation, the use of wind and solar technologies, and the development of geothermal and other new sources of energy.[9]

Carter's comprehensive energy bill was introduced in the House of Representatives by the Democratic Majority Leader Jim Wright on May 2. Various portions of the bill were sent to five different committees, with the Ways and Means Committee charged with reviewing the important tax provisions of the legislation.

On instructions from Democratic Speaker Tip O'Neill, who saw passage of energy legislation as a major test of the new administration and the Democratic Congress, all five committees were ordered to complete their deliberations on the legislation by July 13. The recommendations of the five standing committees were then to be referred to a forty-member Ad Hoc Committee on Energy, which O'Neill had hand-picked to shepherd the combined bill through the House.

In the Ways and Means Committee, it quickly became apparent that the issues that had divided the committee on energy policy during the Nixon and Ford years continued to divide the committee on the Carter energy bill. President Carter and committee Democrats generally favored increased taxes on oil and natural gas as the primary means to reduce energy consumption and promote the alternative uses of energy resources in the United States. Conable and most of the committee Republicans favored the creation of tax incentives to increase the domestic production of oil and natural gas as they had done in the past. The Republicans were able to defeat Carter's standby gasoline tax, which many of the Democrats also opposed, and the committee made some modifications in other administrative proposals. But generally, as a close observer of the Ways and Means Committee during this period has noted, "most Democrats supported the president's approach to energy policy while Republicans continued to criticize increased government regulation of energy markets and the lack of incentives for new oil and gas production." When the committee voted to report the bill, only two Democrats opposed the package, and only one Republican supported it.[10]

In a minority report filed with the bill, Conable and his Republican-led minority explained their opposition to the Ways and Means bill. "The fundamental flaw in the bill is its perspective; it looks back rather than forward," they said.

> As a nation we once used whale oil for lighting, but coal gas later proved more efficient. Subsequently we found that natural gas was cheaper and cleaner. Eventually our inventiveness led to lighting our homes and doing many other things with electricity.
>
> If President Carter and those who have supported this program had been in charge, at the start of our energy evolution, we would now be taxing whalers and large manufacturers in order to reduce demand for diminishing supplies of whale oil; we might have never discovered coal gas, natural gas or electricity; our standard of living

would be so far below what it is today that it would be unrecognizable in a modern context.

The bill represents only half of an energy policy. It lacks reasonable incentives for the development of domestic energy reserves. Without additional production incentives, the nation will be unable to continue to provide reasonable levels of growth and employment and a better way of life.

"The Carter energy package as submitted was not really destined to deal with energy but to tax," Conable and his Republican colleagues wrote. "It sought to force Americans to take certain energy conservation measures by imposing very high tax penalties for the failure to do so. . . . While we must conserve energy, we shouldn't do so by levying huge new taxes which will be used to increase government spending."[11]

As predetermined by the Democratic leadership, the tax provisions reported by the Ways and Means Committee and the various other components of the Carter energy package were then sent to the Ad Hoc Committee on Energy. This committee, working under the tight deadline established by O'Neill, reassembled the energy package for submission to the full House in late July. With the exception of an amendment to restore part of the administration's original gasoline tax, the Ad Hoc Committee made only minor changes in the parts of the plan that had been reported by Ways and Means. The full House rejected the Ad Hoc Committee's gasoline tax amendment, but otherwise approved the energy package, including the tax provisions of the Ways and Means Committee, by a partisan vote of 244 to 177 on August 5.[12]

The outcome, though, was very different in the Senate where the petroleum industry was aggressively lobbying against Carter's energy legislation. In an attempt to rally public support against "the special interests" in Congress, "President Carter unleashed a blistering rhetorical offensive against the U.S. oil industry" on October 13, 1977.

In a televised press conference, President Carter "raised the specter of 'war profiteering' by the companies, which have opposed his energy proposals in the Senate, and suggested that the impending energy crisis could give rise to 'the biggest rip-off in history,'" reported Edward Walsh in the *Washington Post*. "It was the harshest invective the president has yet directed against oil producers, who comprise one of the most financially and politically powerful segments of the American industrial economy."[13]

Carter's rhetorical flourish drew immediate criticism from Republican leaders in Congress, including Conable, who as the

Republican leader of the Ways and Means Committee, wrote Carter a tersely worded letter of rebuke the next day.

> Dear Mr. President,
>
> I feel your remarks relative to the energy bill yesterday were not only intemperate, but destructive. Many of us disagree with the philosophy of your energy policy and do it for reasons other than our attraction to "the special interests." It will be difficult to build cooperation between the presidency and the Congress on such language and I deeply regret rhetoric of this sort. I do not doubt that your motives are good, but many who disagree with you are also trying to take positions which they feel will be in the best interests of the country.[14]

Despite Carter's pressures, the Senate, led by the Finance Committee chairman, Russell Long from Louisiana, would agree only to a small tax on the industrial use of oil and gas and some new tax incentives for energy conservation and production. The House and Senate were unable to resolve the major differences between the two versions of the energy bill, and consequently no energy legislation passed Congress in 1977.

President Carter, however, continued to push for energy legislation as the top priority of his administration, and an energy bill did pass Congress a year later in October 1978. However, the bill Carter signed into law bore little resemblance to the original comprehensive energy package he had introduced in Congress with such fanfare in April of 1977. Of the original plan, only the "gas guzzler" tax and tax incentives for conservation and development of new energy sources survived the final package—a bill much more to the liking of the Republicans and conservative Democrats in Congress than the president and his liberal allies.[15]

Social Security Tax Increase

The second major presidential initiative to come before the Ways and Means Committee in 1977 was President Carter's request for an increase in Social Security taxes to offset the rapidly rising cost of the Social Security program. This issue also illustrates the deep partisan divisions that existed between Democrats and Republicans on the Ways and Means Committee during this phase of Conable's career.

Social Security expenditures had been rising at an alarming rate since 1972. That year, in the fourth year of the Nixon presidency,

Congress raised Social Security benefits by 20 percent and also indexed future benefits to inflation. Payroll taxes had not kept pace with Social Security expenditures during the ensuing period of economic recession, and the Social Security system now found itself on the verge of bankruptcy. In 1977, the Social Security Board of Trustees projected that the system's Disability Insurance fund would exhaust its revenues in 1979 and that the Retirement and Survivors Benefits fund would be depleted by 1983.

Conable now found himself in the ironic position of trying to fix a problem that he and his Republican colleagues had inadvertently helped create several years earlier. In 1972, Conable had been one of the leadership voices on the Ways and Means Committee arguing for indexing Social Security benefits to inflation. "Every year the House and Senate would get into a numbers game to see who could be nicer to the old folks," he recalled. "So we conservatives said, 'Let's index the increase in benefits to inflation,'" thinking the annual inflation rate would be less than the increases Congress was inclined to provide beneficiaries.

But then shortly after indexation went into effect, the economy slid into a deep recession and inflation rose to over 12 percent in 1974 and went even higher in the last two years of the Carter presidency. So Social Security benefits soared because Congress indexed it to inflation.

In hindsight, Conable personally regretted indexing Social Security benefits to inflation, "although the way Congress was at that point, if the inflation rate was 17 percent, Congress would have voted a 25 percent increase. But it was clear," he acknowledged, "indexing Social Security automatically every year raised benefits, where before it had required Congress at least to meet and debate it."[16]

To correct this problem in 1977, President Carter offered a plan for refinancing Social Security that centered on increasing payroll taxes on employers. Honoring a pledge he had made in the 1976 presidential campaign not to increase taxes on low and middle-income workers, Carter would not propose increasing payroll taxes for employees. Carter also proposed an experimental and controversial plan to borrow money from the general treasury to finance the Social Security system during periods of high unemployment. His eight-point plan, Carter said, was designed to provide an additional $83 billion to the Social Security trust funds by 1983 and eliminate the deficit in the Social Security system for the remainder of the century.

Under the Carter plan, there would be a phased-in elimination of the ceiling on the amount of wages on which employers paid payroll taxes, requiring businesses to pay Social Security taxes on the full amount of their employees' wages by 1981. There would be smaller increases in the wage base on which employees paid taxes, with the ceiling lifted to $30,000 by 1985.

To deal with the long-term problem in financing Social Security, Carter's plan also included "decoupling" procedures to correct a flaw in the 1972 law that overcompensated for inflation and allowed some recipients' benefits to exceed their pre-retirement wages. These decoupling techniques proposed by Carter basically separated the process of granting cost-of-living increases for current beneficiaries from the computation of initial benefits for future retirees. Adopting these decoupling techniques, Carter said, would eliminate about half of the projected deficit in the Social Security system.[17]

When President Carter's Social Security bill was referred to the Ways and Means Committee, it created a partisan division within the committee much in the same way Carter's energy bill had done earlier. The Democrats, led by their loyal chairman, Al Ullman, were generally supportive of Carter's plan for refinancing Social Security. The Republicans, led by Barber Conable, supported the decoupling procedures recommended by Carter for correcting the technical flaw in the law that overcompensated for inflation. But they opposed Carter's plan for borrowing money from the general treasury to shore up the Social Security system, and they opposed, with particular vehemence, Carter's plan for an increase in payroll taxes to finance the system, arguing instead for a more long-term solution to the Social Security problem.

The final bill reported by the Ways and Means Committee on October 6 reflected this deep partisan division within the committee on how to fix the Social Security system. Twenty-three Democrats and one Republican voted for a modified version of Carter's tax plan and eleven Republicans and two Democrats voted against the committee bill. Ignoring President Carter's request that payroll taxes not be increased on employees, the committee voted to increase payroll taxes on employees and employers alike from the current rate of 5.85 percent to 7.45 percent by 1990. In an important move, the committee also voted to expand the wage base on which both employees and employers paid Social Security taxes from $16,500 in 1977 to $27,900 by 1990, with automatic adjustments each year thereafter to assure that Social Security taxes would be applied to 90 percent of wages.

To raise additional revenue, and over the strong objection of the Democratic member, Joe Fisher, who represented many federal workers in his northern Virginia district, the committee voted that all federal, state, and local employees, as well as employees in the nonprofit sector, totally about seven million workers, be required to participate in the Social Security system. The committee also voted for the decoupling procedures recommended by President Carter to correct for the overcompensation of inflation, and in one of their most controversial decisions the committee voted to allow the Social Security system to borrow from the Federal Treasury when their reserves fell below a certain level.[18]

As he had done previously on the committee's energy bill, Conable and ten other Republicans filed a minority report opposing the committee's Social Security bill and offering a Republican alternative. "Most Americans are genuinely worried about the future of their Social Security system. They have reason to be. The system is severely deficient, both in money and equity. The people who benefit from it, those who support it, and the following generation of participants, deserve a sound and far-reaching solution to Social Security problems. But they will not get it through the committee bill."

The Republicans criticized the Democrats for raising taxes "too high and too soon," and argued that the committee bill fell "far short of solving the system's long-range financial deficit." They also objected to the provisions of the bill allowing Social Security trust funds to borrow from the Federal Treasury, which they said would only "increase the public debt and ultimately produce higher taxes and greater inflation for all."

"The committee bill has some sensible provisions," the minority report concluded, "but because of the major flaws . . ., our opinion of it can be summed up in one short sentence: There has to be a better way."

As an alternative to the Democrats' approach, Conable and his Republican colleagues offered a fifteen-point proposal for strengthening the Social Security system, which would anticipate in many ways the changes in the program Congress would be forced to make in 1983.

The Republican alternative centered on increasing the Social Security retirement age from sixty-five to sixty-eight. Under the Republican plan, older workers could still retire at sixty-two with slightly reduced benefits, but beginning in the year 2000 the minimum retirement age to qualify for full Social Security benefits would be gradually increased, by three months a year, to sixty-eight by 2011. "We recognize that this is an extremely sensitive issue, one that is politically difficult for our colleagues to embrace," Conable and the other Republicans noted in their minority report. "But we believe it is an issue which the Congress will be forced to face eventually . . ., and we hope our colleagues will have the courage to confront it now."

By raising the Social Security retirement age to sixty-eight and adopting some of the features included by the Democrats in the committee bill, such as the decoupling procedures to correct for the overcompensation of inflation and requiring all federal, state, local, and nonprofit employers to be covered under Social Security, Conable and the Republican minority argued that they could make the Social Security system financially sound for the next seventy-five years with only a 1.2 percent payroll tax increase gradually phased-in by 2000.[19]

Continuing to oppose the committee bill on the floor of the House, Conable moved to recommit the Ways and Means bill to committee with instructions to adopt the Republican alternative. But as expected, Conable's recommittal motion failed, and the Democratic House went on to approve the Ways and Means bill 275 to 146. The full House, however, on the urging of Joe Fisher and after some intensive lobbying by the White House and federal workers, refused to go along with the Ways and Means proposal to include all federal, state, local, and non-profit employees in the Social Security system.

Then on November 4, the more liberal Senate voted by a wide margin to increase the payroll tax to 9.2 percent and raise the wage base on which employers paid taxes. A conference committee quickly resolved the differences between the House and Senate versions of the bill on December 14, siding for the most part with the House bill, raising payroll taxes on employees and employers alike to 7.65 percent by 1990, and raising the wage base on employee and employer taxes to $31,800 by 1982, with provision for automatic increases in the wage base in the future to compensate for inflation.

The conference report sailed through the Senate on December 14 by the lopsided margin of fifty-six to twenty-one, but ran into stiff opposition in the House. Still adamantly opposed to the bill, Conable, using the only remaining power available to him in the minority, tried to persuade the full House not to consider the conference report—a technical, parliamentary maneuver to defeat legislation—arguing that more reasonable alternatives were available to save Social Security. "A vote against this bill will not end Social Security," he told the House. "It will give us a chance to reconsider a major mistake." Conable almost succeeded in this last minute attempt to block the legislation, as the House voted to consider the conference report by a slim three-vote margin of 178 to 175. The House then adopted the conference report by a vote of 189 to 163 following an impassioned plea by Speaker O'Neill.[20]

President Carter signed the ten-year, $227 billion Social Security tax increase—the largest peacetime tax increase in the nation's history—into law on December 20, 1977. "This legislation," Carter said at the signing ceremony, "will guarantee that from 1980 to the year 2030, the Social Security funds will be sound."[21]

"That was a terrible bill," Conable remembered, still railing over the passage of the 1977 Social Security tax increases long after his retirement from Congress. "You know what they did? They increased the wage base with the result that now [in 1999] the covered wage base in Social Security is about $72,000 [and, indexed to inflation, that increased by another $15,000 to $85,000 by 2003], and that's far above average in this country. And, unfortunately, the wage base is part of the formula that determines how big your pension is going to be. So it had the effect of greatly increasing Social Security pensions for the rich. And because so few people are rich, it didn't raise that much money for Social Security. So Carter proclaimed that in 1977 he saved Social Security. By 1982, though, the Social Security system was bankrupt, and Reagan had to create a presidential commission to resolve the crisis."[22]

1978 Tax Act

Though Conable and his fellow Republicans were badly outnumbered and outvoted on most of the legislative issues that came before the Ways and Means Committee during the Carter years, there was one notable exception to this pattern. That exception came with the passage of the Revenue Act of 1978. On that bill a bipartisan group of Republican and Democratic members forged a committee consensus on a major tax bill in a manner similar to the way the committee had worked earlier in Conable's career under the leadership of Wilbur Mills and John Byrnes.

In his 1978 State of the Union message, President Carter indicated that he would ask Congress to pass legislation both to reduce taxes, in part to offset the recent increase in Social Security taxes, and to increase revenue for the coming year. To stimulate the economy, Carter proposed a $24.5 billion tax reduction for 1979. Most of the tax cuts—$23.5 billion—involved personal taxes and were aimed primarily, in traditional Democratic fashion, at taxpayers at the lower end of the income scale. The largest proportional reductions, for example, were to go to families with incomes of $15,000 or less.

To simultaneously increase revenue, Carter proposed a number of reforms to eliminate $9.4 billion in tax deductions and preferences. He recommended that several widely used itemized deductions be eliminated, including special deductions for general sales taxes, taxes on personal property, gasoline taxes, and political contributions. He urged strict limits on business expense deductions for entertainment, meals, and beverages, air travel, and foreign conventions. Importantly, President Carter also proposed an increase in the capital gains tax for higher-income individuals—a tax Republicans and conservative Democrats had never liked and argued should be eliminated or substantially reduced to increase investment and production in the country.[23]

The Carter proposals ran into immediate trouble in the Ways and Means Committee. Responding to a middle-class tax revolt beginning to sweep the country, the committee rejected key elements of Carter's tax package and indicated at a meeting in April that they intended to tilt Carter's proposed tax cuts more toward the middle class. Seizing the initiative on this issue, Conable told the press that he and the other Republicans on the committee, and about half of the Democratic members as well, would insist on more substantial rate cuts for the middle class—at the time generally thought of as families making between $15,000 and $50,000 a year—before they would support ending the itemized deductions.

In an effort to work out a compromise with the White House, a delegation of three Democrats on the committee—Chairman Al Ullman, the second ranking Democrat on the committee, Dan Rostenkowski from Chicago, and the conservative Joe Waggoner from Louisiana—went to the White House on April 20 to tell President Carter that his tax proposals were in serious jeopardy on Capitol Hill. "The committee's actions require a re-evaluation of the whole package," Ullman told the press after the meeting. Waggonner was more blunt. The president "can't win on these reforms," he said. "There is no constituency in the Congress or the country for them."

Of most concern to President Carter and the liberal Democrats on the Ways and Means Committee was a proposal by the young Republican representative from Wisconsin, Bill Steiger, to cut the capital gains tax in half, from 50 percent to 25 percent.[24]

"Bill was one of the brightest members in Congress," Conable recalled, often serving as a catalyst, bringing about workable compromises between opposing committee forces. He had come up with the notion that a rollback of the effective tax rate on capital gains would serve as an economic stimulant, and would be popular. An informal poll taken by Chairman Ullman early in the committee deliberations indicated that 27 of the 37 Ways and Means members would support Steiger's amendment. President Carter, however, strongly opposed any reduction of the capital gains rate as benefiting the rich, whether or not it would benefit the economy.[25]

Faced with these disagreements between the president and the Ways and Means Committee, Al Ullman suspended committee deliberations on Carter's tax bill on April 25 in hopes of working out a compromise that would be acceptable both to the president and a majority of the committee.

Recognizing that Conable was leading the opposition to his tax proposal in the committee, Carter called Conable to the White House about this time to discuss his tax bill. Sitting alone with him in the Cabinet Room, Conable recalled, the president said, "Mr. Conable, you seem like a reasonable man. You've had my tax bill tied up there in Congress, and Chairman Ullman can't seem to do anything about it. I've got a lot of good proposals in that bill. What are you thinking about when you tie this bill up?"

"Well, Mr. President," Conable replied, "you've got to understand that as my colleagues and I see your tax bill, it's mostly an effort to block what you think are bad practices under the tax law, and some of them are bad practices. For instance, you want to eliminate the three-martini lunch as a tax deduction. And you want to prohibit deductions for business purposes of first-class air travel.

"Let's just take the air travel," Conable said. "You've taken care of the first class. So this loathsome business leader will fly into Washington National Airport, be met by a limousine, taken to the Four Seasons Hotel where he'll have a $1,000 a night suite, and he'll be able to deduct everything even though he won't come in first class because it will be business-related."

"Well, all right," Carter said, "let's get rid of the limousine and the Four Seasons Hotel too. Let's make that not deductible."

"That's what we call laundry list taxation," Conable explained to the president. "Every time you prohibit a specific deduction, you test the people who use deductions in their business to find some way of diverting their activity so they can take advantage of some other deduction, and you wind up with a laundry list of prohibitive things which will just test the ingenuity of those who want to use the tax bill to their advantage."

"What do you suggest as an alternative?" Carter asked Conable.

"I suggest that you permit us to put more money into the IRS for enforcement and insist on their exercising a rule of reason on what's deductible and what's not, so that if people are abusing their deductions, you'll have some way of going after them without prohibiting specific things.

"The classic example of yours," Conable told the president, "is that you prohibited the deduction for business purposes of any yacht over forty feet long. Mr. President, do you realize how many thirty-nine-and-a half-feet yachts that will bring about in this country?"

"Well, that's very interesting," Carter replied. "I'll have to think about that."

"The next day the president had a press conference about his tax bill and excoriated people who were using yachts over forty feet for deduction purposes. He didn't listen to me at all," Conable recalled.

On capital gains, the key issue dividing Carter and committee Republicans and conservative Democrats, Conable said: "Quite frankly, Mr. President, your capital gains rate is so high nobody will invest in equipment. The typical American businessman buys a machine, uses it for three years, and then sells it because there's a better machine been made by our remarkable system. If he sells that old machine at a profit and you taxed him at 50 percent on it, he's never going to buy the new machine. We've got to be a more productive society if we're going to be able to compete with the rest of the world."[26]

When negotiations broke down between the committee and the administration on the bill, a bipartisan group of committee members including Conable, Steiger, Ullman, Rostenkowski, and Jim Jones, a conservative Democrat from Oklahoma who also favored more of a middle-class tax cut, was formed to work on an alternative bill. According to a committee staffer who attended the meetings of the group, members of the majority and minority "sat down . . . and negotiated out every single provision in that bill as equals."[27]

After this informal group completed its work, the full Ways and Means Committee approved their alternative plan by a bipartisan vote of twenty-five to twelve on July 27. All twelve Republicans joined thirteen Democrats in supporting the bill. Rather than targeting tax cuts at low-income families and curtailing tax preferences, as Carter had proposed, the new $16.3 billion bill distributed tax cuts fairly evenly, on the average of 5.6 percent, across all income levels, and created new incentives for capital investments by cutting the maximum capital gains rate to 35 percent.

The compromise left the committee's twelve liberal Democrats, accustomed to having their way on the committee, infuriated. One of the most outspoken liberals on the committee, Abner Mikva of Illinois, called the bill "outrageous" and threatened to go to the House Democratic Caucus to rally opposition on the House floor.

But the Republicans were quite pleased with their rare success in achieving a committee victory. "This bill reflects the American people's view of tax reform because it is a tax reduction," Conable said after the committee vote. "It helps the middle class taxpayer in a manner much more substantial than the traditional tax reform bill."[28]

In a last-ditch effort to defeat the compromise bill, two liberal Democrats on the Ways and Means Committee, James Corman from California and Joseph Fisher from Virginia, with the full cooperation of the Treasury Secretary Michael Blumenthal, offered an amendment to the bill on the floor of the House which would have added another $2 billion to the tax cuts and for all practical purposes wiped out the capital gains reform and reinstated deeper tax cuts for wealthy taxpayers as President Carter had originally intended. However, the Corman–Fisher amendment was defeated on the floor by a determined coalition of conservative Democrats and Republicans.

In an elaborate parliamentary maneuver, the House also voted on the controversial Kemp–Roth tax cut proposal before taking a final vote on the Ways and Means bill. Sponsored by Jack Kemp, Conable's Republican colleague from Buffalo, and William Roth, the Republican Senator from Delaware, the Kemp–Roth plan called for a 33 percent across-the-board reduction in income tax rates over the next three years. Supporters of the Kemp–Roth plan argued that a 33 percent across-the-board cut would stimulate savings and investment at the middle and upper-income levels and make the economy grow at a faster rate. The increased economic activity in the country produced by these tax cuts, they believed, would also provide additional revenue to offset the large federal budget deficits. The Kemp–Roth proposal had no realistic chance of passage, but it was seen as an important test vote of the Republican alternative for a much deeper tax cut, and of course in hindsight it was a harbinger of things to come in 1981, during the first year of Ronald Reagan's presidency. All except three Republicans voted for the Kemp–Roth alternative, but this controversial proposal was soundly defeated on the floor.

The House then easily passed the compromise Ways and Means Committee bill, as negotiated by Al Ullman and Barber Conable, by a huge bipartisan vote of 362 to 49 on August 10.[29]

The next day, a jubilant Barber Conable, not accustomed to winning many votes in the Ways and Means Committee and on the floor of the House, wrote Al Ullman a "Dear Al" note saying, "It was a pleasure working with you on this one. We ought to try it again some time." The next morning, Conable reported in his journal, he also saw Ullman and "found him walking on cloud nine, having bucked the president, the Speaker, the secretary of the Treasury and the liberal majority of his party, and having been not only successful, but successful to the degree that it must have enhanced his prestige and given the lie to some of the unpleasant things said about his lack of leadership earlier during our impasse in Ways and Means."[30]

By the lopsided margin of eighty-six to four, the Senate almost doubled the size of the House tax cut to $29.1 billion, for a 10.8 percent average cut in income taxes. A conference committee, that President Carter and Treasury Secretary Blumenthal lobbied intensely to reduce the size of the cuts, resolved the major differences between the two bills in October. But the final $18.3 billion was vastly different from the progressive tax cut Carter had wanted. The House and Senate both agreed to spread the income tax cuts out fairly evenly, on the average of 7.2 percent, for all income groups, with the exception of families below $10,000, who were given additional tax credits, and to lower the maximum capital gains subject to federal taxes from 50 to 40 percent.

Unhappy with the final results of the legislation, President Carter sat on the bill for days before he signed it, quietly and out of sight at Camp David, on November 6, 1978.[31]

Congress Adjourns

The Ninety-fifth Congress adjourned on October 15, 1978, with mixed legislative results. It had not enacted all of President Carter's ambitious legislative agenda. It had not passed, for example, national health insurance, welfare reform, or fundamental revisions in tax and urban policy as Carter had wanted. It had also defeated Carter's request to create a Department of Education.

Despite all its shortcomings, the Ninety-fifth Congress still managed to pass some significant legislation. In addition to the 1977 Social Security Tax increase and the Tax Act of 1978, the

Ninety-fifth Congress also passed a tax stimulus package in 1977, increased the minimum wage to $3.35 an hour, imposed strict new controls on strip mining, updated controls on water pollution, increased subsidies for agriculture, lifted many of the federal regulations on the airline industry, and enacted a major reform of the Civil Service system.[32] Conable supported all of these additional laws, except the 1977 tax stimulus package, the hike in the minimum wage, and increased federal subsidies for agriculture.

As with the work of most Congresses, the evaluation of the Ninety-fifth Congress varied, depending on personal and political perspectives. Though he had not gotten much of his legislative program passed, President Carter was said to be "very proud of this Congress." Seeing the national agenda move more in the Republican direction, the Senate minority leader, Howard Baker of Tennessee, remarked that "we've got a Democratic president singing a Republican song." And the liberal Democratic senator from Massachusetts, Ted Kennedy, said he had "never seen a Congress so captive of special interest," noting the success corporations had in blocking the creation of a consumer protection agency and the health industry's veto of an important hospital cost containment bill advanced by President Carter.[33]

Much of the commentary on the Ninety-fifth Congress centered on President Carter's difficulties in working with Congress. "He didn't get along very well with the 95th Congress," Drummond Ayres wrote for the *New York Times*. "Most members considered his demand for action on a lengthy list of labor, energy, education, tax, welfare, health, and civil service bills to be far too ambitious for a single Congress. They were irked by his seeming unwillingness to compromise and by the sometime amateurish efforts of the [White House] lobbyists."

But Ayres also noted an improvement in Carter's legislative skills during the latter half of 1978. "For the first 18 months of the two-year session, many members of the House and Senate . . . openly laughed at the president's efforts to get action on his agenda. By adjournment Sunday [October 15] the laughter had died. The president had learned in the final months to wheel and deal and the House and Senate had come to respect his new-found ability," perhaps most dramatically illustrated by Carter's ability to get Congress to sustain his veto of a popular water projects bill, which he thought represented the "worst examples" of the "pork-barrel," the last week of the congressional term.[34] Carter's success in negotiating the Camp David peace accords between President Anwar Sadat of Egypt and Prime Minister Menachem Begin of Israel in

September 1978 also enhanced his status in Congress, at least temporarily.[35]

Many journalists and politicians, however, continued to have doubts about Carter's abilities to deal with Congress. A perceptive Hugh Sidey cautioned in *Time* magazine, at the end of the year, that the future of the Carter presidency would ultimately depend on his ability to manage the economy. "Jimmy Carter is preparing for what may be the biggest battle of his presidency," Sidey wrote. "Carter's political fortune largely depends on his success in curbing . . . inflation," which was running at 9 percent at the end of 1978 and the subject of much apprehension in economic and political circles.[36]

Carter's success would also depend on "luck," Barber Conable reminded his constituents near the mid-point of the Carter presidency. "Luck is required," Conable said, "because much that happens in any given four-year period in the nation's history is beyond the power of the presidency to control."[37]

The increasing independence of Congress in the post-Watergate era and the decentralization of power in Congress that had resulted from the institutional reforms Conable and other reformers had pushed through the House over the past decade, also complicated the legislative work of Congress during the Carter years. The abolition of the seniority rule as the sole criteria for selecting committee chairmen, the procedural reforms instituted by the Legislative Reorganization Act of 1970, the increased power given to the party caucuses, and the proliferation of subcommittees had all made the House a more open and democratic body. But these reforms had slowed down the legislative process and made life more difficult for the president and elected leaders of the House. Nowhere were these changes more apparent than in the Ways and Means Committee.

The End of the Carter Years

In November 1978, Conable easily won reelection to his own seat, defeating his Democratic opponent, chairman of the Genesee County Board of Elections, Francis C. Repicci of Batavia, with 72.5 percent of the vote—Conable's largest reelection victory up to that point in his career. Repicci had tried unsuccessfully to suggest that by emphasizing his reputation as a national legislator in Washington, Conable had ignored the local needs of his constituents, particularly the need to create jobs in Genesee County where there had been a number of plant closings and job cutbacks. Conable responded as he always did to such criticism. "I don't think it hurts my people that I'm respected in Washington," he said.[38]

To underscore the respect with which Conable was held in Washington by both Democrats and Republicans, Conable's long-time friend and district assistant, Tom Benton, arranged for the Democratic senator from New York, Daniel Patrick Moynihan, to endorse Conable during his 1978 reelection bid. Moynihan had developed a high regard for Conable from his days as a presidential advisor in the Nixon administration and from working closely with Conable on tax policy as a member of the Senate Finance Committee.

"We were having a testimonial dinner for Barber at the Holiday Inn in Batavia in the spring of 1978," Benton recalled. "It was packed. Across the street in the Treadway Inn Francis Repicci was having the kick-off for his campaign against Barber."

Moynihan was in Buffalo that day, and Benton arranged to have Moynihan stop in at the Conable testimonial dinner as a surprise guest in the evening. "He was late, as usual," Benton said, "and I was outside waiting for him to arrive. Finally he arrived and three or four people got out of the car, including Moynihan."

"You better hurry up," Benton told Moynihan. "Barber is speaking and it is almost over."

"What do you want me to do?" Moynihan asked.

"Just walk right up to the head table," Benton said.

"He did and for half an hour he and Barber stood up there answering questions. It was remarkable. Francis was furious, but Barber cleaned his clock in the election."

Afterwards, Benton asked one of Moynihan's aides why the senator was doing this, and he said, "Some people just don't endorse the right candidate."[39]

Thus, Conable would return to Congress in January 1979 for his eighth term in Congress and his second term as the ranking minority member on the Ways and Means Committee. At the same time attention in Washington was turning to the 1980 presidential campaign.

As Hugh Sidey of *Time* magazine had predicted the previous year, the economy turned out to be the Achilles' heel of the Carter presidency. Unable to control inflation, Carter saw the annual inflation rate rise to over 12 percent by the end of 1979. This high inflation rate, coupled with low economic growth, double-digit interest rates, and a sharp rise in gasoline and oil prices following the overthrow of the Shah of Iran in January 1979, spelled political trouble for Jimmy Carter's reelection.

In July of 1979, Carter returned from a economic summit in Tokyo to find a worsening domestic energy crisis and growing criticism of his own presidential leadership. Gasoline shortages at home had produced higher prices and long lines at service stations. Double-digit inflation continued unabated. A Gallup poll showed that only 29 percent of the public approved of the job Carter was doing as president—the sharpest decline in presidential popularity since the darkest days of Watergate. And a CBS/New York Times poll showed that most Democrats favored Senator Kennedy over Carter for the Democratic presidential nomination.

Rather than making another planned energy speech in July, Carter retreated to Camp David for twelve days to confer with aides, business leaders, academics, religious leaders, and public officials about that state of the country and his own presidency. Emerging from his seclusion on July 15, Carter gave his famous "malaise" speech—a term used by his pollster, Patrick Caddell, to describe the voter alienation and disbelief in major institutions of the country, which Caddell advised the president was impeding the adoption of his energy program and resolution of other national problems. Echoing Caddell's advice, Carter said the nation suffered from a "crisis of spirit" and called on Americans to have more faith in their country and in their own ability to solve great national problems, the most important one of which he continued to believe was the energy crisis.[40]

Though controversial and ridiculed by Republicans and other critics of the Carter administration, the speech gave Carter a temporary boost to his presidency and assisted him in passing additional energy legislation in Congress, most notably a gasoline rationing and emergency conservation bill in October and a huge $227 billion windfall-profits tax on de-controlled oil, which passed both houses by the end of the year and was signed by the president in early 1980.[41] But serious doubts remained about Carter's ability to manage the economy, with inflation still in double digits and interest rates over 14 percent by October 1979.

Then, in November, to complicate Carter's problem further, and in the kind of bad luck that Conable had told his constituents was beyond the power of any president to control, militant Iranians seized the U.S. Embassy in Tehran and held fifty Americans hostage in return for the Shah. For a time, Carter's popularity with the public improved as he rallied the country against the Iranian hostage crisis and also against the Soviet invasion of Afghanistan in December, and he easily fended off a challenge for the Democratic presidential nomination from his rival, Ted Kennedy.[42]

Of more concern for Carter was the challenge to his incumbency from the Republican Party. Widely recognized as the frontrunner for the Republican nomination since he almost defeated Gerald Ford for the nomination in 1976, Ronald Reagan had spent the previous three years crisscrossing the country, making speeches, and raising money to finance another bid for the White House.

Also expressing an interest in the Republican race were two of Conable's colleagues in the House: the conservative Phil Crane from Illinois, who served with Conable on the Ways and Means Committee, and the more liberal John Anderson, chairman of the Republican Conference. Senator Howard Baker of Tennessee was also interested in running, as were John Connally, the former governor of Texas and Nixon's secretary of the Treasury, Senator Robert Dole from Kansas, and Senator Lowell Weicker of Connecticut.

Then on May 1, 1979, Conable's close friend from his early days in the Ways and Means Committee, George Bush, announced that he would also seek the Republican nomination as a more moderate alternative to Reagan and Connally, who were generally seen at that time as the two leading contenders for the Republican nomination.[43]

The day before Bush announced his candidacy, he also announced that Barber Conable would head his national steering committee. Describing Conable as "perhaps the most respected member of the House of Representatives," Bush's campaign manager, James Baker, said, "we are extremely pleased for his support. His acceptance of this position is highly significant for the George Bush campaign. His standing among Republicans throughout the nation will be of enormous benefit to our presidential effort."

In an interview with the press afterwards, Conable indicated that his reasons for supporting Bush were both personal and political. "I sat next to him for four years [1967–1971] on Ways and Means," Conable said. "I feel very comfortable with him. I am a fiscal conservative, and so is Bush. He seems to be more moderate on social issues. Generally, I feel his views are similar to mine."

In addition, Conable liked Bush's breadth of experience in government. After leaving Congress in 1971, Bush had gone on to serve as ambassador to the United Nations, head of the Republican National Committee, representative to China, and director of the CIA. "He has unique experience, but he's still youthful, bright-eyed and idealistic," Conable said of Bush, who was fifty-four at the time. And, in an obvious reference to Jimmy Carter, who was having a hard time in the White House, Conable added, "I don't think outsiders necessarily make the best presidents."[44]

With James Baker managing his campaign and Barber Conable running his steering committee, Bush emerged as Ronald Reagan's chief rival for the nomination. To the surprise of many, he defeated Reagan in the Iowa caucuses on January 21, 1980. Reagan had made the mistake of not campaigning actively in Iowa and Bush had succeeded in attracting many moderate Republicans who were active in President Ford's campaign in 1976.[45]

Bush's victory in Iowa quickly propelled him into front-runner status, prompting some observers to speculate that with his expertise in tax policy, Conable might become the secretary of treasury in a Bush administration. "I'm taking a lot of kidding" from people like Senator Moynihan from New York, Conable told a Rochester reporter at the end of January. "At the windfall profits conference, he turned to me and said, 'I'd like to ask the secretary of the treasury what the policy of the Bush administration will be.'

"That bothers me," Conable told the reporter afterwards. "I don't like to be seen as supporting George Bush out of personal ambition. I went for Bush because I have confidence in him, not because I thought he had a bandwagon. George is still a long shot; he has a long way to go."[46]

Indeed, Bush's front-runner status was short-lived and Conable didn't have to worry for long about becoming Bush's treasury secretary. Adopting a more aggressive campaign style, Reagan defeated Bush by more than a two to one margin in the New Hampshire primary on February 26. Bush came back with a victory in Massachusetts on March 4. Then Reagan won big in South Carolina on March 8 and in three other southern states on March 11. Following more Reagan wins in Illinois on March 18 and three other states in April, Bush bounced back again with impressive victories in Pennsylvania on April 22 and in Michigan on May 20.

With his "competitive juices running," Conable recalled, "George just loved winning those primaries."[47] But it was clear by late May that Reagan had enough delegates to win the Republican nomination. Reagan ended up winning twenty-eight of the thirty-two primaries he entered. He did even better in nonprimary states, winning just under 400 of the 478 delegates chosen through party caucuses.[48]

With Reagan assured of the nomination, Baker and Conable prevailed on Bush to withdraw from the race on May 26. "Jim Baker came around to see me," Conable recalled, "and said, 'Barber, we gotta get him out of this race because all he can do now is show how weak Reagan is and not how strong he is, and it's not going to do him any good.' So I called a meeting of the thirty-seven congressmen who supported George and I said: 'Here's the situation. What do you think we ought to do?' And they all, but one, said: 'We've got to get him out of the race. Maybe he can become vice president.'

"And I told Dave Broder [of the *Washington Post*] that this meeting was going to happen," Conable added. "Dave called me back afterwards to find out what happened at the meeting, and I told him the consensus was that George should get out of the race."

Broder immediately sent a *Washington Post* reporter to New Jersey where Bush was out campaigning with Millicent Fenwick, the liberal Republican congresswoman from New Jersey who had endorsed Bush. Fenwick told Conable that a reporter came up to Bush and asked him what he was going to do. "Why don't you get out of the race?" he asked. "You're behind in it."

"I'm not going to get out of the race," Bush replied.

"But Barber Conable thinks you ought to," the reporter said.

"I had told Dave Broder only that there was a consensus that George should get out of the race, and I shouldn't have done that," Conable remembered.

"According to Millicent," Conable said, "George turned white and said he'd be happy to consider what I had said seriously."

In the meantime, "Jim Baker had closed George's California office. So it was all kind of a put-up job on our part," Conable recalled.

"George didn't speak to me at all. He went home to Houston, was incommunicado for the weekend and finally called me on Monday and, 'Barber, I'm getting out of the race.' "[49]

Reagan went on to easily win the Republican nomination by almost a unanimous vote, receiving 1,939 out of the 1,994 convention delegate votes, at the Republican National Convention in Detroit, Michigan on July 16.[50]

In a strange twist of events, at the Republican National Convention prior to Reagan's nomination, rumors circulated that Reagan might pick former President Gerald Ford as his vice presidential running-mate. "Bob Griffin [the senior Republican Senator from Michigan and long-time Ford friend] and Henry Kissinger both were out there lobbying for Jerry Ford for vice president," Conable recalled. "The theory was that Jerry knew so much about the presidency and Ronald Reagan needed his help."

In the midst of these rumors swirling around the convention hall on the evening of July 16, Conable did an interview with Dan Rather of CBS and said he didn't think a Reagan–Ford ticket was a good idea. "There is no such thing as a co-presidency [which, in essence, is what Ford was demanding as a condition for joining the ticket]," Conable told Rather, "and such an arrangement would be frustrating to both Jerry Ford and Ronald Reagan before they got through with each other. The system never works that way."

"I was told later," Conable added, "that Reagan saw my interview with Rather and asked somebody who I was. He was told who I was and told he should respect me."

Later in the evening, Conable said, "I went over to the hotel where George and Barbara were staying and they invited me into the room. George was sitting there in a tee shirt eating popcorn and Barbara was looking very distressed, and George said, 'Barber, I just got a call from Ronald Reagan and he wants me to be vice president.' He didn't want to do it," Conable said, "and he asked me 'Can I live with it?'"

"Al Hunt says you can live with it," Conable replied. "He told me that the other day, and Al Hunt's a smart guy. Tell me what Reagan told you."

"He said, 'George, let's get one thing straight,'" Bush said. "I want you to be my vice presidential candidate because you're different from me. You have a different constituency in the Republican Party than I do and your constituency and my constituency put together would be a majority. So I don't want you out on the hustings, if you're my vice presidential candidate, to debate me on issues. But I don't want you to offend your own constituency either. That way we will be able to go to Washington together."[51]

Later that evening Reagan made a dramatic post-midnight appearance before the Republican Convention to personally announce that he had picked George Bush to be his vice-presidential running mate. From there, Reagan and Bush went on to wage an aggressive and effective campaign against the Democratic incumbent Jimmy Carter and his running mate Walter Mondale.

Reagan opened his campaign on Labor Day in the financially troubled city of Detroit, Michigan. In a direct appeal to the traditionally blue-collar supporters of the Democratic Party, Reagan blasted Carter for his failure to manage the economy, where interest rates and inflation had soared both into double-digits, and for letting the military defense of the country deteriorate. As president, Reagan promised to do more to improve the economy and to strengthen the military defense of the United States against the Soviet Union.

The centerpiece of Reagan's domestic platform was his long-held belief that reducing the size of the federal government would go a long way toward solving many of the nation's economic problems. In September he proposed eliminating $195 billion from the federal budget by cutting the "waste, extravagance, abuse and outright fraud" he claimed existed in many federal programs. He also promised to freeze federal hiring the day he entered office and said he would try to reduce overall spending levels so the federal budget could be balanced by 1983.

Most controversially, Reagan called for a 30 percent across-the-board reduction in personal income taxes over the next three years to stimulate the economy, an idea known as the Kemp–Roth plan, named for the authors, Congressman Jack Kemp from Buffalo and Senator William Roth of Delaware. To enhance industrial competitiveness, Reagan also proposed a 40 percent increase in the depreciation allowance for American businesses to allow them to more rapidly write off the cost of machinery and equipment, a reform first introduced in Congress some years earlier by Barber Conable and his Democratic colleague on the Ways and Means Committee, Jim Jones of Oklahoma.

In foreign affairs, Reagan advocated the same hard-line approach toward the Soviet Union he had maintained since the 1950s. He called for a substantial increase in the defense budget to combat the influence of what he called "the Moscow–Havana axis." The Russians, he said, have "never retreated from their Marxist dream of one communist world." He believed the second Strategic Arms Limitation Treaty—SALT II, negotiated by President Carter—was "fatally flawed and promised to renegotiate the terms of the treaty after the United States built up its military arsenal."[52]

Seeing in Ronald Reagan another Barry Goldwater, Jimmy Carter tried to discredit Reagan as a dangerous extremist who was "offering simplistic solutions to complex problems. But his frequent allusions to Reagan as a right-winger and a threat to world peace seemed to backfire," *Congressional Quarterly* reported. "Carter's attacks undermined one of the president's strongest assets—his reputation as a politician with a high sense of decency."[53] The deteriorating economy and his own inability to resolve the Iranian hostage crisis also hampered Carter throughout the campaign.

Reagan proved to be an adroit campaigner, deflecting with his easy-going charm and television skills any charges from Carter that he was too extreme and dangerous for the presidency. Reagan was particularly effective in his television debate with Carter on October 28 in swaying many undecided and independent voters his way. "In that debate," Michael Barone noted, "Reagan demonstrated he was not unqualified. He was, indeed, more at ease, more congenial, more confident than the incumbent."[54]

The result was that, one week later, on November 4, Ronald Reagan decisively defeated Jimmy Carter to become the fortieth president of the United States. Reagan received only a bare majority 51 percent of the popular vote to 41 percent for Carter and 7 percent for John Anderson, who ran as an independent candidate after he failed to get the Republican nomination. But in the electoral college, Reagan scored a landslide victory, winning forty-four states and 489 electoral votes to only forty-nine electoral votes for Carter.

Of great historical significance, the Republicans also gained twelve seats in the Senate to give them a majority in the Senate (fifty-three to forty-seven) for the first time since 1953. In the House, however, despite picking up an additional thirty-three seats, the Republicans would remain in a 243 to 192 minority in the new Congress.[55]

Barber Conable easily won his own reelection to Congress, winning 74 percent of the vote, his highest winning percentage in his congressional career, against his Democratic opponent, John Owens, a lawyer from Rochester.[56]

Thinking back on the Carter years long after he left Congress, Conable remembered Jimmy Carter "in many ways [as] the brightest president" of the five presidents with whom he served during his twenty years in Congress. "He had a prodigious capacity for absorbing detail. But that was what he was good at—detail. He didn't have a clear vision for the country, and he wound up judging the Congress and not leading it. He tried to preserve the image of the outsider in the White House. Now by definition, the president of the United States after a while becomes an insider or he's in trouble. And Jimmy never became an insider. So he was in trouble. He was plagued by what he called 'malaise,' but what the American people saw it as was a sense of drift. Nobody had a strong hand on the tiller.

"Let me tell you the kind of thing that happened in the Carter administration," Conable told a public television audience in Rochester in 1998.

> Carter would invite 40 or 50 members of Congress, senators and House members, down to the White House for what he would say would be a kind of bull session. He would sit on a platform in the East Room and behind him would be Ed Muskie, his secretary of state, and Harold Brown, his secretary of defense, to answer questions. And Jimmy would give a *tour d'horizon* as the French would say, a tour of the whole global scene. He would say, "Now here is what the opposition party in Malaysia is doing." He'd have it in tremendous detail and brilliantly laid out. We'd listen to him and find it of great interest, and then he'd open it to questions, and we'd ask questions and

he'd answer them all himself. Poor Harold Brown and Ed
Muskie would never get the chance to answer anything
because Jimmy knew it all.

And a number of us would be driving back up to the
Capitol building to pick up our cars to go home—because
of parking at the White House you went down in
groups—and somebody in the car on the way out would
say, "Gosh, wasn't the president good tonight." And
everybody would say, "Yeah, yeah, he was brilliant."
There'd be a long pause and somebody would say, "How
come we're in so much trouble?"[57]

Interpreting the Election

As was his custom after each election, Conable wrote his constituents
a lengthy newsletter interpreting the results of the 1980 election,
which would have a great effect on his own congressional career.
"Perceptions change, expectations change and then the people speak
and personnel changes," Conable wrote. "Last Tuesday night it all
boiled over as we should have anticipated it would and somehow
Wednesday morning seemed very different. Cynics will say those
who sought dramatic change will be disappointed, and those who
fear change will be reassured, but I believe the reality ultimately will
equal the expectation. The ship of state is more like a battleship than
a destroyer. It turns very slowly, but a steady hand on the tiller can
eventually move it into a different course if it is persistent."

As Conable interpreted the election:

> The mandate was not a personal one for Ronald Reagan—
> doubts about him persisted to the end—and the people
> weren't telling him to do whatever he wants as the
> nation's 40th president. They were telling him to be a
> different kind of president with a different approach to
> government. I am convinced he understands this and
> will carry out these instructions. He has the intelligence to
> understand his mandate and the toughness to carry it out.
>
> You can be sure the Congress has heard the voice of
> the people, also. Most of its liberal leaders were sent
> packing. Congress is fickle, but for a while, anyway, the
> thunder of the public will ring in its ears and it will
> behave conservatively.

The Senate, in Republican hands for the first time since the early
1950s, "will now have mostly conservative committee chairmen

and will take away from the House the initiative on administration measures. At 53 Republicans to 47 Democrats, it will not have a lot of Republican margin, but clearly conservatives will dominate on the floor as they will in the committee chairmanships." The House, on the other hand, with 243 Democrats (about one fourth of whom were conservative) and 192 Republicans, Conable noted, "will have conservative domination on the floor but not in committee," and that is why he believed "most of the successful legislation [in the new Congress] will emerge in the first instance from the Senate."

The tax-writing committees with which Conable was most concerned, he reported, would be "interesting studies." The Senate Finance Committee, "a consensus committee under Russell Long [who had retired], will remain a consensus committee under [the new chairmanship of] Robert Dole. Liberals like [Connecticut's] Abe Ribicoff and dealers like Gaylord Nelson [from Wisconsin], Herman Talmadge [of Georgia] and Mike Gravel [from Alaska] will be gone, leaving the moderately conservative consensus easier than ever."

In the Ways and Means Committee, the chairman for the past six years, Al Ullman, was defeated for reelection, as his eastern Oregon constituents revolted against his advocacy of a national sales tax. Conable believed that Ullman's defeat, plus the departure of two staunch liberals, James Corman and Joe Fisher, and "the expected growth of relative numbers of minority Republicans" on the Ways and Means Committee to reflect the larger Republican minority in the House would "move that committee toward a conservative consensus," regardless of who emerged as the new chairman. With an expanded Republican minority, Conable believed that his "work as leader of the Ways and Means Republicans [would] be much easier" in the new Congress, and he looked forward also to having good relations with officials in a new Republican administration and the Republican majority in the Senate. He was "enthusiastic about the opportunities next year offer[ed], despite [his] continued minority status."[58]

Conable's enthusiasm, however, turned to bitter disappointment in December with the realization that the Democratic majority in the House, under the leadership of Speaker Tip O'Neill and the new chairman of the Ways and Means Committee, Dan Rostenkowski, would probably not agree to an increase in the size of the Republican minority on the Ways and Means Committee in the new Congress. As Conable despairingly wrote his constituents on December 18:

> The realities of party leadership, and the power plays they permit, were brought home forcibly to us this past week

when Speaker O'Neill announced to the Democratic Caucus that while majority to minority party ratios would be five to four on most other committees [to reflect the party ratios in the full House], Rules (which controls the flow of legislation) would be pegged at 11 to 5, and Ways and Means (the tax-writing committee) would be 23-12 [which was roughly the same as the previous Congress with only one less Democrat]. These margins would permit the Speaker and his leaders to control the major provisions of the Reagan program in the House, regardless of mandates elsewhere.

Republican leaders, newly chosen and hoping to get off on a good footing, grimly started negotiating from a position of weakness, not having the votes to overturn the decision but hoping to persuade their majority counterparts that such ratios would force disruption, paralysis and a high level of political contentiousness. The prospects were not happy. Some think the issue is power, some think fairness is more the issue, and clearly President-elect Reagan must think the issue is the enactment of his promised changes.

The Democratic decision not to adjust party ratios on the Ways and Means Committee to reflect a smaller Democratic majority on the floor had particular ramifications for Conable's leadership of the Republican Ways and Means minority. "To be personal, for me the issue is the way we have to do things" on the Ways and Means Committee, he explained to his constituents.

As the leader of the minority on the Ways and Means Committee for the past four years, I have had to plot legislative strategies which assumed the [Democratic] opposition, if it cared, could summon at least twice as many voters as my own group. In such an environment one had to rely on surprises, indirection, division and compromise, constantly worrying about offending members of one's party by going too far in offering compromises to members of the other party to get them to split.

Working in a large group is always hard; working in a large group with the cards stacked against you can be downright dispiriting. So I had a thrill of hope when the election returns showed a close division of the parties for a change, and a close division of the committee was presumed to follow. While it is true that in our system those who have the votes have the power, power should be exercised with restraint and fairness—and so as we go to press and negotiations continue, hope continues as well.[59]

Despite his best hopes, the Democrats refused to budge on the party ratios, thus setting up the circumstances for Barber Conable to go "rushing into the arms of Ronald Reagan"—a man about whom he had not had many kind words to say before—if he was to have any influence at all in the new Congress.[60]

Chapter 12

Cutting Taxes

Anxious to explain himself and his new political situation, Conable held his annual luncheon for the Rochester-area press corps on January 14, 1981, one week prior to Ronald Reagan's inauguration. "Most of you see me as just an assignment and not as a human being," Conable said, reemphasizing a major complaint he had with the press throughout his career. "And I wanted to demonstrate my humanity to you, and one way to do it was over cocktails and food and just talk a little about my job and what I see coming down the pike, to fit myself into a bigger picture than you're able to fit me into in the work-a-day world, where as one of the local congressmen my opinions are sought for agitating the airwaves or the newsprint."[1]

Conable was particularly anxious this year to explain to the local press and others that he would not have as much clout in the new Congress as many assumed he would have. "Around here, everybody says, 'Barber, aren't you thrilled? You'll be able to do anything you want to now. You've got all this clout. What are you going to do with your new clout?' " But Conable wanted the press and others to know that there were "certain political facts of life that have to be taken into account in determining what my influence is actually going to be."

So, after lunch at a Rochester restaurant, Conable, in his typical professorial fashion, described some of the basic political realities that would shape and define his life as a congressman over the next few months.

Political Facts of Life

The first of these political facts of life, Conable said, was "the sense of change that we all feel, the expectancy that always comes with a new president." The expectancy was

> particularly strong now because the mandate for change appears to have been what the electorate wanted to give rather than a personal mandate to Ronald Reagan. They didn't say, "Ronald, we want you to be our president; you do what you think is right." They said, "we want to change things and you appear to be the guy whose more likely to change it than the guy whose been in for four years." And I think Reagan views his mandate in that light.

The second basic political fact of life affecting the new Congress, Conable said, was the "dramatic change" that had taken place in the Senate "because of the dimension of the shift in the electorate." The Senate is "obviously going to be a different place, and the most significant change is the staff," he explained.

> You're sweeping out a legislative bureaucracy of 26-year standing by shifting from Democrat to Republican there.

> Since 1954, you've had a fairly static Senate staff with
> twice as many people in the majority as in the minor-
> ity. That's the old tradition in the Senate. And now the
> Democrats are going to have to get rid of half of their
> people and the Republicans are going to have to double
> the numbers of people in their staff. The staff is terribly
> important in the Senate because those senators are spread
> so thin that they have to rely on staff members to audit all
> these concurrently meeting subcommittee deliberations
> that are going on. So what's happening in the Senate is
> remarkable primarily for the staff changes involved. It
> will change the whole statistical environment. It will be a
> whole new set of characters. I think it's going to slow
> down the organization in the Senate considerably.

Conable, however, did not expect much change in the Senate
Finance Committee—the counterpart to the Ways and Means
Committee in the Senate and therefore the committee with which
he was most concerned—despite the fact that the chairmanship of
the committee changed from Russell Long, the veteran Democratic
senator from Louisiana, who had been "identified with all important tax issues," to the Republican senator from Kansas, Bob Dole.
"My view of the Senate Finance Committee," Conable said, "is that
it's not a terribly ideological place. There are a whole bunch of dealers over there. They like to deal with each other. 'You scratch my
back, I'll scratch yours'—a lot of bilateral contracts of one sort or
another. Russell Long is going to be doing exactly the same sort of
thing he did when he was chairman—help put together deals based
on his understanding of who wants what. Bob Dole, although he
has achieved a level of some stridency in political rhetoric from
time to time in his career, is essentially a pragmatic man, not an ideologue, and I think he'll continue the [non-ideological] traditions of
the Senate Finance Committee."

The third political fact of life, which had a profound effect on
Conable's own role and power in the Ways and Means Committee,
was the ideological change that had taken place in the House as a
result of the election. "Many of the initiating, leading, influential
liberals were defeated in the House," Conable noted.

> For instance, on our Ways and Means Committee we lost,
> through retirement and defeat, all the liberal leaders of
> the committee. Abner Mikva [an articulate liberal from
> Chicago], sick of fighting a conservative constituency,
> midway through last year accepted an appointment to
> the Federal bench by Jimmy Carter. He was an extremely

brilliant, effective fellow. Charlie Vanik retired from Cleveland. Charlie was one of those voices that was always speaking out against appropriations and loved the political game, somewhat on the demagogic side. Jim Corman, the chairman of the Democrats' Congressional Campaign Committee, and therefore a very important fella in the Democratic Party in the House, lost by 760 votes to an anti-busing advocate out in Los Angeles, largely as a result of Jimmy Carter's early concession. [Carter conceded an hour and a half before the polls closed in California, causing the Democrats to lose several congressional elections in the west.]

"Well, the point is," Conable told the reporters, "the Ways and Means Committee is going to be a very different place" in the new Congress, even though it still has Democratic leadership. "Interestingly," Conable thought the Ways and Means Committee would be "more homogeneous for the Democrats" than it had been in the past. "It will be more homogeneous because some of these liberals were so tough, so hard-pressing, so insistent . . ., they caused some backlash among the moderates" on the committee, which made it "easier for me, as the leader of the minority, to drag some of these guys off on specific issues" and form bipartisan, moderate-to-conservative majorities on the committee.

But now, Conable explained, as a result of the loss of the liberals on the committee, "you'll find the Democrats much more easily uniting in opposition to Ronald Reagan than they were able to unite in support of Jimmy Carter. And that's one reason why I think committee ratios is a terribly important issue for me, because I see a 23 to 12 ratio as perhaps tougher in the Reagan administration for me to deal with. Why do I have to deal with it?"

Well, on many issues I have to achieve what I achieve by compromise. I have to attract Democrats to my position by compromising my views, and I have to compromise in ways that will not offend my Republicans and cause them to kick over the fence and go in some other direction. It's a very indirect way of trying to accomplish what I'm trying to accomplish legislatively in my committee, and it's tough to do as you can see, if there's reason for the other side to hold together more than they did in the last Congress.

So I went to Danny [Rostenkowski] and said, "You know, I'm going to sabotage everything you do. I'm going to see that your chairmanship is not a successful chairmanship."

I talked real tough to him, because that's all I could do. When you don't have the votes, all you can do is to be personally unpleasant. So I was being personally unpleasant with him, hoping he'd get the message, go back to Tip and say, "You've got to go back to the caucus and give us a little better ratio." Well, it hasn't worked out that way.

Rostenkowski preferred instead to maintain strong Democratic control over the Ways and Means Committee, though inadvertently, as Conable predicted, he also set into motion committee dynamics that would lead to the enactment of the large Reagan tax cut that the Democrats opposed. But all was not lost to Conable and the Republican minority.

A fourth political fact, Conable explained, which worked to his advantage, was that the Republicans were now in control of the Treasury Department, a most important executive department for the financially oriented Ways and Means Committee and for the Senate, which the Republicans would organize for the first time since 1953. "I'm going to have Treasury with me now," Conable said. "I'm going to be with Treasury, I assume, as long as they're reasonable, instead of trying to pull the rug out from underneath me, as was true in much of the Carter administration.

"I'm also going to have leaders in the Senate," Conable added. "I always got along with Democratic leaders pretty well over there, but now I'll have people who are actually of my party. From a political standpoint, I have that advantage."

A fifth political fact, of great significance, also worked to Conable's advantage and to the advantage of the Republicans generally. "I have the ultimate advantage on the floor of the House," Conable explained, making a key strategic point that in a few short weeks would prove to be decisive in the Republican battle against the Democratically-controlled House.

You see, the way the House is made up, the way the parties are made up, about one-fourth of the Democrats are conservative. The liberals have always run the Democratic Party, but a substantial minority in the party are conservative. About five-sixths of the Republicans are conservative. Therefore, if you look at the floor of the House, you've got a clear conservative majority there. If, through leadership pressure, the Ways and Means Committee, with its atypical party ratio, brings a liberal bill to the floor of the House, it will be rejected by the conservatives in the House if they think the bill is too liberal.

And that gives rise to the major reason I was so upset about committee ratios. I just didn't think it would work very well. I thought the net effect of having a bad committee ratio in the Ways and Means Committee, relative to the power realities on the floor of the House, was that we would shift the initiative in tax matters over to the Senate where an administration and a Republican majority could work together to bring out the kind of tax bill they wanted. . . . [They would not have] all the false starts involved in having to deal first of all with a very political Democratic majority in the Ways and Means Committee, and then try to take that thing through the land mines on the floor of the House, where in all probability conservatives would reject what the Ways and Means Committee had done, if it was atypical of what the conservatives thought should be done in response to popular mandates.

"What do you see happening to the tax cut Reagan proposed during the presidential campaign?" one of the reporters asked Conable in the question and answer period following his presentation. Showing his penchant for instructing presidents as well as journalists, Conable recounted a recent conversation he had had with the president-elect.

Well, the last time I talked to Reagan about it, he was still thinking in terms of a rate cut [in personal income taxes]; that is, something across-the-board, a 10 percent cut [for each of the next three years], something of that sort. And I spoke to him quite frankly about that at the time. It was a meeting of all the ranking minority members of the House with him down at Blair House back two or three weeks ago. I sat next to him at the table and we had a nice chat about taxes.

And I said, "Well now, Mr. President, you're going to have to understand that even if you're committed to a straight rate cut, you're going to be making this recommendation to a Congress made up of a whole lot of people who have been there for a long time and have ideas of their own about taxes. Some of them are going to want to deal with the marriage penalty. Some of them are going to want to deal with further reduction in long term capital gains rates. Some of them are going to want to increase the purposes for which IRAs can be put together. Some of them are going to want to do something better for charities. And to the extent that they make structural changes of that sort, it's going to be a trade off against the rate cuts."

"You're not going to be able to cut tax rates by 30 percent," Conable advised Reagan, "and still not have the deficit go out of sight, if these other things are added to it as well. And so what I hope you'll do is make whatever recommendation you want to make, but then be sure your tax policy people stay very close to both houses of Congress and participate in the process of compromising out an ultimate bill, which will not be a flat rate cut, but something different to some degree."

In advising Reagan to stay on top of his tax proposal once he submitted it to Congress, Conable said he was seeking to help Reagan avoid a "big problem" Jimmy Carter had in his dealings with Congress.

> Jimmy would decide what he wanted to do and announce it and that was the end of it. So my advice to Reagan was, go ahead and recommend whatever you want, but you gotta understand the president proposes and the Congress disposes, and there's a continuum of attitudes about taxes up there in Congress that's going to affect whatever you recommend. So stick with it, stay close to it, and participate in the process. Then you'll come out with a bill that will be much closer to what you want, than if you just say this is the way to do it, and then forget it and go on to something else.

"Barber, none of these things [tax cuts, lower inflation, and lower interest rates, which Conable also discussed] is going to work unless the Congress does something about the budget," one of the reporters said. "What is Congress prepared to do? What is it in the mood to do in terms of cutting back on the overall expenditures?"

> "Well, as of now," Conable responded, "I would expect Congress to be cooperative, but Congress is going to be responsive more than anything else. It's going to reflect the mood of the country. . . ." Congress is not a leadership group. It is a representative group. Our system depends very heavily on executive leadership, on somebody tough taking the heat and saying, this is what you gotta do, vetoing bills when we don't do it, and smacking our paddies in other ways. We're going to continue to try to give people what they want. And if people are in a mood to want more and more, we're likely to give them more and more.
>
> At a time like this, . . . when you have a man who has just been elected president by a wide margin . . . and there is a perceived mandate to cut back on the expectancy

of government, something can be done [to cut the budget] that can't be done normally. . . . The president will take the heat away from Congress, and we're likely to go along with him for a while. During the first 100 days, you're likely to see some fairly dramatic cuts in the Carter budget.

But Conable warned the reporters not to expect "a lot of quick, long-term changes. . . . Changes at the outset are going to be largely on the dramatic side, but not necessarily all that compelling," he said. Reminding the press of the overlapping, presidential sequence in the budgetary process, he noted:

> The budget that President Carter will announce tomorrow is one he's been working on for 14 months and is for the year beginning October 1, 1981. And that is a Carter budget, because he's put it together. Ronald Reagan will then take the Carter budget for the year beginning October 1, 1981 and say, "Well, maybe we can cut out $30 billion by taking $3 billion here or $3 billion there," and so forth. But even there, it doesn't begin to take effect until October 1 of this next year. Reagan will start right now working on the budget for the year beginning October 1, 1982. And that will be the first Reagan budget.
>   So when you look at it in those terms of the time frame of government planning, you realize that all of a sudden on January 21 the whole ship of state isn't going to head over into a new course. It's going to take some time.

One of the key officials responsible for leading the charge for change was the new director of the Office of Management and Budget, David Stockman, a conservative Republican congressman from Michigan whom Reagan had appointed to direct his budget battles in Congress soon after his victory in the November elections. Providing the press some personal commentary on how Stockman had gotten his new job, Conable recounted how Stockman had played the role of the Independent candidate John Anderson and then Jimmy Carter in mock television debates with Reagan during the campaign. "Reagan, who used to be an actor, was just entranced by the extent to which this guy could put himself in the place of Reagan's two major opponents. And that's how Stockman sold himself to Reagan.

"Tomorrow afternoon I'm meeting with Stockman and I think Secretary-designate [Donald] Regan [the former head of Merrill Lynch whom Reagan appointed to be the new secretary of the treasury] and members of the minority in the Ways and Means Committee to try to talk about tax matters. My impression is David Stockman is going to be a very important fella in the Reagan administration if he can time himself so he doesn't work all night for many nights in a row. He's one of those bright-eyed types that just really wants to make a difference and he's going to be very important. I think he'll be pretty much across-the-board in the areas of cuts he comes in with. And I expect the proposals to be announced fairly quickly after Reagan's inauguration."

The luncheon ended on a lighter note as one of the reporters asked Conable what he planned to wear to the presidential inauguration the following week. A few days earlier, Conable had reacted strongly in the press against the inaugural committee's suggestion that members of Congress wear morning coats to the inauguration. "I'm going to wear a dark suit and go there, and if they want to turn me away, then that's their problem," Conable said. "I don't think my people want me to act like a jackass and for that reason I doubt they want me to dress like one. The members of Congress are not being inaugurated. They're spear holders in the rear. We stand there and gossip up there on the stage, while the president raises his hand. Now, he has a right to be dignified. John F. Kennedy wore a high silk hat. If he wants to do that, that's his business. After all, it's his day. But why in the world should we have to go out and pay $54 to rent a morning suit?"

Conable was reminded that Reagan had paid over $1,300 to buy a morning coat for the inauguration. "Now frankly," Conable replied, "I think we'd better investigate whether he can't find a better tailor than that in Washington. A coat that costs $1,350 bucks!"

"Is that tax deductible?" a reporter jested.

"I'd have to consult my tax advisor," Conable replied. "I'll tell you, I wouldn't dare deduct it because I know the Gannett papers would pick that up. . . . 'Do you know what Barber Conable did on his tax return?'"

"What about the dark suit?" another reporter asked. "Is that tax deductible?"

"Gosh, that's a wonderful thought. No, I'm afraid not," Conable said.

"Do you think Reagan is expecting two inaugurations since he went out and spent that money on a new one?" someone else asked.

"You mean he amortized it over two events instead of one? No, I suspect it just demonstrates an unsuspected pinch of liberalism in him," Conable said.

Six days later, on January 20, 1981, Barber Conable, dressed in his dark suit, stood on the inaugural stage, gossiping with the other congressional "spear holders," as Ronald Reagan, dressed in his morning coat, was sworn in as the fortieth president of the United States.

Reagan Proposes a Revolution

President Reagan wasted no time in addressing the economic woes of the country. In a national television address to the country on February 5 and then in an address to a joint session of Congress on February 18, he laid out an ambitious and revolutionary three-part program for economic recovery, similar to the program he had proposed during the presidential campaign.

First, as a long-time critic of excessive federal spending, Reagan proposed reducing federal spending in 1982 by $41.4 billion. Under the Reagan plan, spending for practically all federal departments and programs would be reduced, except for the Department of Defense, where he proposed a substantial increase to strengthen national security and off-set the military buildup of the Soviet Union during the 1970s.[2]

Second, at the heart of Reagan's economic recovery plan, he proposed a 10 percent across-the-board reduction in personal income tax rates for each of the next three years, with an estimated cost to the federal treasury of $44.2 billion in the fiscal year 1982 and $250 billion over the next three years. Under this part of Reagan's plan, marginal tax rates would be reduced in stages from a range of 14 to 70 percent to a range of 10 to 50 percent by January 1, 1984.[3]

This proposal, known as the Kemp–Roth plan, had been an important part of Reagan's presidential campaign. Reagan believed, along with Congressman Jack Kemp and Senator William Roth and other advocates of the "supply-side" theory of economics, that lower tax rates would spur economic growth, produce more revenue for the federal treasury, and eventually—by 1984, according to his budget director, David Stockman—produce a balanced budget.[4]

As a more traditional balance-the-budget conservative, according to Michael Barone, "Conable was always queasy about the tax cut," which, as the ranking minority member of the Ways and Means Committee, he would be expected to introduce in the House. "His instinctive approach was to lower taxes on business and keep income tax rates high enough to get the budget close to balance."[5]

But Conable lost the tax-cut battle to the supply-siders and the more flamboyant Jack Kemp. "As a telegenic celebrity politician and former pro football player," Hedrick Smith of the *New York Times* wrote, "[Kemp] had popularized the supply-side economic theory that cutting tax rates would boost growth and, ultimately, government tax revenues. His star quality and theme politics had given him more clout than the more cautious Conable, especially with the new Reagan team."[6]

Conable, however, was more positive about the third component of Reagan's economic recovery plan, which called for accelerated depreciation allowances for American businesses to make them more competitive in the world market and create more jobs at home. Conable, along with his Democratic colleague, Jim Jones of Oklahoma, had long been an advocate of depreciation reform and enthusiastically welcomed the inclusion of this reform in Reagan's economic recovery package. Under Reagan's accelerated depreciation plan, popularly referred to as "10-5-3" or the "accelerated cost recovery system," businesses would be allowed to write off the cost of plants in ten years, the cost of machinery in five years, and the cost of vehicles and trucks in three years. This part of Reagan's economic recovery plan was projected to cost the federal treasury $9.7 billion in 1982 and $60.8 billion through 1984.

Thus, in the important and shifting world of budget projections that characterized the early days of the Reagan administration, Stockman estimated that the president's economic recovery program would cost $53.9 billion in 1982 ($44.2 billion for individual tax cuts and $9.7 billion for the accelerated business depreciation allowances) and $310.8 billion by the end of 1984 ($250 billion in tax cuts and $60.8 billion in depreciation allowances).[7]

Aware that his economic recovery package did not include all the tax reforms his conservative supporters wanted, Reagan asked Congress in his February 18 address to enact the three major reforms he requested as a matter of "great urgency," and then he said he would seek additional reforms later.[8]

Public reaction to Reagan's well-delivered television speeches was generally positive, but the reaction on Capitol Hill was more skeptical. The second part of the Reagan tax package—speeding up the rate at which businesses could deduct the cost of purchasing new plants and equipment—had the greatest support. However, most observers predicted that Congress would make substantial changes in the individual income tax proposals in Reagan's plan.

The House Budget Committee's chairman, Jim Jones, said he believed the personal-income-tax cut should be limited to one year and "targeted more toward savings and investments in productive assets." The chairman of the Ways and Means Committee, Dan Rostenkowski, predicted that the Reagan package would not emerge from his committee as Reagan had proposed it, but that the final bill would contain "some improvements."

Even in the Republican Senate, where the Reagan tax cuts were expected to have an easier time, the new Senate majority leader, Howard H. Baker of Tennessee, conceded that the tax bill would be the hardest part of Reagan's economic recovery plan to get through Congress. "I expect it would be unrealistic for the tax package to be unchanged," he said. Senate minority leader, Robert C. Byrd of West Virginia, said most Senate Democrats believed that the Reagan tax cuts would be "inflationary, beneficial to the affluent and unfair to poor and middle-class Americans." And many congressional observers agreed with the assessment of the Senate Finance Committee chairman, Bob Dole, that most members would not wait for the next round of tax reform to offer their own individual tax proposals, as the president requested. "If you were a hitchhiker," Dole said, commenting on the way the legislative process usually works, "you wouldn't wait for a second ride."[9]

Back in Rochester, Barber Conable predicted that President Reagan's economic plan must pass Congress quickly, or it might not pass intact. "The whole thing is in trouble unless it holds together," Conable told a local reporter. "David Stockman has done a thoughtful job. But he's reducing a wide range of programs. If part of the cuts are knocked out, the whole thing could collapse."[10]

Rostenkowski's Counterproposal

Almost immediately after Reagan presented his budget proposal to Congress on February 18, Rostenkowski began to formulate a Democratic alternative that he hoped could win the support of Democrats and Republicans on the Ways and Means Committee. At a press conference in March, Rostenkowski indicated that his proposal would include such traditional Republican items as a reform of the so-called marriage penalty, which overcharged couples with two incomes, a reduction in the long-term capital gains rates, and a reduction of maximum individual income tax rate on unearned income—that is, income derived from dividends and investments—from 70 percent to 50 percent. "These [proposals],"

Conable recalled, "constituted Dan's responses to the Reagan program, designed to appeal to conservatives, especially those serving with me on Ways and Means."

Shortly after Rostenkowski's announcement, Conable was called to the White House to talk to the president about tax strategy. Conable had been told in advance that some of Reagan's advisers favored an alternative to a pure Kemp–Roth proposal, but that President Reagan "was adamant in support of broad tax cuts without embellishment." At the meeting, Reagan told Conable that he was "committed to Kemp–Roth" and "expected Ways and Means Republicans to stick with him" on that.

Conable, without any real alternative and now firmly in Reagan's camp if he was to have any influence in the final outcome, responded that he "would do so cheerfully," but that he "did not know if all [his] colleagues would follow, pointing out that they—as well as [he]— really liked some of the provisions that Rostenkowski had talked about." Conable explained that the "Kemp–Roth bill stood little chance in the committee because of the partisan ratio" of 23 Democrats to only 12 Republicans. "In no uncertain terms," Conable recalled, "the president replied that he expected us to go down fighting in defense of Kemp–Roth and instructed me not to participate in any compromise.

"When I left the meeting," Conable wrote later, "I recall thinking that Reagan appeared in complete charge, that his staff seemed far from anxious to tangle with him (at least on this one issue), and that they preferred to have someone like a sacrificial and expendable Conable come down and give the president the bad news when it appeared he might not have his way with the Ways and Means Committee"[11]

A few days later, on April 9, Rostenkowski formally presented the details of his plan in a speech before the Chicago Association of Commerce and Industry. Rostenkowski outlined an alternative one-year tax cut proposal that he said would strike the "essential political and economic balance to pass Congress," and at the same time preserve "the spirit of the president's plan."

Appealing specifically to the Democrats, Rostenkowski proposed a smaller tax cut than Reagan had offered, a cut of $40 billion in 1982 ($28 billion for individuals and $12 billion for business), instead of the $53.9 billion tax cut proposed by Reagan. Under the Rostenkowski plan, marginal tax rates would be reduced for all taxpayers, but not as sharply as the president's 30 percent reduction. Tax brackets would also be widened to prevent slight increases in income from pushing individuals into a higher bracket. The cuts

Rostenkowski proposed would benefit all taxpayers, but were particularly designed to help middle-class individuals earning between $20,000 and $50,000. The standard deduction and the earned income credit would also be liberalized to assist those in the lower income groups.

To appeal to Republicans, Rostenkowski proposed, as he had indicated he would do, to reduce the top marginal rate on investment income from 70 percent to 50 percent, and he also proposed easing the marriage penalty to benefit two-income families. Rostenkowski also called for an increase in the amount of money that could be sheltered from taxes through an Individual Retirement Account—a proposal that Senate Finance Committee Chairman Bob Dole had first made in the Senate in an effort to increase funds available for investment. And finally to appease Republicans, Rostenkowski proposed a dividend reinvestment plan for public utilities and, like Reagan had done in his proposal, a depreciation plan to allow businesses to depreciate their capital investments more easily and quickly.[12]

It now became more obvious why Conable had warned Reagan that it might be hard to hold his fellow Republicans on the Ways and Means Committee together in opposition to the Rostenkowski plan, since Rostenkowski was proposing, short of the three-year 30 percent tax cut Reagan proposed, many of the things Republicans had favored for years. The Rostenkowski plan was, as *Congressional Quarterly* noted, a proposal that "many Republicans will find difficult to ignore."

But in a firm display of leadership on the Ways and Means Committee, Conable was able to hold his fellow Republicans together in opposition to the Rostenkowski bill. Speaking to the press shortly after the Rostenkowski plan was announced, Conable downplayed the bill and said he and the other eleven Republicans on the Ways and Means Committee "would stick by the president's tax plan." He explained the Republicans had little choice but to support the president, since they were so outnumbered by Democrats on the committee. "We have absolutely no clout at all, unless we have the White House behind us. I'd love to be porky and independent like Bob Dole," Conable said—referring to Dole's more independent stance in the Republican Senate where he was in the majority—"but I can't. As long as I think the Reagan plan will improve things, I'll go along."

In a conference with reporters, however, on April 14, Conable, at heart a compromiser, held out prospects for an eventual compromise between the Reagan-supported bill and the Rostenkowski bill.

While Reagan had barred any retreat for the time being, Conable, speaking more openly and candidly than the president would have preferred, said he thought Reagan "might be open to compromise later."

But Reagan was "in no mood to compromise," said Conable's old friend Vice President George Bush. If the Congress approved the smaller, one-year tax cut proposed by Rostenkowski, Bush said, the president "would give the veto very, very serious consideration."[13]

Three weeks later, on May 7, following a dramatic appearance by President Reagan before a joint session of Congress on April 28 after a near-fatal assassination attempt on his life in late March, a coalition of all 190 Republicans and 63 conservative Democrats defeated the liberal Democratic budget resolution, which called for budget cuts of only $15.8 billion for 1982, and replaced it with a budget resolution of their own, drafted by two conservative members of the Budget Committee, Democrat Phil Gramm from Texas and Republican Delbert L. Latta from Ohio. The Gramm–Latta substitute budget resolution set the budget cuts for the fiscal year 1982 at $36.6 billion, more in line with the larger budget reduction Reagan wanted.[14]

So, in his first showdown vote with the House Democratic leadership, Ronald Reagan easily prevailed over his opponents. Reagan called the vote "a historic moment." Some speculated that Reagan would now have an easy time securing his tax cut, but the Democrats said they had assurances of fewer Democratic defections the next time.[15]

All the congressional committees would now have to redraft their bills to place them in the framework of the new Gramm–Latta resolution. This would be no easy task, and if the committees failed to resubmit budget figures consistent with the Gramm–Latta budget resolution, the Republicans warned that another budget resolution might be necessary to force the cuts.

Search for a Compromise

Though the passage of the Gramm–Latta budget resolution enhanced the president's power in the House, it did not automatically assure the passage of the president's proposed tax cut. The tax cut still had to be separately and formally approved by the House.

Now, in a stronger position to negotiate with Rostenkowski and the Democratic leadership in the House, President Reagan instructed Treasury Secretary Donald Regan to begin negotiation with Rostenkowski shortly after the passage of the budget resolution on May 7.

On Monday, May 11, Regan invited Conable to a tax strategy meeting at the White House with himself, David Stockman, Jim Baker, who was Reagan's chief of staff, and several others. What had "caught their attention," Conable wrote in his journal, was "Rostenkowski's *Face the Nation* performance on Sunday in which he said he assumed a compromise could be worked out at two years of rate reductions, rather than the three years the president wanted or one year which he had been advocating himself."[16]

After a "good deal of discussion," Conable asked Regan and company if they wanted him to "feel Danny out about the two-year duration."

"No," they said, "we want to kick this around and bounce it off the president. We'll let you know."

At noon the next day, Tuesday, May 12, presumably having talked to the president, Regan called Conable and asked him "to tell Danny that a call from Danny to the secretary would be accepted and he would be grateful if Danny would call him." Conable again asked Regan if he wanted him "to discuss the two-year period with Danny." Regan said no.

Acting as an intermediary between the treasury secretary and the chairman of the Ways and Means Committee, Conable then called Rostenkowski to relay Regan's message. Conable advised Rostenkowski that "what had attracted their attention at the White House was his discussion of the possibility of a two-year compromise" and that he "should keep that in mind" when he talked to the secretary.

"I was playing both sides a little here," Conable said, as he recounted this conversation.

In his phone call, Conable also suggested to Rostenkowski that he "shouldn't make any deals without being sure that the Senate was brought in"—a possibility that bothered Conable because he knew he "would have trouble with [his] own Republican minority on any deal in which the Senate had not been committed to the final result." Rostenkowski "expressed enthusiasm for the opportunity to speak to Regan [and] said he would call the secretary right away."

The next morning, Wednesday, May 13, Conable recorded in his journal:

> I received a call from Dennis Thomas, one of the secretary's aides, asking if I had delivered the message to

Rostenkowski. I said that I had and asked if Rostenkowski
had not called. He said he had not and asked what
I thought they should do. I suggested they wait until the
middle of the afternoon, and if they had not heard from
him by then that Dennis should himself call Danny and
ask if any message had somehow gone astray.

Immediately following that conversation, however,
I saw Danny on the floor during a vote and asked him
what was happening. He said "nothing." I asked him if
he had called the secretary and he snapped his fingers
and said, "Oh darn, I forgot. I was talking to some people
just after you called and I put it off and I haven't done it."
I said, "I want to repeat to you Danny, the secretary will
be most grateful if you would call him." As a result,
I learned from the secretary that Danny called later that
afternoon and was planning to go down there the
next day.

As planned, Rostenkowski visited with Regan the next day and
called Conable before leaving for his Chicago district in the afternoon to say that he had "a satisfactory meeting" with the secretary,
"but that nothing had been decided." He told Conable that he
wanted to meet with him when he returned from Chicago on
Monday morning to "discuss in detail the options." They arranged
to meet at 9:30 A.M.

The following day, Friday, May 15, Conable received a call from
Bob Dole's office inviting him to "a very private luncheon" with
Dole, Rostenkowski, and Russell Long, the former chairman and
ranking Democrat on the Finance Committee, supposedly, to work
out the details of a tax compromise. The luncheon was arranged for
Monday afternoon and that gave Conable, he thought, "the chance
to discuss Danny's options with him with some care before the
luncheon."

Then, on Sunday morning, May 17, "Senator Dole went on *Face
the Nation* and told forty million people about the secret luncheon
he was going to have with us the next day. He described it as the
beginning of negotiations on a tax bill."

That evening, Conable recalled, President Reagan called him at
his home and talked for about ten minutes, "expressing perplexity
over the Dole announcement that there was to be a luncheon the
next morning." He said, "Barber, you're not going to make any
offers at this luncheon, are you?"

Conable assured Reagan that "I had nothing to offer and I
intended to do what he wanted me to do since I had no way of
influencing the outcome, not having the votes in Ways and Means

unless he was behind me. He said that he thought it was up to the Democrats to make the first compromise. He hoped I would make sure that they did that. He then asked me what Senator Dole intended, something which I could not answer, since I was perplexed that Dole had announced over television what I had thought until that time was to be a secret meeting.

"The president was very nervous about his congressional allies and nervous to the point that after a long day of traveling and speech-making he called to find out what I intended and, if possible, what Dole intended," Conable recorded in his journal.

Monday morning, May 18, Conable met with Rostenkowski, as planned, and despite the pledge he had given Reagan the night before that he would not make an offer to break the deadlock, spent about two hours discussing with Rostenkowski what he thought was "the formula for good start-out negotiations." He suggested that Rostenkowski "offer a package of two years of rate reduction, the 10-5-3 depreciation reforms, and reduction of the tax on unearned income from 70 percent to 50 percent"—a package that embodied substantially Reagan's entire program with a shorter time period of two years. The passage of this first package, Conable suggested, could then be followed by "a second package which would involve some of the targeted savings plan Rostenkowski wanted to include in his bill," which Reagan had agreed he would sign in 1981 if it did not exceed budget limits.

"Danny expressed some enthusiasm for this idea," Conable wrote in his journal, "and I left feeling that he was going to broach it at the luncheon which followed the termination of our meeting. I thought at that point that Danny was going to negotiate."

Conable, Rostenkowski, and Dole all arrived at their noon luncheon at about the same time, "only to find that Senator Long was going to be a half an hour late. It developed later that Long was burned by Dole's announcing the luncheon on television," Conable recalled.

> And well he may have been since there were at least twenty reporters standing outside the room waiting for developments. There was obviously a high expectancy about the meeting. It was a very nice luncheon, with steak for the three of us and hamburger for Dole [a disabled World War II veteran who had the use of only one arm]. But I could not see that anything was being accomplished. I had tried to prompt Danny along the lines of the recommendations I had made to him that morning, reminding him that the president did not feel he should

make an offer at this time, but that the ball was in his court. Even Russell Long told Danny that if he didn't want to deliver the Democratic Party to a handful of conservative Democrats that he should be forthcoming with a plan of his own, understanding that the president always had the option of negotiating with the conservative southerners if the major party leaders would not take the first step to try to resolve the differences. . . .

[But] Rostenkowski kept repeating that he had to talk to Jim Wright [the Democratic majority leader] and "his boys," and it became apparent that he was not going to make any offers that day. We squared our shoulders and walked out the door and told a great battery of microphones that we had not agreed on anything, but it was a very nice meal and that we had a good deal of dialogue about the nature of the problem but nothing about the resolution of the problem. We found the press incredulous that nothing had been accomplished.

Some members of the Washington press corps, however, were acutely aware of the "tightrope" Conable was walking between the Republican White House and Democratic Ways and Means Committee. Writing for the *Wall Street Journal*, Robert W. Merry noted that Conable was one of the most respected and knowledgeable members of the Ways and Means Committee, and would have preferred "to focus some of that intellect on the big tax bill that shortly will be moving through his committee, then on through Congress. He would like to help shape that bill, using some of the vast tax-code knowledge he's accumulated during his 15 years on the committee." But, instead, Merry wrote, Conable was engaged in the "arcane politics" of the Ways and Means Committee, as he tried to hold his fellow Republican committee members together in support of President Reagan's economic recovery package, "even though many are skeptical of its underlying ideas. Many also have an itch to press for their own pet tax provisions, such as incentives for saving or elimination of the tax penalty on two-earner married couples.

" 'Barber has really been tough on those guys,' " one pleased, but surprised administration strategist told Merry.

"The surprise stems from the fact that Mr. Conable's reputation for intelligence isn't matched by a reputation for toughness. Some see him as too prone to compromise, sometimes giving up more than he needs to. 'He's not all that forceful—too quick to deal. . . . He has no instinct for political hardball,' "[17] one top Republican congressional aide said.

On Wednesday, May 20, the same day Merry's article appeared in the *Wall Street Journal*, Conable, showing an increasing willingness to play the political hardball for which he was not well known, decided it was "time to talk to the secretary again." He called and finally reached Regan at the White House and told him that he had "reluctantly concluded" that Rostenkowski and the Democratic leaders in the House were "stalling" in their negotiations on the tax bill in the hopes of forcing a vote in the Ways and Means Committee "over an unvarnished Kemp–Roth bill," which Reagan continued to support and which the Democrats knew they could defeat in committee. The defeat of the Kemp–Roth bill in the Ways and Means Committee, Conable advised Regan, "would put the ball back in the president's court and make it difficult to keep our boys together."

Regan told Conable "that he had come to the same conclusion" and that he "would talk to the president to see what could be done." Conable suggested "that Regan go on *The Today Show* the next morning and say that he was going to start negotiating with the conservative southerners since the Democratic leadership in the House had not been forthcoming." Regan told Conable that he would "get back" to him.

At 12:30 that day, Regan called Conable back and "sounded elated." He said that "not only had the president agreed," but that four of the southern Democrats the administration had been courting—Sonny Montgomery from Mississippi, Phil Gramm and Charlie Stenholm from Texas, and another second-term Democrat from Texas, Kent Hance, who served with Conable on the Ways and Means Committee—"were going to be down at the White House to discuss tax strategy at 4:30 that afternoon. I can assure you," Regan told Conable, "everyone will know that they are here and that will force the Democratic leadership's hand."

At 6:30 Regan called Conable again, "even more elated." He said that "those four had not only come, but had been extremely accommodating and that they wanted 5-10-10—that is, a 5 percent reduction [in personal income taxes] in the first year, 10 percent the second and third years—70 to 50 percent reduction for the maximum income tax, 10-5-3 depreciation reform, and three minor adjustments. Evidently what they wanted," Conable wrote in his journal, "was a further exclusion of dividends and interest from taxation, a phase-in of the marriage tax penalty, and a phase-in of some sort of liberalization of estate taxes." They also "volunteered," Regan said, "to go tell Danny that they had been to the White House, that they had made an offer, and that they would hold off any agreement until such time as Danny had a fair chance to negotiate with the White House himself."

The next morning, informed of the offer the southern Democrats had made to the White House the day before, Rostenkowski called Regan to arrange to see him at the Treasury Department at 11:00 A.M. Barber Conable had already been invited to Regan's office for a 10:00 A.M. meeting, ostensibly to have his picture taken with Regan for a *Time* magazine story on the budget battle, but now, as the timing worked out, this also became an opportunity for Regan to discuss with Conable "how he should handle Danny."

Conable reported in his journal that he "went down and had a nice chat with the secretary, but wasn't able to offer a great deal except to express the opinion that the exclusion of dividends and interest from taxation would not be a great idea. It would be better," Conable told Regan, "to go with something more modest like liberalization of IRA's [Individual Retirement Accounts]," which Regan thought would be "easily accepted" by the southerners, "rather than the original proposal they had made on dividends and interests."

That afternoon, Rostenkowski called Conable to say that he was "not disappointed with the discussion with the secretary." Rostenkowski told Conable he "hoped something could be done," but once again he reiterated that "he couldn't do anything until he talked to 'my boys,' something he planned for the following Thursday." When Conable asked Rostenkowski why it would take so long, Rostenkowski explained that "he couldn't set it up until Wednesday, since Monday and Tuesday were off as part of the Memorial Day weekend." Conable complained to Rostenkowski that "time was dragging on badly" and that he "thought we [including himself and other Ways and Means Republicans with the White House] would have to negotiate further with the southerners unless we could get some assurance from him that he really was interested in negotiating.

"I have great difficulty trying to figure out what Rostenkowski is up to," Conable confessed with some bewilderment in his journal.

> He may be genuinely undecided. He may be held on a very short tender by his liberals, people like Dick Bolling [the Democratic chairman of the Rules Committee], who don't trust him at all and are convinced he is trying to give away the store. He may in fact be having difficulty with the Speaker who in a press conference this past week said he expected to have two votes on taxes—one

on the straight Kemp–Roth and the other on the Rostenkowski bill. Danny tells me he expostulated with the Speaker on learning of this comment, saying he did not have a bill, but only a concept so far. Rostenkowski's plan may also be part of the collective decision to temporize and dodge until such time as the mark-up begins, at which time they will try to force a vote on pure Kemp-Roth for the purpose of putting the initiative for the first offer of compromise back in the presidential court rather than in the court of the House Democrats.

The role of Bob Dole also left Conable "somewhat nervous," as he reported in his journal. "Bob Lightheiser, Dole's top aide, has been quoted to me as saying, 'Rostenkowski and Dole are going to write this bill. We don't need either the White House or Conable.' Dole has made a number of inconsistent statements. I have heard through the grape vine, although not from either of the principals, that he and Rostenkowski are going to meet on Wednesday, the day before the Thursday meeting of the majority on Ways and Means. It may be that these two are trying to cut a deal with each other. I have always said to both of them that the compromise bill should be a Dole–Rostenkowski bill, and maybe they feel if their names are going to be on it they also should decide the contents.

"It is interesting to see too," Conable noted, "that the secretary of the treasury's attitude toward Bob Dole is not good. As I left the picture taking [in the secretary's office], I thanked him for including me in the pictures with the *Time* magazine photographer. He said with an exasperated tone of voice, 'Who do you think I'd have down here to photograph with me, Bob Dole? He's got his wife a great job in the White House; he's had tea in the Rose Garden; he's got all kinds of appointments he's not entitled to; and he continues to make demands. He hasn't done a damn thing for us so far. No, no, Barber, I want you down here to build you up against the day when you will be chairman of the Ways and Means Committee.'"

Rostenkowski did eventually give Reagan and the House Republicans some clear assurance that he was interested in negotiating. After weeks of internal discussion and in preparation for a Ways and Means Committee meeting on June 10 to begin drafting tax cut legislation, Rostenkowski and the Ways and Means Democrats tentatively agreed in early June to go about halfway in meeting the administration's original tax proposal. In place of Reagan's three-year, 30-percent tax cut, Rostenkowski proposed a two-year, 15 percent across-the-board tax cut, 5 percent effective

October 1, 1981 and a 10 percent rate cut effective July 1, 1982, with special relief for the middle class.[18]

Reagan Makes Another Proposal

Despite this major shift in the Democratic position, Reagan decided "to go to the mat" for his three-year cut.[19] "Three years is a matter of principle with me," Reagan told Democratic leaders on June 1. "I'm already backed in a corner and I can't back up anymore."[20]

Asked why the president regarded the third year of the tax cut as so essential, Treasury Secretary Regan said it was "generally because of planning." The administration believed that for investment purposes both businesses and individuals needed to know their tax burden three years in advance.[21]

To preserve his three-year tax cut, Reagan announced on June 4 that he would seek a coalition with the conservative Democrats who had helped him win the battle on the Gramm–Latta House budget resolution on May 7 and with whom his staff had been informally negotiating on the tax cut for the past several weeks. In a televised announcement from the White House Rose Garden, flanked by Conable, Dole, and several other congressional leaders, most notably three southern Democrats—Kent Hance, Conable's Ways and Means colleague, Senator Lloyd Bentsen from Texas, and Senator David L. Boren of Oklahoma—President Reagan outlined his new tax strategy.

Reagan said he would scale back his original three-year, 30-percent tax cut, as the conservative Democratic leaders had suggested in informal conversations with his treasury secretary, to a 25-percent tax cut over three years, with five percent the first year and 10 percent the second and third years. As a further concession to the conservative Democrats, the president also offered to add a series of additional tax cuts to his tax package which the conservative Democrats and some Republicans had been advocating. These additional tax cuts included such things as reducing the top tax rate on unearned income from dividends and investments from 70 percent to 50 percent, easing the marriage penalty tax on two-income families, and reducing estate and gift taxes.[22]

To appeal to Conable and other fiscally conservative Republicans who worried about the effect of tax cuts on the deficit, the administration, armed with fresh statistics from Budget Director Stockman, said the modified tax package would reduce treasury revenues by $37.4 billion, almost $17 billion less than the president's original

$53.9 billion tax plan, and lower the projected fiscal 1982 deficit to less than $30 billion, instead of the original $45 billion deficit projected by the president in February. According to administration estimates, the new Reagan plan would cost about $274 billion over three years ($224.8 billion in individual tax relief and $49.2 billion in business concessions).[23]

On the morning of the president's announcement, Conable was "abruptly called" to the While House to be informed of the new administration proposal and to be asked to introduce the new bill in Congress, along with his Democratic colleague, Kent Hance, to signify conservative Democratic support for the bill. Conable strongly objected to the weakening of the depreciation provisions of the previous package. "A 200 percent declining balance was to be reduced to 150 percent declining balance and the 10 year write-off of depreciable real estate was to be equal to 15 years, thus making the package considerably less attractive from a business viewpoint since we had put together a careful coalition of support for 10-5-3," Conable recorded in his journal.[24] "I told the president in the presence of the secretary of treasury that such a move without adequate preparation of the business community first would have a very bad reaction from his primary constituency. . . . I predicted serious trouble with the business community as a result of this abrupt shift on the issue of depreciation." Treasury Secretary Regan, however, "interjected that he knew something about the business community and what they really wanted was a reduction in the long-term capital gains rates. Of course Regan was a [former stock] broker and that's why he wanted that."

What was important to Conable at this stage of the process was that he be seen standing up to the White House on a matter on which he had considerable expertise and public support. "With my minority sitting there beside me, I continued to press the issue of predicted serious trouble with the business community as a result of this abrupt shift on the issue of depreciation. That I was right has not been of any particular significance to the White House people. [But] at least, my minority heard me negotiating actively for some element of the bill and got the idea that I was not a toady for the Reagan administration, but willing to stand up and argue with them and even the president himself over matters that were within my knowledge. The press has also got the idea that I was less than enchanted with the process and so has described me as 'known to be dissatisfied with White House dictation.' The result is that I am somewhat gingerly handled by Jim Baker, but [thankfully] I am still in full communication with my frustrated minority [on the Ways and Means Committee], some of whom have told me they will not vote for the bill, even though they do not know what will be in the Democratic bill."[25]

Despite Don Regan's confidence, within hours of the president's new economic plan being announced, the business community reacted as Conable predicted. The chief economist of the U.S. Chamber of Commerce, Richard Rahn, called the revised proposal a "breach of faith with the business community."[26] To recapture business support for the plan, the administration hastily restored most of the depreciation cuts promised business in the original plan, resulting in a slightly higher tax cut for 1982 than they had announced on June 4. This revised version of the president's economic recovery plan was then introduced by Barber Conable and Kent Hance in the House on June 9, one day before the Ways and Means Committee was to begin its mark-up session on tax legislation.[27]

In his private journal, Conable disparagingly described the new Conable–Hance bill as a "mongrel" of a bill, signifying the interbreeding of the president's original idea for a clean tax cut with a variety of additional tax cuts to appeal to the conservative Democrats and hopefully win passage of the bill in the House. "How frustrating it is," Conable lamented, "not to have any direct input into the measure that bears your name and not to have sufficient votes so that your position is relevant as an individual and not as a figurehead."[28]

But the sad political fact of life was that the new bill would carry Barber Conable's name as a figurehead—the ranking Republican on the Ways and Means Committee and therefore the president's chief lieutenant in the House on the bill—and he would have to swallow his pride and do the best he could to steer the bill through the Democratic House, where he was outnumbered on the crucial Ways and Means Committee and at the mercy of the conservative Democrats on the floor. He knew there would be a rough road ahead, with perhaps more concessions and unforeseen turns, but he braced himself for battle, the good soldier, the loyal, presidential "spear-holder" he was.

The Bidding War Begins

With the battle lines more clearly drawn between the Reagan tax cut plan and the Democratic alternative, the hunt was on for the votes it would take to pass a tax cut bill in the House and Senate.

The Senate, with its Republican majority and strong bipartisan support for a tax cut, was never a serious problem for Reagan. Despite his early display of independence, the Republican Senate Finance Committee chairman, Bob Dole, cooperated fully with the president in steering his tax cut through the Senate. Pressuring the Ways and Means Committee to act, Dole first attached the Reagan tax bill to a House-passed debt limit measure to enable him to circumvent the constitutional requirement that all revenue measures originate in the House. He then successfully steered virtually the entire Reagan tax package (plus a few additional items the committee added) through the Senate Finance Committee on June 25 by the resounding vote of nineteen to one, with the Democratic senator from New Jersey, Bill Bradley, casting the lone dissenting vote.[29]

The problem for Reagan, as it always had been, was in the House of Representatives. Both sides knew that the outcome of the vote in the House would depend on which way the conservative Democrats decided to vote. With only 190 House Republicans, compared to 242 Democrats, the president had to hold on to all the Republican votes and pick up at least 27 of the 47 members of the Conservative Democratic Forum, 38 of whom had voted with Reagan on the budget resolution. That combination would give Reagan a 217-vote majority in a House, which at the time, with three vacancies, had a total membership of only 432. If, on the other hand, Rostenkowski and the House Democratic leadership could persuade their conservative colleagues to stay within the party, they had a chance to defeat the Reagan tax bill and replace it with one of their own, and, equally important to them, reestablish their partisan control over the House.

The final outcome was far from certain as both sides embarked on a strategy to win the decisive conservative Democratic votes to their side. In a word of caution to Reagan and the Republican strategists, *Congressional Quarterly* warned:

> There are important differences between the coming tax vote and the May 7 vote on the budget. And they will make a second Reagan victory more difficult than the first.
>
> In May, Reagan was riding a crest of personal popularity. As a result, his administration was able to pull out all the stops in lobbying for passage of his budget. . . .
>
> In addition, tax cuts do not have the same popular appeal as budget cuts, particularly in the South and Southwest, where the conservative Democrats' votes are concentrated. In those areas, support is stronger for a balanced budget.

> Many of the conservative Democrats say they fear
> Reagan's more generous tax cut plan will lead to large
> budget deficits in 1983 and beyond. . . . Conservative
> members also worry about inflation, which many of them
> believe is fueled by tax cuts.[30]

On the day Reagan announced his new three-year tax cut plan, Representative Charles W. Stenholm from Texas, coordinator of the Conservative Democratic Forum, confirmed the difficulty Reagan would have in winning their support for his revised tax plan. Stenholm estimated at the time that no more than fifteen to twenty conservative Democrats supported the president's new plan, not enough for Reagan to win in the House, even if he were able to hold on to all 190 Republican votes.[31]

The president, though, was more optimistic. "If we don't have the votes," he told reporters, "we'll get them."[32]

Disorganized and confused, the Democrats' initial response to Reagan's new proposal was to back away from the compromise they had offered earlier that called for a two-year, 15 percent across-the-board cut in individual income tax rates. Rostenkowski announced after a caucus meeting on June 9 that the Democrats were abandoning the idea of an across-the-board tax cut in favor of a tax cut that would benefit individuals primarily in the $10,000 to $50,000 income range. The across-the-board proposal had been made strictly for negotiating purposes with the administration, Rostenkowski said, "but the negotiations have been concluded."[33]

This decision by the Democrats, Conable wrote enthusiastically in his journal, "made us [on the Republican side] feel quite optimistic since it indicated Rostenkowski was moving back toward a more liberal position, thus driving the conservative Democrats more firmly into the arms of Ronald Reagan."[34]

But by mid-June the Democrats had begun to regroup as they considered ways to make their tax cut proposal more competitive with the Reagan plan. They returned to their two-year, 15 percent tax cut plan, with most of the cuts, as Rostenkowski promised, designed to help individuals making less than $50,000 a year. In order to show that their plan was as generous as Reagan's, the Democrats also proposed a third-year, 10 percent tax cut that would be "triggered" if certain economic conditions were met. These economic conditions, however, were so stringent (requiring, for example, an inflation rate of less than 6 percent and a budget deficit of less than $23 billion in 1983), that few Democrats thought the third-year tax-cut trigger could ever be pulled.[35]

On the business side, the Democrats also searched for a depreciation plan which they hoped would be more attractive to business than the Reagan proposal. Sam Gibbons from Florida, the second ranking Democrat on the Ways and Means Committee and head of a task force to draft the Democratic alternative, "set the size of the Republican package as a rough standard" the Democrats would seek to match.

"There seems to have been little controversy over that decision," two congressional scholars noted, but "the question was how to match the Republican offer." In mid-June, the "Ways and Means Democrats pulled a whopper out of their hat; they endorsed 'expensing,' the provision under which a corporation could write-off all the cost of an investment in the first year," instead of depreciating its costs over a period of time, as proposed in the Conable–Hance bill. Observing this bidding war from the Senate, the former Senate Finance chairman, Russell Long, noted that business had always wanted expensing, but "didn't ask for it because they thought they couldn't get it." Now, as a price of victory over Ronald Reagan, the Democrats were prepared to give it to them.[36]

In addition to expensing, the Democrats also proposed a phased-in reduction of the corporate income tax rate from 46 percent to 34 percent by 1986, and they agreed to the administration's proposal to raise the deductions from $7,500 to $15,000 for contributions to a Keogh plan, and to increase deductions for contributions to Individual Retirement Accounts from $1,500 to $2,000. The Democrats also adopted a savings certificate plan—called "allsaver" certificates—similar to one already approved by the Senate to increase savings and help the financially troubled savings and loan industries. And to further encourage savings and investment, the Democrats agreed to let public utilities shareholders exclude up to $1,500 of investment income from taxes if they decided to receive dividends in the form of more utility stock instead of cash.

All and all, the Democrats seemed well on their way toward making their new proposal competitive with the Reagan plan. With the "individual rate cuts, plus some other sweeteners," a hopeful Thomas J. Downey, a young Democratic member of the Ways and Means Committee from New York, noted, "It's conceivable, just conceivable, that our package will be a lot more attractive" than the Conable–Hance bill.[37]

Then on June 26, the bargaining context of the House was dramatically changed once again as the Republicans and their conservative Democratic allies succeeded in winning a crucial vote in a second budget resolution in the House. Concerned that some of the

House standing committees were reneging in their obligation to make the budget cuts required by the first Gramm–Latta budget resolution in May, David Stockman got the Republicans and conservative Democrats to offer another budget resolution—this one called Gramm–Latta II—to force the reluctant Democratic committee chairmen to cut their budgets to bring them more in line with Reagan's recommended budget cuts of $38 billion. This was accomplished in one of the most dramatic maneuvers in congressional history by overturning a rule from the liberal Democratic Rules Committee and forcing the House to vote *en bloc* for the budget allocation of all the House committees. The House had traditionally let each committee submit its own budget request, added up the total, and then voted on the total resolution. The House had never before, since the House Budget Act was passed in 1974, forced such a comprehensive vote on all the standing committees, thus restricting their independence and flexibility.[38]

"It's a terrible way to legislate," Barber Conable said in an impassioned speech for Gramm–Latta II on the floor of the House, "but we have no other alternative unless we [are] willing to lie down and be rolled over by the juggernaut controlled by the floor minority."[39]

Others also agreed that this was a bad way to legislate, but in the end the Republicans and conservative Democrats voted 217 to 211 for Gramm–Latta II, putting in place virtually all of Reagan's budget cuts.[40]

With their impressive victory in Gramm–Latta II, Reagan and the House Republicans now held a decided advantage over Rostenkowski and the House Democratic leadership in their bidding war over tax cuts. "I leave Washington after a bitter battle further extending the coalition strategy of the president," Conable recorded in his journal before leaving Washington for Fourth of July holiday. "The Gramm–Latta conservative Democratic–Republican strategy carried the day on the floor of the House, even though the Democrats had controlled all the committee process up to the moment it hit the floor. And that meant to the White House we could win this tax battle and don't need to compromise as much with the majority of the House controlled by Rostenkowski and O'Neill."

The way the drama was unfolding, Conable expected the vote on the tax cut to be "some kind of replay of the budget confrontation. The administration is expected to substitute on the floor a proposal more acceptable to the president, or whatever comes out of Ways and Means"[41]

Still, the Democrats were not done. Depressed and discouraged by their defeat on Gramm–Latta II, but determined not to be outbid by Reagan and the Republicans on the tax cut, the Democrats returned to Washington after the Independence Day celebration with more offers to sweeten the pie for their conservative colleagues in both parties. First, on July 9, the Democrats adopted several provisions designed to help small businesses. They broadened the corporate income tax brackets to enable more firms to fall into a lower tax bracket than was permitted under existing law, and they lowered the tax rates in each bracket by as much as 10 percent. They increased the amount of money a firm could accumulate before it was subject to an accumulated earnings tax from $150,000 to $200,000. And they agreed to give companies a 25 percent tax credit for new expenditures on research and development.

On July 14, after formally rejecting the Conable–Hance three-year, 25 percent across-the-board tax cut, the Committee on Ways and Means decided in a straight party vote, twenty-two to thirteen, with only the Democrat Kent Hance voting in opposition with the Republicans, to adopt the Democratic two-year, 15 percent tax cut alternative, with three-fourths of the cuts going to individuals earning less than $50,000 a year. The Democratic bill also included the controversial third-year "trigger" mechanism to allow an additional 10 percent tax cut in the third year, if economic conditions warranted.

In addition to the rate cuts and other features the Democrats had already added to their bill to spur savings and investment and attract business support, the Democratic bill also dropped the top rate on investment income from 70 percent to 50 percent, increased the standard deductions, increased the earned income credit for low-income families, reduced the marriage penalty, increased the credit for child care, provided a more generous reduction in estate and gift taxes than that approved by the Senate, and excluded the first $75,000 of income earned abroad from taxes.

Then on July 22, in a bold move to seal the deal with the conservative Democrats, the Ways and Means Committee voted to exempt five hundred barrels of oil a day from the windfall profits tax that had been adopted in 1980, at a cost of $7 billion to the federal treasury over the next five years. This oil "sweetener," a congressional source noted, "emerged from days of negotiation among Democrats anxious to hold the votes of conservative party members—many of whom came from oil-producing states—when the tax bill reached the House floor."[42]

The next day, the Way and Means Committee voted twenty-two to thirteen, with Hance again being the only Democrat voting in opposition, to approve its giant revenue measure, with an estimated cost to the federal treasury of $627 billion through the fiscal year 1986.[43] Confident that they now had outbid Reagan and the House Republicans in their latest appeal to the conservative Democrats, Charles Wilson, a Democrat from Texas sympathetic to the House leadership, categorically declared: "We have the Republicans beat on this bill."[44]

But Reagan and the House Republicans were not to be outbid. Conable wrote in his journal in August: "As soon as Rostenkowski seemed to be locked into his bill, something he had delayed as long as possible, Kent Hance and I, and the other major actors on the congressional scene, went to the White House and negotiated a final package which included almost everything that anyone's heart might desire."[45] There they hastily amended Reagan's 25 percent, across-the-board tax cut and drafted a new tax bill expected to cost over $730 billion through the fiscal year 1986. Added to Reagan's individual rate cuts and accelerated depreciation plans, were tax breaks for oil producers, increased charitable deductions, annual indexation of tax rates at the end of the three-year tax cut to offset for inflation, and a variety of other measures designed to win support of a few swing votes in the House of Representatives.[46]

"The one item that I was probably more responsible for than others was indexing," Conable reported after the White House meeting. Indexing had been part of the original Kemp–Roth bill that inspired Reagan's economic recovery program, but it had not been included in the package of reforms Reagan submitted to Congress in February. "I made clear to the secretary [of the treasury, Don Regan] and Jim Baker [Reagan's chief of staff] that I felt indexing was necessary to attract northeastern support as long as so much had been done to attract the support of agricultural, small business, and petroleum interests in other parts of the country. The White House had been most reluctant about indexing, perhaps indiscreetly acknowledging that they supported it in principle, although they tried to insist it did not belong in this bill, as if the bill was not inclusive of all other beneficial provisions."[47]

Conable, as he later recalled, always saw indexing as "an honesty in taxation device," forcing Congress to raise taxes when it needed more money, instead of automatically relying on inflation to continually push tax payers into higher tax brackets. But Stockman objected when Conable recommended indexation at their White House meeting. "Congress won't have the guts to raise taxes every time we need money. We'll never balance the budget again," Stockman said. "But Jim Baker bought it," Conable recalled, "deciding to index the tax brackets starting after the last year of rate reduction under the Kemp-Roth part of the bill that Reagan liked so much."[48]

Both Republicans and Democrats conceded that their bills were "more products of a political bidding war than blue prints for sound economic policy."[49] "It's terrible that we should be involved in a bidding war," Rostenkowski said. "But it all depends on whether you want to lose courageously or to win. I like to win."[50]

Conable, who also wanted to win, added: "If I were writing this bill, I would write it differently and so would every other member of this Congress." But he said Republicans had little choice "if they wanted to enact the heart of the Reagan economic program."[51]

Even with the latest Reagan bid to the conservative Democrats, Conable was not sure the Republicans could win the vote on the floor of the House. "Kent Hance knew of only 15 hard Democrats," Conable wrote in his journal, "and I could not assure the White House that there might not be as many as 10 Republicans straying across the line the other way, attracted by the weighting of the rate cuts in the Democratic bill, and embarrassed by the appeals to oil which represented the final Reagan bid above the Rostenkowski tenders to the Texans."[52] So, with the House vote set for July 29, both sides prepared for the final battle.

Reagan Rallies Support

According to Pamela Fessler of *Congressional Quarterly*, "the Republicans rolled out their heavy artillery." On Friday, July 24, in a speech before the House Republican Conference on Capitol Hill, President Reagan personally urged Republicans to stick together in "these last critical days," calling the tax cut "the most critical item left on our agenda for prosperity."[53]

Two days later, on Sunday, July 26, the president invited fourteen wavering members to a barbecue at Camp David. The visiting congressmen generally reported no change of mind, two observers noted, but "in the end a sense of being personally courted could not have hurt, as 11 of them did back the president."[54]

On Monday evening, July 27, two days before the scheduled congressional vote, President Reagan delivered a dramatic television address from the Oval Office that proved to be decisive to the final outcome. In an infuriating piece of deception to the Democrats and a masterful stroke of persuasion to the Republicans, Reagan explained the difference between his bill and the Democratic alternative as a choice "between a tax cut or a tax increase." Although the Democratic Ways and Means bill called for a 15-percent tax cut, Reagan explained, there was a 22 percent tax increase built into the system over the next three years with Social Security tax increases and inflation, thus still leaving the taxpayer with a 7 percent tax increase for that period. "Our bill"—the Conable–Hance bill—on the other hand, he said, called for a 25 percent tax cut over the next three years, "wipes out the tax increase . . . with a little to spare . . . and gives you [the taxpayer] an on-going [3 percent] cut. . . . Even more important," Reagan said, "if the tax cut goes to you, the American people, [that money] won't be available to the Congress to spend. And that, in my view, is what the whole controversy comes down to. Are you entitled to the fruits of your own labor or does government have some presumptive right to spend and spend and spend?"

Reagan ended his dramatic television address by urging voters "to contact your senators and congressmen [and] tell them of your support" for the economic recovery program when it came up for a vote in Congress later in the week.[55]

Conable had given a speech himself to a business group in New York City on Monday evening and had missed the president's speech. So he was "unprepared for the onslaught of telephone calls that came from all over the country the next day," he wrote in his journal.[56]

Indeed, the *Washington Post* reported the next day that the Capitol Hill "switchboards [were] ablaze" with phone calls supporting the president's program. And the White House received more than 4,000 phone calls and 1,200 telegrams and mailgrams on the tax cut, with the calls running six to one in the president's favor and telegrams ten to one.[57]

The president and his allies also continued their lobbying campaign after the speech. "In every way available to a president," two scholarly observers noted, "Ronald Reagan sought votes for his tax plan, the centerpiece of his program to change the course of American government."[58]

By the next morning Tip O'Neill all but conceded defeat. "We are experiencing a telephone blitz like this nation has never seen," the Speaker said. "It's had a devastating effect."[59]

Conable, too, sensing a Republican victory, noted in his journal:

> Clearly the rolling tide of contacts from constituents engulfed many uncertain congressmen and created an environment in which it was easy for them to switch.

Of course, the president continued his personal lobbying efforts and many Democrats visited the White House on Tuesday and early Wednesday. The Democrats, having started this period comfortably ahead and confident the embarrassment of Gramm–Latta budget votes was a thing of the past, planned no special devious strategy from the Rules Committee, and the straight up and down vote on the [Conable–Hance] substitute was the easy result of the Rules Committee deliberations [that took place on Tuesday with testimony from both Conable and Rostenkowski].[60]

Under the "closed rule," which prohibits amendments, there would be three straight up and down votes on the tax cut alternatives. First, there would be a vote on a liberal Democratic alternative, sponsored by Morris K. Udall of Arizona, that called for a one-year tax cut and a balanced budget by 1982, along the lines previously proposed by the 1980 Democratic National Convention. That proposal, in the opinion of most observers, had no chance of passing. Then there would be a vote on the bipartisan Conable–Hance substitute favored by President Reagan. If that failed, there would be a final vote on the committee bill sponsored by Rostenkowski and the other Democratic members of the Ways and Means Committee.[61]

"By early Tuesday evening," Conable recorded in his journal, the Democrats "began to look glum as they saw their edge being dulled, and then broken in the face of the onslaught of phone calls from presidential blandishments. By Wednesday morning," with O'Neill and the Democratic leadership openly acknowledging the effectiveness of the Reagan lobbying campaign, "they knew they were beaten. But I did not know they were beaten until I saw how many Republicans wanted to speak in favor of the bill."[62]

The House Votes

The House convened the next morning at nine o'clock. After the routine morning business and formal adoption of the rule from the Rules Committee, the House resolved itself into the Committee of the Whole—technically a smaller body than the full House, requiring a quorum of only one hundred members, but with practically all of the members of the House remaining on the floor this day—for consideration of the three tax-cut bills being debated. As expected, the Udall, liberal alternative calling for a one-year tax cut and a balanced budget by 1982 was defeated by the lopsided margin of 288 to 144.

The House then proceeded to debate the Conable–Hance substitute. As the Republican floor manager for the bill with responsibility for deciding who would speak for the bill, Conable reported in his journal that he "made long lists and ceded for purposes of control small blocks of debate time to various groups, including the Boll Weevils [the conservative southern Democrats who had defied their party's leadership to support President Reagan] and the Gypsy Moths [an informal caucus of about two dozen northeastern and midwestern Republicans who were also strong supporters of Reagan's economic plan] so that I would not have to decide which of these special caucuses were to speak for that point of view."

When his time came to speak, Conable found that he only had three minutes left for himself in the one hour of debate time allocated to the Republican side, "a terribly inadequate time in which to get into any substantial matters which should have been discussed, if the merits of the bill were to be talked about at all. I thought we were clearly ahead on the merits, since Reagan's economic philosophy was still intact, despite all the add-ons, and I would have liked to have pointed out the advantages we had over Rostenkowski's efforts at counter-punching." But with his time lapsing, and privately feeling "robbed of the major role [in the debate] by the pressure of my colleagues for debate time," Conable had time only to offer a brief summary of the bill, in which he stressed the two parts that he had had the greatest role in crafting: the accelerated depreciation plan for business and indexing of the tax brackets, which he described as "probably the most significant long-term change in this bill," since, as he said, it made "the tax cut permanent [by] in effect taxing real income for the first time, instead of nominal income."[63] With no time left for debate—a painful fact for a man who liked to talk and who described the events of that week as "probably the most significant week of my life"[64]—Conable then had time only to say: "I trust the members of this body will support the Conable–Hance substitute."

It fell to the minority leader, Bob Michel of Illinois, to more completely state the case for the Republicans.[65]

> The philosophy underlying the Conable–Hance bill is the antithesis of the committee bill. The two bills are worlds apart philosophically. . . . Conable–Hance is a dramatic departure from the past. It is not only a three-year reduction of 25 percent but also provides for automatic

adjustments thereafter through indexing. The Conable–
Hance substitute gives back to the people what is theirs to
begin with. Conable–Hance means that those who govern
must get their license to govern—to spend and tax—from
those who are governed. No more will there be taxation
without representation and without debate, without a
single hearing, without our voting the financing mecha-
nisms up or down on future wild spending programs.

When the time came for Rostenkowski, as chairman of the Ways
and Means Committee, to make the case for the Democratic bill, he
also explained the differences between the two bills as a philosophical difference between the two political parties.

As Democrats, we believe that . . . middle-income workers, families who make up the largest part of our society
deserve the largest share of this tax cut. . . . The president's approach ignores economic distinctions in the
country. His across-the-board tax cut favors the wealthy—
assuming that they, not the middle class are the rightful
decision makers in this country.

Democrats dread the potential consequences of an
automatic third-year cut, followed by indexation. The
"certainty" of tax reduction that the president demands
for Wall Street may well promise certain disaster—rather
than certain prosperity.

The larger issue, though, Rostenkowski said, in a pointed criticism of Conable and the other Republican Ways and Means members, was

whether laws should be written by political strategists in
the basement of the White House or by men and women
elected to serve in this legislature. The tax cut we are
about to judge bears little imprint of Republicans elected
to serve on the Ways and Means Committee. The president's approach to the legislative process is an insult to
those committee Republicans who pride themselves as
legislators, who pride themselves on their experience and
their understanding of taxation and economics.

Republicans, especially my colleagues on the Ways and
Means Committee, have little reason to be proud of the
final White House version. Some feel a quiet shame for
what has been forced upon them, and, as a legislator and
committee chairman, I share your sense of frustration.
I know that few of you are free to oppose the president's
substitute.

The general debate on the Conable–Hance bill was concluded by a stinging speech from Speaker O'Neill, who, in a rare appearance on the floor of the House of Representatives, warned his colleagues of the risk they were taking by enacting the Republican tax cuts.

> By 1986 the Republican substitute will cost $754.8 billion in anticipated revenues for the treasury. Its proponents maintain that reducing taxes will generate more revenue for the treasury. This proposition has no precedent. It is a terrible gamble. If it fails, the consequences for the nation will be horrible. Deficits will soar, inflation will persist, budgets will be cut. . . .
> The Democratic plan seeks only an opportunity after two years, to see if the cuts are working, if the administration's economic projections are correct. If inflation and unemployment are reduced and if business prospers, further cuts would follow. If the administration is wrong, then we could take steps to reduce high interest rates and high deficits.
> There is a lot at stake in how we vote today. A lot more than a political victory for Republicans or Democrats. . . . I believe that if all of you vote what you truly believe is the wisest and best course for this nation to follow in the 80s, then you will join me in voting against the Republican substitute.

With the time for general debate on the Conable–Hance substitute expired, the chairman of the Committee of the Whole, Bill Natcher of Kentucky, called "the question on the amendment in the nature of the substitute offered by the gentleman from New York."

The vote was taken by electronic device, with the results, member by member, displayed on a large tote board over the Speaker's chair. There were 238 ayes, 195 nays, and two members not voting. By a comfortable margin, 48 Democrats—30 of the Boll Weevils from the south and 18 others—had joined 190 Republicans in voting for the Conable–Hance substitute.

The Committee of the Whole, following the normal parliamentary procedure used in such matters, then rose and reported the bill back to the House. James Jeffords, the lone Republican voting against the bill (and the same independent-minded Republican from Vermont who would shift the balance of the Senate twenty years later by abandoning the Republican Party) moved to recommit the bill to the Committee on Ways and Means in a traditional last-ditch effort to defeat the legislation. The motion to recommit was rejected, and the Speaker, by then back in the chair, ordered a vote on the passage of the bill. The question was taken and by an even larger bipartisan majority of 328 to 107 the full House of Representatives passed the Conable–Hance substitute.

After the vote, Conable reported in his journal, he "went over to a very glum Rostenkowski standing in the middle of his supporters, shook hands and said to him, 'You're a good guy, Danny, I hope we can work together to avoid this kind of polarization on Social Security,'" the next major reform item on the Reagan agenda, which would test the president's leadership as well as that of the Congress. "Rostenkowski said virtually nothing in return," Conable reported, "and shook hands without enthusiasm."[66]

Confident of victory only days earlier, Rostenkowski had "ordered twenty cases of champagne and had potted palms set up in the Ways and Means hearing room where he was going to have a great celebration when he won on the floor. Well, he didn't win," Conable recalled, with the obvious pride of someone still savoring his victory years later, "and all the champagne was put away for another occasion."[67]

On July 29, the Senate also tentatively approved a similar version of the Reagan tax cut by a huge bipartisan margin of 89 to 11, with 37 of the Senate's 47 Democrats voting for the bill and only one Republican, Charles McC. Mathias Jr. of Maryland, voting against it. In deference to the House's constitutional prerogative to initiate revenue matters, the Senate stopped short of final passage until it had received the House bill on July 31.[68]

The Conference Committee and Final Passage

With the House and Senate now having passed slightly different versions of the Reagan tax cut, a conference committee was called for late Friday afternoon, July 31, to work out the differences between the two versions of the bill. "We were anxious to get it behind us, so that the tax cut could take effect this year rather than having to wait until after the October 1st effective date," Conable wrote in his journal.

> The conference convened Friday afternoon at 4:00 o'clock and on time, but a time made necessary by Rostenkowski's refusal to give up a Friday morning date to see his daughter graduate from nursing school.
> On the House conference committee there were five Democrats and three Republicans. . . . On the Senate

side there were four Republicans and three Democrats. Rostenkowski was the chairman of the conference, it being his turn with the usual rotation between Ways and Means and the Senate Finance Committee.

Rostenkowski had us meet in H-208, a steamy small room next to the House chamber, reflecting his prejudice against open meetings. Although the conference was technically open, in H-208 there was room, in addition to members and staff, for only a few reporters and for virtually none of the unfortunate and disorderly lobbyists, clustered in the hall, sometimes numbering as many as 150, and laying hands on the persons of the conferees unlucky enough to have to leave occasionally for purposes of personal comfort or otherwise.

I stayed in the conference room virtually the entire time, except when the House members caucused in the lobby of the House chamber, at which time the Senate caucused in the Speaker's room on the floor below.

Although at discouraging times in the night we wavered occasionally in our determination, it was assumed that we would go until we had completed the somewhat more than 100 differences in the two versions of the tax bill, many of which were more imagined than real.[69]

"The big issues as expected," Conable recalled a few days later, "turned out to be oil, commodity straddles, qualified stock options, capital gains holding period, and some differences affecting charity." These issues and other minor differences were resolved without too much difficulty in the course of an all-night session and

at 8:00 o'clock the next morning we all signed the conference report and staggered off without much sense of mutual satisfaction, but sufficiently exhausted that we knew we had been through something. In fact, looking back on it, I feel we had done rather well. Most of the significant things in the tax bill were not subject to the scope of the conference. The matters which survived are not bad. The bill has a lot of garbage in it, but all tax bills do. The Reagan economic program is totally intact and sufficiently clearly understood to transfer the responsibility for government and the state of the economy to him, [though] more totally than reality should require. [Conable believed that the economy responded more to the forces of the marketplace than any form of governmental intervention.] In the view of the public, Reagan is totally in control, and if anything will help inflationary expectations and improve the optimism of the American people over the effectiveness of their government, that should do it.[70]

With the conference committee work done, a compromise bill, satisfying both the House and Senate conferees, was submitted to the full House and Senate on August 1. After a brief but unsuccessful attempt by liberals in the Senate and House to scale down the tax breaks for independent oil producers and royalty owners, the Senate passed the bill on August 3 and the House on August 4.

As agreed to by the conference report, the final version of the Economic Recovery Act of 1981 included the heart of Reagan's economic program: a 23 percent across-the-board reduction in individual income taxes over three years and accelerated depreciation for capital investment to spur productivity and economic growth.[71] To gain congressional support, the new law also included future indexing of income taxes to offset the effects of inflation, which Conable had successfully added to the bill in the bidding war that took place in July, and the long list of tax breaks—on oil production, interest income, charitable contributions, child care, estate and gifts, etc.—which had been added to the bill to secure passage in the House and Senate.[72]

In signing the massive five-year $749 billion Economic Recovery Act and a three-year $130 billion budget-cutting bill (which included an immediate $35.2 billion budget cut for 1982) into law on the same day, Reagan said from his mountain-top ranch in California on August 13 that he did not know how many more budget cuts would be required in the next three years to meet his goal of a balanced budget by 1984. But he acknowledged that deficits in the coming years might be higher than originally forecast because Congress had not cut domestic spending as much as he requested and had cut taxes more than he requested. "It just means that we are going to have to try to get more additional cuts than we might have had to get before," a cheerful president told the press.[73]

As it turned out, Congress refused to make many more cuts in domestic spending, the tax cuts did not produce the immediate results many had expected, and the economy slid into recession in 1982. As a result, instead of achieving the balanced budget Reagan officials had originally projected for 1984, the budget deficit soared from the $79 billion Reagan inherited from Jimmy Carter in 1981 to $185 billion in 1984, and Reagan was forced to go back to Congress for a tax increase in 1986. "If Rostenkowski had been willing to bargain a little about Kemp–Roth at the outset rather than trying to out-bid Reagan for special interest votes, this tax increase would not have been necessary," Conable maintained.[74]

Despite this tax increase in 1986, however, the deficit continued to climb throughout the Reagan and Bush presidencies, reaching a high of $290 billion in 1992, before beginning to decline and eventually disappear during the latter half of the Clinton presidency in the late 1990s, only to rise again under the second Bush presidency in the early part of the twenty-first century.[75]

Thus, as the chain of fiscal events unfolded in the 1980s, Barber Conable—the long-time fiscal conservative and advocate of a balanced-budget amendment—ironically ended up contributing, with the Conable–Hance tax-cut bill he was compelled to steer through the House, to the largest budget deficits in American history. Barber Conable, the professor, had been right when he advised President-elect Reagan in December 1980 that, "You're not going to be able to cut tax rates by 30 percent and still not have the deficits go out of sight, if these other things are added to it as well."[76]

But in the trenches of the Ways and Means Committee, Barber Conable, the pragmatic politician, outnumbered two to one by the Democrats, and "forced into the arms of Ronald Reagan," as he said, if he was to have any influence at all, was not able to head off the fiscal disaster the professorial side of him had warned the president-elect about before the battle began. He had privately tried to get Rostenkowski to bargain with Reagan for a smaller tax cut which he thought would be acceptable to the White House, but when that failed, he completely allied himself to the president. And in the midst of battle, with his own competitive juices flowing and no room for retreat, Conable had even come to rationalize the merits of the legislation and admire the leadership ability Ronald Reagan had shown in getting his economic reforms through Congress.

"I must say," Conable wrote in his journal the week Congress enacted the Economic Recovery Act into law, "I have grudgingly come to admire and be entertained by the willingness of this president to provide leadership. I have become so cynical about government I thought all political types were more interested in survival than in accepting any degree of responsibility. Reagan, a man who is not all that admirable personally, and certainly not all that traditional politically, appears to be a man willing to give leadership of significant mention to a country which probably needs leadership more than affection or admiration or political tradition."

As for his own role in enacting the tax cut into law, Conable was particularly pleased that he had been able to add indexing to the legislation. "Indexing changes the whole manner of American taxation. Of all the elements of the bill, indexing is probably the most significant and probably the greatest source of trouble for the politicians of the future. . . . The old days are gone forever when every two years we reduce taxes, claim credit, and in fact return the people no farther than to place them where they would have been if bracket creep had not constantly pushed them into a higher bracket."

Conable realized, though, that his relations with Rostenkowski had been damaged as a result of the political process it had taken to enact the Conable–Hance bill into law. "Danny was convinced he could detach from Republican solidarity some of the more vocal and brighter members of my minority on the Ways and Means Committee, and he totally failed," Conable wrote, appraising his own role in holding the Republican Ways and Means members together.

> In one way or another I hung in there and became an effective force for change, [if] only through negotiations with the White House. Rostenkowski has been resentful of my persistence, referring many of the matters of contention between us back to the stacking of the Ways and Means Committee in favor of the Democrats. It took him a long time to realize that he had forced me into the arms of Ronald Reagan on substantive tax matters, if I was to have any influence in the outcome of tax legislation in his totally dominating committee. It also took him some time to understand that I had very little enthusiasm for maintaining the prerogatives of the House if these prerogatives were as totally concentrated in his own control of the committee, when the alternative was accepting some degree of White House dictation, a White House with which I had some respect and possibly even a little influence.

At the end of the all night conference session,

> probably elated that he had turned back the depletion efforts [to freeze oil depletion allowances] in our bill, Rostenkowski shook hands with some enthusiasm with Bob Dole and Russell Long, but although I was sitting directly in front of him, he did not tender his hand to me. I got up and extended my hand to him, saying something of a mollifying nature, [to] which he did not respond except for a perfunctory handshake. From all this and from his natural competitiveness, as well as the edge he

has given himself in all of his dealings within the committee, I assume that I will continue to have a difficult time as far as Ways and Means is concerned. I also assume that this difficulty will be extended into the next Congress since it is unlikely we will pick up control of the House after two years of a high silhouette, high risk administration.

"Despite his vindictiveness, his competitiveness," Conable consoled himself,

> Rostenkowski is basically a decent man. He enjoys a non-intellectual, comparatively vulgar camaraderie with the people with whom he serves. He is not unintelligent, and when not riled by failure, his instincts are friendly. I must make a serious effort at friendliness and must try to plan the campaigns of the future, modest though they may be compared to the immediate past, with an eye to including him and enlisting his cooperation and urging that course out of others who have to deal with our committee. I do not see any devolution of party politics in what remains for us in the 97th Congress. [But] I do expect the issues for the next year and a half to be less wrought with tension and substantive significance than the issues with which we have already dealt.[77]

Conable's expectations for a less contentious remainder of the Ninety-seventh Congress, however, were not fully realized, as Congress was thrown almost immediately into the interrelated problem of rescuing the Social Security system from bankruptcy. Once again, Conable would have to deal with Rostenkowski and the House Democratic leadership on one of the most controversial issues of American politics, but in a different, far less visible manner than had been the case on tax cuts.

Figure 13. Congressman Conable meeting with presidential candidate Richard M. Nixon in 1967. (Credit: Box 80, Barber B. Conable Papers, #2794. Division of Rare and Manuscript Collections, Cornell University Library.)

Figure 14. Conable interviews University of Rochester political science professor, Richard F. Fenno Jr., for a television show broadcast to his constituents in the late 1960s. (Credit: Barber B. Conable Jr.)

Figure 15. Conable with Rumsfeld's Raiders, a reform group in the House founded by Illinois Republican Congressman Donald Rumsfeld to democratize the rules and procedures of the House in the late 1960s. The group is pictured in front of a 1909 Mitchell Flyer to symbolize one of the last years in which major changes were made in House rules. From left to right are William Steiger (Wisc.), William Brock (Tenn.), Barber Conable, Donald Rumsfeld, Robert Taft (Ohio), Charles Whalen (Ohio), James Cleveland (N. H.), and Frederick Schwengel (Iowa), October 1969. (Credit: Box 80, Barber B. Conable Papers, #2794. Division of Rare and Manuscript Collections, Cornell University Library.)

Figure 16. Conable points to a map of his congressional district with two of his legislative interns, Tim Collins (left) and Kevin Bell (middle), July 1969. (Credit: Box 80, Barber B. Conable Papers, #2794. Division of Rare and Manuscript Collections, Cornell University Library.)

Figure 17. Conable advises his old friend and mentor, President Gerald R. Ford, on congressional affairs in the Oval Office in 1975. (Credit: Barber B. Conable Jr.)

Figure 18. Conable types a constituent newsletter in his Washington office, Janury 1978. (Credit: Jimmy Carter Library.)

Figure 19. Conable at the presidential signing of the Social Security Reform legislation. Standing behind President Reagan from left to right are: Alan Greenspan, Daniel Rostenkowski, Robert Dole, J. J. "Jake" Pickle, Claude Pepper, Robert Michel, Daniel Patrick Moynihan, Thomas P. "Tip" O'Neill, Barber Conable, Howard Baker, and George Bush, April 20, 1983. (Credit: Barber B. Conable Jr.)

Figure 20. Conable with other members of the House Republican leadership. Standing from left to right are Silvio Conte, Jack Edwards, Guy Vander Jagt, James Quillin, Richard Cheney, Barber Conable, and Robert Lagomarsino. Seated left to right are James Martin, Trent Lott, Minority Leader Robert Michel, and Jack Kemp, September 1983. (Credit: Barber B. Conable Jr.)

Figure 21. Conable discusses tax legislation with his friend and influential member of the Senate Finance Committee, Senator Daniel Patrick Moynihan of New York, fall 1984. (Credit: Barber B. Conable Jr.)

Figure 22. Conable in his House office with his long-term administrative assistant, Harry Nicholas, in 1984. (Credit: Barber B. Conable Jr.)

Figure 23. Conable back home in Alexander, New York after his retirement from Congress, summer 1985. (Credit: Barber B. Conable Jr.)

Figure 24. As president of the World Bank, Conable meets with his old friend and former Ways and Means colleague, President George Bush, in the Oval Office, September 14, 1989. (Credit: George Bush Presidential Library.)

Figure 25. Conable with the author, James S. Fleming, and two of his students, Laura Scarpelli (left) and Elizabeth Luc, at the Conable home in Alexander, New York, October 1992. (Credit: James S. Fleming. Photo taken by another student, Richard Alfvin.)

Chapter 13

Saving Social Security

"Social Security faced a very simple problem in the early 1980s: it was going broke fast," in the words of Paul Light, a political scientist in Conable's office, who closely followed the details of the crisis and later wrote a book on the subject.

> More money was going out in benefits than was coming in, outstripping taxes by $10 to $15 billion a year. The reserve ratio, a measure of trust fund savings, had dropped to an all-time low and threatened to fall below zero in 1982. At the height of the crisis, Social Security

was spending about $3,000 more per minute than it was taking in. Still, it seemed like a simple problem: just raise more revenues or cut benefits.[1]

But finding a solution to this simple problem, as Light demonstrates, proved to be complicated, and one of Barber Conable's most significant contributions as a legislator who had been deeply involved in the Social Security issue for almost twenty years. It was, in fact, as Conable later recalled, "the high point of my legislative career."[2]

The basic cause of the Social Security crisis in the early 1980s was the poor economic conditions of the country during the second half of the Carter presidency. Just three years earlier, Congress had passed a $227 million Social Security tax increase which President Carter said would guarantee the solvency of Social Security until 2030. By 1980, however, the economic conditions of the country had deteriorated and seriously threatened the future of Social Security. With high inflation and weak economic growth, a crisis seemed inevitable in the Social Security system. The 1979 cost-of-living-adjustment for inflation, or COLA as it is called, was 9.9 percent. The 1980 inflation rate was expected to be even higher. At the beginning of the year, President Carter had proposed a series of incremental adjustments to shore up the trust fund. By mid-year, however, the Social Security Administration recognized that the program was in serious financial trouble, but everyone knew that nothing realistically could be done to solve the problem until after the 1980 presidential election.[3]

"The Social Security crisis," as Light explains,

> actually fell into two time periods. The short-term crisis ran from 1980 to 1989. According to most economic forecasts, that crisis would end in 1990 with yet another tax increase from Carter's rescue legislation. Between 1990 and 2015, the program would enter two decades of good times, the "golden years" of Social Security. Though the elderly population would continue to grow, it would be offset by the huge baby boom generation, born in the 1950s and 1960s. With the baby boomers working and paying taxes, Social Security would build a substantial surplus during the golden days. Around 2015, however, the baby boomers would start to retire themselves, driving the ratio of workers to retirees down to just over two to one. The program would spend the golden surpluses quickly, entering an indefinite period of crisis lasting well into the middle of the next century, as far as the projections could see.[4]

The exact size of both the short-term and long-term crisis was hard to estimate with certainty. But, depending on the economic and demographic assumptions that were used, most experts placed the size of the short-term crisis at somewhere between $50 and $212 billion. Adjusted for inflation, the size of the long-term debt after 2015 was around $1.5 trillion, or an even more staggering $5 to $6 trillion when not adjusted to inflation.

Rather than focus on these incredibly large sums of money, planners and politicians preferred instead to talk about the percentage payroll taxes would have to be increased to solve the financial crisis. Depending on the assumptions used, most analysts believed the combined payroll taxes for employees and employers would have to be increased somewhere between 1.8 and 6.5 percent to solve the long-term problem. By virtue of Carter's 1977 rescue package, the FICA (Federal Insurance Contribution Act) tax rate was already scheduled to increase to 7.65 percent on both employees and employers by 1990 (with 6.2 percent of that being the Social Security tax and 1.45 percent the Medicare tax). Even at the minimum increase, an additional 1.8 percent FICA tax increase would drive payroll taxes up to 8.55 percent on both employees and employers for a combined 17.1 percent tax rate. Either taxes would have to be increased by that amount or benefits would have to be cut by an equal amount to solve the long-term crisis in Social Security after 2015.[5]

The political parties tended to differ in their solution to this most recent Social Security crisis, as they had disagreed historically on financing Social Security over the years. The Democrats argued either that the current financial crisis was only a temporary problem that would be corrected with an improved economy or that payroll taxes should be increased to make up for any future deficit. The Republicans, on the other hand, emphasized the gravity of the current crisis and argued for a reduction of benefits and a substantial restructuring of the Social Security system.[6]

As somewhat of an exception to this partisan division, the conservative Democratic chairman of the Social Security Subcommittee in the Ways and Means Committee, Jake Pickle from Texas, favored a substantial restructuring of the Social Security system to resolve the current crisis and put the program on sound financial footing. Pickle had a Social Security reform bill ready to introduce in the House several weeks before Ronald Reagan was inaugurated president in January 1981. Though there was no assurance Pickle's bill would pass, he had the implicit support of the Ways and Means chairman, Dan Rostenkowski. So when Pickle's bill finally passed the subcommittee on April 8, he had some reason to hope for favorable action by the full Ways and Means Committee and eventual passage by the House.

"From a conservative standpoint," as Light notes, the Pickle bill "was not a bad bill. Despite general revenue and accounting games in the short term, it carried a deep benefit cut in the long term. By raising the retirement age from 65 to 68, it slashed the early retirement option. Workers could still retire at age 62, but with much lower benefits. It was just the kind of cut conservatives wanted. Coming from a Democratic subcommittee in a Democratic House, it was a good starting point for serious negotiations."[7]

But just as Pickle's bill was being referred to the full Ways and Means Committee, the White House introduced a controversial proposal that substantially altered the politics of the Social Security debate. Under intense pressure to find additional savings to off-set the huge Reagan tax cut, Reagan's budget director, David Stockman, proposed cutting $45 billion from future Social Security expenses. Like Pickle, Stockman proposed reducing the early retirement benefits when workers retired at sixty-two, but where Pickle's bill would have cut the early retirement option 16 percent starting in 1990, Stockman's proposal would have cut the option 25 percent on January 1, 1982. About half of Stockman's proposed savings—$20 billion—would have come from reducing the early retirement options. In addition, Stockman proposed a $4 billion cut in basic benefits, a $5 billion three-month COLA delay, and $16 billion of other savings. Some sixty million retirees would have been affected by the benefit cuts proposed by Stockman and presented by President Reagan to Congress on May 12, 1981.

The response to the Reagan–Stockman proposal to cut Social Security benefits was immediate and overwhelmingly negative on Capitol Hill. What had quietly started out as a legislatively inspired effort in the Ways and Means Committee to reform Social Security had now turned into a full-blown conflict between the Congress and new president.[8]

"By any calculation, the administration has launched the most fundamental assault on the Social Security system since its inception 46 years ago," the House Committee on Aging reported. "These cuts constitute a breach of contract. . . . Millions of people, who will retire in the next few years, will have their benefits slashed by 30 or 40 percent. . . . Now we find that Social Security is a punching bag, an open sesame from which to fund large tax cuts and budget deficits."[9]

In the House, the octogenarian Claude Pepper from Florida and long-time advocate for the elderly, said the administration's package was "insidious" and "cruel." The Democratic Speaker of the House, Tip O'Neill, agreed, calling the plan "despicable" and "a rotten thing to do," and accused Reagan of being "stonehearted" in his approach to the elderly.

In the Republican Senate, the administration's proposal to cut Social Security was also severely criticized. The ranking Democrat on the Senate Finance Committee, Senator Daniel Patrick Moynihan from New York, introduced a strongly worded "Sense of the Senate" resolution condemning the administration's plan as "precipitous and severe . . . and a breach of faith with . . . aging Americans who have contributed to the Social Security system." The Republicans were able to defeat the Moynihan resolution with a slim forty-nine to forty-eight majority. But the Senate then went on to pass a slightly watered-down and more focused resolution offered by the Finance Committee chairman, Bob Dole of Kansas. Sensitive to the widespread criticism of the administration's proposal, particularly its plan to reduce the benefits of early retirees, the Dole resolution promised specifically that "Congress shall not precipitously and unfairly penalize early retirees." With the passage of the Dole resolution on a ninety-six to zero vote, the Reagan–Stockman plan for reforming Social Security, or simply cutting Social Security as a means of funding the Reagan tax cuts and budget deficits as the Democrats charged, was effectively dead.[10]

Reagan Creates a Presidential Commission

With the administration's Social Security proposals going nowhere on Capitol Hill, the Senate majority leader, Howard Baker, urged Reagan to establish a bipartisan presidential commission to study the Social Security problem. Following Baker's suggestion, Reagan announced on September 24 that he would create a bipartisan National Commission on Social Security Reform. The commission would be asked, Reagan said, "to review all the options and come up with a plan that assures the fiscal integrity of Social Security and that Social Security recipients will continue to receive their full benefits."

Reagan's announcement to create a presidential commission to study the Social Security problem was not well received in Congress, where few of the major legislative leaders had been consulted in advance. "It was a classic cover-your-ass maneuver," one Senate aide said. "There was absolutely no need for another commission on Social Security [the fourth major study in three years]. It had been studied to death already."

Barber Conable, who was widely regarded as one of the leading authorities on Social Security in Congress, also agreed that there was no need for yet another commission to study Social Security. "We do not need another study," he told his young legislative assistant. "If we don't straighten out Social Security this fall, the sensitivity to the political election cycle will prevent us from doing it for another four years."[11] But there was very little Conable or anyone else in Congress could do to stop the commission, once Reagan had made the announcement.

In the meantime, though, Conable tried one more time to forge a legislative solution to the Social Security crisis with his Democratic friend and chairman of the Ways and Means Subcommittee on Social Security, Jake Pickle. The Pickle bill would have wiped out most of the Social Security system's anticipated $1.56 trillion, long-term deficit over the next seventy-five years. Pickle's proposal, which Conable co-sponsored, would have gradually increased the retirement age to sixty-six, changed the annual cost-of-living formula, and cut payments for new beneficiaries by revising the initial benefit formula. The Pickle–Conable bill, though, was rejected by a largely partisan vote of fourteen to eighteen in the Ways and Means Committee. In rejecting the bill, Conable felt at the time, along with most of the other Republican members, that the committee was just putting off a serious problem that would get worse. After the vote, Conable said with uncharacteristic disgust, "It's a disgrace the way we've turned tail and run on Social Security and that includes the administration, and everyone in this room" who voted against the bill.[12]

With the Pickle–Conable bill going nowhere in Congress, Conable eventually accepted membership on Reagan's fifteen-member presidential commission, despite the strong objection of Ways and Means Chairman Rostenkowski. "Danny told me not to go on the commission," Conable recalled later. "He thought I would come back to the Ways and Means Committee committed to something that wouldn't be the committee's work. But I said to him, 'Danny, we've copped out of this issue [in the Ways and Means Committee], and I'm not going to refuse to try to get this thing straightened out. And it's not going to get straightened out any other way.' "[13]

As the man who Senator Daniel Patrick Moynihan said "probably [knew] more about Social Security than any member of Congress," Conable was a natural choice for the commission.[14] In addition to Conable, the minority leader, Bob Michel, who got to choose two Republicans for the commission, also chose the arch-conservative Bill Archer from Houston, Texas, who was the ranking Republican member of the Ways and Means Subcommittee on Social Security.

Speaker O'Neill selected three liberals for the commission: Claude Pepper from Florida; the former Democratic Congresswoman Martha Keys from Kansas, one of Conable's colleagues on the Ways and Means Committee from the 1970s and a strong proponent for the greater protection of women in Social Security; and the former Social Security Commissioner Robert Ball, who from all accounts would be the "Speaker's man" on the commission.

The Senate was also asked to select five members for the commission. To fill the Republican slots, Republican Majority Leader Howard Baker chose three of the Republicans' leading experts on Social Security: Dole, the pragmatic chairman of the Senate Finance Committee, which had jurisdiction over Social Security in the Senate; the conservative William Armstrong from Colorado, who headed the Social Security Subcommittee; and the more moderate John Heinz of Pennsylvania, who chaired the Special Aging Committee in the Senate.

To represent the Senate Democrats, Minority Leader Robert Byrd appointed Senator Moynihan and AFL-CIO President Lane Kirkland. Moynihan was the ranking Democrat on the Social Security Subcommittee and the author of the May resolution condemning the Reagan–Stockman proposal to cut $45 billion from Social Security. Kirkland, of course, represented organized labor's interest in Social Security and would bring his many years of experience as a negotiator to the commission.

Rounding out the fifteen-member presidential commission were five members chosen by the executive branch. As chairman, President Reagan chose the respected New York City economist, Alan Greenspan, who had been the chairman of the Council of Economic Advisors under Gerald Ford and someone who was acceptable to both conservatives and moderates in the White House. The four other executive appointees were all strongly pro-business. Alexander Trowbridge was president of the National Association of Manufacturers. Robert Beck headed the Business Roundtable Social Security Task Force. Mary Falvey Fuller was vice president of a large California consumer products corporation, and Joe Waggoner was a former conservative congressman from Louisiana who had been Conable's colleague on the Ways and Means Committee from 1967 to 1979. Two of the four appointees—Trowbridge and Waggoner—were Democrats as Reagan had promised, but all four strongly opposed tax increases and favored benefit cuts as the best way to solve the Social Security crisis.

With the commission in place, there were various ways to characterize the membership. Reagan talked about the eight to seven Republican majority on the commission, emphasizing the fact that he had appointed two Democrats. O'Neill, on the other hand, stressed the more purely ideological division on the commission. Since the two Reagan Democratic appointees—Trowbridge and Waggoner—rarely met with the five congressional Democrats, O'Neill was probably more realistic in emphasizing the ten to five split between conservatives and liberals on the commission.

From a practical point of view, perhaps the most important breakdown on the commission was the division between the seven legislators and eight outside members. The commission included an unusual combination of legislators and lobbyists in one advisory group. Under these circumstances, there would be no need to consult outside interest groups in making recommendations on Social Security reforms, since their representatives were already on the commission. If the lobbyists and legislators could agree among themselves on how to rescue Social Security within the commission, chances were the Congress and president would go along.[15]

Conable Pushes Congress to Set a Deadline

Before the newly formed National Commission on Social Security Reform could hold its first meeting in February 1982, Congress set a deadline for resolving the Social Security crisis. With a deadline engineered in large part by Barber Conable, and indirectly perhaps his most significant contribution to the resolution of the crisis, Congress gave itself until July 3, 1983, to resolve the Social Security crisis. Without a specific deadline for legislative action, Conable convinced his colleagues that Congress would not take the necessary steps to resolve the crisis.

The circumstances for setting the deadline came unexpectedly with a conference committee for restoring some fairly minor benefit cuts in Social Security in November 1981. Earlier in the year, Congress had tentatively agreed to cut minimum Social Security benefits, which provided a basic income floor of $122 a month for anyone eligible, regardless of past taxes or earnings, as part of Reagan's controversial budget package for 1981. Responding to public protest, the House and Senate both subsequently voted to restore these benefit cuts, which affected nearly three million people, mostly elderly women. But the two houses differed substantially on the legislative details for restoring the cuts. The House simply voted 405 to 20 to restore the minimum benefit cuts in Social Security, without specifying how the benefits would be paid, assuming that the financial crisis would pass with improved economic conditions and that there would be sufficient revenue in the trust fund to pay for the benefits when the time came. The Senate, however, led by Finance Committee Chairman Dole, was more alarmed by the weak financial condition of Social Security and the latest projection that the Old Age and Survivors Insurance program, the largest of the three Social Security trust funds responsible for paying for the minimum benefits and other benefits, would run out of funds in late 1982, possibly as early as October. To avert this disaster and provide Congress more time to solve the larger Social Security problem, Dole proposed, and the Senate unanimously concurred, that the Old Age and Survivors Insurance trust fund be allowed to borrow from the other two trust funds in the Social Security system—the Disability Insurance fund and Medicare, which were running a large surplus—for up to ten years.

Thus, what started out as a minor conference committee on how to restore the minimum benefit cuts in Social Security now turned into a conference of major significance on how to shore up the entire Social Security system. Would the conference committee go along with Dole's temporary, ten-year solution of interfund borrowing as a way of buying time to solve the inevitable Social Security crisis in the future? Or would the conference committee seek a more immediate and permanent, long-term solution to the Social Security problem?

Confronted with this dilemma, the conference committee convened on November 16, 1981, to decide what to do. The basic question confronting the members was how to set a deadline for future congressional action on Social Security reform. On the one hand, if they decided to extend the interfund borrowing option, they would simply be postponing the inevitable crisis. On the other hand, the conferees realized that Social Security reform was such a controversial issue they could not possibly take any congressional action on the problem prior to the November congressional election in 1982.

Acutely aware of this dilemma, and at the same time very much wanting Congress to move sooner than later on resolving the Social Security crisis, Conable pushed hard for a compromise that would allow the conference committee to set a one-year deadline on interfund borrowing that would expire at the end of 1982. As a political realist, Conable believed that the most likely time for congressional action on Social Security reform would be in a lame-duck session of Congress just after the congressional elections in November 1982. A lame-duck session would include retiring and defeated members who would no longer have to calculate the political consequences of controversial votes on Social Security. A lame-duck session would also be a full two years away from the next congressional elections, a long enough time for incumbent members to mollify any disgruntled constituents.

There were obvious risks in setting the one-year limit on interfund borrowing. If the lame-duck session of Congress refused to address Social Security after the midterm elections in November 1982, the next Congress would be forced to deal with the matter early in 1983, at about the same time the new Reagan budget arrived on Capitol Hill. Social Security would once again be entangled in the budget battle, and it would be difficult to devise an acceptable package to which all parties could agree.

But "in the end," as Paul Light reports,

> the conference committee adopted Conable's deadline. "If you want my vote," Conable . . . told the conference, "this is my price. But maybe you don't need me?" Faced with Conable's threat not to sign the final agreement, the conferees voted to terminate the interfund borrowing privileges on December 31, 1982. Without Conable's signature on the conference report, House Republicans would not support the agreement.
>
> To give Congress a little extra time under Conable's crisis, the conference allowed the Social Security trust fund to borrow at least six months of reserve in December. As a result, the crisis would occur on July 3, 1983, at the start of the seventh month of the year. That was the day the checks would not go out. If the 1982 lame-duck session failed, the House and Senate would have just over six months to build a package, move it through the committees, get it past the floor, and have it on the president's desk.

With a deadline set for solving the Social Security crisis, the House and Senate conferees signed the conference report. The Senate unanimously adopted the conference report on December 11. The House approved the report five days later, and President Reagan signed the bill into law before Christmas.

Led by Conable, "a small band of Social Security leaders in the House and Senate had designed the perfect device for congressional pressure," Light notes. "Though they had not been able to draft any kind of serious reform, they had been able to do the next best thing: create an inescapable crisis. Since Congress [is] a crisis-activated body, the key was making sure the members knew that a crisis was coming. . . . Now the question was how Congress would respond."[16]

Gang of Seventeen

The National Commission on Social Security Reform held its first meeting at the Washington Sheraton Hotel on February 27, 1982. The commission's staff director, Robert Myers, briefly discussed the history of Social Security and the financial crisis facing the system. The chairman, Alan Greenspan, urged the commission to approach its work with "a spirit of compromise." President Reagan also sent the commission a letter to wish them luck and reminded them of the bipartisan nature of their task.[17]

It quickly became apparent that the National Commission would not be able to make much progress in a volatile election year, with both political parties using the Social Security issue to their own advantage. The economic conditions of the country continued to worsen and Budget Director David Stockman was now projecting huge budget deficits in the neighborhood of $100 billion for each of the next four years. Some resolution of the Social Security problem seemed more urgent than ever.

In an effort to find some quiet, behind-the-scenes way to resolve the Social Security problem and related budget issues, the White House and congressional leaders decided in late March that they would create a secret, ad hoc negotiating group to see what could be done to hammer out a 1982 budget agreement that would also include a resolution of the Social Security issue. The National Commission on Social Security Reform would continue to meet, but it would now serve only as "a cover" for the more significant private negotiations that would take place outside the commission and outside the normal legislative and executive processes as well. The Social Security problem, in other words, was being pushed further and further from public view in an effort to find a solution.

Dubbed the Gang of Seventeen—apparently in a parody of China's Gang of Four who had tried to seize power in China after the death of Mao Ze Dong in 1976—this secret negotiating group included twelve congressional leaders (seven from the House and five from the Senate) and five White House officials.

Conable was one of the first House members asked to join the group. Also joining the group from the House were Ways and

Means Chairman Rostenkowski; the chairman of the Budget Committee, Jim Jones from Oklahoma; Richard Bolling of Missouri, who chaired the House Rules Committee; Del Latta of Ohio, the senior Republican on the House Budget Committee; and the rising conservative star from Mississippi, Trent Lott. The five senators in the Gang of Seventeen were Finance Committee Chairman Dole; the ranking Democrat on the Finance Committee, Russell Long from Louisiana; the chairman of the Budget Committee, Pete Domenici from New Mexico; Reagan's long-time friend, Paul Laxalt from Nevada; and the Democratic senator from South Carolina, Ernest Hollings. Representing the White House in the secret negotiations were Budget Director Stockman; Reagan's chief of staff, Jim Baker; his deputy chief of staff, Richard Darman; the head of the White House Congressional Liaison Office, Kenneth Duberstein; and the Treasury Secretary Donald Regan. Together, this group of seventeen leaders would secretly try to forge out an agreement on the 1982 budget and the related Social Security crisis before the interest groups could attack their plan.

"Though Republicans outnumbered Democrats twelve to five," according to Light, "only two people mattered: Reagan and O'Neill. The gang would have to keep the principals informed, and would have to get their approval before cutting any deals. . . . Like a House–Senate conference committee, the Gang of Seventeen was designed to resolve the differences between two positions. Unlike a conference, the gang was not bound by any formal rules or legislation. It was up to the group to define the range of problems and solutions. . . . The gang was noticeably short of ideologues. It was structured to provide an opportunity for a compromise and was not accountable to any outside group beyond Reagan and O'Neill."

In early April, one of the House participants recalled: "We all received a call from the White House telling us to gather in a driveway of the Rayburn House Office Building to be picked up by unmarked limos. The big boys themselves did not attend—Senate Majority Leader Baker, O'Neill, or the president—sending representatives whose actions they could disavow if the meetings blew up." Richard Bolling apparently represented O'Neill and Jim Baker spoke for Reagan.

The first meeting of the Gang of Seventeen was held at Vice President George Bush's home. "The rest of the meetings were held at Blair House, across from the White House. The gang usually arrived at the new Executive Office Building and sneaked through an alley to the back door. 'The press was particularly frustrated,' one gang member said. 'They apparently never learned where we were being picked up. Stakeouts were put on some of the members to try to find out where the meetings were being held. Once they learned that we were meeting at the White House, the press stood guard at the gates. Thundering herds rushed from one gate to the other as it appeared that we were entering or leaving. Gamesmanship, in short, became an entertaining sidelight of our press relations.' "

The group had some initial success in agreeing on the size of the budget deficit they faced. With no increase in taxes or spending cuts, they concluded that the deficit for 1983 would approach $182 billion, and then rise to $216 billion in 1984 and $233 billion in 1985—deficits which were far larger than Reagan and Stockman had originally predicted.

The Gang of Seventeen, however, ran into serious difficulty in late April in deciding how to resolve the financial crisis in Social Security, which was seen from the start as a major part of the larger deficit problem. The Democrats wanted Reagan to cancel the third year of his 1983 tax cut, and the Republicans wanted the Democrats to freeze the 1983 Social Security COLA. Unable to negotiate their differences, the group decided that the only way to resolve the disagreement was for Reagan and O'Neill to meet in a face-to-face summit. Light describes what happened at the interesting meeting that took place between Reagan and O'Neill on Capitol Hill on August 28.

> With the entire gang gathered in a sweltering hearing room in the Capitol building, Republicans offered their compromise: a three-month delay in both the Social Security COLA and the 1983 Reagan tax cut, pushing both back from July to October. "There was quite a pause there," one member said, while Reagan mulled over the figures. "In order to get that [the COLA delay] I agree [to the three-month delay in the tax cut]," he said. But O'Neill refused. "I will not discuss COLAs—they're off the table," the Speaker replied, later describing the three-month double delay as a trade of "an apple for an orchard." O'Neill then presented the Democratic plan: a three-month delay in the 1983 COLA in return for complete elimination of the third-year tax cut. Reagan refused. He could take some pain on his tax cut, but not that much, not in exchange for a simple three-month COLA delay. "I can crap a pineapple" the president told the Speaker, "but not a cactus."[18]

"That was it," Light reports; "three weeks of negotiations down the drain. The summit meeting was over; the Gang of 17 was finished."

Each side blamed the other. "We had hoped for give and take," one White House participant concluded, "and what we found from the other side was mostly take and very little give." But in the view of Tip O'Neill, the only Reagan "concession was to allow a slight three-month pause in his program of giving billion-dollar tax cuts to the rich." In return, O'Neill charged, Reagan "wanted the Democratic Party to become his accomplice in making more brutal cuts in programs such as Social Security."[19]

The November Collapse

Conable's earlier hopes that Congress could find a solution to the Social Security problem in a lame-duck session after the midterm congressional election on November 2, 1982, were quickly dashed by the intense party bickering that took place during the fall election campaign over the Social Security issue. All across the country, the Democrats, led by their eighty-two-year-old champion of the elderly in the House, Claude Pepper of Florida, lambasted the Republicans for the cuts they wanted to make in Social Security. The Republicans lost twenty-six seats in the House, ending any hope of finding a solution to the Social Security problem in a lame-duck session after the election. In a national television interview, Speaker O'Neill said that Social Security reform would not be on the agenda of the lame-duck session planned for late November and December. O'Neill, in fact, had already warned his fellow-Democrats in a pre-election letter that "many of our Republican colleagues will be defeated this coming week precisely because they voted to cut Social Security. To allow these same members another crack at Social Security would be an insult not just to their constituents but to the American electorate as a whole."

The Republicans were quick to respond to O'Neill's announcement. With the National Commission on Social Security Reform scheduled to meet in a three-day meeting, November 11–13, "the Republicans feared another political disaster," writes Light. At stake now was not only the 1984 congressional elections, but also the presidency. "I'm not backing into that buzz saw again, and I'm sure not walking straight into it," Senator Dole said. In an effort to coordinate efforts with his fellow Republicans on the National Commission, Dole sent them a telegram after the election recommending that

> we [do] not attempt to draft a final commission position next week. After the very partisan debate that has

surrounded Social Security in recent weeks, there should be a cooling off period and time for reflection by those who have the responsibility for preserving the system. . . . I do not believe the commission members should be trapped by leading partisans who seek political gain rather than solutions to a serious Social Security financing problem. If those who have been doing all the talking have a solution, we should hear about it in advance of any final commission report.[20]

"Since the Republicans favored benefit cuts, it would be far better to let Democrats take the first step," Light explains. "It was already clear that the tax increases could not solve the short-term crisis. Further, Dole reminded the Democrats that the House would have to produce a reform package if the commission failed. 'There is no need and little value for the commission to rush forward in an attempt to reach agreement next week,' Dole said. 'After all, the House of Representatives has the constitutional obligation to institute Social Security financing legislation.' Perhaps the responsibility would sober the Democrats into hard bargaining."[21]

On the House side, Barber Conable was also "dismayed by the general fear tactics used by the Democrats" in the course of the election campaign of 1982. "Pat Moynihan, for instance," he wrote in his journal,

despite having a totally inconsiderable opponent in Florence Sullivan—an assemblywoman from Brooklyn who spent only $100,000 while he spent 20 times that amount, and who is a pathetic speaker and candidate generally—felt he wanted to exploit the Social Security issue, because his wife had persuaded him that he was going to be beaten. Since Pat is my friend and I consider him a man of some quality, I was dismayed by this. I heard radio commercials in which he claimed twice to have saved Social Security from cutbacks by Republicans and in which he promised that if the people of New York would reelect him, he wouldn't let "them touch it." It was a demagogic performance, making Pat sound like a "know nothing," and I was so angry that I voted for him with reluctance and gave an interview to *Newsweek* which was published a week after the election, in which I said he had rendered himself useless to the Social Security Commission by his tactics during the campaign. I said he had engaged in "unconscionable blather on the issue."[22]

"Here's a brilliant man," Conable told *Newsweek*, "who totally flipped."[23]

At the first day of the planned three-day commission meeting shortly after the *Newsweek* article hit the newsstand, Conable wrote in his journal, "Pat came up to me without a smile on his face, put his finger in my chest, and said to me, 'You, sir, have engaged in an ethnic slur.'"

"Well, Pat," Conable retorted, "if you're going to engage in blather, you've got to expect to be called a blatherer."

"The conversation went downhill from there and we were obviously both disturbed by the falling out we had had," Conable recalled afterwards.[24]

"Negotiations of the commission during this three-day meeting were widely televised and largely unsuccessful," Conable also recorded in his journal.

> We did agree on the dimensions of the problem, finding that the Social Security system had a short-term deficit between now and 1990 of $150 to $200 billion and that it had a long-term deficit of 1.8 percent payroll [that is, the amount of immediate increase in Social Security taxes it would take to put the program on sound financial footing into the middle of the twenty-first century.] That the commission was able to come up with such a statement of the nature of the problem was astonishing since some commission members, most notably Claude Pepper, had been campaigning two weeks before, all over the country, on the grounds that there was nothing wrong with Social Security that couldn't be corrected by getting people back to work. Claude had been in 41 congressional districts, putting his arm around the Democratic candidate and saying to the people of that district, "If you'll vote for my friend here, he'll promise not to touch Social Security."
>
> We were able to agree on some other modest matters such as the desirability of putting everyone at some sacrifice rather than loading the whole burden on any one group. We were also able to agree that federal employees should be covered by Social Security, although the details were not in any way nailed down due to the fierce opposition of Lane Kirkland, a member of the commission, whose public employees' unions are now the cutting edge of his AFL-CIO organized labor movement, and who fear that if they were covered by Social Security, Congress would find some way to water down federal retirement plans. Congress will never do that.

"Beyond that," Conable wrote, "we were not able to agree at all and after three days of negotiations, mostly off camera, we adjourned subject to the call of the chair. The commission is due to go out of existence, after a presidential extension having been granted, on January 15. It was apparent that no progress would be made without the full participation and consent of the principals, namely Tip O'Neill and Ronald Reagan."

In a last-ditch effort to get the principals to the negotiating table, Conable made an impassioned plea to the Speaker on the first day of the lame-duck session of Congress. "It's not too late," Conable told the Speaker in a speech on the floor of the House on November 29. He summarizes the speech in his journal: "The chances of resolving the Social Security crisis with lame-duck votes were considerably greater than the chance of our resolving it with the first votes of freshmen [in the next Congress], many of whom would not be there if they had not used the Social Security issue prominently in a negative way . . . It would take some time to organize the new Congress and [since] interfund borrowing had been terminated as of January 1, 1983, . . . the crisis would be on us [with only six months of extended interfund borrowing permitted under the 1981 law] before July 3, 1983. . . . My words might as well as fallen into a black hole, so completely did they disappear and so little stir did they create."

Failing with O'Neill, Conable "then wrote a long letter to President Reagan telling him that there was no chance of this issue being resolved if he did not pick up the phone and say to Tip, 'We've got to get together and discuss this as principals.' I take it that my letter was read at the White House" he recalled, "but there was no apparent response. As a result, the 97th Congress went to its reward with no progress on Social Security except for the definition of the nature of the problem."[25]

Thus, Conable failed with his 1981 conference-committee strategy to get Congress to enact Social Security reform during the lame-duck session of the Ninety-seventh Congress at the end of 1982. But the six-month extension on interfund borrowing, which had also been part of the 1981 law to give Congress a little extra time to solve the crisis, would now force the new Congress, with even more urgency, to find a solution to the Social Security problem before the system went bankrupt in July 1983.

Gang of Nine

With the deadline for the commission report set for January 15 and the Social Security system projected to go bankrupt in July, the new Ninety-eighth Congress convened on January 3, 1983.

Following the swearing in of new members in the Senate, as Conable tells the story, Pat Moynihan followed Bob Dole back to his office and said to Dole: "Are we going to leave this where it is? Are we going to let the checks not go out in July?"

"What in the hell do you expect?" Dole said. "You guys killed it."

"Well now, let's not get too excited about this," Moynihan said. "I could go for making some of the changes you [Republicans] have been suggesting."

Encouraged by what he heard, Dole immediately called the commission chairman, Alan Greenspan, in New York and said, "Pat's here in my office and he says he could go along with some of the changes we want to make."

"Well, I'm coming right down," Greenspan said. "Hold him there and let's talk."

Greenspan immediately flew down to Washington. Later he called Jim Baker, Reagan's chief of staff, to tell him about the conversation he had with Dole and Moynihan.

Seeing some possibility for a breakthrough, Baker said, "Let's have some secret discussion [like they had previously with the Gang of Seventeen] and see if we can figure out what we can do here."[26]

As Conable recalled it later, the three of them—Dole, Moynihan, and Greenspan—then met with Baker. "They needed to get enough people so that they could reach everybody in the various levels of ideology. They figured that with Dole and Moynihan, they had the Senate taken care of. But they needed somebody who would appeal to the liberal Democrats more fairly than Moynihan could, and they settled on Bob Ball, the former commissioner of Social Security who was a real liberal. Then they said, 'We gotta get somebody from the House,' and Moynihan said," still feeling bad about the derogatory comments Conable had made about him in the press following the November elections, " 'Let's get Barber Conable. He thinks I'm not worth anything. I want him to know I'm working on it.' " So they decided to have Conable represent the House.[27]

Representing the White House in these secret negotiations were Jim Baker, his deputy chief of staff, Richard Darman, Budget Director Stockman, and the head of the White House congressional liaison office, Kenneth Duberstein. All four had been members of the Gang of Seventeen in 1982 and were thoroughly versed in the politics of Social Security reform. Together, they would work with the four representatives from Congress and Bob Ball—now collectively dubbed the Gang of Nine—to see what could be done to rescue Social Security by the January 15 commission deadline.

The operating rules of the Gang of Nine would be the same as the rules established earlier for the Gang of Seventeen. None of the members were allowed to bring any of their staff. All meetings would be held in secret "with no records or transcripts." Though they would not be present at the meetings, everyone knew from the start that the two principal figures were Ronald Reagan and Tip O'Neill. There would be no agreement unless Reagan and O'Neill both consented. Stockman would represent Reagan and Ball would be the spokesman for O'Neill.

The National Commission essentially became a "front" organization for the secret negotiations conducted by the Gang of Nine, as it had been earlier for the Gang of Seventeen. Once the Gang of Nine finished its negotiations, it would report back to the National Commission, which hopefully would then be able to make a strong recommendation for resolving the Social Security crisis acceptable to the president and Congress. The normal legislative process had broken down, and the leaders of the two branches now sought secret negotiations as a way out of their impasse.

The group held its first meeting on Wednesday morning, January 5, 1983, at Jim Baker's home on Foxhall Road. The White House did not offer a formal proposal at the first meeting. "They didn't want specifics," one participant revealed. "Just proportions; a 50-50 deal. It would be up to Congress to fill in the blanks." Though Ball and Moynihan objected, thinking they could get a better deal for the congressional Democrats, the White House pushed for a reform package that would be 50 percent benefits cut and 50 percent tax increases.

After about an hour of general discussion, the first meeting adjourned. White House limousines returned for a second round of negotiations at four o'clock. The negotiations quickly turned into an exchange between Stockman and Ball. "Every hour," another participant recalled, "Baker would announce that he could not guarantee the president's support. And one of the Democrats would say they could not guarantee the Speaker's support. It was a ritual. The Republicans would say, 'You have to give us something we can take to the president,' and the Democrats would say, 'You have to give us something we can take to Claude Pepper.'"

The group met again on Friday, January 7, and on Saturday, January 8. On Saturday afternoon, they took time off to watch the Washington Redskin-Detroit Lions football game. "The Skins-Lions game was an important diversion and helped cool us off," one White House participant remembered. "There was already an almost self-fulfilling drive for an agreement. Things like the football game helped us reestablish our commitment after we had some pretty serious fights. We were able to get together and root for the home team."

They also found themselves playing "games with the media." Though the media quickly found out about the secret meetings, the discussions themselves were never revealed. "This is a very open town," Conable confided to Light at the time. "Everyone knows about the meetings and wants to find out who said what.. We're going to hold the meetings in different locations, try to confuse the press, and hope that nothing slips out. It's fun in a way, relieves the tension. We all like to play cops-and-robbers."

Each of the nine members of the group played important but different roles in the discussions. Stockman and Ball, "the two numbers men," took the lead in the negotiations, "throwing statistics around . . . and debating the basic formulas. It was up to them to sift through the technical bull, and up to us to make the political decisions," one member said.

The other White House representatives—Baker, Darman and Duberstein—were quiet during most of the negotiations, as were Conable, Dole and Moynihan. With negotiations at a critical phase, they all wanted to wait until an agreement was almost at hand before revealing their positions.

Commission Chairman Greenspan was also quiet during the meetings. "He's really a very shy man," one participant observed, "and not used to hard bargaining. He was great when it came time to define the problem. People trusted his judgment, and thought he was fair. But when it came time for some hardball politics, he wasn't cut out for it."

With Stockman and Ball leading the way, "it was clear by Saturday, January 8, that the Republicans were willing to accept some tax increases while Democrats were willing to take some COLA cuts. The major question was, how much?"

The two sides spent the next week in intense negotiations trying to hammer out their differences. By Friday, January 14, one day before the commission was scheduled to go out of business, they had reached substantial agreement on a number of issues. After discussing dozens of options for solving both the short- and long-term crises in Social Security, the Democrats agreed to a permanent, six-month COLA delay, with an estimated savings to the system of about $40 billion. They also agreed to bring new federal employees, hired after December 31, 1984, into the Social Security system, a concession worth another $20 billion.

In exchange, the Republicans agreed to accelerate the planned 1990 payroll tax increase (called for in the 1977 law that had been enacted during the Carter administration) in two parts. They agreed to an early payroll tax increase in 1984 and another one in 1988, bringing the total Social Security tax rate to 7.65 percent, a full two years ahead of the original starting date. To balance out the Democrats' concession on the COLA delay, this Republican concession also amounted to about $40 billion. In addition, the Republicans agreed to accept higher Social Security taxes on the self-employed, worth another $18 billion.

These concessions, plus a few others, notably an accounting maneuver involving military benefits, amounted to about $140 billion in the short run and covered a third of the projected long-term debt in Social Security. As impressive as these concessions were, however, the group still needed to find more money to solve both the short-term and long-term crises in the system. But neither side seemed willing to accept more taxes or benefit cuts.

The compromise solution came at the eleventh hour when both sides reluctantly agreed to tax Social Security benefits. By taxing Social Security benefits at the upper-income level, they estimated that they could raise an additional $36 billion in the short run and finance one-third of the long-term debt.

The idea of taxing Social Security benefits had originated with the liberal commissioner, Bob Ball. "He had won the Speaker's support for the idea in November, and he had talked with most of the commission members about the proposal. Though the Senate had rejected the notion twice in 1981, it did raise a great deal of money. More important," as Paul Light notes, "it was all things to all people. Consider the label: 'taxation of benefits.' Was it a tax increase or a benefit cut? In fact, it was both. 'It could be called taxes or benefits, depending on which ax you wanted to grind,' a White House participant said. 'It was a tax increase to Democrats, but a benefit cut to Republicans.' In reality, it was a deep benefit cut for upper-income retirees, achieved through the income tax."

With the gang's agreement to accept taxation of benefits as part of the final package, negotiations proceeded swiftly toward a conclusion. As one of the White House participants noted: "That was the breakthrough, if there was one. Once we broke through with that, everything else was easy. That put us at around $160 to $170 billion, and that's all we needed in the short run."

But the gang still faced a sizable long-term problem. Even with the taxation of benefits, the package would cover only about two-thirds of the long-term debt, or 1.2 percent of the needed 1.8 percent increase in taxable payroll. The Gang of Nine could not agree on the final one-third of the long-term solution. The Democrats advocated another tax increase to close the gap, while the Republicans favored an increase in the retirement age. Unable to resolve this conflict, the group decided to leave the final decision to Congress. "Besides," as one member noted, "Danny Rostenkowski [as chairman of the Ways and Means Committee] would need something to do anyway," once the commission's recommendations were submitted to Congress.

Before sending the package to Reagan and O'Neill, the Gang of Nine submitted its recommendations to the National Commission on Social Security Reform. The commission "had provided the cover for secret bargaining," and now it would have the responsibility of acting on the gang's recommendations for saving Social Security. With only hours to go before the January 15 deadline, Greenspan called the commission into session for the first time since December 10. "We wanted at least an 11 to 4 vote," one commissioner recalled. "It had to look like the commission was in agreement." The major obstacles to a strong, bipartisan majority would be Claude Pepper and the representatives of the business community.

Pepper was the first one to accept the compromise package. Conable remembered sitting in the front room of the Blair House where the meeting was held and hearing Bob Ball explain the package to Pepper on the phone.

"You haven't cut anything have you?" Pepper asked Ball.

"Well technically not, but . . . you should understand there's a six-month COLA that's going to be dropped out and never picked up, and you could call that a cut."

"Oh no, no, it just sounds like a little postponement to me," Pepper said.

"He turned down his hearing aid. He wanted to go along in other words," Conable recalled. "He realized he was in trouble, despite the fact that he claimed that there was nothing wrong with Social Security."[28]

The business representatives, however, were more reluctant to accept the compromises. They had strong reservations about the size of the tax increases. The most outspoken critics, Senator Armstrong and Congressman Archer, were hoping to persuade all four business representatives to vote against the compromise package, leaving a nine-to-six majority, hardly the ringing endorsement supporters sought.

The business opposition remained strong until Saturday afternoon when the White House entered the battle with force. "You should have seen it. Fuller, Beck, and Trowbridge all got calls from the president," a gang member recalled. "It was tremendous pressure. I'll never forget the look on Mary Fuller's face after she got her call. She was white as a sheet and told us that she was going to support the package." Joe Waggoner, however, Conable's former Ways and Means colleague and the fourth outside representative of business interest on the commission, remained unshakable and joined Archer and Armstrong in opposition to the compromise package.

Late in the afternoon, there were still some last-minute calls to be made. As Greenspan remembered: "The last thing was the tricky problem of getting everybody within an hour's time to all agree to this document, all contingent on everyone else's agreement. What we had going is that the president would agree if the Speaker would agree, if the commission would agree."

Around four o'clock, a call was placed to O'Neill in Palm Springs, California, where he was playing golf with Rostenkowski in the Bob Hope Desert Classic. While they waited for Rostenkowski to return the phone call, some of the commission members watched a Redskins-Vikings football game, and Stockman and Baker walked over to the White House to discuss the agreement with Reagan.

Despite Rostenkowski's initial reluctance to endorse the commission's recommendations, O'Neill called back early in the evening and said that he would accept the package. Reagan also agreed. "In the span of not more than twenty minutes," Light notes, "the two principals agreed, the commission debated the package, and the final vote was taken." The National Commission agreed to the compromise package submitted by the Gang of Nine by a vote of twelve to three, with the archconservatives Archer, Armstrong, and Waggoner voting against the agreement.

"It was pretty tense up to the end," Conable reported after the vote. "We would meet for two or three hours, then go consult with our principals or interest groups. It is impossible to say who blinked first."

Despite all their hard bargaining, however, the commissioners did not allow themselves to celebrate after the vote. "We were concerned that cheers would break . . . [the agreement] apart," another commissioner added.

The Gang of Nine proposal now became the National Commission agreement. This is the way it was labeled throughout the congressional debate that followed. Members who did not like the package would be able to say they were just following the commission's recommendations. "The commission label," as Light points out, "would provide a shield against public outcry and a way to explain a painful vote back home. The package would be sold as the product of a year-long bipartisan study, not two weeks of secret negotiations."[29]

Congress and President Approve Commission Recommendations

With the adoption of the Gang of Nine's compromise package by the National Commission, full attention turned to selling the plan to Congress. Though the president, the Speaker, and the majority leaders in both houses backed the commission recommendations, passage of the plan was by no means a certainty. "This so-called compromise is a very fragile one," a lobbyist for the elderly cautioned. "If any one component is knocked out, it will all fall like a house of cards."

To prevent the unraveling of the package, the supporters of the commission plan designed a three-pronged strategy. First, they would try to push the package through Congress as fast as possible, hopefully before the Easter recess which began on March 25, and before the interest groups had a chance to mobilize their opposition. Second, they would try to prevent the adding of any unrelated amendment to the package which could slow down or defeat the entire legislation. Third, they would present the package as "an all-or-nothing proposition." The compromises within the package were all delicately balanced, Conable warned, and "any change in the basic balance [would] threaten . . . the whole package." Unfortunately, however, the National Commission had left one-third of the long-term problem unresolved, and Congress would have to do something to solve that part of the problem.[30]

Putting this strategy in place, Rostenkowski, now fully behind the National Commission's efforts, began hearings on the commission recommendations in the Ways and Means Committee on February 1. In front of national television cameras, the commission chairman, Alan Greenspan, explained the commission's recommendations and took questions from members of the committee. The following exchange Greenspan had with his fellow commissioner, Barber Conable, now back in his chair as the Republican leader of Ways and Means, reflected the basic legislative strategy for getting the commission's compromise package adopted and the friendly atmosphere that existed in the Ways and Means Committee:

> *Conable*: Is there any part of this, Mr. Greenspan, that you think could be taken out and the compromise still preserve its essential outline?

> *Greenspan*: I am certain that if you press me for every single line and word, I might suggest that it is possible, but anything substantive, anything which resembles a critical element in the negotiation, I would say no. We struggled very hard.
>
> *Conable*: In your long-standing capacity as an economist associated with the government in various ways, have you made any effort to estimate what might happen if this agreement fails?
>
> *Greenspan*: In the event that somehow or by some means Congress fails to resolve this question . . . I am most fearful that the international financial markets would take this as a terribly negative signal, that our domestic markets would perceive it as a verification of their already deep-seated view that the Federal budget is out of control, that it will create a reign of inflationary forces, and that . . . would push long-term interest rates up from where they are, would abort a nascent recovery and I think create a problem for this nation which I have very great difficulty even contemplating.[31]

After three days of Ways and Means hearings, Rostenkowski referred the commission recommendations to the Subcommittee on Social Security for further deliberations. The major dispute in the subcommittee centered on how to resolve the one-third of the long-term deficit problem. Continuing to push his own reform agenda, the subcommittee chairman, Jake Pickle, advocated gradually raising the retirement age from sixty-five to sixty-seven and reducing benefits for early retirees. While individuals would still be able to take early retirement at age sixty-two, under the Pickle plan their benefits would be reduced from the current 80 percent of full benefits to 70 percent in 2027.

Pepper, on the other hand, who had become chairman of the Rules Committee in the new Congress, continued to oppose an increase in the retirement age and vowed never to let such a proposal come to a vote on the House floor. He preferred instead to increase payroll taxes (by an additional half percentage point in 2010) as a way to solve the long-term deficit problem.

Seeking to avoid a divisive conflict on this issue in the Ways and Means Committee, Rostenkowski worked out a deal with the Speaker to allow both Pickle and Pepper to present their respective solutions on the floor of the House when the bill came up for a vote.

With this arrangement fully understood, the Ways and Means Committee voted thirty-two to three on March 2 to report the Social Security package to the House. Reminiscent of Conable's early days in Congress when Wilbur Mills and John Byrnes ran the Ways and Means Committee, Dan Rostenkowski and Barber Conable had succeeded in putting together a strong bipartisan coalition on a major piece of legislation. Conable and all but three of his Republican colleagues voted with the twenty-three Democrats on the committee to report a Social Security bill that closely resembled the package recommended by the National Commission.

The bill, as reported by the Ways and Means Committee, brought all new federal employees into the Social Security system for the first time, raised payroll taxes by accelerating the scheduled 1990 tax increases, delayed the July COLA for six months, and taxed Social Security benefits for high-income individuals. The package agreed to by the Ways and Means Committee was expected to raise about $165 billion—enough to meet the system's immediate financial need—and also solve about two-thirds of the long-term crisis in Social Security going into the twenty-first century. The full House was left to decide between the Pickle amendment to raise the retirement age and the Pepper amendment to raise payroll taxes as the best way to finance the additional one-third of the long-term debt.

According to the rule agreed to by the Rules Committee, the House would first vote on the Pickle amendment and then the Pepper amendment. If for some reason, both amendments passed, the Pepper amendment to raise payroll taxes would supersede the Pickle amendment to increase the retirement age.

On the day of the dramatic floor vote on March 9, few observers gave the Pickle amendment much chance of passage. But to the surprise of many, seventy-six Democrats voted with all but fourteen of the 166 Republicans to pass the Pickle amendment by a margin of 228 to 202. Continuing their cooperation on Social Security reform, Rostenkowski and eleven of the Democratic members of the Ways and Means Committee joined with Conable and all twelve Republicans in supporting the Pickle amendment raising the retirement age.[32]

Shocked by the passage of the Pickle amendment, Pepper then made an impassioned plea for the House to enact his tax increase amendment and turn aside the Pickle amendment. "He spoke for 34 minutes on this issue and then came to me [as the Republican floor manager for the bill] and asked if I would give him some of my time," Conable wrote in his journal afterwards.

> I was not planning to have much debate on it since we had already passed the Pickle amendment, which called

for the raising of the retirement age, but it was subject to substitution by the Pepper amendment if the majority wanted to do so. After consulting with my Republican leadership, I refused to give him any of my time and brought the issue to a vote as quickly as possible, substantially foreclosing a large number of Democrats who wanted to rise and use any available time to reassert the Republican determination to cut benefits rather than raising the money in some other way. Claude wept on the floor when we beat him on this issue [396 to 132], then voted, after some delay, for the final product, thus assuring the large majority of Democrats would support it. The bare majority of the Republicans supported it also, and so the issue passed comfortably [282 to 148] and then went to the Senate where it was also comfortably passed [88 to 9].[33]

Anxious to pass the Social Security legislation before Congress adjourned for the Easter-recess, a conference committee convened at 9:00 A.M. on March 24 to resolve the few remaining differences between the House and Senate versions of the bill. With Rostenkowski and Conable leading the House conferees, the House prevailed on most of the items on which the two chambers were in disagreement.

At ten o'clock that evening the House met for final passage of the legislation. "Rostenkowski rose to praise the conference; Pickle rose to praise Rostenkowski and Conable; Conable rose to praise the House. It was, in the words of one House member, 'a love feast.'"

"We all relinquished some long-cherished objectives in the process," Conable told the House. "It was painful, but the sacrifice was well worth the effort and the result. This conference report may not be a work of art, but it is artful work."[34]

With less than twenty minutes of discussion, the House of Representatives passed the conference report by the huge margin of 243 to 102 with 88 members having already left for the Easter recess. The House had already passed the Social Security bill once, and now all they needed to know was that they had prevailed on most of the disagreements with the Senate before moving on to final passage. Despite his opposition to the higher retirement age, Pepper voted for the legislation as did most of the Democrats, while a majority of the Republicans voted against the compromise package.

"Conable's first words upon leaving the floor were, 'It was just like the good old days.' Ways and Means was once again the great legislative engine on Social Security, rolling up a large committee majority on its bill, and winning easily on the floor and in conference. Conable and his Republicans were once again part of the game, a key part of Rostenkowski's strategy for passing the bill. Little wonder," Light notes, "Conable was reminded of the good old days."[35]

Passage of the Social Security rescue package was more problematic in the Senate, which had lost to the House on most of the legislative issues in the conference committee and where a group of disgruntled conservative Republicans were strongly opposed to the final package. But thanks to impassioned pleas from Senator Moynihan, who now saw his work on the National Commission jeopardized in the Senate, and from the Republican Majority Leader Howard Baker, the Senate also passed the conference report by the surprisingly comfortable margin of fifty-eight to fourteen, with twenty-eight senators having already departed for the holiday.

The White House decided to wait until Congress returned from Easter recess for Reagan to sign the bill. Then, on April 20, before a large audience on the lawn of the White House, the president signed the bill into law. "None of us here today would pretend that this bill is perfect," Reagan said. "Each of us had to compromise one way or another. But the essence of bipartisanship is to give a little in order to get a lot." In a bipartisan gesture to the Democrats, Tip O'Neill was invited to speak to the audience before the signing, describing the occasion as "a happy day for America." Howard Baker also addressed the crowd, noting: "There are issues that are more important than any of us, or perhaps all of us, taken together. The preservation of the Social Security system is one of those issues."

After the speeches, President Reagan signed the Social Security Amendments Act of 1983 into law. Barber Conable, Dan Rostenkowski, Claude Pepper, Tip O'Neill, Bob Dole, and Pat Moynihan were all given souvenir pens to commemorate their struggle. The long battle to save Social Security was over—at least for the time being.[36]

Thus, the deadline Conable had gotten Congress to set in November 1981 for resolving the Social Security crisis by July 3, 1983, had worked to push Congress toward a resolution of this crisis. "Once again," Conable wrote in his journal afterwards, Congress had shown its tendency to act "only at the last possible moment and that our system of government is a crisis-activated system of government."[37]

"Some things just aren't pretty to watch or easy to do," Conable later said, reflecting on the political process that produced the Social Security reforms of 1983.

> I've never seen a glamorous opossum or a graceful giraffe. Divorces are never comfortable. The seriously overweight should stay away from short shorts. Deep mud doesn't make light movements. A politician has a hard time looking relaxed when found with his hand in the cookie jar.
> In the same way, government, which has a great time making people happy by allotting surpluses, always looks awkward—and sometimes downright foolish—when it tries to deal with shortages. If that government is a democracy, it will go through the most remarkable contortions to avoid unpleasant duties, even when everyone understands the necessity and yearns for grace under pressure.[38]

Looking Back and Forward

I asked Conable in August 2000 if he thought the reforms he had helped enact in 1983 had worked.

"You bet they have," he responded with obvious pride in what he had helped accomplish.

"I found it ironic, though, that after twenty years in Congress and being such a strong advocate of open representative government, you would end up describing your participation on the Social Security Commission and secretive Gang of Nine as 'the high point of [your] legislative career,'" I said.

"So did I," he replied. "But I came to regard the sunshine laws to be less important and useful than I had originally thought, and certainly they were not very helpful in resolving the Social Security crisis we faced in 1983. The press was so anxious to see everything that happened in Social Security that Social Security was called the 'third rail of American politics; you touch it and you die.' So we were determined not to have contact with the press."[39]

"Is Social Security going to be there for the young generation?" asked a young student assistant who accompanied me on the interview.

"Yes," Conable responded. "Congress will never let Social Security fail. They'll find a way to save it, even if they have to dump general treasury money into it. They will do it, because Social Security is so important to people. So I wouldn't worry about it.

If they let Social Security fail, they'll be all executed by some state tribunal."

"What kind of decisions do you think will have to be made over the next fifty years to save Social Security?" I asked.

"The big decision that has to be made is raising the retirement age," he said.

"Again?" I asked.

"Oh, hell yes," he said. "If you ran a poll nowadays, people will tell you that people are getting old when they are seventy-five, not when they are sixty-five. . . . And there is the terrible problem that we're going to be short labor. And so we've got to stop giving people an economic incentive to retire at sixty-five."

"What do you think would be a good retirement age for Social Security?" I asked. "I think it should be set well in advance, like the 1983 reforms, to go up very gradually, to seventy or whatever age can be agreed to. The savings between sixty-five and seventy are hundreds of billions of dollars over a period of time. That's the best thing to do. I would not favor raising the Social Security tax, because, as I've always said, it's a regressive tax. It hits poor people harder than it hits rich people."[40]

The Social Security reforms that Conable helped enact in 1983 were enormously successful in extending the life of Social Security into the twenty-first century. But these reforms did not guarantee the solvency of the system indefinitely, as the recent creation of yet another presidential commission on Social Security reform by President George W. Bush in 2001 indicates. According to 2002 estimates, payroll taxes will not be sufficient to pay benefits after 2016 as the baby boomers born in the 1950s begin to retire and receive benefits. By 2043, as the young generation today starts to retire, the Social Security Trust Fund will become exhausted and the system will be able to finance only 75 percent of current benefits from payroll taxes.[41]

At some point, therefore, in the near future Congress will face another financial crisis in Social Security, which, like the last crisis, will activate Congress into either raising taxes or reducing benefits. Future reform efforts are no more likely than the last reforms to be a "work of art," but they will require, as Conable said, the "artful work" of compromise if they are to be successful.

Chapter 14

Concluding a Congressional Career

"I am not seeking reelection in 1984," Conable announced in a brief one page statement he released to the press in Washington and back home in his district on February 4, 1984. He had hinted as far back as 1978 that he might retire from Congress to pursue other interests. But when his final decision to leave actually came, it was a surprise and disappointment to many of his colleagues and constituents.

"I have enjoyed my job," Conable said.

It is good to be a participant in interesting events, to have responsibility and the challenge of diversity. Service as a representative is a privilege which should not be granted or received lightly. The work is not easy, but it is made easier by the patience of family and friends and the faith and support of good people. I am grateful for these. It would be difficult not to be proud of the individuals and communities in western New York I have been representing for 20 years.

Representative government is more important to the American people than many realize. For all its flaws, it does tend to give the public what the public wants, and the responsibility flows both ways. Representative institutions remain vigorous only if there is a frequent infusion of new ideas so that each generation can have its own expression of the dialogue of representation, which constantly changes with popular expectations and circumstances. Everyone is entitled to his own time-frame: for me, 20 years is long enough.[1]

In talking to the press after his announcement, Conable said that he did not know what he would do after his retirement from Congress, but indicated that he would probably return to his home in western New York. He emphasized, however, that he would definitely not become a Washington lawyer or lobbyist. "There is nothing wrong with being a Washington lawyer," he said, "only that it would be an uncomfortable role for me."[2]

Public Reaction

Conable's retirement announcement "caught most of his colleagues by surprise," and according to the *Washington Post*, "produced expressions of regret far stronger than is customary."

"I'm really disturbed. I just wish he was staying, because he's one of the most brilliant men I've ever known," said Rep. John J. Duncan of Tennessee, next in line to succeed Conable as the ranking Republican on the Ways and Means Committee. "I'd rather be second in line and have him there as ranking."

Conable "is a remarkable intellectual and moral force in Congress," the Ways and Means Chairman Dan Rostenkowski noted. Conable's old friend, Vice President George Bush, hailed him as "one of the most sane and able men in the whole United States Congress."

"He's one of the finest people that I know," said Democratic colleague on the Ways and Means Committee, Sam Gibbons of

Florida. "He's independent and he's got a very bright brain and [he's] got a great grasp. I just am terribly disturbed that he's retiring. He's the kind of person that has to strain to be partisan. He's always thinking of the best for the country."

"I think he's one of the giants of this place on either side of the aisle, and I don't use those words frequently," another Republican Ways and Means colleague, Bill Gradison of Ohio, observed.

Noting that Conable was the fifth senior Republican to announce his retirement at the end of the term, House Minority Leader Bob Michel blamed Conable's retirement, and the exodus of other senior Republicans, on the "unfair treatment of the Republican minority by the Democratic majority."[3]

District officials and constituents were equally shocked and saddened by Conable's announced retirement. With 80 percent of Conable's congressional district now in metropolitan Monroe County, the rural and small-town Genesee County Republicans, who had always formed the backbone of Conable's congressional career, were particularly concerned about losing the seat to Monroe County. "We've always known that after we lose Barber [the seat would] probably go to Monroe County, because they're bigger," the head of the Genesee County Republicans, Amy Torrey, noted. "We feel pretty bad about it. But it was Barber's decision and he gave it a lot of thought."[4]

The chairman of the Monroe County Republican Party, Ron Starkweather, who was always one of Conable's strongest local supporters, was equally distressed at the news of his retirement. "He's not just a western New York figure, he's a national figure," Starkweather said. "Nobody's indispensable, but Barber Conable comes as close as anyone I've known in public life."[5]

Local Democratic leaders also regretted Conable's departure. "I'll be very sorry to see him leave," Thomas P. Ryan, mayor of Rochester, said. "Despite obvious philosophical differences, he has been a very good congressman to work with, very knowledgeable, a very decent person."[6]

Louise Slaughter, a Democratic state assemblywoman from Monroe County, who would eventually succeed Conable in Congress in 1987, agreed. "I think he is an extraordinary man, extremely capable and [he] represented us well. . . . His reason and intellect are going to be missed."[7]

Karl Buchholtz, Conable's old friend at the Genesee Hardware Store in Batavia where he had been meeting with friends for Saturday morning coffee and donuts since 1952, was particularly distressed with Conable's decision to leave Congress. "When he came to Batavia, he was just a young man," Buchholtz told a Rochester reporter. "Not many people knew him. In no time at all, he went to the top. I bleed that he's leaving."

"Buchholtz's words were echoed from Main Street Batavia to Rochester, as Conable's varied friends lamented his decision to leave Congress," Chris Lavin wrote for the *Rochester Times-Union* the day after Conable announced his decision to retire.

> Conable, they said, is a special kind of politician, a man who abhors pork barrel legislation, a man who uses honesty and a strong mind to win over rural residents, city dwellers—Republicans and Democrats alike.
>
> "I'm very sad," said Donald Hess, a University of Rochester vice president, who often worked with Conable on higher education legislation. "He was far better than a congressman. He was a statesman. He didn't localize issues. He would give us a fair hearing and then decide in the national interest. . . . We're about to lose a giant."
>
> Hess said Conable's quick grasp of complex issues and his seniority in the House may be impossible to replace. "I don't know if anybody can equal him," Hess said.[8]

With his decision to retire, Conable's reputation among the national press corps and his House colleagues soared even higher. In a February 8 editorial entitled "The Conable Conscience," the *New York Times* paid special tribute to Conable's service in Congress. "As a Republican and an incumbent, he has always stood to gain from an electoral system that heavily depends on campaign financing from special interests," the *New York Times* wrote. "But since 1967, when he joined Ways and Means, Barber Conable has refused to accept campaign contributions of more than $50. . . . Mr. Conable has announced that he will not run again this year. It will be a loss not only for his constituents but for us all."[9]

A few days later in a long editorial on February 13, the *Washington Post* tried to put Conable's twenty-year congressional career in broader, historical perspective.

> For years it has been a tradition for districts in rural America, stretching from New England west through upstate New York to the midwest, to elect some of the most talented young men to the House of Representatives. If the district is wise enough to pick a man of longevity and character and intellect, he can hope to become one of the natural leaders of the Republicans in the House.
>
> Barber Conable, who announced his retirement from the House last week, is a good example.

When he was first elected to the House in 1964, he was a 42-year-old Cornell-trained lawyer and ex-Marine, one-term state senator from Alexander, N.Y.—a hamlet near Rochester settled in the rush westward along the Erie Canal route in the early 19th century. Elected in a year his party was routed, Mr. Conable was scarcely noticed as he entered the House and, two years later, became a member of the Ways and Means Committee.

Now his departure from the House is widely regretted, and not just by his constituents or his fellow Republicans. One of Mr. Conable's achievements has been to bring an unusual degree of civility and intellectual integrity to legislative deliberations—and fights. On a committee that considers tax legislation worth billions, he has decided issues on their merits, and his example has moved others to do so too. He has recognized a duty to his party—with unfortunate results, in our view, in his sponsorship of the Reagan administration's tax cut measures in 1981. But his work on Social Security and trade, and on tax measures generally has been exceedingly valuable. He has elevated, and by a considerable measure, the workings of the legislative process.[10]

In April, Conable's House colleagues voted him the "most respected member" of the House of Representatives from either political party in a survey conducted by the *U.S. News and World Report*. Conable outpolled some of the major leaders of the House, such as Majority Leader Jim Wright, who came in second in the poll, Speaker Tip O'Neill, who was third, Mo Udall of Arizona, who came in fourth, and Minority Leader Bob Michel, who was ranked fifth in the poll.[11]

Though this award gained Conable considerable recognition in the press, he himself took it all in stride, noting in his journal, with his characteristic blend of realism and detachment: "My colleagues voted me in the *U.S. News and World Report* annual poll the 'most respected member' of the House and they voted Howard Baker [the Senate Republican majority leader from Tennessee, who had also announced his retirement at the end of the term] the 'most respected member' of the Senate, leading me to believe that statesmanship is somewhat closely related to the announcement of retirement."[12]

In early June, as if the Washington journalists were trying to see who could outdo whom in their praise of the retiring Barber Conable, the conservative columnist George Will weighed in with the most flattering piece yet on Conable in an editorial he wrote for *Newsweek*.

The framers of our Constitution were framing away just fine in Philadelphia in 1787 until they got to the eighth paragraph of the ninth section of the first Article, where they committed an 11-word blunder: 'No title of nobility shall be granted by the United States.' . . . Talk about tossing out the baby with the bath water. . . . We should repeal this prohibition on titles and establish a House of Lords. . . .

This thought acquires special urgency from the fact that one of my pinups, Rep. Barber Conable of New York, ranking Republican on the Ways and Means Committee, is calling it quits after 20 years in Congress.

There never has been a better congressman and, judging by the newsletter he writes, if he now does what he ought to do—starts writing a column—the rest of us in the business will be competing for only the silver medal. No one can blame Conable from growing weary of life in the minority, a life of predictable defeats. It is like being regularly bashed in the back of the head with a sock full of wet sand, and it is not likely to change soon for House Republicans. Conable also is, no doubt, weary of running for reelection every two years. Truth be told, he should not have to. In a rationally designed society it would be a flogging offense to try to unseat a congressman this good.

Will's preferred solution to Conable's retirement was the creation of an American House of Lords with Conable and other senior statesmen appointed to an

upper-upper House, which will meet in the Capitol, in the old Supreme Court chamber, hard by the Senate. It will be easy to swell the ranks with persons whose guile, charm and wisdom have enlivened public life. We can start by making Melvin Laird (former congressman, defense secretary and other things) the Laird of Wisconsin. . . . Stir in Gene McCarthy, John Connally, Bob Strauss, Beverly Sills, Murray Kempton, Earl Weaver, Mayor Koch [and] Clare Luce. You think cable television coverage of Tip O'Neill's wrath is entertainment? Let the government put my House of Lords on pay television and we can balance the budget. We could have balanced it already if more of Conable's peers (not that he really has any) in the House had listened to him. It would be nice to balance it by selling the public the privilege of listening to him and the rest of the peerage.

Conable is talking about doing some teaching. But he, like sex and Victorian novels, would be wasted on undergraduates. If he will consent to become Earl of Upstate

New York, I will promise to tug my forelock wherever I am admitted to his presence. But then, I do that anyway.[13]

Reasons for Retirement

Much of the press reporting about Conable's retirement centered on the reasons for his retirement.[14] Why would a man at the relatively young age of sixty-one suddenly step down from one of the most prestigious positions in Congress? Conable had made no secret of his growing frustration in being a member of the Republican minority for nineteen years, but this was only one of several personal and political reasons for his retirement.

"No politician does anything for just one reason," Conable reflected in his journal on April 20, 1984. "I announced my retirement in February and there were many reasons for me to do it," not all of which were as candidly reported in the media as they were in his journal. "First," he said, "I was tired. I have noticed that increasingly I have had a short fuse and tended to lecture my friends, shaking my fists under their noses and behaving in general something like an elderly baby would. I don't like myself very well under these conditions, and there didn't seem to be much prospect that my disposition would improve if I were to stay here longer."

Also, Conable wrote, "I didn't like the political signs."

> The Reagan administration is headed for an uncertain renewal. I don't doubt that the president will win with an almost landslide proportion. But I doubt that he will have coattails and that when all the votes are counted, he will have significant tools to govern. I also don't doubt that he will have an extremely difficult economic situation and, as a lame duck president, reduced capacity to deal with it.
>
> If Reagan had not announced for reelection, I might very well have to run again to be of assistance to Bush whom I would still support for the presidency.[15]

Then in an interesting aside on the Reagan presidency, not typically reported in the press, Conable, never a big fan of Ronald Reagan, wrote in his journal,

> I must say that this year I've been increasingly uneasy about Ronald Reagan as president, since he appears to be no better clued in to the details of governing or the need for his personal attention to affairs of state than he

was when he first became president. I go to leadership
meetings and find him still sealed inside an envelope of
anecdote and as elusive as he ever was in a substantive
sense. My impression of him continues to be that he's
a very bright, but very lazy president.

Another important reason for his retirement, Conable wrote,
was his desire to have an active, productive life after Congress.

If I were not to quit now, I would be at least 64 years old
[by the next congressional election in 1986] and possibly
66 years old [by the next presidential election in 1988]
before I tried to do something else. Inevitably, that something else would be simply the mowing of my lawn back
in Alexander rather than the more active options that are
available to me if I stop now. Then from a personal point
of view, there seems to be 'a tide in the affairs of men'
indicating that right now my opportunity to stop will
leave me with the best possible taste in my mouth and the
best possible prospects for the future.

In addition,

my wife has phased out her job at George Washington
University [where she had spent five years as an administrator in the Women's Studies Program], and so she
does not have to be pulled out by the roots if we leave at
this point. She's uncertain what she wants to do . . ., but
inevitably before an option of the future is chosen, she
must be a full participant in the decision. I'm not sure
what her decision would have been if I had tried to get
her to walk away from her job two years ago or four years
ago. But obviously it would have been more difficult for
her than it is now.

Next, Conable observed, reflecting with some dispassion on
what many thought was his most important reason for retiring:

My situation in the Congress is not going to be easier since
it is apparent that Chairman Rostenkowski is getting better
and better control of the [Ways and Means] Committee,
using devices available to him to do so. Starting with a
stacked committee, moving through personal vindictiveness to those who cross him, and finally negotiating an
arrangement with subcommittee chairmen whereby he
supports what they bring out of subcommittee, whatever
it is, in return for their supporting whatever he wants to do

in conference committee. Danny has put himself in a position where he is constantly able to dominate the rather divergent Senate in conference and to do a great deal of real legislating in what used to be a form of give and take between senators and congressmen.

Danny has been very nice to me during the past year. He has acceded to my wishes as a matter of grace on many occasions. He's adroit and understanding when he is interested, although his substantive interests still are far behind his desire to exercise power.

The point is that whatever he gives me is a matter of grace and not a true exercise of true legislative give and take, and I do not have any illusions that this [situation] will improve, since he seems to be so successful in the management of the committee. I have no desire to be a supplicant for crumbs rather than a true participant, whether or not Rosty is good to me. And so I can see nothing but growing frustration in the years ahead.

"I have also been increasingly alarmed by the stridency of the young Republicans [in the House]," Conable added as another reason for his retirement.

As I have said on many occasions . . . they are performing the act of renewal that young people usually do, but they are doing so in a way that is not constructive for the party. They will not support their president, who is ideologically much closer to them than he is to me. Many of them are avid [Jack] Kemp supporters, willing to accept his fantasy of critical understanding. They give Bob Michel [the Republican minority leader] fits. They are not easy to live with and show no signs of mellowing, although I do not doubt that eventually they will accept some responsibility for government and stop posturing over in the corner. Surprisingly few in number in proportion to their stridency, they nonetheless are a very divisive element in our party and somewhat reduce my pleasure in service.

"Besides all this," Conable said, giving his final rationale for retiring, "twenty years is a nice round number and nobody can claim that I am quitting or running away."[16]

Endorsing a Successor

No sooner had Conable announced his decision to retire than a fight broke out in his district to see who would succeed him in

Congress. As with so much else in Conable's congressional career, the fight to succeed him was closely followed not only by the local and national press, but by political scientists as well. In fact, two political scientists at Syracuse University, Linda L. Fowler and Robert D. McClure, used Conable's retirement announcement as a research opportunity to study the politics of replacing such a popular, well-established incumbent.[17]

Of particular importance in choosing Conable's successor was the fact that his congressional district had been reapportioned in the early 1980s to include more of Rochester and the western suburbs of Monroe County. The district still included all of Genesee County, but only the northern parts of Livingston and Ontario counties. So a strong candidate from Monroe County, which now comprised about 80 percent of the district, as opposed to 60 percent previously, would have a decided advantage in replacing Conable in Congress.

The front-runner to succeed Conable in Congress from the outset, as Fowler and McClure show, was the former state senator from Rochester, forty-three-year-old Fred Eckert, who was then serving as ambassador to the Fiji Islands. A native of Rochester and graduate of North Texas State University, Eckert had established a successful public relations firm in Rochester in the 1960s. Then in 1970, at the age of twenty-eight, he was elected supervisor of the town of Greece, a Rochester suburb and the largest town in the district. Two years later, Eckert won a seat in the New York Senate, where he gained the reputation as a maverick and very conservative member. A strong supporter of Ronald Reagan, Eckert was appointed ambassador to the Fiji Islands in 1982.

Fred Eckert tried in many ways to present himself as another Barber Conable. He was a strong admirer of Conable, as were others in the district, and he had played an important role as a media consultant in Conable's 1974 campaign against Midge Costanza. Like Conable, Eckert was also a fiscal conservative and he tended to be a hawk on national security issues. But Eckert, as one local Republican leader put it, "was no Conable."[18]

To begin with, Eckert was much more conservative than Conable and more conservative than most other Republicans in the district. Closely aligned to the national conservative movement in the Republican Party, Eckert ironically resembled the right-wing Republicans in the House Conable had found so distasteful during his last years in Congress. Often described as a "right-wing ideologue," Eckert was a staunch supporter of Reaganomics. He opposed the Equal Rights Amendment and abortion rights, and he supported a constitutional amendment to allow prayer in schools.[19]

Eckert was also known as a very tough, aggressive, even "mean-spirited" campaigner. He saw himself as "honest" and "candid." Others, in both parties, saw him as "abrasive," "intemperate," "blunt," "acerbic," "a barracuda," "a shark," "the Jesse Helms of the north," and a man who "doesn't suffer fools gladly." "In one election," Fowler and McClure wrote, "Eckert pressed his attack so relentlessly during the public debate that his opponent finally left the hall and became violently ill." Such was the nature of Eckert's reputation, both politically and stylistically, which put him poles apart from the man he sought to replace.[20]

Over the next several weeks, several other prominent Republicans in the district expressed an interest in Conable's seat. But in the end the contest boiled down to a choice between Eckert and his young, thirty-seven-year-old former aide, Don Riley, who had succeeded him as supervisor of the town of Greece when he was elected to the state Senate in 1972. A more moderate, consensus-minded politician than Eckert, noted for his affable, low-key personal style, Riley posed a serious threat to Eckert's nomination. Through a series of endorsements by local officials and party leaders and some aggressive campaigning on his own part, however, Eckert edged out the less assertive Riley at the district party convention at the end of May. Though local Republican leaders were uneasy with Eckert's abrasive personality and right-wing views on many of the issues, they were in the end more impressed with his knowledge of the issues, his experience in government, his ability to raise money from conservative political action committees in Washington, his reputation for integrity and hard work, and above all his presumed ability to win and hold Conable's seat in Congress for the party. Eckert's nomination, as Fowler and McClure demonstrate, was "a stunning example of the pragmatism that governs American partisan politics."[21]

Meanwhile the Democrats were busy choosing their own nominee to replace Conable. The leading Democratic contender was the fifty-two-year-old liberal New York assemblywoman, Louise Slaughter, from the Rochester suburb of Fairport. A good campaigner, and very popular with organized labor and women's groups, Slaughter was seen as a strong challenger for Conable's congressional seat. In the end, however, Slaughter decided that the time was not right for her, personally or politically, to seek a seat in Congress.[22]

With Slaughter out of the race, the Democrats then turned to a man who was remarkably like Barber Conable, both personally and politically, as their candidate for Congress, the popular forty-three-year-old sheriff of Genesee County, Doug Call. Like Conable, Call could trace his ancestry in western New York back to the early nineteenth century. Like Conable, Call's family had long been active in local Republican politics, and they had been friends and strong supporters of Conable during his congressional career, some even joining the congressman in the backroom of the Genesee Hardware Store for Saturday morning coffee and donuts.

Also like Conable, Call attended Cornell University as an undergraduate, and after law school and military service, he returned to the region, his hometown of Batavia in Genesee County, in 1973 to practice law, where Conable had also practiced law in the 1950s. Uncontented with his law practice, Call soon enrolled in the Colgate Rochester Divinity School to pursue a masters degree in theology and in 1975 he became the assistant attorney for the Genesee County Department of Social Services, where he provided legal counsel on neglected and abused children, and public assistance. Not until 1980, at the age of forty, did Call finally decide to seek elective office, about the same age Conable also was when he ran for the state Senate.

In 1980, Call was urged by some of his young Republican friends to challenge the unpopular Republican sheriff of Genesee County, much as Conable had been urged by his young Republican friends to challenge the incumbent Austin Erwin for the New York Senate in 1962. Unable to wrestle the nomination away from the Republican incumbent, Call was offered the Democratic nomination for sheriff of Genesee County and went on to win the election with 76 percent of the vote, capturing every election district in the county. As sheriff, Call combined a humanistic approach toward sentencing of minor offenders with a tough law and order stance against drunk drivers. Now, after four successful years as sheriff, Call was recruited by the district's Democratic Party to seek Conable's seat in Congress.

Call was more liberal than Conable on some national issues. He supported a nuclear freeze, which Conable opposed. Conable advocated a balanced budget amendment, which Call opposed. And on economic issues, the two men also had some philosophical differences. "Underneath Conable's moderate image had always been a core of hard-headed capitalist thinking that observers frequently missed because they judged him mainly on his style. In contrast," Fowler and McClure noted, "Call's upstate conservatism was softened too much by his reformist leanings and humanist[ic] impulses for him to be comfortable with the streak of rugged individualism found in Conable."

But, "at the heart of both Conable's and Call's approach to politics," Fowler and McClure observed, "was a lack of dogmatism, a rural attachment to community, and a sense of noblesse oblige inculcated by their families; in these respects Call and Conable were nearly identical."[23]

Despite the similarity between Conable and Call and close ties between the two families, party loyalty won out in the end, and Conable issued a strong public endorsement of Fred Eckert in the fall general election. Conable had usually stayed out of local elections and not endorsed anyone. But for reasons still controversial and debated within political circles of western New York, Conable issued a widely publicized endorsement of Eckert during the fall campaign, which most observers, in both political parties, considered decisive in the final outcome.

"If there was a local issue in this campaign," Fowler and McClure noted,

> it was the question of which candidate was in the tradition of Barber Conable. Call's campaign suggested that he was, and as long as Conable did not act the claim was credible. But when Conable so forcefully and visibly endorsed Eckert, Call's basic issue—his one genuinely local appeal—was cut out from under him.

Conable's "sweeping public endorsement of Eckert," which was repeatedly cited by Eckert in his television and radio advertisements leading up to the election, "took Call's campaign by complete surprise."

> Although Conable had endorsed Eckert quietly in July in a perfunctory press release, that had been expected by everyone. He had always been helpful to the party's candidates, but never before had he thrust himself and his prestige into the very center of local politics. His endorsement of Eckert was an abrupt departure from his past behavior.

The question that Fowler and McClure asked, and the question many others in the district asked at the time, was: "Why did Conable do it? Why did he break his usual pattern of noninvolvement in local elections? Why would he deliberately undermine the campaign of a politician who shared his deep attachment to the values and people of rural upstate New York and endorse a man with whom he had a number of fundamental differences?"

Through their interviews, Fowler and McClure "heard from many sources in the Republican Party and outside it that Conable was not pleased to be succeeded by Eckert. It rankled him," they were told, "that he was being replaced by the very kind of new Republican politician who had given him so much trouble in his last years in the House."

"In the end, however," Fowler and McClure concluded,

> Conable's displeasure over his successor's political style was not equal to his deep sense of party loyalty and feelings of political obligation to Eckert. Throughout his career in Congress, Conable had been a party man: accommodating, loyal, and a good soldier. Indeed his only serious election scare in politics was in 1974, and this was due in part to his being one of the last Republicans to abandon Richard Nixon during his Watergate troubles. Later, in Ronald Reagan's era, Conable again carried the burden of his party on taxes and Social Security, which led him often to express his annoyance in private but seldom in public. In addition, Conable was indebted to Eckert. Eckert had helped him win the election in 1974, and Conable could not resist Eckert's heavy pressure to return the favor. Also, on the fiscal issues that mattered to Conable, such as the balanced budget, he felt Eckert was right and Call wrong.

On election day on November 6, 1984, "Conable got what he wanted." Fred Eckert was elected the new congressman from the Thirtieth Congressional District. But Eckert's victory was not as impressive as many had expected. Despite some sizable advantages—an almost two-to-one party registration edge, a large campaign chest (Eckert outspent Call $206,000 to $103,000 with most of his money coming from outside the district), a professional staff, an extensive media campaign, the endorsement of local politicians, a popular president at the head of the ticket, and a disorganized Democratic Party—Eckert defeated Call by only a margin of 55 percent to 45 percent. This margin was below the 60 percent Reagan polled in the district and well below the 68 percent Conable had received in 1982. Most observers in both political parties believed that Conable's strong endorsement of Eckert had provided him the decisive margin of victory.[24]

As the new congressman from the Thirtieth Congressional District, Eckert tried in many ways to be another Barber Conable and focus on the legislative aspect of his job. To help with his legislative work, he retained Conable's long-time administrative assistant, Harry Nicholas, as his chief aide in Washington. With Conable's help, and the assistance of the other Monroe County congressman, Frank Horton, who was New York's representative on the Republican Committee on Committees, he obtained a position on the much sought after Energy and Commerce Committee.

At home, Eckert also embarked on an ambitious public relations campaign to improve his negative image in the district. He set up a district office in the strongly Republican, rural Genesee County, which he had lost in the election and where he was not well known. At Conable's suggestion, he began to hold a series of town meetings throughout the district, where he met individually with constituents to discuss their concerns. He faithfully attended local party meetings, even showing up at one meeting in the midst of a blizzard.[25] And he continued Conable's successful practice of sending newsletters to his constituents, although his newsletters, as his administrative assistant, Nicholas, noted, tended to be "more partisan, more argumentative" than Conable's newsletters had been, confirming the view many had of Eckert as an overly partisan right-wing politician.[26]

But Eckert quickly grew tired of the daily grind of congressional life, particularly the need to balance his legislative responsibilities in Washington with the needs of his constituents at home. Preferring to tend to legislative business in Washington, Eckert increasingly resisted the efforts of his staff to arrange press conferences or appearances for him in the district. "Often he would cancel planned events at the last minute, or, even worse, just fail to show up," Fowler and McClure noted.

Eckert later confessed to Fowler and McClure "that this was a side of politics he found both distasteful and rather pointless. 'The angel Moroni makes appearances,' he joked. 'The Virgin Mary makes appearances. A congressman should accomplish something, not just be content with making appearances.' "

In the final analysis, Fowler and McClure noted, "it appears that Eckert went to Washington with the idea of following in Barber Conable's footsteps, but without realizing that Conable had spent many years laying the groundwork for the trust and leeway he enjoyed in the district that enabled him to be a statesman in Washington. 'I don't think Fred ever understood how much person-to-person stuff Conable did,' " one Republican told Fowler and McClure.

Sensing Eckert's vulnerability at home, Louise Slaughter, the liberal Democratic assemblywoman who had opted out of the 1984 race to succeed Conable, announced in early March 1986 that she would challenge Eckert for reelection. With the strong support of women, organized labor, the local and national party organizations, and an enthusiastic band of local volunteers, Slaughter waged an aggressive and well-financed campaign of over half a million dollars against Eckert. Arguing that Eckert had been an ineffective legislator, out of touch with the mainstream of his district, and inattentive to the needs of his constituents, Slaughter defeated Eckert by 3,300 votes (51 percent to 49 percent) on election day to become the new congresswoman from Barber Conable's old district.[27]

A Year of Reflection

Nineteen-eighty-four was a special year of reflection for Barber Conable. It was his final year in Congress, and it was only natural for him, as the master teacher–legislator he was, to try to sum-up the cumulative lessons and observations of his twenty years in Congress. All members of Congress, at the end of their careers, even the most unreflective among them, must ponder what they have learned from their experiences. But few retiring members had Conable's pedagogical ability to put these lessons into words, and fewer still commanded the respect and attention Conable had among his constituents, colleagues, the media, and academic community. Conable was, after all, in the words of his Democratic colleague, Dan Glickman of Kansas, the "E. F. Hutton of Congress. . . . When Barber Conable speaks, people listen."[28]

In one of his final newsletters in April 1984, Conable reflected broadly and philosophically on what he had learned about representative government from his years in Congress. "My terminal legislative condition has caused me recently to muse more than usual about the interesting job that has claimed my energies over the past 20 years. To oversimplify my conclusions," Conable said,

> I believe that representative government is alive and well here in Washington, that the governmental system conceived by the Founding Fathers was wise and a continuing part of our heritage, that a realistic expectancy of government and an understanding of how it functions are probably more important than any of the specific things government does, and that I am blessed in this skeptical age to have had the experience which brings these conclusions forth.
>
> This optimistic assessment seems to fly in the face of the well-known mess which at any given time clutters up

the Washington landscape. Why, you may well ask, are not our problems solved if government is functioning as it should? Why aren't we more secure, happier, and more satisfied that our prospects are brighter than those of our ancestors? Maybe messes result from governments trying to do too much, not too little.

I didn't say representative government was efficient or that the government was dealing well with our problems, only that it is working out the way it was intended and that we are the better for it. Those who want a government that solves everybody's problems efficiently should turn to some other system than representative democracy. When decision rests on the consent of the governed, it comes slowly, only after consensus has built or crisis has focused public attention in more unusual ways. The representatives in the meantime hang back until the signs are unmistakable. Government decision, then, is not the cutting edge of change but a belated reaction to change.

Fortunately, our society has many decision makers outside Washington, in the churches and non-profits, in the other levels of government, in the private sector, in the schools and the university organizations. In short, the involved citizens of America do their own thing, bring about change, and then drag government kicking and screaming into recognizing that change has occurred and that it should be reflected in the way the government does business.

The irony is that the traditional American liberal believes that this conservative lagging force should be the major instrumentality of change in our society. Liberal thinkers describe the way government ought to be, not the way it is, far behind the curve because accountability makes it so. In effect, they are yearning for philosopher-kings with the power and the will to do for the people what the people are not yet ready for, rather than for representatives.

One of the lessons of history is that people with the power to be philosopher-kings quickly become more kings than philosophers, and not comfortable purveyors of liberalism. It's safer to let the people decide first, even though it's not very inspiring to have a laggard government. Don't expect too much: realism about the way government functions is better in the long run than the disillusionment that follows wishful thinking.

The Founding Fathers didn't want efficient, adventurous governments, fearing they would intrude on our individual liberties. I think they were right, and I offer our freedom, stability and prosperity as evidence. I'm not indicting our government when I describe it in these terms, but I'm saying that its role was properly designed not to damage the dynamics of a free society.[29]

In his next to last newsletter on October 18, 1984, Conable, the philosopher, gave way to Conable, the pragmatic politician, as he offered some practical advice to his would-be successors. In an advisory newsletter, entitled "Passing the Torch," which was also reprinted in newspapers in his district, Conable wrote:

> Age hath its privilege. Experience talks. Time must have a stop, and so must any job. As I leave Congress, many people ask me what I'd like to say to some new person, just arriving in these windy halls, about how to have a good time and a successful time here. One who's already stepped in the potholes ought to describe their location and depth to those who follow down the same road.
> Realizing that few who read these words will want to run for Congress, I nevertheless offer this gratuitous "advice to a new member," hoping that others may glean some understanding of an institution which affects us all.
> 1. It's a good job here in the House, worth having and worth working hard to keep. Some think it's an unpleasant way station on the road to a greater glory, but someone willing to be a legislator, not just a politician without function, can make a distinguished career. Commitment is needed and if you do it right you will not make much money or take many vacations, but there's a lot of satisfaction in participating in government on this level.
> 2. The status of the job, considerable though it is, is more than offset by all the inconveniences, tensions and loss of privacy which cannot be avoided. That's why you need a sense of purpose to motivate and sustain you. The ones who leave disillusioned have no cause, and therefore no possible satisfactions beyond hollow status.
> 3. Independence is important, but so is party loyalty. The political parties run the Congress. You need standards of your own, but as one of 435 you also need a team and the predictability a label gives you. Then there are those issues when party standards are not enough. A label is no substitute for moral courage.
> 4. Have a better reason for what you do than that everybody does it. Don't raise more campaign money than you need. Don't imitate others; every personality and constituency is different, and success

ultimately depends on finding a truth that's true for you.

5. If something goes wrong, deal with it promptly and directly. Don't be afraid to say you were wrong, because nobody expects you to be infallible. Total consistency is impossible because circumstances change. A legislator must look ahead—not back—and will be better liked if he stresses the positive.

6. If you haven't got a good staff, get one. With the volume of mail, legislation and constituency obligations, you need professionals. Direct and control them if only to find out what's being done in your name, but listen to them and remember you're not always right just because you're boss.

7. Judgment is the one quality you'll need most. Advocacy is overworked here, and not in as short supply as judgment. That's another way of saying that balance is a magic word and that if anything seems simple to you, it's probably wrong.

8. Make yourself accessible to people who are affected by your legislation. They probably know more about it than the people who are uninterested, and you shouldn't legislate in a vacuum. You can learn from lobbyists, but there's almost always another side as well which you may have to look for.

9. Reach out to people who disagree with you. Confrontation dulls dialogue and dialogue is needed in a democracy. Political types usually need to have their prejudices tested rather than confirmed. One of the biggest mistakes you can make is to narrow your circle of friends because it's more comfortable.

"I wouldn't claim this is all you need to know," Conable concluded in his advice to his successors, "but if you turn out to be like me, it will help if you tell these things to yourself occasionally here in the House."[30]

Finally, a month later, in his last newsletter to his constituents, the philosopher and pragmatic politician gave way to the happy private citizen, about to embark on a new life after Congress. "For me, it all began 20 years ago," Conable wrote in his "Hail and Farewell" on November 29, 1984.

As one year slid into another, patterns and expectations emerged. We all have patterns in our lives or our insecurities would consume us, but the pattern of a national legislator is a particularly intense one: biannual elections, annual budgetary cycles, contentious weeks and hectic weekends, surges of mail from concerned constituents, outraged or inebriated phone calls in the night, the rise and fall of political rhetoric, even the yearning for a quiet, uncommitted hour. We all learn to live with what life deals us; but for most of us finally a shining moment of perception shatters the old accepted pattern, telling us that we have more control over our future than the life-style of the past will permit. Happy 20 years! Happy moment of truth! Happy anticipation! Thank you all sincerely.[31]

A Final Tribute

As Conable was reflecting on Congress and his own career, his colleagues, constituents, and the media were reflecting on him: what kind of man he was, what kind of congressman he had been, and what his contributions had been to representative government.

On the evening of October 3, 1984, in a special session organized by his Rochester colleague, Frank Horton, the House of Representatives paid special tribute to Conable's long service in the House. For the next hour and a half, from 10:30 until almost midnight, sixty of Conable's colleagues, from both sides of the aisle, praised Conable for his service to the House. Seventeen others later added their comments to the *Congressional Record*.

Each of Conable's colleagues had a little something special to say about Conable and their association with him. Some talked about his personal background growing up in western New York, his college days at Cornell, and his service in World War II. Others emphasized his legislative accomplishments as the ranking Republican on the Ways and Means Committee and his service on the National Commission on Social Security Reform. Many stressed his character and personal traits: integrity, knowledge, intelligence, independence, conscientiousness, civility, thoughtfulness, wit, and penchant for reciting poetry.

But running throughout the comments of Conable's colleagues that evening was a clear recognition and appreciation of the educational and pedagogical qualities that defined Conable in his relationship with his colleagues and others. Time and again, Conable was described as: "an intellectual giant," "a genuine scholar," "the think tank of the Republican Party," "an intellectual with the ability to understand the whole and not just the parts," "a polished academic with a unique ability to reduce complex issues to a form and substance that can be generally understood," "a student and teacher of the legislative process," and "a walking textbook [on] the far reaching complexities of the House Ways and Means Committee."

Several members even thanked Conable, very much as grateful students might thank their professor at the end of the semester, for what he had taught them about the legislative process and public policy. "I will never forget Barber for what he has taught me in the last four years," one young Republican congressman from Minnesota, Steve Gunderson, said. Another colleague from New York, Richard Ottinger, thanked Conable for "interrupting one of his weekends to come to my district to explain to my constituents the many changes in the Social Security system which the [National] Commission recommended." And one of Conable's Republican colleagues on the Ways and Means Committee, Bill Frenzel of Minnesota, noted: "Of all the people in the Congress, I suppose that I shall miss Barber the most, because I was most reliant on him to do my thinking, to be my counsel on the Ways and Means Committee. My opportunity to serve with him was wonderful and enjoyable, but unfortunately I am a slow learner, and I wish that he had stayed a few more years."

This rare ability Conable had to combine thought with action— "he thought like a man of action and acted like a man of thought" as one colleague put it—made Conable in the eyes of many of his colleagues "a tremendous force in the House," "one of our brightest stars," "the ideal congressman," "the epitome of what the ideal legislator should be."

In the final analysis, though, what was most distinctive about Conable's legislative career, was summed up by his young Democratic colleague, Dan Glickman from Kansas.

> The respect that those of us in the House feel for this man stems in large part from the respect he has shown for the institution. He has treated this public trust with the greatest care. By limiting [the] campaign contributions he accepts, he has left not a shadow of a doubt about the basis of his decisions; by speaking his mind, he has made sure we each know where he stands and why. Through hard work and dedication, he has risen to a position of considerable influence. That position is one he well deserves and one from which he has contributed much.[32]

Thus, Conable had come full circle in his House career. He had started out his House career, twenty years earlier, by attending the

American Political Science Association's orientation session for the freshmen members of the Eighty-ninth Congress. With a political scientist looking over his shoulder, observing how new members were socialized to Congress, Conable and his freshmen colleagues had heard the Speaker of the House, John McCormack, and other senior members of Congress describe some of the rules of success in the House: "learn parliamentary procedure," "do your homework," "specialize," "work hard in committee," "be in attendance on the floor," "don't speak 'till you know what you are talking about," and "be courteous to your colleagues."

"The House is the best judge of its own members," the senior members advised the newcomers, and "we spend a lot of time sizing each other up." The members who followed these standards of behavior, they said, stood the best chance of winning the "confidence," "respect," and "trust" of their colleagues—what Richard F. Fenno described in his study of Conable's freshman year as "the most enduring basis of influence in the House."[33]

Conable was a quick study, and as Fenno discovered in following him around his freshman year, it did not take Conable long to learn and apply the rules of success in the House. He, in fact, already knew and instinctively understood the norms of the House from growing up and living in the small communities of western New York and from his previous two years in the New York Senate. He was used to living in small communities where members were regularly sized-up by their neighbors and peers, and he liked and thrived in living in such communities.

So, as we have seen, Conable quickly took to the rules of success in the House and soon became recognized as one of its most distinguished members. Now, at the twilight of his career, Conable quietly sat on the floor of the House, listening, somewhat embarrassed, he later recalled, to his colleagues describe him in the same glowing terms he and other freshmen had heard the ideal congressman described in 1965.

Back in his district, too, Conable was being honored for his service in Congress. "It seems that everyone wants to say goodbye," one Rochester reporter noted.[34]

First in October, a group of four hundred Republicans from Genesee County met to say goodbye to Conable in his small hometown of Alexander. From the small towns and rural communities all across Genesee County, this was Conable's oldest and most loyal constituency. They had worked hard for his election to the New York Senate in 1962, and they had been his most devoted supporters during his years in Congress. They had been regular readers of his congressional newsletters, and they had gladly contributed their $50 to his reelection campaigns.

One of the guest speakers for the evening, the Republican nominee, Fred Eckert, who hoped to succeed Conable in Congress, said he knew it would be "hard to follow in Conable's footsteps." But it is "better to go chasing high standards than mediocre ones," he said. Quoting Rudyard Kipling's famous poem, "If," Eckert described Conable, as many did, as a man who could "walk with Kings," and yet never lose "the common touch."[35]

When it came time for Conable to speak, he also used poetry— a love sonnet from Shakespeare—to express his gratitude and feelings toward his constituents. Gazing out at the crowd of friendly faces, the neighbors and friends who had been with him from the beginning and formed the backbone of his political career, Conable movingly recited Shakespeare's Sonnet 29, a love poem on the importance of other people—in his case his constituents—in shaping individual worth and happiness.

> When, in disgrace with fortune and men's eyes,
> I all alone beweep my outcast state
> And trouble deaf heaven with my bootless cries
> And look upon myself and curse my fate,
> Wishing me like to one more rich in hope,
> Featured like him, like him with friends possess'd,
> Desiring this man's art and that man's scope,
> With what I most enjoy contented least;
> Yet in these thoughts myself almost despising,
> Haply I think of thee, and then my state,
> Like to the lark at break of day arising
> From sullen earth, sings hymns at heaven's gate;
> For thy sweet love remember'd such wealth brings
> That then I scorn to change my state with kings.

"It seems strange not to be running again after all these years," Conable said at the end of his comments. When he started out with his election to the state Senate in 1962, he said, he had no reason to believe that he would end up having all the opportunities he had had. "I just guess I'd better say thank you for all of that," his voice breaking a bit at the end of the speech. "It's been a great opportunity for me. I look forward to seeing more of you in the future. . . . Thanks."[36]

Then in November more than 1,100 people, many of them wearing old Conable campaign buttons, gathered at a downtown Rochester hotel to put the finishing touches on the district's tribute to Conable. They came from all over the Thirtieth Congressional District, from Rochester and the suburbs of Monroe County and the rural counties to the west. They came to honor Conable for the same reason the Genesee County Republicans had gathered earlier, but now on a somewhat grander scale. They came to honor Conable, not only for his service to his district, but also for the national prominence he had gained in Washington as a legislator. "I've admired the conscientious way he has gone about his job," one of Conable's constituents at the dinner said. "He has been a credit not only to this area, but to the entire nation, as you can see by the attention devoted to his retirement."[37]

Conable had started out his career wanting to be a national legislator. The individual constituent services were important, he said, and with the help of his staff he would take care of them. But more than anything else, he said in his first newsletter on February 3, 1965, he wanted to focus on the legislative aspect of his job, what he thought was his "real reason for being" a congressman.[38] And over the years, through his carefully crafted newsletters and important positions and contacts he had in Washington, he had been very successful in carving out a local reputation as a prominent national legislator.

To help recognize and celebrate the national stature Conable had attained in Washington, the district organizers arranged for the Senate majority leader, Howard Baker, to give the main speech for the evening. A man very much like Conable in many ways, a moderate well-liked Republican, with deep local roots in his native Tennessee, Baker had also distinguished himself in Washington as a national legislator and party leader. Baker's presence in Rochester that evening, as the organizers intended, clearly gave the local celebration of Conable's career an added national significance.

Conable though, in his typical fashion, tried to make light of the evening, as all the recounting of his accomplishments had grown a bit heavy at the end. Standing next to Baker at a press conference before the dinner, Conable quipped before Baker could speak: "We're here to bury Barber, not to praise him." Then, when Baker described Conable as an "institution" in the Congress, Conable laughed and said, "Oh now, come on."

Seriously, Baker retorted, he had come to Rochester "to praise Barber, not to bury him. Really," he said, making the essential point so many others had made since Conable announced his retirement in February, "as the senior Republican on the Ways and Means Committee, he has brought not only the Republican viewpoint and the strength of his own convictions to tax policy over these many years, but he has also established a precedence of quality of service and dedication to his responsibility that others will, I'm sure, want to follow and will follow for years to come.

"Barber will be missed in the House, but I expect you'll hear more from Barber Conable," Baker added. "He's a man of great vigor and great intellect, and I suspect he has much yet to contribute."[39]

As Conable's colleagues and constituents spent much of the fall of 1984 remembering and honoring his service in Congress, so did the media, as they sought one last time to get Conable's observations and explanations on Washington and at the same time sum-up and praise his career.

In November, for example, the editors and reporters of *Congressional Quarterly* invited Conable to offer his observations on his two decades on Capitol Hill. Asking a question that was on many peoples' mind, the editors ask Conable "what it was like to be part of the minority" for twenty years. Putting his most positive public face on this question, Conable replied.

> A lot of people think I'm quitting because I'm frustrated. Well, there's frustration involved in being in Congress and being in the minority. But if you want to look at frustration, I'm not as frustrated as Danny Rostenkowski is. I sit six inches from him [on the Ways and Means Committee]. He has to touch more bases than the Baltimore Orioles. Nobody expects much from me, because they know I've only got 12 votes and he's got 23.
>
> The point is I've been able to affect more legislation as the minority leader of the Ways and Means Committee than I would be able to affect as the chairman of some other lesser committee. So my frustrations are not justified on the basis that I'm a minority.
>
> Now, [there are] a lot of personal things, too. Danny has a very modest substantive interest. He's a political leader. He knows that I can give him fits on some substantive issues. So Danny tends to try to work around me. . . . He's more interested in something that's central to the political battle. The result is that I've been able to have quite an impact on a lot of legislative areas simply because of my interest and willingness to work on it. . . . So I don't have any right to be all that frustrated in that role.

"But I'll tell you," Conable added, "there is a certain amount of frustration built into the collective decision-making process. A lot of folks who come here, who think they are going to change the world overnight, wind up very quickly frustrated, because there are 534 other people who think they're going to change the world overnight, too."[40]

In early December, the MacNeil-Lehrer News Hour on PBS did a special profile on Conable's congressional career, which they headlined "Barber Conable: Setter of Standards." Quoting Senator Daniel Patrick Moynihan's tribute to Conable, Judy Woodruff of the News Hour, noted: "Some men meet standards; others set them. Barber Conable has been one of the others."

What set Conable apart from his colleagues, Moynihan told Woodruff, was his mastery of the nation's tax system.

> He has been a master of detail in the taxing process and the whole revenue system of government, and really, in the end, became very discouraged that nobody wanted to know about complexity in these matters. He is, in one sense, one of the great complexifiers. He does not make simple that which is not simple. He makes comprehensible that which is complex.

"It's a different quality," Moynihan noted, which distinguished Conable and provided a whole new standard of congressional excellence, which others would find hard to emulate, but which Moynihan, a master teacher–legislator himself, greatly admired.[41]

In the middle of December, Hugh Sidey paid special tribute to Conable in a column he wrote for *Time* magazine. Noting that Conable "had studied medieval history at Cornell and American history throughout his adult life," Sidey, who like other Washington journalists had come to rely on Conable for his own reporting, praised Conable for the historical perspective he brought to American politics, particularly on the presidency, which was Sidey's primary beat.

> For two decades, Conable played a role in the political drama [in Washington], and always the events of history whispered to him "to avoid the pressures of the moment" and consider a broader perspective. In the capital, [Conable] became a ray of wry wisdom amid the constant drizzle of somber buncombe [the claptrap, the empty and insincere talk of Washington, which today we might call the "spin," that Conable constantly sought to avoid as a congressman]. He toughed his way into power like the Marine he was in World War II and Korea. He became the ranking member of the Ways and Means Committee. More important, he gathered a grateful flock of admirers, among them scholars, journalists, and politicians.[42]

Finally, on January 2, 1985, the day before Conable's congressional career formally ended, Read Kingsbury, a local reporter who had covered Conable throughout his career, wrote an editorial tribute to Conable for a Rochester newspaper, entitled "Extraordinary Instructor."

> From tomorrow on, this community . . . will no longer be represented by Barber Conable in Congress. Some of us will feel as if we've lost our security blanket. . . .
>
> Much flattery has been heaped on the man from Alexander. It is gratifying that people across the country also held him in high regard and regret as we do the loss of his incisive mind and problem-solving skills in the high councils of government. . . .
>
> Rather than add to the encomiums, it may be more appropriate for constituents to reflect on what he has taught us during his 20 years in Congress.
>
> Make no mistake, Barber Conable is, above all else, a teacher. He seems to enjoy nothing so much as describing to his neighbors of the 30th Congressional District the strange workings of Congress and the complex issues of the day. . . . Readers of his newsletters and columns must be among the best-informed citizens in the nation, not only because Conable has so often been at the center of matters but because he can make the complex clear.

Then, using two personal vignettes to make his point, Kingsbury recalled two educational encounters he had with Conable during this congressional career. In the first vignette, Kingsbury remembered the time in the late 1960s when he was doing a story on "a period of turmoil" at the Monroe County Department of Social Services. The story involved a national recession that was occurring at the time and a shift in welfare policy in the Nixon administration. For background on the story, Kingsbury sought an interview with Conable, who supported Nixon's policy reforms and had jurisdiction over welfare policy as a member of the Ways and Means Committee.

Conable replied that he would be in Rochester with "some free time" the following Saturday afternoon and offered to meet Kingsbury at a ribbon-cutting ceremony he had to attend in the district. So Kingsbury met Conable at the ceremony and afterwards took him home to talk about welfare policy.

"We are deep in the complexities of the matter," Kingsbury recalled, "when I went into the kitchen to fix tea. Conable arose and followed so as to continue without a break."

Kingsbury, like practically everyone else who came into contact with Conable over his long congressional career, was "impressed" by Conable's "compulsion to communicate," an impression that was "reinforced" for Kingsbury when he spent a day following Conable around in Washington a few years later.

"One of the spring chores of a congressman is to greet students from home and have their familiar picture taken, the group strung up the glaring marble east steps of the Capitol," Kingsbury wrote, as he recounted the second vignette on Conable's pedagogical style.

> The class on this balmy day was from the School of the Blind in Batavia and so Conable took particular pains to paint the scene: the Library of Congress and the Supreme Court buildings beyond the green park in front of them, House office buildings on their right, Senate offices on their left, and the White House down Pennsylvania Avenue behind them on the far side of the Capitol. . . . He wove the scene into a mini-lecture on the Constitution and the separation of power that was almost breath-taking in its clarity and power.

There was, of course, "something in Barber Conable deeper than a relish for communication." It was his interest in the "substance of legislation" that came before the House. "It was this interest," Kingsbury concluded, "served by a first-rate mind, that made Conable such an authority in Ways and Means subjects—taxation, trade, Social Security, welfare policy—and a key figure in finding a way out of disputes in these areas. . . . It was this interest that led him to travel abroad at his own expense to learn about trade issues, this interest that makes him such an effective leader."

"Standing above any issue" though, was

> Conable's obvious love for the legislative process and the democratic way. My mind goes back to that spring day in 1973 when he led the group from the School of the Blind into the House, pausing in the Speaker's Lobby to describe the blue carpet, the crystal chandeliers, the gilt-framed portraits. In the chamber he sat them down and spoke.
>
> "There are no black and white issues here," he said. "It's difficult to decide if a bill is 52 percent good and you should vote for it or only 48 percent good and you shouldn't."
>
> What they should remember, he said, is that government is "ordinary people trying to do the best we can with difficult and complex issues."

"It is a lesson he often taught," Kingsbury concluded. "Barber Conable is not ordinary, but the fact that he thinks of himself so has made his public service extraordinary."[43]

Going Home

At noon, on January 3, 1985, Fred Eckert was sworn in as the new congressman from the Thirtieth Congressional District in New York, and Barber Conable became a private citizen for the first time in twenty-two years. A Renaissance man, with wide-ranging interests and talents, Conable had said for some time that he wanted to retire from Congress at an early enough age so that he would have time to pursue other interests after Congress. Now, at the relatively young age of sixty-two, Conable would have a chance to put his retirement plans into effect.

Some had assumed that, with his national reputation, Conable would stay in Washington after his retirement from Congress, as so many former members do. But Conable's local roots and orientation—indeed, his very identity as "just a country boy from western New York"—were always stronger than any attraction for Washington. The first and most important decision the Conables made about their life after Congress was to go back to the home they had bought in the small town of Alexander, New York, in the late 1950s. An early nineteenth-century farmhouse, surrounded by a large five-acre yard and dozens of trees Conable had planted from various parts of the world, this place had always been a special haven for the Conables on their trips home during the congressional years. And now it would once again be their permanent home as they returned to Alexander for good.

Conable also accepted a prestigious teaching position as Distinguished University Professor at the nearby University of Rochester, only an hour's drive from his home in Genesee County. So Congressman Conable would become in retirement what in many ways he had always been, Professor Conable, but now with the more formal educational tasks of teaching undergraduate and graduate students in political science and management at the University of Rochester.

Widely admired in academic circles, Conable had also been offered the presidency of Bucknell University and teaching positions at Harvard, Yale, Stanford, Xavier University, and the University of Virginia. He told the press at the time that he had been "sorely tempted" to accept the endowed chair he was offered at

Harvard. But in the end, he decided to accept the offer at the University of Rochester so he could be close to home. "After all these years" in Washington, he told a reporter, "we finally decided if we didn't go back. . ., we'd always feel rootless."[44]

To pursue his writing talents, as George Will and other Washington journalists had urged him to do, Conable also began writing a biweekly column for *U.S. News and World Report* (alternating with David Gergen, the former White House communications director), hoping to bring to a national audience the same candid analysis of current events he had brought to his constituents through his newsletters and newspaper columns. Conable's first column, "The Messy Budget Process," appeared the first week of February 1985.[45] But Conable's career as a journalist was short-lived as his penchant for candor soon ran counter to the financial interest of the *U.S. News and World Report*.

In September Conable wrote an editorial critical of the federal civil service pension system, which he argued provided an excessive level of compensation to some retired federal workers. More than 325,000 pensioners, he said, using data with which he was well familiar, were receiving pensions bigger than the salaries they once earned in government and some of these were receiving pensions approaching $100,000 a year.

> Some reasonable limit [should be] imposed on growth of the federal pension system [before] its excesses . . . exacerbate our deficit problem . . . and eventually bring about a popular reaction punitive to the interests of retired public employees. It would be reassuring if this group would, by its leadership or acquiescence, point the way toward a responsible entitlement formula for the future.[46]

"So many retired federal workers in the Washington area canceled their subscriptions after the editorial," Conable recalled years later, "that I was told by the people at the magazine that my editorial services were no longer needed."[47]

Conable of course was also in great demand as a Washington lawyer and lobbyist after his retirement from Congress. Although he had clearly indicated on the day of his retirement announcement on February 6, 1984, that he would not follow the retirement track of many of his colleagues and stay in Washington as a lobbyist, he received a number of offers to do just that. "By the amount of money offered me," he recalled, "they had a right to own me. I didn't want to be owned by a big law firm. I was either going to be a stuffed exhibit on display for corporate clients, or I was going to be a lobbyist. I didn't want to do either," he told a reporter after he returned home.[48]

Conable, however, did accept a number of positions on corporate and charitable boards after his retirement. Gerald Ford, who continued to be Conable's mentor after he left Congress, called Conable and told him "not to accept more than eleven" corporate directorships.

"Eleven?" Conable replied.

"Yeah, that's what I've got," Ford said.

From the twenty-five corporate directorships Conable was offered, he picked four, he said, "each one different from the other so I could learn something different from each one": the large pharmaceutical giant, Pfizer, Corning Glass Works in nearby Corning, New York, the Honeywell Corporation, and the American International Group, the largest insurance company in the world, headquartered in New York City. These were all paid positions and contributed significantly to Conable's retirement income.

Conable was also invited to join the boards of the New York Stock Exchange, the Dole Foundation, and the Independent Sector, and he continued his chairmanship of the Museum of the American Indian in New York City, which he had begun while in Congress.

In addition, Conable became a senior fellow at the American Enterprise Institute, a nonpartisan conservative think-tank in Washington, where he joined in the institute's ongoing study of Congress and spent some time editing the private journal he had kept during his years in Congress.[49] While in Washington, Conable also agreed to give a three-day lecture on tax policy at the University of Oklahoma in the fall, which was later published as a book.[50]

Shortly before leaving Washington, Conable also donated the large number of nineteenth-century prints of the U. S. Capitol he had collected over the years to the Capitol Historical Society. These prints, several of which had hung in Conable's congressional office, now are handsomely displayed on the walls of the House Restaurant and directly across the hall in the Speaker's Dining Room, with a small plaque on the wall acknowledging Conable's parting gift to the Capitol.

Sometime later, on May 29, 1986, several of Barber's House colleagues also planted a tree (a Tulip Poplar) in his honor on the east front of the Capitol to commemorate his long service in Congress. There the Conable tree has taken root with trees honoring other former members—such as Speaker Sam Rayburn of Texas,

Speaker Joe Cannon from Illinois, Congressman Richard Bolling of Missouri, and most recently Conable's long-time friend, Senator Daniel Patrick Moynihan of New York.[51]

Finally, in late June, Conable headed back home to Alexander, New York. "I'm going home where I belong," he told reporters in Washington just before driving out of town. He said he stayed so long in Washington after his retirement because "I had trouble selling my house."[52]

Soon after arriving back in Alexander, Patrice Mitchell, who had covered Conable off and on during his congressional career, wrote a long piece for a Rochester newspaper which nicely captured the exuberance Conable felt in being back home. "Like a proud father, Barber Conable is poking about his rambling, 150-year-old farmhouse, his 'pool of tranquility' in Alexander, Genesee County," Mitchell wrote as she followed Conable around his farmhouse. "Cup of coffee in hand, he treads on sneakered feet from room to well-appointed room, showing the antiques, the Indian artifacts, the valuable old books he has collected over the many years. . . . He steps outdoors into the flower garden, slapping the swarming wood flies from his neck and head. He leads the way towards the vast yard, reciting many of the 90 varieties of trees he has planted—Swiss stone pine, weeping beech, gingko, European fern leaf beech, corkscrew willow. He waves an arm towards his 170-acre wood lot populated with grouse, turkey and deer."

"I love this environment," Conable told Mitchell. "I feel my little soul expand here."

Retirement, Conable said, had enabled him to put some "space" back in his life. He was now free of the hectic congressional routine and had more time for his leisurely activities, which included classical music, poetry, reading and visiting with two of his children who lived in the area. "I don't want to run around a lot," he said. "That's part of the process of scheduling some space in my life."

But Conable was retired in name only, as Mitchell and others observed. Sitting at his often-photographed 1874 Wooten desk, which had been shipped from his Washington office to his Alexander study, Conable leafed through his appointment book. Upcoming entries for the year included meetings at the University of Rochester where he'd join the faculty in the fall, committee meetings of the New York Stock Exchange, a meeting of the Museum of the American Indian in New York City, meetings of the various corporate boards on which he had agreed to serve, speeches at IBM and the Rochester Rotary Club, and lectures on tax policy at the Albany Law School and the University of Oklahoma.

Explaining the apparent contradiction between putting some space back in his life and the heavy schedule he had arranged for himself for the fall, Conable explained to Mitchell: "You taper off slowly so you don't sit around and brood a lot."

In tapering off into retirement, Conable also remained in touch with his congressional colleagues, for personal reasons and to keep up with legislative developments for his speeches and seminars. On a trip to Washington a few weeks earlier, he had had lunch with his former administrative assistant, Harry Nicholas, and talked to the Ways and Means Committee staff members about taxes. "He seems just as active as he was in Congress," Nicholas noted. "He's got a dozen balls in the air. . . . He certainly has lost no interest in Congress."

But Conable's primary interests were now back home in western New York and in the life he had carved out for himself after Congress. If he had not come back to Alexander, he told Mitchell, as he repeated to many other people, he would have "felt rootless."

"That was his dream to come back home," his long-time friend, Karl Buchholtz at the Genesee Hardware Store, added. "Can you blame him? Alexander is a nice town."

Conable's neighbors in Alexander had also assumed that he'd come home to stay after he retired from Congress. "In the 20 years he spent in Washington, neighbors kept a watchful eye on his house." If he drove up "late one weekend night in a rental car, they'd come over to make sure it was him.

" 'It gives you a sense of belonging,' " Conable, the "old country boy," said, as he happily reflected on his reasons for coming home.[53]

"You want to know the real reason I came back to Alexander?" Conable asked, recalling a farewell dinner given in his honor in Washington before he left for Alexander.

> Dave Broder and a lot of the Washington press were there. Nice people, good friends of mine. They got up and said the usual stupid lies about me. I didn't want to be maudlin. So I said, everybody's been asking me why in the world would I come back to a place like Alexander. I said, I want to tell you why.
>
> I said, the story revolves around a guy by the name of Paul Pautler. He used to be our justice of the peace there in Alexander. He got cancer and he died, and they had a very formal funeral for him. All the Masons came in their aprons, and all the state police came with their lights flashing. The solemn cortege moved down to the Alexander Village Cemetery. The cemetery is right next to

the Schmieder's cow pasture, and the Schmieder's cows came and put their long, lugubrious faces over the fence and tried to figure out what was happening when this big cortege arrived. They behaved very well until the final prayer, and then a bee stung one of them. They all ran mooing off across the pastures with their tails up and their udders swinging, and the Schmieders were so humiliated their cows behaved so badly. It was the talk of the town for about two weeks about the way the Schmieder's cows behaved at Paul Pautler's funeral.

I heard about that, and I went right over to the Schmieders, and I said, I've just bought six cemetery plots for my family right next to the fence, and I want you to promise me that if anything happens to me, you'll let your cows come to my funeral. I said, now there isn't another person in this room who has any idea where he's going to be buried, much less who's coming to his funeral. I need the stability of knowing, the security of knowing things like that, and that's why I'm gong back to Alexander instead of staying here in Washington and wandering around, as if I were still important, when I'm not. Since that time one of my daughters has married one of the Schmieder boys, and so we can be fairly confident they'll live up to their share of the bargain.[54]

Chapter 15

Life After Congress

In February 1986, Conable was settling into his new life back in western New York when he received a surprise phone call from Treasury Secretary James Baker that would radically change his life for the next five years. Conable had known Baker since they worked together on George Bush's presidential campaign in 1979–80.

Conable had also worked closely with Baker on a variety of tax issues when Baker served as President Reagan's chief of staff in the early 1980s, and then again when they both were members of Reagan's Presidential Commission on Social Security Reform in 1982–83.

Baker called Conable to discuss the difficulty the Reagan administration was having in finding a successor to Alden W. Clausen, whose five-year term as president of the World Bank expired on July 1, 1986. Formerly called the International Bank for Reconstruction and Development, the World Bank was established by the United States and its allies in 1944 as a means of providing long-term loans to developing countries for capital investment after World War II.

According to Jochen Kraske, an historian of the World Bank, "Federal Reserve Chairman Paul Volcker and Labor Secretary William E. Brock . . . turned down the job [and] others, such as former Treasury Secretary William Simon and former Navy Secretary J. William Middendorf, did not find support among the other major shareholders" of the Bank.[1] Baker and Secretary of State George Shultz were growing increasingly concerned that the failure to fill the position with an American might lead the Europeans to submit their own candidate for the presidency of the World Bank. By tradition, all previous presidents of the Bank had been Americans, and all previous presidents of the closely related International Monetary Fund—which had also been created in 1944 as a means of providing short-term flows of money to developing countries to facilitate international trade—had been Europeans.

"At this point," writes Kraske, "Baker called his old friend Barber Conable . . . to ask permission to mention his name as a potential candidate, so as to illustrate the caliber and stature of the person who should be nominated" for the presidency.

> Conable was reluctant. He had left politics a year before and had returned to an enjoyable life, divided between some teaching and his hobbies, in upstate New York. He had no desire to return to Washington, and he knew nothing about the World Bank. . . . Baker assured him that this was strictly a tactical move and that nothing would come of it.
>
> Two weeks later, however, Baker called him again. "Barber, I am sorry to tell you, you're the only guy we can agree on." Conable protested, but Baker pointed out that if he was not prepared to take the job, it would be left to the Europeans to find a candidate.

"Baker's appeal to Conable's sense of public duty was effective," Kraske writes.

> Conable had an old-fashioned notion of public service. One had an obligation, he thought, to respond affirmatively when asked to take on a position of importance in the broader public interest. When he said he thought he was totally unqualified for the job, Baker took that as a promise that he would do a good job. Conable did not know much about the World Bank, but it was one of those institutions that he had vaguely considered worthy of support. In fact, Conable later said he went back to look up his voting record and was relieved to find that he had been supportive of the Bank.

"Conable was the first career politician to be appointed president of the Bank and the only one without substantial Wall Street experience." Some of the representatives of the banking industry, such as Robert D. Hormats, vice president at Goldman, Sachs and Company, and C. Fred Bergsten, director of the Institute for International Economics, noted that "the World Bank presidency was a little out of line with Conable's background. But they praised his appointment because of his statesmanlike qualities, his financial knowledge, and his solid grasp of complicated trade and tax issues. . . . He was a big-picture person well suited for the job," they said.

Though Conable was well known and respected in Washington, he was little known within the international banking community. "Barber who?" the executive directors of the World Bank anxiously asked when they heard President Reagan's choice to head the Bank. "Conable was completely unknown among the Bank's borrowers" in the developing world. "European bankers also knew little about him and expressed surprise at his choice." But in time, as Kraske has pointed out in his study, "Conable's political skills, his ability to listen and communicate, would help him overcome this handicap and become as well liked among the Bank's members as he had been on Capitol Hill."

> As developed as his political skills were, however, they did not prepare him to be a manager and leader of a major bureaucratic organization. Indeed, Conable himself joked that the largest organization he had ever headed was the small staff in his personal congressional office. His lack of experience became evident early in his tenure, when he undertook a major reorganization of the Bank that proved disruptive and traumatic.

Despite the bitter controversy over that reorganization [which resulted in the reduction of almost four hundred employees at the Bank], Conable warmed to his job. He enjoyed having a platform from which to speak about major development issues. He took a keen interest in, and often spoke about, reviving the Bank's focus on alleviating poverty. He thought that during the Clausen years [1981–86] the Bank, in its emphasis on structural adjustment, had lost sight of the importance of fighting poverty. He was personally committed to this fight and to other issues that became important to the Bank in the 1980s. Publicly, he advocated increasing the Bank's attention to environmental problems, promoting programs to curtail population growth, and advancing the role of women in development. Those positions won him admirers among the executive directors, within management and the staff, and in the leadership of the nongovernmental organizations (NGOs) that were pressing the Bank on environmental and social issues in the 1980s.[2]

The five years Conable spent as president of the World Bank also had a profound effect on him personally, expanding the global perspective to which he had aspired even as a young congressman. He and his wife, Charlotte, who was an important partner with him in this adventure, as she had been throughout his political career, traveled to more than fifty countries during their years at the World Bank. "While I was closeted with big shots learning of their virtues," Conable recalled in a personal travelogue he wrote on his World Bank experience later, "Charlotte was on a separate schedule visiting schools, slums, women's groups, and informal contacts learning the truth, and as a result my horizons were greatly expanded in every country we visited."[3]

As Conable said in his last major address as president of the World Bank on July 10, 1991:

> When I came to Washington as a freshman congressman from upstate New York, Americans thought about themselves as more or less self-sufficient. Today you can't look anywhere even in my tiny home village of Alexander, New York, without finding evidence of foreign ties. More than ever before, growth in the United States is linked to growth overseas, not least of all in developing countries. We can sell the future short, put our heads in the sand, and pretend the link does not exist, but it does exist. . . .
>
> We live in an increasingly interdependent world. People in all industrial nations must think internationally. We must find common solutions.

> I came to the World Bank five years ago without a
> great deal of knowledge about development, but with
> an open mind. I'm leaving with a closed mind about the
> importance of the work of the World Bank and other
> multilateral institutions.[4]

Back at home in Alexander, Conable resumed his many local activities that had been interrupted by his return to public service. Once again, he faithfully made the six-mile trip from his home in Alexander to Batavia every Saturday morning to have coffee and donuts with his long-time friends at the Genesee Hardware Store. As a newly returned local celebrity, he was much in demand by the media, civic groups, and local colleges for his perspective on national and international affairs. His alma mater, Cornell University, invited him to join the Board of Trustees.[5]

Closer to home he joined the board of the Genesee Country Village and Museum, an "educational living museum" in nearby Mumford, New York, full of nineteenth-century homes, schools, shops, and churches relocated from various parts of the state to depict life in nineteenth-century western New York—a life Conable's great grandparents, Rufus and Sophia Conable, would have known well when they migrated from western Massachusetts to western New York in the 1820s. There on the steps of an early nineteenth-century town hall in the Village Square, Conable could be seen during his congressional days and for nearly twenty years after his retirement, dressed in the attire of the period, reciting the Declaration of Independence with vigor on the Fourth of July. Now, he also spent his time in the board room helping direct the educational activities of a museum that captured so much of his own nineteenth-century heritage.

One of Conable's favorite local activities continued to be giving talks on the history of western New York, and particularly the Native American history of the region, which he had first learned as a boy growing up in Warsaw. As the head of a local historical society proudly said in introducing Barber at a talk he gave on the early history: "As our congressman, Barber was known by the national press for his abilities and honesty. But he has always been an historian, often speaking to historical societies long before he ran for Congress."

Besieged in retirement by weighty questions about the World Bank and global poverty, Conable responded that it "was nice not to talk about poor people for a while." Instead, he talked that evening about Ebenezer "Indian" Allan, a pioneer and early settler of western New York (1744–1816), known among other things for his polygamous lifestyle. Showing his old political skills of relating both to his audience and subject, Conable told the audience: "In doing some research on some of my relatives in western Massachusetts, I discovered that some of my family belonged to a sect that believed in free love, and I'm not sure that I'm even a Conable."

It was just like old times that evening, as Conable delighted his audience with his humor and fascinating details of Indian Allan's life and the early development of Rochester. "It's too bad we don't have a congressman like that any more," a former constituent said as she left the talk.

Another young college student in attendance, wowed by Conable's performance, said, "We should start a draft Barber Conable movement for Congress again."

Conable looked at him and laughed and said, "I'm crazy, but not that crazy."[6]

In addition to his many local activities, Barber was also invited to resume his membership on three of the corporate boards from which he had resigned after accepting the presidency of the World Bank in 1986: Pfizer, Corning Glass, and the American International Group.

As the former head of the World Bank, Conable's life took on a larger significance than it had before. As much as he liked spending time with his children and their families (three of whom lived nearby), having coffee and donuts every Saturday morning with "the boys" at the Genesee Hardware Store, and giving talks to local historical societies, his elevated status as the former head of the World Bank brought with it greater expectations and opportunities. He may have seen himself as a "country boy" and enjoyed spending most of his time in the country, but others saw him as a senior statesman and world leader, the local boy who had made good, who as much as anyone they knew combined the parochial qualities of small town, rural western New York with the broader national and international perspective of a world citizen.

As visitors drove up to Conable's house in the small village of Alexander, it was sometimes hard for them to imagine that the former Republican leader of the Ways and Means Committee and president of the World Bank lived here. But Alexander is where he did live and felt most at home, as deeply rooted, but yet as expansive as the wide assortment of trees from around the world that adorned his backyard for all to see as they drove into his driveway.

Responding to the greater opportunities for national and international participation after his retirement from the World Bank, Conable accepted membership on the United Nations Commission on Global Governance, and he chaired the National Committee on U. S.–China Relations, a prestigious nonprofit organization, funded by the Rockefeller, Ford, and Luce Foundations, to foster good relations between the United States and China. He became particularly committed during his retirement to improving those relations, and he often traveled to China to meet with high-ranking Chinese officials and helped entertain visiting Chinese dignitaries when they visited New York and Washington. In addition, he served on the boards of both the Museum of the American Indian and the American History Museum of the Smithsonian, and he chaired the Executive Committee of the Board of Regents of the Smithsonian as well.

Along the way, Conable was showered with local honors and recognition. A building (the Conable Technology Building) was dedicated to honor him and his wife at the local Genesee Community College in Batavia, and an endowed chair in international studies was established in his name at the Rochester Institute of Technology where he was a frequent and popular guest speaker.

Though Conable's five-year presidency of the World Bank overshadowed his twenty-year congressional career in the minds of many observers, his congressional years continued to be remembered by his colleagues, constituents, journalists, and academicians. Long after he left Congress, political scientists continued to cite his legislative accomplishments and observations in their scholarly work.[7] Most recently, one of Conable's former congressional colleagues, Lou Frey, a Republican congressman from Florida from 1969 to 1979, asked Conable to write a chapter on his experience in the Ways and Means Committee for a book he and a young political scientist at Colgate University were editing on the inner workings of Congress. As when he was in Congress, Conable's colleagues and political scientists continued to remember him as someone who could clearly explain and illustrate to the outside world how the Congress really works.[8]

Privately, though, Conable often lamented in retirement that his work in Congress had been fruitless, "written on the wind," as he liked to say, describing how easily the laws he had helped craft were changed or eliminated after he left Congress. He particularly regretted Congress's abandoning the federal revenue-sharing program with state and local governments which he had been instrumental in passing during the Nixon years, and the type of program more than any other that symbolized Conable's Jeffersonian commitment to decentralization of power in American politics.[9] Though he wanted to contribute more to the legislative process and longed to become chairman of the Ways and Means Committee where he could have more firmly put his imprint on the laws of the country, he still left behind a legislative record for which he and his supporters could be proud.

As a freshman member of the Science and Astronautics Committee, he was in on the ground floor of the American space program and helped develop congressional and public support for this important initiative. He was a major contributor to the partisan and institutional reforms of the House in the 1970s that led to the modification of the seniority system for committee chairmanship and the greater democratization of the House as an institution. He was a member of the Republican leadership of the House for fourteen years and one of the key House Republican leaders calling for the resignation of Richard Nixon from the presidency in 1974. As the ranking Republican member of the Ways and Means Committee for eight years, he was his party's chief spokesman on taxes and economic policy in the House. He took major roles in indexing both Social Security benefits and the income tax to inflation. He was an important participant in the negotiations that led to the Social Security reforms of 1983. Of particular significance, as we have seen throughout this book, he was a committed and effective informer and teacher of the legislative process for his younger colleagues, constituents, journalists, and academic community in general. And for all these and other reasons, mostly having to do with the exemplary character he displayed during his years in Congress, he was voted by his colleagues on both sides of the aisle the "most respected member" of the House of Representatives from either party in 1984.[10]

But still there was much more he longed to accomplish legislatively and could perhaps have achieved if he had been blessed with majority status for at least part of his tenure. So it came as a particular surprise to him in 2000 when he learned that *Pensions and Investments* magazine had chosen him as one of the runners-up for "men of the century" for originating 401(k) pension plans when he was a member of the Ways and Means Committee in 1979. The two top recipients of this award went to none other than the industrialist Andrew Carnegie, who is credited with creating the world's first advance-funded pension funds in the early years of the twentieth century, and a brilliant young graduate student, by the name of Harry Markowitz, who pioneered the idea of portfolio diversification a half century later.

In singling Conable out as one of the ten runner-ups for men of the century, the editors of *Pensions and Investments* wrote:

> When Rep. Barber Conable, Rochester, N.Y., inserted section (K) into Section 401 of the Internal Revenue Code in 1979, little did anyone know the impact it would have.
>
> He acted to protect constituent companies from threats of IRS interference. The Treasury Department said the provision would not have any effect on U. S. government revenue.
>
> But it drew the attention of Theodore Benna, a benefits consultant at The Johnson Cos., Newton, Pa. The company adopted the first 401(k) plan.
>
> Mr. Benna then lobbied the government to allow such arrangements arguing 401(k) plans would do a better job of stimulating savings than would expanding individual retirement accounts. The IRS agreed.[11]

Conable himself was totally surprised by this award. "I had a very strange experience this year, " he said in an interview at his home in the summer of 2000. "I was shown in January a copy of a magazine called *Pensions and Investments*, and they had chosen me as one of the dozen or so men of the century, because I had originated the 401(k)."

"You originated that?" I asked with surprise.

"Well, that's what they said," Conable replied with equal surprise.

> This was announced at an American International Group board meeting that I was at. And everybody was saying, "Oh Barber, you did such a wonderful thing!" I said, "I don't think I did." This was twenty years after the fact. I finally called up the Ways and Means staff and said, "Would you check to see if I had anything to do with 401(k)?" And they called back to me and said, "Yes you did. You changed the law to protect the Kodak pension and profit sharing plan in such a way that a Pennsylvania industrialist a year or two later, looking at that section of the tax code, said 'I could make a pretty good pension plan out of that.' "

"It was totally inadvertent on my part," Conable said. "I'd been thinking that everything I did in Congress was written on the wind, that it had all been amended and expired and that I had had no affect at all. But then I find out that something that I did to try to ensure my constituents who worked for Eastman Kodak didn't get their profit sharing and pension plans taken away from them made possible the 401(k).

"Isn't that fascinating, really incredible," he said, with the detached amusement of a man who had inadvertently stumbled into the kind of national legislative prominence to which he had always aspired. It was paradoxical, also, because here was a congressman who deliberately downplayed the constituent services aspect of his job in favor of a more national focus, but who in the end found his way to perhaps his most significant national accomplishment inadvertently through an effort to help the employees of one of the major firms in his district.[12]

And then in 2002 another surprise came Conable's way when he was credited with "the birth of America's current beer renaissance," with a bill he introduced and President Carter signed into law in 1978 authorizing the production of beer in the home.

"Some people joked that Carter passed the law on behalf of his brother, Billy, who tried marketing his own eponymous brew," two young Rochester journalists who reported this story noted.

> Yet few know the legalization of American home-brewing—and the microbrew craze that soon followed—has Rochester roots, and the credit goes to Barber Conable.
>
> That's right, the Republican congressman, who represented Monroe and Genesee counties from 1964 to 1984, sponsored the bill that removed the bootlegging stigma from homebrewing, a hobby now enjoyed by more than 2 million Americans.
>
> For his part, Conable doesn't remember much about the 1978 legislation. At the time he recalls being busy arguing for public-financing for elections, and the homebrewing bill must not have generated much opposition.

"I did not consider it a big deal," Conable, who did not drink beer, told the reporters.

Indeed, there too Conable had to examine his records to see if he had sponsored the legislation. He found a letter he had written his old friend, Senator Daniel Patrick Moynihan, asking him to sponsor similar legislation in the Senate. "A small beer-kit manufacturer in Rochester will appreciate it," Conable wrote Moynihan.

Julie Johnson Bradford, editor of *All About Beer* magazine in Durham, North Carolina, called the 1978 legislation "a significant milestone in the history of American brewing. It was really an oversight that homebrewing remained illegal when Prohibition was repealed," she said. "People still did it, but it was an underground activity."

After homebrewing was legalized in 1978, the hobby became more popular and the industry grew.

"Homebrewing can take a lot of credit for the beer revolution," Bradford said. "The first cohort of microbrewers got their start as homebrewers. . . . Now, we've got a lot more diversity from top to bottom because of homebrewing."

Calling Barber Conable "a champ," Bradford told the two Rochester reporters, "Tell your town they can feel pride."

"I thought most of what I had done in Congress was written on the wind and changed a few years after I left," Conable said, as he typically stressed his own legislative insignificance in Congress.

"Lucky for us," the two Rochester reporters noted, "he was wrong."[13]

So now, in the twilight of his life, looking back on his aspirations and accomplishments, in search of some reassurance that it had all been worthwhile, Conable was delighted with the recognition and accolades that continued to flow his way late in life. "Most of us enjoy having our efforts recognized and appreciated," he told a small group of students in the spring of 2001. And throughout his life, he said, mindful of the importance of his parents in growing up, "I like to think that I have not moved far from the original values that my parents put in me as a boy."[14]

Conable took especially to heart his father's advice to him as a young lawyer in Batavia in the early 1950s that "you've got to put a lot into the community if you're going to take a lot out of it."[15] Remembering too the silent pledge he had made to his fallen comrades at Iwo Jima in 1945 "to do a little of [their] work as well as [his] own, to make the world a little better than it otherwise would be,"[16] Conable had thrown himself wholeheartedly into every public service he had ever attempted. Always trying to balance his commitment to public service with his many private interests, he remained true throughout his life to the democratic ideals first instilled in him by his parents.

There is no perfect or even good way to end the biography of any man's life, particularly a man as complex and accomplished as Barber Conable, as we search for just one more clue or story that might provide the deeper truth and ultimate meaning of that man's life.

But in Conable's case, the truth is probably no more complicated than the simple answer he gave to a student in April 2001. "What motivates you to do all the things you have done with your life?" the amazed and inspired student asked.

"It's good to be a participant. It's good to be a participant," Conable said.

> I don't see the issues being all that different between the Board of Supervisors and the Congress of the United States. Same cast of characters, perhaps a little less sophisticated on the Board of Supervisors, but the same kinds of debates, same kinds of decisions that have to be made. What democracy is all about is it gives extraordinary responsibilities to ordinary people. And you hope that they can rise to the point where they can participate in the decisions related to those responsibilities in significant ways. I used to come home and say to my wife, "Does this remind you of anything that happened back in Batavia?" And I'd tell her something that happened in the Congress, and she'd say, "Remember when we had that big fight in the county building?" And that's true. That's one of the things about democracy. It does not rely on philosopher kings. It relies on people who have representative views and express them effectively.

True to his participatory tradition, Barber Conable recited the Declaration of Independence on the steps of the Genesee Country Museum townhall for what would be the last time on July 4, 2003. Shortly after his 81st birthday, he died on November 30, 2003. Following his wishes, he was buried in the small graveyard less than a mile from his Alexander, New York home in a private ceremony attended by family and close friends.

Barber B. Conable Sr. was right in the advice he gave his son in 1952. "You've got to put a lot into a community if you're going to take a lot from it." From Alexander, New York to Washington D. C., to the world community, the evidence is in the life and accomplishments of his son, Barber B. Conable Jr.[17]

Notes

1: Introduction

1. Courtney R. Sheldon, "Movers and Shakers in Congress," *U.S. News and World Report*, 23 April 1984, 38.

2. George F. Will, "An American House of Lords," *Newsweek*, 4 June 1984, 92.

3. Jane Perlez, "Rep. Conable, After 20 Years in Congress, Plans to Retire," *New York Times*, 7 February 1984.

4. Charles O. Jones, political science professor at the University of Virginia, conversation with the author, 2 September 1988.

5. See, for example, Nelson W. Polsby, ed., *Congressional Behavior* (New York: Random House, 1971), 136–7.

6. For an illustration of other congressional styles, see *50 Ways To Do the Job of Congress* (Washington, D.C.: Congressional Quarterly, Inc., 1999).

7. Barber B. Conable Jr., *Washington Report* (Conable's congressional newsletter), 18 October 1984.

8. William Safire, *Safire's New Political Dictionary* (New York: Random House, 1993), 620.

9. Conable, "Washington Report," 13 February 1975.

10. Harry Nicholas, administrative assistant to Congressman Barber B. Conable Jr. from 1965 to 1985, interview by author, 9 June 1989.

11. "A Tribute to Barber Conable," *Congressional Record*, 3 October 1984, H 11189.

12. Ibid., H 11177–96.

13. Ibid., H 11183.

14. Ibid., H 11189.

15. Ibid., H 11196.

16. Ibid., 14 October 1984, E 4276.

17. Ibid., 3 October 1984, H 11197.

18. Conable, "Washington Report," 5 April 1984.

19. Ibid., 13 May 1970.

20. For an analysis of their newsletters, see Clem Miller, *Member of the House: Letters of a Congressman*, edited by John W. Baker (New York: Charles Scribner's Sons, 1962), and Robert L. Peabody, ed., *Education of a Congressman: The Newsletters of Morris K. Udall* (Indianapolis: The Bobbs-Merrill Co., Inc., 1972).

21. Conable, "Washington Report," 14 November 1974.

22. Ibid., 18 March 1982.

23. Barber B. Conable Jr., interview by author, 28 September 1991.

24. Charles Collins, art history professor at the Rochester Institute of Technology, conversation with author, 18 July 1989.

25. Raymond Downs, retired Kodak engineer, interview by author, 8 March 1988.

26. Conable, "Washington Report," 18 March 1982.

27. Pam Trenholme, administrator at the State University of New York College at Brockport, interview by the author, 5 April 1991. For a detailed analysis of how Conable used his congressional newsletters to educate his constituents, see James S. Fleming, "The House Member as Teacher: An Analysis of the Congressional Newsletters of Barber B. Conable, Jr.," *Congress and the Presidency* 20 (Spring 1993): 53–74.

28. Albert R. Hunt, "Ways and Means' Unsung Mr. Conable," *Wall Street Journal*, 9 July 1973.

29. Albert R. Hunt, "In Defense of a Messy Congress," *The Washingtonian*, September 1982, 187–9.

30. David Broder, "Rep. Conable Cuts Through the Puffery," *Rochester Democrat and Chronicle*, 10 April 1974.

31. Bob Woodward and Carl Bernstein, *The Final Days* (New York: Simon and Schuster, 1976), 153–60, 378–9.

32. Safire, *Safire's New Political Dictionary*, 723.

33. Godfrey Sperling, interview by the author, 10 January 2002.

34. Read Kingsbury, "Extraordinary Instructor," *Rochester Times-Union*, 2 January 1985.

35. Richard F. Fenno Jr., "The Freshman Congressman: His View of the House," in Polsby, *Congressional Behavior*, 129–35.

36. Richard F. Fenno Jr., *Home Style: House Members in Their Districts* (Boston: Little, Brown and Company, 1978).

37. Richard F. Fenno Jr., *Watching Politicians: Essays on Participant Observation* (Berkeley: Institute of Government Series Press, 1990), 13.

38. Thomas Fitzpatrick, "Watching Politicians," *Rochester Review*, Spring 1991, 12–17.

39. Richard F. Fenno Jr., political science professor at the University of Rochester, conversation with the author, 28 March 1996.

40. See, for example, John F. Manley, *The Politics of Finance: The House Committee on Ways and Means* (Boston: Little, Brown and Company, 1970), 84–5; Nelson W. Polsby, *Congress and the Presidency* (Englewood Cliffs: Prentice Hall, 1986), 116; William F. Connelly Jr. and John J. Pitney Jr., *Congress' Permanent Minority?* (Lanham: Rowman and Littlefield Publishers, Inc., 1974), 8, 14–15, 157–8; Stephen Bates, ed., *The Media and Congress* (Columbus: Publishing Horizons, 1987), 23; Peter Woll, *Congress* (Boston: Little Brown and Company, 1985), 269–72; Walter J. Oleszek, *Congressional Procedures and the Policy Process* (Washington, D.C., 1989), 135; James L. Sundquist, *Constitutional Reform and Effective Government* (Washington, D.C.: The Brookings Institution,

1986), 4, 10, 105; Roger H. Davidson and Walter J. Oleszek, eds., *Governing: Readings and Cases in American Politics* (Washington, D.C.: Congressional Quarterly, Inc., 1987), 506–8; Morris P. Fiorina, *Congress: Keystone of the Washington Establishment* (New Haven: Yale University press, 1989), 69–70; and Lou Frey Jr. and Michael T. Hayes, eds., *Inside the House: Former Members Reveal How Congress Really Works* (Lanham: University Press of America, Inc., 2001), 152–6.

41. Paul Light, *Artful Work: The Politics of Social Security Reform* (New York: Random House, 1985).

42. *Congress: We the People* (A telecourse produced by WETA in Washington, D.C. and the American Political Science Association with funding from the Annenberg/CPB Project, 1984).

43. Linda L. Fowler and Robert D. McClure, *Political Ambition: Who Decides to Run for Congress* (New Haven: Yale University Press, 1989).

44. Barber B. Conable Jr., with A. L. Singleton, *Congress and the Income Tax* (Norman: University of Oklahoma, 1989).

45. Michael Clements, "Professor Conable: Congressman to Teach at UR," *Rochester Democrat and Chronicle*, 7 December 1984.

46. Barber B. Conable Papers, 1960–1985, Collection Number 2794. Courtesy of the Division of Rare and Manuscript Collections, Cornell University Library.

47. Conable's newsletters and newspaper columns were both entitled the "Washington Report." In his newsletters, Conable typically discussed three or four issues of importance to his constituents. His newspaper columns, on the other hand, were devoted to a lengthier discussion of one issue. Unless otherwise indicated, the "Washington Reports" cited in the notes refer to the newsletters.

48. Conable, *Congress and the Income Tax*.

49. Barber B. Conable Jr., Personal Journal, 1968–1984.

50. Barber B. Conable Jr., letter to the author, 19 July 2000.

51. Conable interview, 22 March 1992.

52. Ibid., 1 May 1997.

2: Roots in Western New York

1. Barber B. Conable Jr., "The Global Economy," speech delivered at the Economic Forum Luncheon, sponsored by the Boy Scouts of America, Riverside Convention Center, Rochester, New York, 30 March 1990.

2. Barber B. Conable Jr., conversation with the author, Summer 1985.

3. John S. Conable, interview by the author, 18 December 1990.

4. Barber Conable, interview by the author, 24 August 1993.

5. John G. Wilson, "One Man's Family," *Historical Wyoming*, January 1984, 71.

6. Anita Ripstein, "The Conables of Wyoming County," *Historical Wyoming*, January 1984, 62.

7. John S. Conable interview, 18 December 1990.

8. Barber Conable interview, 24 August 1993.

9. John S. Conable interview, 18 December 1990.

10. Ibid.

11. Ripstein, "The Conables of Wyoming County," 63.

12. Barber Conable interview, 24 August 1993.

13. Ibid.

14. John S. Conable interview, 18 December 1990.

15. Ibid.

16. John G. Wilson, interview by the author, 18 December 1990.

17. John S. Conable interview, 18 December 1990.

18. Robert Ingersoll, 1833–1899, was a noted New York lawyer known for his controversial critique of the Bible published in *The Gods and Other Lectures* and *Some Mistakes of Moses*; Thackeray, 1811–1863, was best known for his 1848 novel *Vanity Fair*; Kipling, 1865–1936, famously glorified British imperialism.

19. Barber Conable interview, 24 August 1993.

20. For a published example of Conable's expertise on local Indian history, see Barber B. Conable Jr., "Early Inhabitants of Wyoming County," *Historical Wyoming*, January 1976, 53–6.

21. John S. Conable interview, 18 December 1990.

22. Barber Conable interview, 24 August 1993.

23. Wilson interview, 18 December 1990.

24. Barber Conable interview, 24 August 1993.

25. Frederick G. Marcham, "Letter to a Freshman," *Cornell Magazine*, September 1993, 20–4.

26. Stephen Madden, "A Man of Quiet and Luminous Joy: Remembering Professor Frederick Marcham," *Cornell Alumni News*, April 1993, 7–8.

27. Barber Conable interview, 24 August 1993.

28. Barber Conable interview, 15 June 1994.

29. Barber B. Conable Jr., "Homily Delivered at Marine Corps/45th Anniversary of the Battle of Iwo Jima," National Cathedral, Washington, D.C., 19 February 1990.

30. Barber Conable interview, 15 June 1994.

31. Conable, "Homily."

32. Barber Conable interview, 15 June 1994.

33. Tom Brokaw, *The Greatest Generation* (New York: Random House, 1998).

34. Conable, "Homily."

3: Becoming a Lawyer and Politician

1. Barber B. Conable Jr., interview by the author, 15 June 1994.

2. R. P. Sibley, assistant dean, College of Arts and Sciences, Cornell University, letter to Professor D. G. Yorkey, secretary, Cornell Law School, 28 April 1942.

3. Frederick G. Marcham, professor of history, Cornell University, letter to secretary, Cornell Law School, 5 May 1942.

4. Conable interview, 15 June 1994.

5. *Telluride Association* (Ithaca, N.Y.: Telluride Association, undated).

6. Conable interview, 15 June 1994.

7. Barber B. Conable Jr., application to the Telluride Association, 26 June 1946.

8. Conable interview, 15 June 1994.

9. Eric Pell, interview by the author, 8 June 1994.

10. Conable interview, 15 June 1994.

11. Karl Buchholtz, interview by the author, 8 June 1993.

12. Conable interview, 15 June 1994. For interested local historians, the other three New Yorkers chosen for this honor were Robert B. Adams, the president of a Buffalo department store; the mayor of Middletown, Louis F. Mills; and an optometrist in Binghamton active in community affairs, William I. Roberts. For details on this award, see "Batavian is Included by the State Jaycees as Outstanding Leader," *The* [Batavia] *Daily News*, 28 February 1954.

13. Conable interview, 15 June 1994.

14. The first of three Conable daughters, Anne, was born on 26 November 1954. Jane came along a short time later on 6 June 1956, and Emily was born on 15 January 1958.

15. Conable interview, 15 June 1994.

16. Miles Cunningham, "Senator Erwin Ending 52 Years of Public Life," *Rochester Times-Union*, 27 December 1962.

17. Conable interview, 15 June 1994.

18. "Batavia Attorney Announces Candidacy for State Senator Opposing Long-Term Official," *The* [Batavia] *Daily News*, 17 April 1962.

19. "Indications Mount Sen. Erwin Will Not Be Candidate Again," *The* [Batavia] *Daily News*, 19 May 1962.

20. "Senator Erwin Decides to Retire to Devote Full Time to Law," *The* [Batavia] *Daily News*, 23 May 1962.

21. "Emery Announces Candidacy," *Livingston County Leader*, 14 June 1962.

22. Conable interview, 15 June 1994. The fourth child, Sam, had been born on 27 May 1961.

23. "GOP Endorses Barber Conable," *The* [Batavia] *Daily News*, 12 June 1962; "Conable Endorsed by Wyoming's GOP," *The* [Batavia] *Daily News*, 19 June 1962; "Conable Gains Orleans Backing," *The* [Batavia] *Daily News*, 27 June 1962; and "Livingston GOP Endorses Sheriff, *The* [Batavia] *Daily News*, 20 June 1962.

24. "Four Candidates Battle for Senatorial Nomination," *Livingston County Leader*, 23 August 1962; "Sheriff Emery Campaigns Hard for State Senate," and "Conable Steps Up Campaign for State Senate," *The Livingston Republican*, 30 August 1962.

25. "Onus on Genesee GOP," *The* [Batavia] *Daily News*, 5 September 1962.

26. "GOP Readies Campaign 'To Get Out The Vote' for Conable Candidacy," *The* [Batavia] *Daily News*, 5 September 1962.

27. "Genesee's Candidate Scores Smashing Win," *The* [Batavia] *Daily News*, 7 September 1962.

28. "Very Grateful, Says Conable," *The* [Batavia] *Daily News*, 7 September 1962.

29. Conable interview, 15 June 1994.

30. "Conable Wins Erwin Seat in Senate," *Rochester Times-Union*, 7 November 1962.

4: Mr. Conable Goes to Albany

1. Barber B. Conable Jr., letter to Peter Dragon, *Albion Advertiser*, 11 January 1963. Barber B. Conable Papers, 1960–1985. Collection Number 2794, Box 4. Courtesy Division of Rare and Manuscript Collections, Cornell University Library.

2. "Senator Conable Draws Glares in First Speech," *Rochester Times-Union*, 27 February 1963.

3. "Conable Defends Home Rule Issue," *The* [Batavia] *Daily News*, 28 February 1963.

4. "Senator Conable Draws Glares in First Speech."

5. Robert McEwen, interview with the author, 25 June 1993.

6. Barber B. Conable Jr., "Albany Report," 17 January 1993.

7. Ibid., 24 January 1963.

8. Ibid., 14 March 1963.

9. Tom Benton, interview with the author, 18 May 1988.

10. "Albany Report," 14 March 1963.

11. Ibid., 21 March 1963.

12. Barber B. Conable Jr., letter to district newspaper editors, 5 April 1963, Conable Papers.

13. Orville Allen, Genesee Valley Press, *The Breeze* and *The Express*, Dansville, N.Y., letter to Barber B. Conable Jr., 8 April 1963, Conable Papers.

14. Barber B. Conable Jr., letter to George Questa, *Olean Times Herald*, Olean, N.Y., 6 July 1963, Conable Papers.

15. Barber B. Conable Jr., press release, 30 July 1963, Conable Papers.

16. Barber B. Conable Jr., letter to George Questa, *Olean Times Herald*, Olean, N.Y., 6 July 1963, Conable Papers.

17. Barber B. Conable Jr., memorial service for John F. Kennedy, Batavia, N.Y., 24 November 1963, Conable Papers.

18. Barber B. Conable Jr., interview with the author, 8 December 1990.

19. "Conable Candidate; Ostertag Retiring," *The* [Batavia] *Daily News*, 25 February 1964. Also see "Conable Wins Support for Ostertag Post," *Rochester Times-Union*, 25 February 1964.

20. "Conable Candidate; Ostertag Retiring."

21. Ibid.

22. Al Walkley, letter to Barber Conable, 28 February 1964, Conable Papers.

23. "Sen. Conable is Opening Campaign for Congress," *The* [Batavia] *Daily News*, 27 March 1964.

24. Theodore H. White, *The Making of the President 1964* (New York: Atheneum Publishers, 1965), 200–31.

25. Conable interview, 24 August 1993.

26. "Senator Conable Views Political Parties with Relation to National Progress," *The* [Batavia] *Daily News*, 7 August 1963.

27. Conable interview, 8 December 1990.

28. White, *The Making of the President*, 253–308.

29. Charles O. Jones, "The 1964 Presidential Election—Further Adventures in Wonderland," in Donald G. Herzberg, ed., *American Government Annual, 1965–1966* (New York: Holt, Rinehart, and Winston, 1965), 114–15.

30. Neil Bubel, interview with the author, 20 March 1997.

31. "Q and A on What They Say: Candidates for the HR," *Rochester Democrat and Chronicle*, 28 October 1964.

32. Kathleen Smith, "Mrs. Conable Manages Many Things on Campaign Trail," *The* [Batavia] *Daily News*, 22 August 1964.

33. Michael Telesca, interview with the author, 5 May 1997.

34. John Riedman, interview with the author, 6 July 1988.

35. "Conable Praised Miller," *The* [Batavia] *Daily News*, 24 October 1964.

36. Telesca interview, 5 May 1991.

37. Conable interview, 8 December 1990.

38. Bubel interview, 20 March 1997.

39. Tom Benton, interview with the author, 18 May 1988.

40. Conrad Christiano, "Williams, Horton Battle for District 36 Seat," *Rochester Democrat and Chronicle*, 18 October 1964.

41. "To Represent Us in Congress: Horton, Conable, Quigley," *Rochester Democrat and Chronicle*, 27 October 1964.

42. "Conable Wins House Seat, Genesee Aids," *The* [Batavia] *Daily News*, 4 November 1964.

43. Mitchell Kaidy, "Tide Bucked by Horton, Conable," *Rochester Democrat and Chronicle*, 4 November 1964.

44. "It was an Avalanche with Debris Everywhere," *Rochester Democrat and Chronicle*, 4 November 1964.

45. Thomas F. Hicks, "7 Area Counties Go For Johnson," *Rochester Democrat and Chronicle*, 4 November 1964.

46. Peter Behr, "Senate Race Paved Way: Conable Carries Rural Counties to Win," *Rochester Times-Union*, 4 November 1964.

47. "Conable Promises De-centralist Role," *Rochester Democrat and Chronicle*, 5 November 1964.

48. "Victory Brings Problems," *Rochester Times-Union*, 4 November 1964; "Conable Buys Maryland Home for His Family," *The* [Batavia] *Daily News*, 18 November 1964.

5: A Freshman in the Eighty-Ninth Congress

1. "A Hectic First Day for Conable," *Rochester Times-Union*, 4 January 1965.

2. Richard F. Fenno Jr., "The Freshman Congressman: His View of the House," in Nelson W. Polsby, ed., *Congressional Behavior* (New York: Random House, 1971), 129–35.

3. Ibid.

4. Robert L. Peabody, *Leadership in Congress, Stability, Succession, and Change* (Boston: Little, Brown and Company, 1976), 100–1.

5. Barber B. Conable Jr., interview by the author, 22 March 1992.

6. Peabody, *Leadership in Congress*, 100–48.

7. Conable interview, 22 March 1992.

8. Fenno, "The Freshman Congressman," 132–4.

9. Conable interview, 22 March 1992.

10. Fenno, "The Freshman Congressman," 135.

11. Richard F. Fenno Jr., *Home Style: House Members in Their Districts* (Boston: Little, Brown and Company, 1978). Conable was one of the eighteen congressmen Fenno studied for this book. Fenno classified Conable's home style anonymously as that of "Congressman H," a congressman from a heterogeneous, urban-suburban-rural district who felt most comfortable and drew his strongest support from the rural portions of his district (154–7).

12. Conable interview, 11 August 1988.

13. James S. Fleming, "Frank Horton: Twenty-Five Years in the United States Congress, 1962–1987," booklet prepared for the testimonial dinner in honor of Congressman Frank Horton, Rochester (N.Y.) Riverside Convention Center, 11 December 1987.

14. Conable interview, 24 October 1992.

15. Barber B. Conable Jr., "Washington Report," 3 February 1965.

16. Ibid., 25 January 1967, 13 April 1970, and 14 November 1974.

17. For a detailed analysis of how Conable used his congressional newsletters to develop the trust and support of his constituents throughout his congressional career, see James S. Fleming, "The House Member as Teacher: An Analysis of the Newsletters of Barber B. Conable Jr.," *Congress and the Presidency* (Spring 1993): 53–74.

18. Conable, "Washington Report," 3 February 1965.

19. Ibid., 17 March 1965.

20. Ibid., 14 April 1965.

21. Ibid., 17 February 1965.

22. Ibid., 7 July 1965.

23. Ibid., 23 June 1965.

24. Ibid., 20 October 1965.

25. Ibid., 15 June 1966.

26. Ibid., 31 March 1965.

27. Ibid., 3 February 1965.

28. Ibid., 31 March 1965.

29. "House Freshman Presidential Support-Opposition Scores," 1965 *Congressional Quarterly Almanac* (Washington, D.C.: Congressional Quarterly, Inc., 1966), 1746.

30. Conable, "Washington Report," 22 September 1965.

31. "House Freshman Presidential Support-Opposition Scores." A related study by *Congressional Quarterly* revealed that Conable was generally more supportive of President Johnson than his conservative rhetoric would indicate. On the sixty-six legislative issues on which President Johnson took positions during the first seven months of his presidency, *Congressional Quarterly* found that Conable tied with Tim Lee Carter of Kentucky in leading the twenty House Republican freshmen in support of the president, voting with Johnson 58 percent of the time, a full 20 percent above the average freshman Republican supporting the president.

32. Conable, "Washington Report," 3 March 1965.

33. Ibid., 28 July 1965.

34. Ibid., 18 May 1966.

35. Ibid., 12 April 1965.

36. Linda McLaughin, Congressman Conable's personal secretary and office manager from 1975 to 1985, interview by the author, 17 August 1988.

37. Conable, "Washington Report," 20 October 1965.

38. Stephen Frantzich and John Sullivan, *The C-SPAN Revolution* (Norman: University of Oklahoma Press, 1996).

39. Conable, "Washington Report," 12 April 1965.

40. Ibid., 28 September 1966.

41. Ibid., 23 March 1966.

42. Ibid., 12 April 1965.

43. Ibid., 9 February 1966.

44. Ibid., 1 June 1966.

45. Ibid., 27 July 1966.

46. Ibid., 26 January 1966.

47. Ibid., 9 March 1966.

48. Ibid., 6 April 1966.

49. Ibid., 17 March 1965.

50. Ibid., 23 June 1965.

51. Ibid., 28 July 1965.

52. Ibid., 12 April 1965.

53. Ibid., 26 January 1966 and 15 June 1966.

54. Ibid., 18 April 1966.

55. Ibid., 2 November 1966.

56. Gerald R. Ford, conversation with the author, 28 October 1992.

57. Charles Collins, art history professor at the Rochester Institute of Technology, conversation with the author, 18 July 1989.

58. Jan Sturdevant, "Conable, Horton Victories Again," *Rochester Democrat and Chronicle*, 9 November 1966.

59. *1966 Congressional Quarterly Almanac*, 1387.

6: Appointment to the Ways and Means Committee

1. See, for example, John E. Simonds, "Conable Backed for Key Post," *Rochester Democrat and Chronicle*, 12 January 1967. Simonds reported that on January 11 the fifteen-member New York Republican delegation in the House had unanimously endorsed Conable for a seat on the Ways and Means Committee.

2. Barber B. Conable Jr., "Washington Report," 25 January 1967.

3. Barber B. Conable Jr., interview by the author, 22 March 1992.

4. In a side note, Conable recalled that Bush's appointment to the Ways and Means Committee was closely tied to the interparty politics in the House at the time. Omar Burleson of Texas announced that he would give up his chairmanship of the House Administration Committee to seek a seat on the Ways and Means Committee, but Burleson lost his bid by one vote in the Democratic Caucus to Jack Gilbert from New York City. "I remember Jerry Ford put out a statement," Conable recalled, "saying the Democrats don't care about Texas, but the Republicans do and for the first time in many years a freshman from Texas, George Bush, is going on the Ways and Means Committee."

5. John E. Simonds, "Conable Named to Ways and Means," *Rochester Democrat and Chronicle*, 26 January 1967.

6. Conable interview, 22 March 1992.

7. Conable, "Washington Report," 8 February 1967.

8. Laurie Bennett, "Before There Was an Attica, There Was a Judge Conable," *Rochester Times-Union*, 7 January 1984. Barber's mother, Agnes Conable, the other major influence on his early life, would live another seven years, dying in Warsaw at the age of eighty-nine on March 6, 1975.

9. Barber B. Conable Jr., with A. L. Singleton, *Congress and the Income Tax* (Norman: University of Oklahoma, 1989), 15–21.

10. For the historical details on how the Democratic members of the Ways and Means Committee came to serve on the Democratic Committee on Committees in 1911, see James S. Fleming, "Re-establishing Leadership in the House of Representatives: Case of Oscar W. Underwood," *Mid-America*, 54 (October 1972): 234–50.

11. Conable, *Congress and the Income Tax*, 17–19.

12. Ibid., 19.

13. For a detailed analysis of Mills's chairmanship of the Ways and Means Committee, see Julian E. Zelizer, *Taxing America: Wilbur Mills, Congress, and the State, 1945–1975* (Cambridge: Cambridge University Press, 1988). Also see John F. Manley, *The Politics of Finance: The House Committee on Ways and Means* (Boston: Little, Brown and Company, 1970), 98–150.

14. Conable interview, 11 August 1988.

15. See, for example, "Rep. Conable Sets Laudable Example," *Utica Dispatch*, 26 November 1968, and "Conable Returns Donation," *Rochester Times-Union*, 15 November 1968, Barber B. Conable Papers,

1960–1985. Collection Number 2794, Box 30. Courtesy Division of Rare and Manuscript Collections, Cornell University Library.

16. *1967 Congressional Quarterly Almanac* (Washington D.C.: Congressional Quarterly Inc., 1968), 892–916.

17. Ibid., 643–53.

18. *1968 Congressional Quarterly Almanac*, 263–78.

19. Barber B. Conable Jr., Personal Journal, 27 March 1968.

20. *1968 Congressional Quarterly Almanac*, 263–78.

21. Conable, "Washington Report," 22 February 1967.

22. John Machacek, "Conable's 'Twilight': Leaving Imprint on Tax System—And Doodle Pad," *Rochester Times-Union*, 1 October 1984.

23. "They Hope to Earn a Boodle With His Doodles," *Rochester Democrat and Chronicle*, 29 September 1985.

24. Conable interview, 22 March 1992.

25. "Barber Conable Thanked for Committee Work," *LeRoy Gazette*, 24 October 1968, Barber B. Conable Papers, 1960–1985. Collection Number 2794, Box 30. Courtesy Division of Rare and Manuscript Collections, Cornell University Library.

26. *1968 Congressional Quarterly Almanac*, 89–92A.

27. Barber B. Conable Jr., "Washington Report," 13 June 1968 (newspaper column).

28. *1968 Congressional Quarterly Almanac*, 979–98.

29. Ibid., 1013–53. For historical perspective on this election, see Michael Barone, *Our Country: The Shaping of America from Roosevelt to Reagan* (New York: The Free Press, 1990), 411–53.

30. Barber B. Conable Jr., Personal Journal, 20 September 1968.

31. Gerald R. Ford, speech at a dinner honoring Rep. Barber Conable, Batavia, New York, 3 October 1968. Gerald R. Ford Library, Ann Arbor, Mich.

32. Conable, "Washington Report," 24 October 1968 (newspaper column).

33. Conable, Personal Journal, 17 November 1968.

34. "It's a Breeze for Horton, Conable," *Rochester Democrat and Chronicle*, 6 November 1968.

7: Support for Richard Nixon

1. *1969 Congressional Quarterly Almanac* (Washington, D.C.: Congressional Quarterly Inc., 1970), 28–29A.

2. Barber B. Conable Jr., "Washington Report," 5 March 1969.

3. *1969 Congressional Quarterly Almanac*, 35–86A.

4. Barber B. Conable Jr., "Washington Report," 6 November 1969 (newspaper column).

5. *1969 Congressional Quarterly Almanac*, 77–97.

6. *Congress and the Nation 1969–1972*, vol. 3 (Washington, D.C.: Congressional Quarterly 1973), 899–906.

7. Conable, "Washington Report," 25 June 1969.

8. *1969 Congressional Quarterly Almanac*, 1017–19.

9. Conable, "Washington Report," 22 October 1969.

10. *1969 Congressional Quarterly Almanac*, 88–91A.

11. Ibid., 87, 1017–18; *Congress and the Nation 1969–1972*, 899–906.

12. "House Seniority Study," *Congressional Quarterly Weekly Report*, 20 March 1970, 783.

13. Conable, "Washington Report," 18 June 1970 (newspaper column).

14. "Capitol Roundup," *Congressional Quarterly Weekly Report*, 16 October 1970, 2578.

15. Barber B. Conable Jr., interview with the author, 10 October 1997.

16. "The House: New Leaders of Democratic Majority," *Congressional Quarterly Weekly Report*, 22 January 1971, 176–9.

17. Conable interview, 10 October 1997.

18. For background on Rumsfeld's Raiders, which included future President George Herbert Walker Bush as a member, see the 1968 *Congressional Quarterly Almanac*, 647–54 and Conable's "Washington Report" for 18 June 1968.

19. Conable interview, 10 October 1997.

20. Andrew J. Glass, "Legislative Reform Effort Builds New Alliances Among House Members," *National Journal*, 25 July 1970, 1607–14; "No 'Secret' Votes is Conable Aim," *Rochester Times-Union*, 8 July 1970. Conable presented and explained the coalition's proposed amendments in the *Congressional Record* on July 13, 1970, E24008–10.

21. *1970 Congressional Quarterly Almanac*, 447–61.

22. Even more surprising, Mayhew found that the Nixon-Ford 93rd Congress (1973–1974), in the midst of the Watergate crisis, also enacted twenty-two major laws, thus equaling the 89th and 91st Congresses as the most legislatively productive Congresses in the post-World War II era. For the details on this, see David Mayhew, *Divided We Govern: Party Control, Lawmaking, and Investigations, 1946–1990* (New Haven: Yale University Press, 1991), 75.

23. For an extended explanation of Conable's opposition to the Voting Rights Act of 1970, see "Washington Report," 18 December 1969 and 26 March 1970 (newspaper columns). Though Conable was from a partially agricultural district, he traditionally opposed federal subsidies for agriculture and "supported a plan to phase out the present subsidies and move gradually to a market economy for the major crops." For details on his position, see his "Washington Report," 13 August 1970 (newspaper column). Conable offered no formal explanation to his constituents on his opposition to the 1970 expansion of the food stamp program, though he later recalled in a July 2, 2003, conversation that he opposed the escalating cost of the program and worried about reports of widespread abuse in the program.

24. "Conable Coasts to Victory," *Rochester Times-Union*, 4 November 1970.

25. Conable, "Washington Report," 12 November 1970 (newspaper column).

26. Conable, "Washington Report," 1 October 1970 (newspaper column).

27. *1970 Congressional Quarterly Almanac*, 22.

28. "Family Assistance," *Congressional Quarterly Weekly Report*, 27 November 1970, 2852; James Reichley, *Conservatives in an Age of Change: Nixon and Ford Administrations* (Washington, D.C.: The Brookings Institution, 1981), 142–8; Daniel P. Moynihan, *The Politics of a Guaranteed Income* (New York: Random House, 1973).

29. "Nixon and Albert: Clashing Views on the 91st," *Congressional Quarterly Weekly Report*, 8 January 1975, 35.

30. Mayhew, *Divided We Govern*, 61–2.

31. Conable, "Washington Report," 3 February 1971.

32. *1971 Congressional Quarterly Almanac*, 9–12.

33. *1971 Congressional Quarterly Almanac*, 2–5A.

34. Phil Currie, "Conable: In Congress to Do a Job," *Rochester Times-Union*, 17 February 1971. "In recent weeks," Currie noted, "Conable was mentioned by *Newsweek* magazine as one of six 'up-and-coming' congressmen, and *Life* magazine's Hugh Sidey had a reference to Conable in a column on the president and Congress."

35. "Republican House Leadership: Contests Foreseen," *Congressional Quarterly Weekly Report*, 25 December 1970, 3092; "The House: New Leaders of Democratic Majority," *Congressional Quarterly Weekly Report*, 22 January 1971, 177.

36. Conable, "Washington Report," 3 February 1971.

37. Ibid., 12 May 1971.

38. Conable interview, 10 October 1997.

39. Cabinet Room Conservations, 9 March 1971 to 10 July 1973, Nixon Presidential Matters, National Archives, Washington, D.C.

40. Conable interview, 10 October 1992.

41. *1972 Congressional Quarterly Almanac*, 638–9.

42. "Barber B. Conable Jr.," in Charles Moritz, ed., *Current Biography Yearbook 1984* (New York: The H. W. Wilson Company, 1984), 91.

43. Conable interview, 10 October 1997.

44. *Congressional Record*, 22 June 1972, 22048–9.

45. Reichley, *Conservatives in an Age of Change*, 159–65; Conable, "Washington Report," 22 June 1972.

46. Mayhew, *Divided We Govern*, 84–5.

47. *1969 Congressional Quarterly Almanac*, 1047; *1970 Congressional Quarterly Almanac*, 1129; *1971 Congressional Quarterly Almanac*, 83; *1972 Congressional Quarterly Almanac*, 49.

48. Nancy Weinberg and Pauline Jennings, "Barber B. Conable Jr.," Ralph Nader's Congressional Report, *Citizens Look at Congress* (New York: Grossman Publishers, 1972), 14.

49. Conable, "Washington Report," 8 September 1971. Conable's wife was also an active supporter of the Equal Rights Amendment and

later wrote a book on the unequal treatment of women at her alma mater, Cornell University. See Charlotte Williams Conable, *Women at Cornell: The Myth of Equal Education* (Ithaca, N.Y.: Cornell University Press, 1977).

50. Barber B. Conable Jr., "Washington Report," 20 July 1972 (newspaper column).

51. "Not Bad After All," *Rochester Democrat and Chronicle*, 21 October 1972.

52. *1972 Congressional Quarterly Almanac*, 1011–20.

53. "Conable Credits His Rival," *Rochester Times-Union*, 8 November 1972.

54. Conable, "Washington Report," 29 November 1972.

8: The Watergate Betrayal

1. Barber B. Conable Jr., interview by the author, 15 June 1994.

2. *1972 Congressional Quarterly Almanac* (Washington, D.C.: Congressional Quarterly Inc., 1973), 42.

3. Conable interview, 15 June 1994.

4. Ibid.

5. Barber B. Conable Jr., Personal Journal, 7 September 1972.

6. Ibid., 26 March 1973.

7. "A Cast of Characters for the 93rd Congress," *Time*, 15 January 1973, 18–19.

8. Albert R. Hunt, "Ways and Means' Unsung Mr. Conable," *Wall Street Journal*, 9 July 1973.

9. Conable, Personal Journal, 8 May 1973.

10. Ibid., 21 May 1973.

11. Ibid., 5 June 1973.

12. *Congress and the Nation 1973–1976*, vol. 4 (Washington, D.C.: Congressional Quarterly Inc., 1977), 931–61.

13. Personal Journal, 21 September 1973.

14. "Presidential Support: Nixon Score Hits Record Low," *Congressional Quarterly Weekly Report*, 1 September 1973, 2344–8.

15. See, for example, John Omicinski, "Conable No. 1 Lawman as Nixon Supporter," *Rochester Democrat and Chronicle*, 9 September 1973.

16. Conable, Personal Journal, 21 September 1973.

17. *Congress and the Nation*, 956–7.

18. "Republican Policy Committee Chair," *Congressional Quarterly Weekly Report*, 16 December 1973, 3300; "House GOP Elects Conable to Post," *Rochester Times-Union*, 13 December 1973.

19. Barber B. Conable Jr., "Washington Report," 9 January 1974.

20. Conable, Personal Journal, December 1973.

21. Conable, "Washington Report," 6 February 1974.

22. *Congress and the Nation*, 937.

23. Ibid., 983.

24. *Congress and the Nation*, 938.

25. Bob Woodward and Carl Bernstein, *The Final Days* (New York: Simon and Schuster, 1976), 153–4.

26. Conable, Personal Journal, 9 May 1974; Woodward and Bernstein, *The Final Days*, 154.

27. Woodward and Bernstein, *The Final Days*, 157.

28. Conable, Personal Journal, 9 May 1974.

29. Ibid., 26 June 1974.

30. John Omicinski, "Conable Dines Aboard Presidential Yacht," *Rochester Times-Union*, 30 May 1974.

31. Conable, Personal Journal, 26 June 1974.

32. *Congress and the Nation*, 959.

33. Albert R. Hunt, "The Persuaders: Small Group in House Holds Key to Size of Impeachment Vote," *Wall Street Journal*, 29 July 1974.

34. *Congressional Record*, 1 August 1974, 26348.

35. Conable, Personal Journal, 1 September 1974.

36. *Congress and the Nation*, 947.

37. Conable, Personal Journal, 1 September 1974. Also see Woodward and Bernstein, *The Final Days*, 379; John Omicinski, "Put Ford in Oval Office, Conable Says," *Rochester Democrat and Chronicle*, 6 August 1974; John Omicinski, "Conable Has Image of 'Doer' in the House," *Rochester Democrat and Chronicle*, 14 August 1974; and "The Transition: Nixon Resigns, Ford Takes Over," *Congressional Quarterly Weekly Report*, 10 August 1974, 12071.

38. For example, see Richard L. Lyons and William Chapman, "GOP Leaders Seen Voting to Impeach," *Washington Post*, 6 August 1974.

39. William Safire, *Safire's New Political Dictionary* (New York: Random House, 1993), 723.

40. *Congress and the Nation*, 948.

41. Conable interview, 29 July 1989.

42. Ibid., 15 June 1994.

9: The Toughest Reelection

1. "It'll be a Tough Campaign," *Rochester Democrat and Chronicle*, 21 May 1974.

2. John Machacek, "Conable A '50–50 Conservative,' Says Challenger Carman," *Rochester Times-Union*, 29 August 1974.

3. Ibid.

4. John Machacek, "Conservative Backing Shaky for Conable," *Rochester Times-Union*, 13 September 1974; "Political Unknown Upsets Conable," *Rochester Times-Union*, 14 September 1974.

5. Scott Spreier, "Conable Blames Rocky, Amnesty for Primary Loss," *Rochester Democrat and Chronicle*, 15 September 1974.

6. Phil Hand, "Midge: Next Target—Conable," *Rochester Democrat and Chronicle*, 11 September 1974.

7. Midge Costanza, interview by the author, 18 December 1994.

8. Barber B. Conable Jr., Personal Journal, 1 December 1974.

9. Peter Regenstreif, interview by the author, 12 December 1994.

10. "Rivals Say Conable 'Tardy' on Nixon," *Rochester Times-Union*, 7 August 1974.

11. Regenstreif interview, 12 December 1994.

12. Ironically, Fenno's intervention in Conable's campaign changed forever his relationship with Barber Conable, but not in ways Fenno had anticipated. As Fenno later wrote, reflecting on this important episode in his own professional career, Conable "never forgot that telephone call. And I became, in his eyes, an ally who had stood with him in his toughest election fight. The personal relationship between us became too close to be professional. Having entered the fray and won, I had paradoxically lost the very scholarly resource I had sought to protect. Having crossed over the boundary as wholeheartedly as I did, I could not return. . . . I could not and did not do any more research on Barber Conable." For further details on Fenno's intervention in the Conable campaign, see Richard F. Fenno Jr., *Watching Politicians: Essays on Participant Observation* (Berkeley: Institute of Government Studies, University of California at Berkeley, 1990), 12–14.

13. Conable, Personal Journal, 1 December 1974.

14. Regenstreif interview, 12 December 1994.

15. Michael Zeigler, "Big-name Democrats Target In on Conable," *Rochester Democrat and Chronicle*, 9 October 1974.

16. "Ford Plan Would Hurt Many, Georgian Says," *Rochester Times-Union*, 9 October 1974.

17. Michael Zeigler, "'Twas Midge's Campaign, but Carter's Show," *Rochester Democrat and Chronicle*, 10 October 1974.

18. "Text of Testimony," *Rochester Times-Union*, 11 October 1974.

19. Mary Anne Pikrone, "Conable Says '73 Meeting is Non-Issue," *Rochester Times-Union*, 11 October 1974. See also Michael Zeigler, "Conable Gets Vague '73 Scandal Report," *Rochester Democrat and Chronicle*, 11 October, 1974.

20. "Conable Splashed by Watergate," *Rochester Times-Union*, 15 October 1974.

21. Zeigler, "Big-Name Democrats Target in on Conable."

22. R. W. Apple Jr., "Democrats Await a Flood of Votes . . . While Ford Does What He Can With a Blotter," *New York Times*, 13 October 1974.

23. Michael Zeigler, "Conable Reluctant, Has Fund-Raiser," *Rochester Democrat and Chronicle*, 12 October 1974.

24. Mary Ann Pikrone, "Conable vs. Costanza: The Choice Is Between Images," *Rochester Times-Union*, 1 November 1974.

25. Scott Spreier, "Conable-Costanza: Their Styles Poles Apart," *Rochester Democrat and Chronicle*, 13 October 1974.

26. Pikrone, "Conable vs. Costanza."

27. Spreier, "Conable-Costanza."

28. Pikrone, "Conable vs. Costanza."

29. Spreier, "Conable-Costanza."

30. Pikrone, "Conable vs. Costanza."

31. Mary Ann Pikrone, "Eckert Engineered Late Conable Tactics," *Rochester Times-Union*, 13 November 1974.

32. "Something That Needs Saying About Barber Conable: By Some People You May Know," *Rochester Democrat and Chronicle*, 1 November 1974.

33. Dan Lovely, " 'Everyone's Disgusted About Most Everything,' " *Rochester Democrat and Chronicle*, 3 November 1974.

34. Conable, Personal Journal, 1 December 1974.

35. Michael Zeigler, "A Worrier for a Time, A Winner in the End," *Rochester Democrat and Chronicle*, 6 November 1974.

36. Michael Zeigler, "Tough Run to Conable," *Rochester Democrat and Chronicle*, 6 November 1974.

37. Scott Spreier, "Conable Gives Party Reason for Cheering," *Rochester Democrat and Chronicle*, 6 November 1974.

38. Barber B. Conable Jr., interview by the author, 3 August 1994; Midge Costanza, interview by the author, 18 December 1994.

39. Pikrone, "Eckert Engineered Late Conable Tactics."

40. Conable, Personal Journal, 1 December 1974.

41. "House Democrats Roll Up Landslide," *Rochester Democrat and Chronicle*, 6 November 1974.

42. "The Results: A Major Sweep for the Democrats," *Congressional Quarterly Weekly Report*, 9 November 1974, 3059–60.

10: A Friend in the White House

1. Barber B. Conable Jr., interview with the author, 28 September 1991.

2. In addition to Conable and Bush, Ford also met individually with Elford Cederberg, the senior Republican congressman from Michigan; the long-time House Republican whip, Leslie Arends, from Illinois; Senate Minority Leader Hugh Scott from Pennsylvania; Senator Robert Griffin of Michigan; Arizona Senator Barry Goldwater; House Republican Minority Leader John Rhodes, also from Arizona; and Senator John Tower of Texas. "The Daily Diary of President Gerald R. Ford," August 11, 1974, Gerald R. Ford Library, Ann Arbor, Mich.

3. Conable, Personal Journal, 1 September 1974.

4. Conable interview, 15 June 1994.

5. Conable, Personal Journal, 1 September 1974. For the newspaper coverage of Conable's comments, see John Omicinski, "Conable Talks with Ford: Rocky, Bush, VP Choices," *Rochester Times-Union*, 13 August 1974.

6. Conable, Personal Journal, 1 September 1974.

7. *1974 Congressional Quarterly Almanac* (Washington, D.C.: Congressional Quarterly Inc., 1975), 917–21.

8. The following account of Ford's presidential style is taken from Sidney M. Milkis and Michael Nelson, *The American Presidency: Origins and Development* (Washington, D.C.: Congressional Quarterly Inc., 1999), 328–9.

9. Ibid., 329. Also see Mark J. Rozell, *The Press and the Ford Presidency* (Ann Arbor: University of Michigan Press, 1992), 31–85.

10. Conable interview, 2 April 1999.

11. Bob Woodward, "Gerald R. Ford," in Caroline Kennedy, ed., *Profiles in Courage for Our Time* (New York: Hyperion, 2002), 315.

12. "The Results: A Major Sweep for the Democrats," *Congressional Quarterly Weekly Report*, 9 November 1974, 3059–60. Also see Conable's analysis of this election, anticipating the many institutional reforms that would follow, in his *Washington Report* for 14 November 1974.

13. "New Congress Organizes; No Role for Mills," *Congressional Quarterly Weekly Report*, 7 December 1974, 3247–53; *1975 Congressional Quarterly Almanac*, 26–34.

14. "Wilbur Mills Incident," *Congressional Quarterly Weekly Report*, 12 October 1974, 2841.

15. *1974 Congressional Quarterly Almanac*, 36.

16. "New Congress Organizes."

17. *1975 Congressional Quarterly Almanac*, 30.

18. "New Congress Organizes"; *1975 Congressional Quarterly Almanac*, 26–34.

19. Conable, "Washington Report," 12 December 1974. These important committee and institutional changes in the House in 1974 and 1975 also attracted the attention of political scientists. See, for example, Catherine E. Rudder, "Committee Reform and the Revenue Process," in Lawrence C. Dodd and Bruce I. Oppenheimer, eds., *Congress Reconsidered* (New York: Prager Publishers, 1977), 117–39 and Randall Strahan, *New Ways and Means: Reform and Change in a Congressional Committee* (Chapel Hill: University of North Carolina Press, 1990), 91–138.

20. "Ulman Unlikely to Assert Power of Mills . . . But Chairman's Strength Was Slipping Anyway," *Congressional Quarterly Weekly Report*, 7 December 1974, 3248–9.

21. "Republican Caucus," *Congressional Quarterly Weekly Report*, 7 December 1974, 3253.

22. *1975 Congressional Quarterly Almanac*, 8–11A.

23. Conable, Personal Journal, 22 January 1975.

24. Gerald R. Ford, *A Time to Heal* (New York: Harper and Row, Publishers and The Reader's Digest Association, Inc., 1979), 258–9; *1975 Congressional Quarterly Almanac*, 95–111.

25. A. James Reichley, *Conservatives in an Age of Change: The Nixon and Ford Administrations* (Washington, D.C.: The Brookings Institution, 1981), 367.

26. Conable, Personal Journal, 29 April 1975.

27. Conable interview, 16 October 1998.

28. Conable, Personal Journal, 29 April 1975.

29. Conable, "Washington Report," 8 May 1975.

30. Conable, Personal Journal, 7 May 1975.

31. "Republicans: On the Sidelines," *Congressional Quarterly Weekly Report*, 15 March 1975, 516.

32. *1975 Congressional Quarterly Almanac*, 211–14; Strahan, *New Ways and Means*, 117.

33. "House Passes Stripped Down Energy Tax Bill," *Congressional Quarterly Weekly Report*, 21 June 1975, 1275–6.

34. Reichley, *Conservatives in an Age of Change*, 367–8.

35. *1975 Congressional Quarterly Almanac*, 207–19.

36. Ibid., 220.

37. Conable, Personal Journal, 12 July 1975.

38. Jack Marsh, "Conable Says He'll Retire Soon Enough for a New Career," *Rochester Times-Union*, 14 January 1976.

39. Conable, Personal Journal, 9 June 1975.

40. Conable, Personal Journal, 12 July 1975.

41. Ford, *A Time To Heal*, 328.

42. Conable interview, 16 October 1998.

43. Ford, *A Time To Heal*, 333–4.

44. Conable, Personal Journal, 26 February 1976.

45. John Robert Greene, *The Presidency of Gerald R. Ford* (Lawrence: University of Kansas, 1995), 164–7.

46. Conable, Personal Journal, 4 May 1976.

47. Ibid., 12 May 1976.

48. Ibid., 21 May 1976.

49. Ford, *A Time To Heal*, 387–9.

50. *1976 Congressional Quarterly Almanac*, 900; Ford, *A Time To Heal*, 389.

51. Greene, *The Presidency of Gerald R. Ford*, 170–1.

52. Conable, Personal Journal, 31 July 1976.

53. *1976 Congressional Quarterly Almanac*, 892.

54. Greene, *The Presidency of Gerald R. Ford*, 172–3.

55. Conable, Personal Journal, 23 August 1976.

56. Ford, *A Time To Heal*, 409.

57. Greene, *The Presidency of Gerald R. Ford*, 175–86.

58. James Cannon, *Time and Chance: Gerald Ford's Appointment with History* (New York: Harper Collins, 1994), 408.

59. Conable, Personal Journal, 10 October 1976.

60. Greene, *The Presidency of Gerald R. Ford*, 186.

61. Conable, Personal Journal, 1 December 1976.

62. Conable interview, 10 October 1998.

63. Greene, *The Presidency of Gerald R. Ford*, 187.

64. Conable, Personal Journal, 1 December 1976.

65. *1976 Congressional Quarterly Almanac*, 823–31.

66. Michael Ziegler, "Conable Easily Keeps 35th Seat," *Rochester Democrat and Chronicle*, 3 November 1976.

67. Conable, Personal Journal, 1 December 1976.

68. *1977 Congressional Quarterly Almanac*, 3–8.

69. Conable, "Washington Report," 11 November 1976.

70. Conable, Personal Journal, 1 December 1976.

71. "Meeting Carter—A Tale of Foe," *Rochester Democrat and Chronicle*, 29 December 1976.

72. Conable, Personal Journal, 13 December 1976.

11: Republican Leader of Ways and Means

1. Barber B. Conable Jr., "Washington Report," 17 February 1977 (newspaper column).

2. Barber B. Conable Jr., Personal Journal, 16 February 1977.

3. Barber B. Conable Jr., interview by the author, 2 April 1999.

4. Conable, Personal Journal, 16 February 1977.

5. Ibid., 23 October 1977.

6. *1977 Congressional Quarterly Almanac* (Washington, D.C.: Congressional Quarterly Inc., 1978), 21–3E.

7. Ibid., 23–5E.

8. Conable, "Washington Report," 5 May 1977.

9. *1977 Congressional Quarterly Almanac*, 23–5E; Randall Straham, *New Ways and Means: Reform and Change in a Congressional Committee* (Chapel Hill: University of North Carolina Press, 1990), 119; Charles O. Jones, *The Trustee Presidency: Jimmy Carter and the United States Congress* (Baton Rouge: Louisiana State University Press, 1988), 135–43.

10. Strahan, *New Ways and Means*, 119.

11. House Committee on Ways and Means, *Tax Act of 1977*, 95th Cong., 1st sess., 1977, H. Rept. 496, 241–7.

12. Strahan, *New Ways and Means*, 119–20.

13. Edward Walsh, "Carter Rips Oil Firms, Defends Energy Plan: Harsh Criticism Brings Response by Industry, Hill," *Washington Post*, 14 October 1977.

14. Barber B. Conable Jr., Letter to President Jimmy Carter, Congressional Liaison File, Jimmy Carter Library, October 13, 1977. Inadvertently, this letter was incorrectly dated, since the comments to which Conable refers were made on October 13.

15. Strahan, *New Ways and Means*, 120; *1978 Congressional Quarterly Almanac*, 639–67.

16. Conable interview, 2 April 1999.

17. "Social Security Crisis: Committee to Weigh Financing Alternatives," *Congressional Quarterly Weekly Report*, 3 September 1977, 1874–7.

18. *Congress and the Nation 1977–1980*, vol. 5 (Washington, D.C.: Congressional Quarterly Inc., 1981), 235–8; *1977 Congressional Quarterly Almanac*, 161–72.

19. House Committee on Ways and Means, *Social Security Financing Amendments of 1977*, 95th Cong., 1st sess., 1977, H. Rept. 702, 296–304.

20. *Congress and the Nation 1977–1980*, 235–8; *1977 Congressional Quarterly Almanac*, 161–72.

21. Quoted in Paul Light, *Artful Work: The Politics of Social Security Reform* (New York: Random House, 1985), 89.

22. Conable interview, 2 April 1999.

23. *Congress and the Nation*, 238–9; Strahan, *New Ways and Means*, 122.

24. *1978 Congressional Quarterly Almanac*, 226–30.

25. Barber B. Conable Jr., with A. L. Singleton, *Congress and the Income Tax* (Norman: University of Oklahoma, 1989), 51.

26. Conable interview, 2 April 1999.

27. Cited in Strahan, *New Ways and Means*, 122.

28. *1978 Congressional Quarterly Almanac*, 228.

29. *1978 Congressional Quarterly Almanac*, 233; *Congress and the Nation 1977–1980*, 241.

30. Conable, Personal Journal, 13 August 1978.

31. *1978 Congressional Quarterly Almanac*, 210–48; *Congress and the Nation 1977–1980*, 238–44.

32. David Mayhew, *Divided We Govern: Party Control, Lawmaking, and Investigations, 1946–1990* (New Haven: Yale University Press, 1991), 51–99.

33. *1978 Congressional Quarterly Almanac*, 9–11.

34. Cited in Mark Rozell, *The Press and the Carter Presidency* (Boulder: Westview Press, 1989), 102.

35. For a review of Carter's relations with Congress during his first two years, see Jones, *The Trustee Presidency*, 123–68.

36. Hugh Sidey, "The Crux of Leadership," *Time*, 11 December 1978, 44.

37. "Washington Report," 6 July 1978 (newspaper column).

38. Michael Zeigler, "Conable Smashes to 8th Term," *Rochester Democrat and Chronicle*, 8 November 1978.

39. Tom Benton, interview with the author, 18 April 1988.

40. Michael Barone, *Our Country: The Shaping of America from Roosevelt to Reagan* (New York: The Free Press, 1990), 128–40; Burton I. Kaufman, *The Presidency of James Earl Carter* (Lawrence: University of Kansas Press, 1993), 144–50; and Rozell, *The Press and the Carter Presidency*, 144–50.

41. Jones, *The Press and the Carter Presidency*, 175–79.

42. Kaufman, *The Presidency of James Earl Carter*, 159–79.

43. "Candidate Bush Pledges 'New Candor,'" *Rochester Times-Union*, 1 May 1979.

44. Louis Peck, "Conable To Support George Bush Campaign," *Rochester Democrat and Chronicle*, 1 May 1979.

45. "Carter, Bush Win Iowa Precinct Caucuses," *Congressional Quarterly Weekly Report*, 26 January 1980, 187–9.

46. Louis Peck, "Conable Hitched to Rising Star—Bush," *Rochester Democrat and Chronicle*, 26 January 1980.

47. Conable interview, 2 April 1999.

48. *1980 Congressional Quarterly Almanac*, 40–6B.

49. Conable interview, 2 April 1999; see also "Frontrunners Win; Bush Stops Campaigning," *Congressional Quarterly Weekly Report*, 31 May 1980, 1467.

50. *1980 Congressional Quarterly Almanac*, 31–4B.

51. Conable interview, 2 April 1999.

52. *1980 Congressional Quarterly Almanac*, 40–6B.

53. Ibid., 4B.

54. Barone, *Our Country*, 594.

55. *1980 Congressional Quarterly Almanac*, 3–17B.

56. Richard Whitemire, "Conable Stature Gains for 9th Term," *Rochester Times-Union*, 5 November 1980.

57. Barber B. Conable Jr., interview with WXXI Public Television, Rochester, New York, 1998.

58. Conable, "Washington Report," 13 November 1980.

59. Ibid., 18 December 1980.

60. Conable interview, 2 April 1999.

12: Cutting Taxes

1. My thanks to Dick Fenno at the University of Rochester for his tape recording of this January 14, 1981, press luncheon on which this transcript is based. Though Fenno did no more formal research on Conable's congressional career after the 1974 election when he had been inadvertently drawn into the campaign as a political participant himself, he continued to have a personal interest in Conable's career, often speaking with the congressman, chairing his student internship selection committee, and attending political events in the district. For the press coverage of Conable's luncheon, see John Stewart, "Conable Predicts Tax Cuts Will Take Time," *Rochester Democrat and Chronicle*, 15 January 1981, and Bill O'Brien, "Transition: Down-Home Republican Finds 'Tinge of Liberalism' in Reagan Wardrobe," *Rochester Democrat and Chronicle*, 15 January 1981.

2. *Reagan's First Year* (Washington, D.C.: Congressional Quarterly Inc., 1982), 113–6.

3. "A Program for Economic Recovery," *A White House Report* (Washington, D.C.: U.S. Government Printing Office, 18 February 1981), 30.

4. For a more technical definition and understanding of supply-side economics, or Reaganomics as it was known at the time, see any basic economics textbook, such as Campbell R. McConnell and Stanley

L. Bruce, *Macroeconomics: Principles, Problems, and Policies* (New York: McGraw-Hill, 1999), 343–5. Also, for a short history of supply-side economics and how Ronald Reagan came to endorse the Kemp-Roth tax cut in his 1980 presidential campaign, see the account by one of his principal advisers on the subject, Martin Anderson, *Revolution* (New York: Harcourt Brace Jovanovich, 1988), 140–63.

5. Michael Barone, *Our Country: The Shaping of America From Roosevelt to Reagan* (New York: The Free Press, 1990), 621.

6. Hedrick Smith, *The Power Game: How Washington Works* (New York: Ballantine Books, 1988), 44–5.

7. Most of the reporting on Reagan's economic recovery proposal emphasized, as I have done here, the cost of the program for the first three years. However, the White House also released figures showing that the five-year cost of the program was much higher, $718.3 billion ($554 billion in individual tax cuts and $164.3 billion in accelerated depreciation allowances for business), a figure which was not much below the final five-year $749 billion package Reagan signed into law on August 31, 1981. For further details, see "A Program for Economic Recovery."

8. *Reagan's First Year*, 115.

9. "Reagan Tax Cut Meets Skeptical Hill Reception," *Congressional Quarterly Weekly Report*, 21 January 1981, 336–7.

10. John Stewart, "Plan Must Pass Quickly to Stay Intact: Conable," *Rochester Democrat and Chronicle*, 20 February 1981.

11. Barber B. Conable Jr., with A. L. Singleton, *Congress and the Income Tax* (Norman: University of Oklahoma, 1989), 54–5.

12. *1981 Congressional Quarterly Almanac* (Washington, D.C.: Congressional Quarterly Inc., 1982), 96–7.

13. Dale Tate, "Tax Cut Compromise Barred as Committee Markups Near," *Congressional Quarterly Weekly Report*, 18 April 1981, 670–1.

14. Dale Tate, "House Provides President a Victory on the 1982 Budget," *Congressional Quarterly Weekly Report*, 9 May 1981, 783–5.

15. Helen Dewar, "Reagan's Budget Plan Wins Easily in House," *Washington Post*, 8 May 1981; Pamela Fessler, "Doubts Voiced on Reagan Tax Cuts," *Congressional Quarterly Weekly Reports*, 16 May 1983, 841.

16. The following account of the events leading to the tax-cut bill comes from Barber B. Conable Jr., Personal Journal, 26 May 1981.

17. Robert W. Merry, "Mr. Conable Walks a Tightrope," *Wall Street Journal*, 20 May 1981.

18. "Reagan and Rostenkowski Modify Tax Cut Proposals to Woo Conservative Votes," *Congressional Quarterly Weekly Report*, 6 June 1981, 979–80.

19. Ibid., 979.

20. Quoted in Joseph White and Aaron Wildavsky, *The Deficit and the Public Debt: The Search for Responsible Budgeting in the 1980s* (Berkeley: University of California Press, 1989), 162.

21. "Reagan and Rostenkowski Modify Tax Cut Proposals to Woo Conservative Votes," 979–80.

22. Ibid.

23. *1981 Congressional Quarterly Almanac*, 97.

24. Conable, Personal Journal, 1 July 1981.

25. Ibid.

26. "Reagan and Rostenkowski Modify Tax Cut Proposals to Woo Conservative Votes," 979–80.

27. Pamela Fessler, "Testing Time for Reagan Economic Plan," *Congressional Quarterly Weekly Report*, 13 June 1981, 1027–9.

28. Conable, Personal Journal, 1 July 1981.

29. *1981 Congressional Quarterly Almanac*, 97–8.

30. Irwin B. Arieff, "Conservative Southerners Are Enjoying Their Wooing as Key to Tax Bill Success," *Congressional Quarterly Weekly Report*, 13 June 1981, 1023–4.

31. White and Wildavsky, *The Deficit and the Public Debt*, 165–6.

32. "Reagan and Rostenkowski Modify Tax Cut Proposals to Woo Conservative Votes," 979–80.

33. *1981 Congressional Quarterly Almanac*, 97.

34. Conable, Personal Journal, 1 July 1981.

35. White and Wildavsky, *The Deficit and the Public Debt*, 167; Pamela Fessler, "House Floor Battle Looming on Tax Cut Bill," *Congressional Quarterly Weekly Report*, 25 July 1981, 1323–6.

36. White and Wildavsky, *The Deficit and the Public Debt*, 167.

37. *1981 Congressional Quarterly Almanac*, 99.

38. Dale Tate, "House Ratifies Savings Plan in Stunning Reagan Victory," *Congressional Quarterly Weekly Report*, 27 June 1981, 1127–9.

39. *Congressional Record*, 20 June 1981, 14658.

40. Tate, "House Ratifies Savings Plan in Stunning Reagan Victory," 1127–9.

41. Conable, Personal Journal, 1 July 1981.

42. *1981 Congressional Quarterly Almanac*, 99–100.

43. Ibid.; Pamela Fessler, "House Floor Battle Looming on Tax Cut Bill," 1323.

44. White and Wildavsky, *The Deficit and the Public Debt*, 173.

45. Conable, Personal Journal, 3 August 1981.

46. *1981 Congressional Quarterly Almanac*, 100.

47. Conable, Personal Journal, 3 August 1981.

48. Barber B. Conable Jr., interview with the author, 21 August 2000.

49. *1981 Congressional Quarterly Almanac*, 100.

50. White and Wildavsky, *The Deficit and the Public Debt*, 174.

51. *1981 Congressional Quarterly Almanac*, 100.

52. Conable, Personal Journal, 3 August 1981.

53. Fessler, "House Floor Battle Looming on Tax Cut Bill," 1323.

54. White and Wildavsky, *The Deficit and the Public Debt*, 176.

55. *Reagan's First Year*, 122–6.

56. Conable, Personal Journal, 3 August 1981.

57. Lou Cannon and Kathy Sawyer, "President's Speech Has Hill Switchboards Ablaze," *Washington Post*, 28 July 1981.

58. White and Wildavsky, *The Deficit and the Public Debt*, 178–9.

59. *1981 Congressional Quarterly Almanac*, 103.

60. Conable, Personal Journal, 3 August 1981.

61. Thomas B. Edsall, "Senate All But Wraps Up Work on Tax-Cut Bill," *Washington Post*, 29 July 1981.

62. Conable, Personal Journal, 3 August 1981.

63. *Congressional Record*, 29 July 1981, 18254.

64. Conable, Personal Journal, 3 August 1981.

65. The following account of the House debate is found in *Congressional Record*, 29 July 1981, 18254–63.

66. Conable, Personal Journal, 3 August 1981.

67. Conable interview, 8 December 1990.

68. *1981 Congressional Quarterly Almanac*, 100.

69. Conable, Personal Journal, 3 August 1981.

70. Ibid.

71. The law reduced individual income tax rates from a range of 14 to 70 percent to a range of 11 to 50 percent by 1984. "The final cut was 23 percent instead of 25 percent," Pamela Fessler of *Congressional Quarterly* explained, "because the rate reductions each succeeding year [was] applied to a smaller base." For details, see Pamela Fessler, "Reagan Tax Plan Ready for Economic Test," *Congressional Quarterly Weekly Report*, 8 August 1981, 1433.

72. Broken down by the three principal parts, the final five-year $749 billion Economic Recovery Act included $557 billion in individual income tax cuts, $154 billion in accelerated business depreciation allowances, and $38 billion in add-ons to win special-interest votes. For budgeting details on the law, see U.S. Congress, Joint Committee on Taxation, *General Explanation of the Economic Recovery Tax Act of 1981* (Washington, D.C.: U.S. Government Printing Office, 29 December 1981). Also see Matthew Bender's *Analysis of the Economic Recovery Act of 1981* (New York: Matthew Bender Company, 1981).

73. Lee Lescaze, "President Signs Budget-Cutting Tax Legislation: Concedes Future Deficits May Exceed Predictions," *Washington Post*, 14 August 1981.

74. Conable interview, 21 August 2000. However, "the attention paid to the special-interest battle," White and Wildavsky note in their detailed study of the Reagan tax cut, "should not be allowed to obscure the fact that if that battle had not occurred and the president had won his original [February 18, 1981] leaner bill [which cost $718 billion over five years, only $31 billion less than the final package], deficits would still have been huge. The fiscal crisis that followed," they conclude, "had far more to do with the original plan than with the add-ons." Indeed, a close examination of the final legislation indicates that the add-ons amounted to only five percent (or $38 billion) of the total $749 billion economic recovery package that President Reagan signed into law on August 13, 1981. For their discussion on these figures, see White and Wildavsky, *The Deficit and the Public Debt*, 181–2.

75. *Statistical Abstract of the United States: 2000* (Washington, D.C.: U.S. Census Bureau, 2000), 339; Jonathan Weisman, "Budget Deficit May Surpass $450 Billion," *Washington Post*, 15 July 2003; David Firestone, "Dizzying Dive to Red Ink Poses Stark Choices for Washington: How a Huge Surplus Became a Vast Deficit, Fast," *New York Times*, 14 September 2003.

On the more positive consequences of the Reagan economic policy, economists Campbell R. McConnell and Stanley L. Bruce have noted that

> the Reagan years did in fact witness significant declines in inflation and interest rates, a record-long peacetime economic expansion, and eventual attainment of full employment [which is generally defined by economists to be an unemployment rate of no more than 5.5 percent, which the Reagan administration achieved in 1988]. These years were also characterized by a resurgence of the spirit of entrepreneurialism. Nevertheless, it is fair to say that, as such, supply-side economics largely failed to increase aggregate supply more rapidly than its historical pace. There is little evidence [as a skeptical Barber Conable predicted from the outset] that this program had any significant positive impacts on saving and investment or incentive to work. The savings rate, in fact, tended downward throughout the 1980s. Productivity growth surged in 1983 and 1984, as it usually does during recovery from recession, but was disappointingly low in the rest of the 1980s. Most economists attribute the post-1982 economic recovery to the demand-side expansionary effects of the Reagan tax cuts and not to the use of tax cuts as a pro-growth, supply-side measure. [For more elaboration on the effects of the Reagan Economic Recovery Program, which remain controversial even today, see McConnell and Bruce, *Macroeconomics: Principles, Problems, and Policies*, 343–5.]

76. Conable, Rochester Press Luncheon, 14 January 1981.
77. Conable, Personal Journal, 3 August 1981.

13: Saving Social Security

1. Paul Light, *Artful Work: The Politics of Social Security Reform* (New York: Random House, 1985), 89. Light, a political scientist from the University of Virginia, spent 1982–83 as an American Political Science Association Congressional Fellow in Conable's office. "After looking over the list of members and range of issues [on which he could work],"

Light recalled in the Introduction of his book, "I picked Conable and Social Security. I bet a year of my time that Conable would be in the eye of the legislative storm [on Social Security reform] and would tell me what was happening. . . . I followed him to all the Social Security negotiations, talked with him as often as possible, hounded him at times, and sat in on many meetings as his staff assistant. Though I rarely offered more than trivial advice, he gave me invaluable access and information. More than anyone else, Conable was my Social Security teacher." Much of the material in this chapter is indebted to Light's book.

2. Barber B. Conable Jr., letter to author, 19 July 2000.

3. Light, *Artful Work*, 89.

4. Ibid., 90. Actually, the first boomers were born in 1946 and will turn sixty-five in 2011. Since it is possible to take Social Security retirement benefits starting at age sixty-two, there will be boomer Social Security recipients starting in 2008, potentially pushing up the beginning date of the projected long-term crisis by several years.

5. Ibid., 96–7.

6. Ibid., 99–101.

7. Ibid., 117.

8. Ibid., 117–22.

9. Ibid., 122.

10. Ibid., 124–8.

11. Ibid., 133.

12. Ibid., 135; Pamela Fessler, "Social Security," *Congressional Quarterly Weekly Report*, 7 November 1981, 2165. For Pickle's account of these events, see Jake Pickle and Peggy Pickle, *Jake* (Austin: University of Texas Press, 1997), 157–68.

13. Barber B. Conable Jr., interview by the author, 21 August 2000.

14. Daniel Patrick Moynihan, *Came the Revolution: Argument in the Reagan Era* (New York: Harcourt Brace Jovanovich, 1988), 131.

15. Light, *Artful Work*, 164–7.

16. Ibid., 133–8.

17. Ibid., 167.

18. Ibid., 142–5.

19. Ibid., 146.

20. Ibid., 169.

21. Ibid., 170–1.

22. Barber B. Conable Jr., Personal Journal, 1 April 1983.

23. Peter McGrath, "The Next Two Years in the New Congress," *Newsweek*, 15 January 1982, 38. Though this issue of *Newsweek* was dated January 15, 1982, it was released the previous week, as is customary.

24. Conable, Personal Journal, 1 April 1983; Conable interview, 21 August 2000.

25. Conable, Personal Journal, 1 April 1983.

26. Conable interview, 23 August 1993.

27. Ibid. For a similar recounting of these events, see Moynihan, *Came the Revolution*, 131. The following account of the negotiations by

the Gang of Nine, unless otherwise noted, comes from Light, *Artful Work*, 180–95.

28. Conable interview, 21 August 2000.

29. Light, *Artful Work*, 190–2.

30. Ibid., 196–7.

31. Ibid., 203–4.

32. Ibid., 204–12; *1983 Congressional Quarterly Almanac* (Congressional Quarterly Inc., 1984), 222–4.

33. Conable, Personal Journal, 1 April 1983.

34. Light, *Artful Work*, 224. Light took the title of his book from this quote by Conable to describe the process that produced the Social Security reforms of 1983.

35. Ibid.

36. Ibid., 224–8; *1983 Congressional Quarterly Almanac*, 223–6.

37. Conable, Personal Journal, 1 April 1983.

38. Light, *Artful Work*, 5.

39. "After the adoption of the sunshine laws in the 1970s," Conable also noted, the "locus of decision-making simply shifted to smaller groups of like-minded members who would meet behind closed doors to arrange votes that were later taken in public. Also the sunshine laws played into the hands of the lobbyists who were in frequent attendance at committee meetings to keep an eye on the members" (Conable interview, 21 August 2000).

40. Ibid.

41. Steven Thomma, "Lots of Talk About Social Security, No Solutions," *Rochester Democrat and Chronicle*, 13 October 2002.

14: Concluding a Congressional Career

1. Barber B. Conable Jr., Press Release. U.S. House of Representatives, 30th District, New York, 6 February 1984.

2. Jan Perlez, "Rep. Conable, After 20 Years in Congress, Plans to Retire," *New York Times*, 7 February, 1984; Jeffrey H. Birnbaum, "Top GOP Member of Ways and Means Panel, Barber Conable, Won't Seek Reelection," *Wall Street Journal*, 7 February 1984; Pamela Fessler, "Conable's Retirement to Leave House Gap," *Congressional Quarterly Weekly Report*, 11 February 1984, 243; and Michael Clements, Scramble for Conable's Job," *Rochester Democrat and Chronicle*, 7 February 1984.

3. Martha M. Hamilton, "Rep. Conable to Retire After Term: Peers Regret Losing 'One of the Giants,'" *Washington Post*, 7 February 1984.

4. "Conable Won't Run Again," *The* [Batavia] *Daily News*, 6 February 1984.

5. "Accolades Flow for Congressman," *The* [Batavia] *Daily News*, 7 February 1984.

6. " 'His Reason and His Intellect are Going to be Missed,'" *Rochester Democrat and Chronicle*, 7 February 1984.

7. Ibid.

8. Chris Lavin, "Conable's Touch Hard To Equal, Friends Say," *Rochester Times-Union*, 7 February 1984.

9. "The Conable Conscience," *New York Times*, 8 February 1984.

10. "Mr. Conable Retires," *Washington Post*, 13 February 1984.

11. Courtney R. Sheldon, "Movers and Shakers in Congress," *U.S. News and World Report*, 23 April 1984, 38.

12. Barber B. Conable Jr., Personal Journal, 20 April 1984.

13. George F. Will, "An American House of Lords," *Newsweek*, 4 June 1984, 92.

14. See, for example, John Machacek, "Conable Felt Frustrated in His Role," *Rochester Times-Union*, 6 February 1984; and Fessler, "Conable's Retirement to Leave House Gap," 243.

15. In the end, this was the decisive factor pushing Conable toward retirement. As he told a Rochester reporter at the time: "My personal friend is George Bush. I had the feeling that if Reagan was not going to run, I might regret moving into retirement and being in a position where I couldn't help my friend. That was the main reason I was uncertain [about retirement]." For elaboration on this point, see Michael Clements, "Reagan Decided To Run, So Conable Chose Not To," *Rochester Democrat and Chronicle*, 12 February 1984.

16. Conable, Personal Journal, 20 April 1984.

17. Linda L. Fowler and Robert D. McClure, *Political Ambition: Who Decides to Run for Congress* (New Haven: Yale University Press, 1989).

18. Ibid., 22.

19. Ibid., 156.

20. Ibid., 154–61.

21. Ibid., 171–3.

22. Ibid., 113–15.

23. Ibid., 175–8.

24. Ibid., 193–5.

25. Ibid., 202.

26. Harry Nicholas, interview with the author, 9 June 1989.

27. Fowler and McClure, *Political Ambition*, 204–22.

28. "A Tribute to Barber Conable," House of Representatives, *Congressional Record*, 3 October 1984, H11187.

29. Barber B. Conable Jr., "Washington Report," 5 April 1984. This newsletter was so well done it was later reprinted in the Capitol Hill newspaper, *Roll Call*, 19 April 1984, 19, and in Roger H. Davidson and Walter J. Oleszek, eds., *Governing: Readings and Cases in American Politics* (Washington, D.C.: Congressional Quarterly, Inc., 1987), 507–9.

30. Conable, "Washington Report," 18 October 1984. Also see "Conable Directs Words of Wisdom to New Legislators," *Rochester Democrat and Chronicle*, 11 November 1984.

31. Conable, "Washington Report," 29 November 1984.

32. "A Tribute to Barber Conable," 3 October 1984, H11177–96; 4 October 1984, E4266–77; 5 October 1984, E4369; 9 October 1984, E4384–7; 10 October 1984, E4413, E4456, E4470–1; 12 October 1984, E4517–18.

33. Richard F. Fenno Jr., "The Freshman Congressman: His View of the House," in Nelson W. Polsby, ed., *Congressional Behavior* (New York: Random House, 1971), 134–5.

34. Kathy Lindsley, "An Intimate Supper for Conable's 1,000 Friends," *Rochester Times-Union*, 10 November 1984.

35. Roger Muehlig, "400 Say 'Thanks' to Conable," *The* [Batavia] *Daily News*, 18 October 1984.

36. Ibid.

37. Michael Clements, "Conable, His Achievements Are Praised: 1,000 Attend Tribute for Veteran Congressman," *Rochester Democrat and Chronicle*, 11 November 1984.

38. Conable, "Washington Report," 3 February 1965.

39. Clements, "Conable, His Achievements Are Praised." Also see Lindsley, "An Intimate Supper," and Muehlig, "400 Say 'Thanks' to Conable."

40. "Conable: A 20-Year Perspective on Congress," *Congressional Quarterly Weekly Report*, 3 November 1984, 2870–1.

41. The MacNeil-Lehrer News Hour, Educational Broadcasting and GWETA, transcript number 2396, 3 December 1984.

42. Hugh Sidey, "A Student of Leadership," *Time*, 17 December 1984, 49.

43. Read Kingsbury, "Extraordinary Instructor," *Rochester Times-Union*, 2 June 1985.

44. Patrice Mitchell, "Barber Conable Is Coming Home," *Rochester Times-Union*, 7 December 1984. Also see Michael Clements, "Professor Conable: Congressman to Teach at UR," *Rochester Democrat and Chronicle*, 7 December 1984. After his retirement from Congress, Conable was also offered the presidency of the National Trust for Historic Presentation, a national, nonprofit membership organization chartered by Congress to promote the protection and continued use of the nation's historic sites. The National Trust had been indebted to Conable for his help in changing the federal tax law to support the rehabitation of old buildings.

45. "Conable Begins Writing Columns for *U.S. News*," *Rochester Times-Union*, 6 February 1985.

46. Barber B. Conable Jr., "A Formula With a Future," *U.S. News and World Report*, 30 September 1985, 80.

47. Conable interview, 27 April 2001.

48. Patrice Mitchell, "Home Again to Alexander," *Rochester Times-Union*, 24 August 1985.

49. Conable interview, 30 June 1995.

50. Barber B. Conable Jr., with A. L. Singleton, *Congress and the Income Tax* (Norman: University of Oklahoma Press, 1989).

51. *Memorial and Historic Trees of the Capitol: A Self-Guided Tour* (Washington, D.C.: United States Capitol Historical Society, undated).

52. "Conable Finally Going Home," *Rochester Democrat and Chronicle*, 26 June 1985.

53. Mitchell, "Home Again to Alexander."

54. Conable interview, 1 May 1997.

15: Life After Congress

1. The following account of Conable's selection as president of the World Bank comes from Jochen Kraske, with William H. Becker, William Diamond, and Louis Galambos, "Barber B. Conable: Dedicated to Public Service," *Bankers With a Mission: The Presidents of the World Bank, 1946–1991* (Oxford: Oxford University Press, 1996), 247–50.

2. Ibid.

3. Barber B. Conable Jr., "The World Bank Period," an unpublished recollection, 1994.

4. Barber B. Conable Jr., "Address to the Annual Meeting of the Bretton Woods Committee," Washington, D.C., 10 July 1991, in *The Conable Years at the World Bank: Major Policy Addresses of Barber B. Conable, 1986–1991* (Washington, D.C.: The World Bank, 1991), 175–7.

5. Bill Kauffman, "The Power Broker Who Came Home," *The American Enterprise*, November/December 1999, 32–3, 88; Bill Kauffman, *Dispatches from the Muckdog Gazette: A Most Affectionate Account of a Small Town's Fight to Survive* (New York: Henry Holt and Company, 2002), 104–16.

6. Barber B. Conable Jr., "First Settler Indian Allan," Wheatland Historical Association, Scottsville, New York, 9 April 1992. For an interesting history of Indian Allan, see Blake McKelvey, "Indian Allan's Mills," *Rochester History I* (October, 1939): 1–24.

7. See, for example, Morris P. Fiorina, *Congress: Keystone of the Washington Establishment* (New Haven: Yale University Press, 1989), 69–70; Linda L. Fowler and Robert D. McClure, *Political Ambition: Who Decides to Run for Congress* (New Haven: Yale University Press, 1989), 1–24; Richard F. Fenno Jr., *Watching Politicians: Essays on Participant Observation* (Berkeley: Institute of Government Studies Press, 1990), 13; and Roger H. Davidson and Walter J. Oleszek, *Congress and Its Members* (Washington, D.C.: Congressional Quarterly Inc., 1998), 128.

8. Barber B. Conable Jr., "Congress and Ways and Means," in Lou Frey Jr. and Michael T. Hayes, eds., *Inside the House: Former Members Reveal How Congress Really Works* (New York: U.S. Association of Former Members of Congress and University Press of America, Inc., 2001), 152–6.

9. Barber B. Conable Jr., interview with the author, 22 March 1992.

10. Courtney R. Sheldon, "Movers and Shakers in Congress," *U.S. News and World Report*, 23 April 1984, 38.

11. "Men of the Century," *Pensions and Investments*, 27 December 1999, 1, 34–5. Conable was in distinguished company in receiving this recognition. The other nine runner-ups for "men of the century" were Warren Buffet, "the pre-eminent active investor of the 20th century"; Benjamin Graham, "the father of fundamental investing"; William F. Sharpe, the winner of the 1990 Nobel Prize in economics for devising a means of measuring the volatility of individual stock against the stock market; Edward G. Leffler, founder of the first mutual fund, the Massachusetts Investors Trust in 1924; George B. Back, Jr., who started the pension actuarial consulting business before World War II; William L. Fouse, originator of the index fund; Senator Jacob Javits of New York, the first to introduce legislation in Congress to require minimum vesting, funding, and fiduciary standards; and Conable's former House colleagues, John Dent (D-Pa.) and John Erlenborn (R-Ill.), who sponsored bipartisan legislation to protect pension plan participants.

12. Conable interview, 21 August 2000.

13. Patrick Flanigan and Rick Armon, "Toast Barber Conable for the Homebrewing Boom," *Rochester Democrat and Chronicle*, 27 August 2002.

14. Conable interview, 27 April 2001.

15. Ibid., 15 June 1994.

16. Barber B. Conable Jr., "Homily Delivered at Marine Corps/45th Anniversary of the Battle of Iwo Jima," Washington, D.C.: National Cathedral, 19 February 1990.

17. Conable interview, 27 April 2001.

Index

Abzug, Bella, 207
"accelerated cost recovery system,"
    276, 283, 285, 289
accelerated depreciation: allowances
    for business, 276, 407n7, 409n72;
    plan for business, 300
Adams, Robert B., 389n12
Ad Hoc Committee: on Energy, 239;
    gasoline tax amendment, 240
Afghanistan, Soviet invasion of,
    255
AFL-CIO: Committee on Political
    Education, 185
Agnew, Spiro T., 124, 153, 164, 197
aid to education, 192
aid to Turkey, 190
ailing economy and national energy
    crisis, 208
"Albany Report," 55–57, 59–60, 89
Albert, Carl, 139, 143–44, 202–3,
    231
All About Beer, 382
Allan, Ebenezer "Indian," 377–78,
    415n6
"all-saver" certificates, 293
American Enterprise Institute, 369
American History Museum, 379
American Independent Party, 125
American International Group, 369,
    378, 381
American Political Science
    Association, 9, 84, 359–60,
    387n42, 410n1
Anderson, John, 164, 170, 172, 182,
    208, 231, 256, 261, 273
Annenberg/CPB Project, 387n42

Anthony, Susan B., 16
anti-poverty program, 100, 102
Apple, R. W., Jr., 189
Arab oil embargo, 208, 238
Archer, Bill, 204, 315, 330–31
Arends, Leslie, 79, 111, 144, 164, 208,
    401n2
Armstrong, Anne, 226
Armstrong, William, 315, 330–31
Arthur Burns, 209, 233
Avon Rotary Club, 186
Ayres, Drummond, 252

Back, George B., Jr., 416n11
Baker, Howard H., 226, 252, 256,
    277, 313, 315, 336, 343, 362–63
Baker, James, 256–58, 281, 289, 296,
    320, 326–28, 331, 373–75
balanced budget, 305, 352
Ball, Robert, 315, 326–30
Barone, Michael, 260, 275
Bartlett, Joseph, 176
Batavia Republican Committee, 43
Batavia Rotary Club, 41, 59, 60
Beach, James, 44, 46–47
Beck, Robert, 315, 330
Becker, William H., 415n1
Begin, Menachem, 252
Benna, Theodore, 381
Bentley, Robert, 45
Benton, Thomas, 55, 57, 69, 185, 254,
    390n9, 391n39, 405n39
Bentsen, Lloyd, 288
Bergsten, C. Fred, 375
Bernstein, Abraham, 54

Bernstein, Carl, 7, 168
Bishop, Richard, 188
Black, Gordon, 183–84
Blair House, 271, 320, 330
Bliley, Thomas J., 5
Blumenthal, Michael, 250–51
Boggs, Hale, 144
Bolling, Richard, 231, 286, 320, 370
Boren, David L., 288
Bork, Robert, 164
Boulenger, Jacques, 36
Bow, Frank, 121
Boy Scouts, 19, 387n1
Bradford, Julie Johnson, 382–83
Bradley, Bill, 291
Brock, William E., 374
Broder, David, 7, 258, 371
Brokaw, Tom, 31
Brooke, Edward, 225
Brown, Harold, 261–62
Browning, Robert, 23
Bruce, Stanley L., 410n75
Bubel, Neil F., 69–72, 391n30, 391n38
Buchholtz, Karl, 40–41, 65, 341–42, 371, 389n11
Buckley, James L., 181, 217–18, 230–31
Buffalo News, 48
Buffet, Warren, 416n11
Burke, Edmund, 99, 133
Burleson, Omar, 394n4
Burns, Arthur, 209, 233
Burton, Phillip, 202, 231
Bush, George H. W., 11, 18, 112, 114, 120–21, 128, 139, 170, 198–99, 256–59, 280, 306, 320, 340, 345, 373, 394n4, 396n18, 401n2, 413n15
Bush, George W., 338
Butler, Caldwell, 222
Butterfield, Alexander, 147, 161
Byrd, Robert C., 277, 315
Byrnes, John, 11, 114–18, 120–21, 123, 137–38, 149–51, 159, 173, 237, 246, 334

Caddell, Patrick, 255
Call, Doug, 350–52

Callaway, Howard, 83
Cannon, James, 227
Cannon, Joseph G., 115, 203, 370
Cape Kennedy, 82
capital gains tax, 247, 248–50, 271, 277, 289
Capitol Hill, 77, 98, 170, 222, 247, 276, 297–98, 312–13, 318, 321, 363, 375, 413n29
Capitol Visitors' Center, 97
Capra, Frank, 52, 61
Carlson, Clifford, 157
Carman, Clarence E., Jr., 180–82, 195
Carnegie, Andrew, 380
Carter, Jimmy, 11–12, 185–87, 189, 222, 227–29, 233–44, 246–56, 259–61, 268–70, 272–73, 305, 329, 382, 404n14, 405n35; comprehensive energy proposal, 237; Social Security bill, 243; standby gasoline tax, 239
Carter, Tim Lee, 393n31
Case, Clifford, 225
Cederberg, Elford, 401n2
Cheney, Richard, 227
Chicago Association of Commerce and Industry, 278
Chicago Tribune, 168
Chili [N.Y.] Women's Republican Club, 65
Christian Science Monitor, 7
Churchill, Winston, 91
Civil Rights Act, 68, 73
Clark, Champ, 76
Clausen, Alden W., 374, 376
Clawson, Del, 164, 231
Clean Air Act, 143
Cleveland, Grover, 38
Cohen, William, 187
COLA. *See* Social Security: cost-of-living-adjustment for inflation
Colgate Rochester Divinity School, 350
Colgate University, 379
Collins, Charles, 386n24, 393n57

Committee of the Whole, 139–40, 299, 302

Committee to Reelect the President, 153, 157, 186, 188, 191

committee system, 35, 56, 138, 202, 207

Conable Technology Building, 379

Conable, Agnes Gouinlock, 16–17, 19, 21–22, 394n8

Conable, Anne, 389n14

Conable, Barber B., Sr., 16–24, 26, 30, 38, 40, 42, 51, 113–14, 383–84

Conable, Benjamin Barber, 15–16

Conable, Charlotte Williams, 39–40, 43, 49, 63, 69, 74–75, 178, 346, 367, 376, 379, 397–98n49

Conable, Emily, 389n14

Conable, Jane, 389n14

Conable, John S., 15, 17–20, 22, 24–25, 31, 34, 38, 48, 387n3, 387n7, 388n9, 388n14, 388n17, 388n21

Conable, Maud, 16

Conable, Rufus, 15, 19, 377

Conable, Sam, 389n22

Conable, Samuel, 19

Conable, Sophia, 15, 377

Conable, William, 17, 19, 22, 34

Conable–Hance bill, 290, 293, 298–303, 306–7

Conference on Inflation, 200

Congress: abandoning the federal revenue-sharing program with state and local governments, 379; in Crisis, 158; a lame-duck session of, 141–43, 318, 322, 325; veto-proof, 181

Congress, 2, 3, 5, 7–11, 32, 76, 84, 86, 88, 99–100, 103–6, 340; Eighty-ninth, 11, 73–75, 77–78, 80, 88, 90, 100, 103–5, 107, 140, 202, 360, 396n22; Ninetieth, 104–5, 107–9, 111, 123, 126; Ninety-first, 137, 140–42, 149, 396n22; Ninety-second, 138, 141, 143–45, 148–49, 152; Ninety-third, 154, 158, 396n22; Ninety-fourth, 202–3, 208, 232;

Ninety-fifth, 229, 231, 233, 236, 251–52; Ninety-six, 85; Ninety-seventh, 85, 308, 325; Ninety-eighth, 325

Congressional District: Conable's, 73, 118, 341, 348; the four rural counties in, 62; Thirtieth, 8, 352, 362, 365, 367; Thirty-fifth, 194; Thirty-sixth, 72–73; Thirty-seventh, 64, 98, 105

Congressional Quarterly, 92–93, 107, 119, 152, 157, 162–63, 166, 204, 224, 260, 279, 291, 297, 363, 393n31, 409n71

Congressional Record, 140, 358, 396n20

"Congressman H," 392n11

Connally, John, 147, 256, 344

Connor, John, 46

Conservative Democratic Forum, 291–92

Conservative Party, 141, 180–82, 217, 229–30, 295

contributions, political, 247

Corman, James, 250, 263, 269

Corman–Fisher amendment, 250

Cornell Law Quarterly, 34

Cornell University, 2, 10–11, 16–17, 22–23, 27, 32–33, 35, 38, 350, 358, 377

Corning Glass, 369, 378

Costanza, Margaret "Midge," 11, 182–95, 202, 229, 233, 348, 400n7

Council of Economic Advisors, 209, 315

Cox, Archibald, 160–61, 163–64, 189

Crane, Philip, 236, 256

Currie, Phil, 397n34

Daley, Richard J., 150

Darman, Richard, 320, 326, 328

Dean, John, 161, 175

Democratic Caucus, 115, 144, 202–7, 209, 213, 231, 250, 264, 394n4

Democratic Committee on Committees, 115, 138, 205, 394n10

Democratic National Committee
    Headquarters, 158, 185
Democratic National Convention,
    124, 299
Democratic National Headquarters,
    157
Democratic Party, 71, 83, 115–16,
    144, 154, 157, 207, 259, 269–70,
    284, 322, 350, 352
Dent, John, 416n11
Department of Defense, 275
Department of the Treasury, 150,
    270, 286, 381
depreciation allowance for
    American businesses, 260
depreciation reform, 10-5-3, 285
Derounian, Steven, 109
Dewey, Thomas E., 44
"dialogue of representation," 5, 87,
    340
Diamond, William, 415n1
Dirksen, Everett, 98–99
Disability Insurance fund, 317
Dole, Robert, 12, 226, 256, 263, 268,
    277, 279, 282–83, 287–88, 291,
    307, 312–13, 315, 317, 320,
    322–23, 326, 328, 336, 369
Dole–Rostenkowski bill, 287
Domenici, Peter, 320
Donaldson, Sam, 176
Dong, Mao Ze, 319
Downey, Thomas J., 293
Downs, Raymond, 386n25
draft reform, 134
Drake, Francis, 218
Duberstein, Kenneth, 320, 326,
    328
Duncan, John J., 236, 340
Durant, Will, 36

Eagleton, Thomas F., 153
Eastman Kodak, 63, 69, 182, 381
Eckert, Fred, 193–95, 348–49, 351–54,
    361, 367
Economic Forum Luncheon, 387n1
Economic Opportunity Act, 101

Economic Opportunity, Office of,
    139, 153
Economic Recovery Act of 1981,
    305–6, 409n72
Economic Recovery program, 298
Educational Broadcasting and
    GWETA, 414n41
Ehrlichman, John D., 159
Ehrmann, Max, 109
eighteen-year-old vote, 193
eight-point plan, 242
Eighty-Ninth Club, 82
Eisenhower, Dwight D., 66, 127, 146
election reform, 134
Elementary and Secondary
    Education Act of 1965, 91–92
emergency conservation bill, 255
Emery, James, 49–50
Energy and Commerce Committee,
    80, 353
energy crisis, 190, 208, 238, 240, 255
Energy Plan, 237
Equal Rights Amendment, 152, 348,
    397n49
Erlenborn, John N., 168–69, 188, 208,
    416n11
Erwin, Austin, 44–50, 53, 55, 62, 350
Erwin, Austin, Jr., 46, 48–49
estate tax, 285
excise tax bill, 121

"family assistance system," 133
federal: civil service pension system,
    368; income maintenance, 133;
    income tax, 67, 132; Insurance
    Contribution Act, 311; rent
    subsidies for low income
    families, 99; Reserve Board,
    209; subsidies for agriculture,
    125, 252, 396n23; tax law,
    414n44; Treasury, 244, 275–76,
    295–96
Fenno, Richard F., Jr., 8–9, 76–78,
    81–82, 84–85, 184–85, 360,
    392n11, 400n12, 406n1
Fenwick, Millicent, 258

Fessler, Pamela, 297, 409n71
Feynman, Dick, 37
FICA. *See* Federal Insurance
    Contribution Act
FICA tax increase, 311
Fillmore, Millard, 38
financing Social Security, 243, 311
Fisher, Carlton, 39, 44
Fisher, Joseph, 243, 245, 250, 263
Foley, Tom, 9
Food for Peace, 83
food stamp program, 141, 143,
    396n23
Foote, Donald, 63
Ford, Gerald R., 11–12, 76, 78–81, 90,
    105, 109–10, 120, 126, 137, 139,
    144–46, 152, 160, 164, 172,
    176–77, 181, 185, 191, 197–202,
    208–15, 217–30, 238–39, 256–59,
    315, 369, 379, 393n56, 394n4,
    395n31, 401n2, 402n8; energy
    proposal, 209, 213
Foreign Affairs Committee, 110
Forhan, Eugene, 49
Fouse, William L., 416n11
Fowler, Linda L., 9, 348–53
Fox, Fanne, 203
Frelinghuysen, Peter, 127
Frenzel, Bill, 4, 236, 359
Frey, Lou, 379
Fuller, Mary Falvey, 315, 330–31

Galambos, Louis, 415n1
Gang of Nine, 325–27, 329–32, 337,
    412n27
Gang of Seventeen, 319–21, 326–27
Gardner, John, 119
"gas guzzler" tax, 238, 241
gasoline: rationing, 255; taxes, 209,
    238, 241, 247
General Kuribayashi, 30
Genesee Community College, 379
Genesee Country Village and
    Museum, 377, 384
Genesee County Republican
    Committee, 44

Genesee Hardware Store, 40, 44, 341,
    350, 371, 377–78
Gergen, David, 368
Gerhard, Norman, 128
Germond, Jack, 185
Gibbons, Sam, 139, 293, 340
Gilbert, Jack, 394n4
Glickman, Dan, 5, 354, 359
Goldman, Sachs and Company, 375
Goldwater, Barry, 66–74, 80, 153,
    260, 401n2
Goodell, Charles, 78, 100, 110–11
Gouinlock, George, 40
Gouinlock, Margaret, 16
Gouinlock, William C., 16–17
Gradison, Bill, 341
Graham, Benjamin, 416n11
Gramm, Phil, 280, 285
Gramm–Latta: II, 294–95; budget
    resolution, 280, 288, 294; budget
    votes; 299
Gravel, Mike, 263
Gray, Thomas, 20–21, 23
Great Society program, Johnson's,
    68, 88, 90–93, 99, 102, 106, 125,
    140
Green, William, 5
Greenspan, Alan, 12, 209, 315, 319,
    326, 328, 330–33
Gregg, Hugh, 219
Griffin, Robert, 78, 146, 258, 401n2
Gunderson, Steve, 359
Gypsy Moths, 300

Haig, Alexander M., Jr., 168–69, 172
Haldeman, H. R., 159, 161, 164, 168,
    175–76
Hall, Sam, 4
Halleck, Charles, 78–80, 105
Hance, Kent, 285, 288–90, 295–97
Hanks, Paul, 63
Hansen, Clifford, 127
Hansen, Julia, 137
Harvard University, 9, 38, 114, 160
health care, 93, 144, 190, 192
Hed, Kenneth, 106

Heinz, John, 315
Helms, Jesse, 220, 349
Hemingway, Ernest, 36
Hess, Donald, 342
Hinman, George, 199
Hodgson, Russ, Andrews, Woods and Goodyear, 38
Hollings, Ernest, 320
Holy Trinity Lutheran Church, 39
Honeywell Corporation, 369
Hormats, Robert D., 375
Horton, Frank, 72–73, 86, 353, 358, 392n13
House Administration Committee, 109, 394n4
House Appropriations Committee, 110–11, 121
House Budget Act, 294
House Budget Committee, 277, 320
House Committee on Aging, 312
House Judiciary Committee, 164, 167, 172, 174, 176, 187, 208; impeachment inquiry, 195
House of Representatives, 5, 8, 11–12, 56, 73, 75–77, 81–82, 84–85, 87, 89, 97, 100, 103, 106, 112, 118–19, 128, 136, 140–41, 145, 164, 166, 170, 196, 202–3, 225, 229, 238, 256, 291, 296, 302–3, 323, 335, 342–43, 358, 380; rules and procedures, 140
House Republican Conference, 164, 297
House Republican Policy Committee, 208–9
House Rules Committee, 139, 150, 202, 204–5, 225–26, 286, 294, 299, 320, 333–34
House Ways and Means Committee, 4–7, 11–12, 65, 108–23, 111, 115–16, 123, 125, 137–39, 142, 148–50, 159, 165, 175, 199, 202–7, 209, 213–15, 232, 236–43, 246–51, 253–54, 256, 260, 263–64, 268–71, 274–75, 277–79,

281, 284–85, 287, 289–91, 293, 295, 299, 301–2, 306–7, 311–12, 314–15, 330, 332–34, 340, 343–44, 346, 358–59, 362–65, 371, 378–80, 394n1, 394n4, 394n10, 394n13; bills, 119, 150, 204–6; Democratic members of, 115, 138, 299, 334, 394n10; legislation and politics, 110, 122; Subcommittee on Social Security, 314–15; Trade Subcommittee, 236
Hruska, Roman L., 157
Humphrey, Hubert H., 68, 124–28
Hunt, Albert R., 7, 159, 174, 259, 386nn28–29
Hutton, E. F., 354
Huxley, Aldous, 36

income tax, 65; cuts in, 260, 277; indexing the tax brackets, 296; marriage penalty tax on two-income families, 271, 277, 279, 285, 288, 295; maximum individual rate on unearned income, a reduction of, 277; negative income tax program, 133; personal and corporate, surcharge on, 119, 121; special deductions for general sales taxes, 247
indexing: Social Security, 242; both Social Security benefits and the income tax to inflation, 380; of the tax brackets, 296–97, 300
Individual Retirement Accounts, 271, 277, 279, 286, 293, 381
inflation, 118, 120, 185, 190–91, 199–200, 208, 229, 242–46, 253–55, 259, 272, 292, 296, 298, 302, 305, 310–11, 380, 410n75
Ingersoll, Robert, 21, 388n18
Institute for International Economics, 375
interest equalization tax, 122

interest rates, 272, 410n75
International Monetary Fund, 374
Iranian hostage crisis, 255, 260
IRAs. *See* Individual Retirement Accounts

Jagt, Guy Vander, 1
Javits, Jacob, 67, 225, 416n11
Jaworski, Leon, 164, 173
Jefferson, Thomas, 96
Jeffersonian: commitment, 58, 380; decentralist, 74; democracy, 19; Republican, 151; values, 20
Jeffords, James, 302
Jet Propulsion Laboratory, 90
Johnson, Endicott, 117
Johnson, Luci Baines, 98
Johnson, Lyndon, 65, 68, 70–71, 73–74, 79–80, 88–93, 103–4, 107, 109, 118–22, 124–25, 140, 153, 202, 393n31
Johnson, Mrs. "Lady Bird," 89
Joint Committee on Taxation, 409n72
Jones, Charles O., 2, 385n4
Jones, James, 249, 260, 276–77, 320
Judiciary Committee, 53; additional taped presidential conversations subpoenaed by the, 168; the evidence produced by the, 171, 175; Nixon's willingness to cooperate with the, 169; request for more White House tapes, 169; substantial misleading of Republican members of the, 176; White House's effort to cooperate with the, 169
Junior Chamber of Commerce, 43, 47, 53

Keating, Kenneth, 67, 70, 73
Kemp, Jack, 250, 260, 275–76, 287, 297, 305, 347
Kemp–Roth: bill, 250, 260, 275, 278, 285, 296; tax cut proposal, 250, 407n4

Kempton, Murray, 344
Kennedy Foundation, 201
Kennedy, Edward, 98, 252, 255
Kennedy, John F., 44, 61, 65, 68, 144, 274
Kennedy, Robert F., 70, 73, 124–25
Kesselring, Leo, 181
Keys, Martha, 315
Khanh, Nguyen, 89
Kierkegaard, Soren, 3
Kingsbury, Read, 8, 365–67
Kipling, Rudyard, 21, 361, 388n18
Kiplinger Washington Letter, 6
Kirkland, Lane, 315, 324
Kissinger, Henry, 134, 147, 167, 172, 213, 258
Koch, Mayor, 344
Kraske, Jochen, 374–75, 415n1
Kunzig, Bob, 127

Labor Day, 153, 259
Laird, Melvin, 83, 110–11, 344
Landgrebe, Earl, 195
Landon, Alfred, 73
Latta, Delbert L., 280, 320
laundry list taxation, 248
Lavin, Chris, 342
Laxalt, Paul, 320
Leffler, Edward G., 416n11
Legislative Reorganization Act of 1970, 140, 159, 253
Liberal Party, 69, 182
Library of Congress, 96–97, 366
Liddy, G. Gordon, 157–58
Life, 397n34
Light, Paul, 9, 309–10, 312, 318, 320–23, 328–29, 331, 336, 410n1, 412n34
Lightheiser, Bob, 287
Lincoln, Abraham, 83
Long, Russell B., 142, 241, 263, 268, 282–84, 293, 307, 320
Lott, Trent, 320
Luce, Clare, 344
Luce Foundation, 379

MacAdam, David L., 69, 72, 182
Macaluso, Michael, 182, 229, 231
MacNeil-Lehrer News Hour, 364, 414n41
Mahoney, Walter, 43, 47, 53, 73, 77
Management and Budget, Office of, 273
Manley, Robert H., 64
Marcham, Frederick G., 24–26, 34, 389n3
Marine Corps, 11, 27–28, 30–32, 34, 37–38, 64, 66, 93
Markowitz, Harry, 380
Mathias, Charles McC., Jr., 303
Mayhew, David, 140, 151, 396n22
McCaffery, Minnie, 16
McCarthy, Eugene, 124, 344
McClory, Robert, 169
McClure, Robert D., 9, 348–53
McConnell, Campbell R., 410n75
McCormack, John W., 75, 77, 81, 84, 139, 143, 360
McEwen, Robert, 54–55, 80, 390n5
McFall, John J., 231
McGovern, George, 153–54, 178
McLaughlin, Linda, 96–97, 393n36
McNamara, Robert S., 89
Meagher, John, 236
Medicare tax, 311
"Men of the Century," 416n11
Merry, Robert W., 284–85
Michel, Robert, 2, 208, 231, 300, 314, 341, 343, 347
Middendorf, J. William, 374
Middle East, 172, 190
Mikva, Abner, 250, 268
Miller, George P., 82
Miller, Jack, 127
Miller, William, 68, 70
Mills, Louis F., 389n12
Mills, Wilbur, 11, 114–23, 125–26, 149–51, 173, 175, 194, 202–7, 213, 215–16, 232, 237, 246, 334, 394n13
Minh, Ho Chi, 89
Mississippi Freedom Democratic Party, 83

Mississippi Test Facility, 82
Mitchell, Patrice, 370–71
Mondale, Walter, 259
Monroe County Republican Committee, 63
Montgomery, Sonny, 285
Morton, Thruston, 83
Moynihan, Daniel Patrick, 2, 12, 133, 230–31, 254, 257, 313–15, 323, 326–28, 336, 364, 370, 382
Museum of the American Indian, 369–70, 379
Muskie, Edmund S., 125, 261–62
Myers, L. H., 36
Myers, Robert, 319

Nader, Ralph, 152–53
Natcher, Bill, 302
National Aeronautics and Space Administration, 82
National Archives log, 148, 397n39
National Association of Manufacturers, 315
National Commission on Social Security Reform, 313, 316, 319, 322, 330–31, 358
National Committee on U.S.–China Relations, 379
National Democratic Campaign Committee, 185
National health insurance, 251
National lottery system for the military draft, 134
National Science Foundation, 90
National Trust for Historic Presentation, 414n44
National War College, 66
Nelson, Gaylord, 263
Nessen, Ron, 226
"New American Revolution," 144
"New Federalism," 58, 132, 144
New York *Daily News*, 174
New York Times, 3, 7, 189, 252, 255, 276, 342

Newsweek, 194, 323–24, 343, 397n34

Newton, George D., 45

Nicholas, Harry, 3, 111, 122, 175, 353, 371, 385n10

Nixon, Richard Milhous, 7, 11, 44, 124–37, 139–44, 146–54, 156–80, 182–85, 187–88, 191–92, 195, 197–98, 200–202, 208–9, 211, 229–30, 238–39, 241, 254, 256, 309, 352, 365, 379–80, 396n22; domestic reforms, 132; Presidential Matters, 397n39; revenue-sharing program, 149; Vietnam policy, 134; wage and price-control policies of 1971, 208

nongovernmental organizations (NGOs), 376

Nugent, Patrick, 98

Nunn, Lucien L., 34–35

O'Brien, Paul A., 186–89, 191

Occupational Safety and Health Act, 143

Office of Economic Opportunity, 139, 153

oil and gas: depletion allowances, 209; tax on the industrial use of, 241

Old Age and Survivors Insurance program, 317

Older Americans Act, 192–93

Omnibus Crime Control Act, 143

O'Neill, Thomas P. "Tip," Jr., 2, 139, 144, 202, 231, 239–40, 246, 263–64, 294, 298–99, 302, 313, 315–16, 320–22, 325, 327, 330–31, 336, 343–44

Onondaga County Young Republican Club, 67

Ostertag, Harold C., 62–64, 70, 72, 86, 110

Ottinger, Richard, 359

Oval Office, 70, 124, 146, 161, 175, 198, 218–19, 297

Owens, John, 261

Paris peace talks, 134–36

Pautler, Paul, 371–72

payroll tax, 113, 118, 242–43, 245, 311, 333–34, 338

Peabody, Robert L., 78

Peace Corps, 153

"peace with justice," 134, 136

Pell, Eric, 37, 389n9

Pensions and Investments, 380–81, 416n11

Pepper amendment, 334–35

Pepper, Claude, 312, 315, 322, 324, 327, 330, 333–36

Pettis, Jerry, 199, 208

Pfizer, 369, 378

Phillips, Martha, 236

Pickle, J. J. "Jake," 4, 311, 314, 333–35

Pickle amendment, 334; and Conable bill, 314

Playboy, 227

Policy and Steering Committee, 203

PPR. *See* registration, permanent personal

Profile in Courage Award, 201

public utilities, a dividend reinvestment plan for, 279

Rahn, Richard, 290

Railsback, Thomas F., 169

Rather, Dan, 258–59

Rayburn, Sam, 369

Reagan, Ronald, 12, 147, 152, 199, 217, 219–26, 246, 250, 256–62, 265–67, 269–85, 287–300, 303–7, 311–16, 318–22, 325–27, 330–31, 336, 343, 345, 348, 352, 374–75, 407n4, 409n74, 413n15; accelerated depreciation plan, 276; economic program, 297, 304, 410n75; economic recovery plan, 275–77, 407n7; tax cut, 270, 290, 303, 312, 321, 409n74, 410n75

Reagan–Stockman proposal and plan for reforming Social Security, 312–13, 315
Reed, Clarke, 225
Reed, Daniel, 111, 114
Regan, Donald, 273, 280–82, 285–86, 288–90, 296, 320
Reaganomics, 348, 406n4
Regenstreif, Peter, 183–86, 400n9, 400n11, 400n14
registration, permanent personal, 53–54
Repicci, Francis C., 253–54
Republican Campaign Committee, 83, 110
Republican: clambake in Rochester, 59; GOP leadership meetings, 146; minority leader, 2, 99, 109, 146, 164, 347; research for, 145;
Republican Committee in Batavia, 42–43
Republican Committee on Committees, 78–79, 109–11, 115, 138, 205, 353
Republican Conference, 80, 83, 138, 164, 171, 208, 231, 256, 297
Republican National Committee, 126, 170, 198, 226, 256
Republican National Convention, 124, 225, 258
Republican Party, 4, 11, 22, 42, 44–45, 48, 51, 53, 62, 66–67, 78, 80, 83, 100, 105, 110, 118, 126–27, 137–38, 145, 156, 158–59, 164–65, 181–82, 185, 188, 198, 217–19, 223, 256, 259, 302, 341, 348, 352, 358
Republican Policy Committee, 100, 164, 173, 232, 236
Republican Research and Planning Committee, 100, 145, 236, 246
Republican State Committee, 127
Republican Task Force on Economic Opportunity, 100–101
Republican Truth Squad, 126–28
Revenue and Expenditure Control Act, 122

revenue-sharing: bill, 148, 150; law, 151–52; during the Ninety-first Congress, 149; proposal in the Ninety-second Congress, 148
Rhodes, John, 100, 164, 170–73, 175–77, 208, 221, 231–32, 401n2
Ribicoff, Abraham, 263
Richardson, Elliot, 160, 163
Riedman, John, 69, 391n34
"right-to-work" laws, 92, 99
Riley, Donald, 349
Ringwood, Mrs., 98
Riverside Convention Center, 387n1
Roberts, Bill, 222
Roberts, William I., 389n12
Robinson, Jackie, 43
Robison, Howard W., 78, 110–11
Rochester Democrat and Chronicle, 72, 111, 194
Rochester Institute of Technology, 379
Rochester papers, 48
Rochester Times-Union, 8, 54, 342, 386
Rockefeller, Nelson, 45, 58, 66, 92, 150, 181, 198–200, 217–19, 226, 379
Roosevelt, Franklin, 19, 23, 26, 73, 235
Roosevelt, Theodore, 235
Rose Garden ceremony at the White House, 90
Rosenbaum, Richard, 199, 223
Rostenkowski, Dan, 117, 150, 247, 249, 263, 269–70, 277–87, 291–92, 294, 296–97, 299–301, 303–8, 311, 314, 320, 330–36, 340, 346, 363; performance on *Face the Nation*, 281
Roth, William, 250, 260, 275
Roukema, Marge, 5
Ruckelshaus, William, 163, 226
Rumsfeld, Donald, 78, 126, 138–39, 218–9
Rumsfeld's Raiders, 139, 396n18
Rusk, Dean, 89
Ryan, Joseph, 42
Ryan, Thomas P., 341

Sadat, Anwar, 252
Safire, William, 3, 7, 177
SALT II. *See* Strategic Arms
    Limitation Treaty
Saturday Morning Club, 41
"Saturday Night Massacre," 163
Scheuer, James S., 76
Schneebeli, Herman, 214, 232
Schweicker, Richard, 224–25
Science and Astronautics
    Committee, 77, 80–82, 90, 105,
    109, 380
Scott, Hugh, 146, 401n2
Scowcroft, Brent, 227
Scranton, William, 66
Sears, John, 224–26
Security Trust Company of
    Rochester, 162
Senate Campaign Committee, 83
Senate Finance Committee, 44–45,
    47, 142, 214, 254, 263, 268, 277,
    279, 291, 304, 313, 315
Senate Watergate Committee, 158,
    161
Senate Watergate hearings, 147
Seniority Task Force, 137
"Sense of the Senate" resolution, 313
Shah of Iran, 254
Shakespeare, William, 23, 361
Sharpe, William F., 416n11
Shriver, Sargent, 92, 153
Shultz, George, 147, 374
Sibley, R.P., 388n2
Sidey, Hugh, 253–54, 364, 397n34
Sills, Beverly, 344
Simon, William, 209, 213, 374
Simonds, John E., 394n1
Sirica, John J., 162–63
Slaughter, Louise, 341, 349, 353–54
Smith, Alfred E., 18
Smith, Hedrick, 276
Smoking Gun, The, 7, 157, 173,
    176–77, 195
Social Security, 12; benefits, 113,
    118–19, 125–26, 134, 242, 244,
    312, 316, 329, 334, 380; cost-of-
    living-adjustment for inflation,

310, 312, 321, 328–30, 334; crisis,
310–11, 314, 316–18, 320, 321,
325, 327, 328, 336–37;
expenditures, 241–42, 312;
financing problem, 323; fiscal
integrity of, 313; greater
protection of women in, 315;
history of, 319; legislation, 119,
125, 243–44, 334–35;
negotiations, 411n1; organized
labor's interest in, 315; pensions
for the rich, 246; problem, 98,
243, 313, 317, 319, 322, 325;
program, 241; proposals, 313;
recipients, 411n4; refinancing
of, 242–43; reform, 9, 316,
337–38, 380, 411n1, 412n34;
reform bill, 311; reform, 2,
politics of, 326; retirement and
survivors benefits fund, 242;
saving, 12, 309, 330; system,
242–46, 308, 310–14, 317, 324–25,
328, 334, 336, 359; tax increase,
237, 241, 246, 251, 298, 310;
taxes, 241, 243, 246, 311, 324,
329, 338; teacher, 411n1; trust
funds, 242, 244, 317–18, 338
Social Security Amendments Act of
    1983, 336
Social Security Board of Trustees, 242
Social Security Commission, 313,
    315, 323, 337
Social Security Subcommittee of the
    Ways and Means Committee,
    311, 315, 333
Social Security Task Force, the
    Business Roundtable, 315
social-welfare system, 67; programs,
    101
SOS Club, 83, 105, 110
Space Committee, 81, 113
Special Aging Committee, 315
Spencer, Stuart, 222, 227
Spencer, Terrence, 182
Speno, Edward J., 54
Sperling, Godfrey, 7–8, 386n33
Stanford University, 9

Starkweather, Ron, 341
State and Local Fiscal Assistance Act, 151–52
State of the Union: address, 144, 148, 208–9; message, 146, 149, 209, 246
St. Clair, James, 167–69, 176
Steiger, Bill, 222, 236, 247–49
Stenholm, Charles W., 285, 292
Stennis, John C., 163
Stevenson, Adlai, 127
Stockman, David, 273–77, 281, 288, 294, 296, 312–13, 315, 319–21, 326–28, 331
Strategic Arms Limitation Treaty, 260
Strauss, Robert, 344
Sullivan, Florence, 323
Sunshine laws, 337, 412n39
supply-side economics, 406–7n4, 410n75
Syracuse University, 69, 348

Taft-Hartley Act, repeal of Section 14(b) of, 92, 99
Talmadge, Herman, 263
Task Force on Seniority, 137
tax: cuts, 2, 246–47, 249–51, 272, 276–78, 288, 290–92, 294, 302, 305, 308, 312–13, 322, 407n7, 409n72, 410n75; increases, 328; law, 6, 9, 38, 110–11, 114, 117–18, 122–23, 248, 414n44; legislation of the Ways and Means Committee, 118; policy, 5, 9, 254, 257, 272, 362, 369–70; reform, 134, 166, 190, 215–16, 250, 251, 277. *See also* capital gains tax, estate tax, excise tax, gasoline tax, income tax, payroll tax
Tax Act of 1978, 237, 246, 251
tax incentives for: conservation and development of new energy sources, 241; energy conservation and production, 241

taxes: oil and natural gas, increased, 239; on personal property, 247
taxing Social Security benefits, 329
Taylor, Zachary, 128
Telesca, Michael, 69–70, 391n33, 391n36
Telluride Association, 34–36, 389n5
Telluride House, 35–38
"10-5-3" *See* accelerated cost recovery system
The [Batavia] *Daily News*, 49–50, 64
Thackeray, William, 21, 388n18
Thomas, Dennis, 281
Time, 158, 194, 253–54, 286–87, 364, 398, 405, 414
Timmons, William, 168, 172
Tofany, Vince, 63
Tonkin Gulf Resolution, 212
Torrey, Amy, 341
Tower, John, 128, 401n2
Trenholme, Pam, 386n27
Trowbridge, Alexander, 315–16, 330
Truman, Harry S., 31
Twenty-fifth Amendment, 93, 197, 200
"two-way communication," 5, 87

Udall, Morris K., 2, 144, 299, 343
Ullman, Al, 207, 209–10, 213–16, 232, 243, 247–49, 251, 263
United Nations Commission on Global Governance, 379
United States Chamber of Commerce, 290
United States Circuit Court of Appeals, 162–63
United States Naval Academy, 97
University of Rochester, 8–9, 76, 183–84, 342, 367–68, 370, 406n1
University of Virginia, 9
urban policy, 251
U.S. News and World Report, 343, 368

Vanik, Charles, 269
Vanity Fair, 388n18

Veterans of Foreign Wars, 200
Vietnam amnesty program, 201
Vietnam Moratorium Committee, 135
Vietnam war, 70, 93, 99, 106–7, 109,
    118–19, 124–25, 134, 153, 200,
    212–13
Vietnamization plan, 135
Volcker, Paul, 374
Voting Rights Act of 1965, 93; 1970
    extension of the, 141, 396n23

Waggoner, Joe, 247, 315–16, 331
Walkley, Al, 41, 64–65
Wall Street Journal, 7, 159, 174, 284–85
Wallace, George C., 125, 128
Walsh, Edward, 240
War on Poverty, 65, 68, 73, 91, 101
Washington, George, 73, 346
Washington Post, 7, 79, 194, 240, 258,
    298, 340, 342
"Washington Report," 86, 102, 135,
    396n23, 387n47, 402n12
Washington Star, 185
Watergate, 11, 156–79, 201, 396n22
Weaver, Earl, 344
Weevils, Boll, 300, 302
Weicker, Lowell, 256
Weidenbaum, Murray, 150
Welch, Marc, 45, 49
welfare reform, 119, 133–34, 142,
    144, 166, 251
WETA, 387n42
White House, 7, 12, 87–90, 98, 122,
    128, 146–48, 157, 159–61, 167–70,
    172–73, 177, 186, 188, 197–200,
    209–10, 212, 215–17, 221, 224–25,
    232, 235, 237, 245, 247–48, 252,

256, 261–62, 278–79, 281, 284–89,
    294, 296–99, 301, 306–7, 312, 315,
    319–22, 325–31, 336, 366, 368,
    407n7; effort to cover up the
    Watergate scandal, 161;
    Republican leadership
    meetings, 147
White, Clifton, 218
White, Joseph, 409n74
White, William S., 79–80
Wiggins, Charles, 177, 208
Wildavsky, Aaron, 409n74
Wilkinson, Bud, 128
Will, George, 2, 343, 368
Williams, John C., 72
Wilson, Bob, 83, 105
Wilson, Charles, 296
Wilson, John G., 20, 23, 388n16,
    388n23
windfall-profits tax, 255, 295
Wolfe, Thomas, 36
Woodruff, Judy, 364
Woods, Rose Mary, 164
Woodward, Bob, 7, 168, 201
World Bank, 12, 14, 28, 122, 178,
    374–79, 415n1
Wright, Jim, 2, 231, 238, 284, 343

Xavier University, 9

Yale University, 9
Yearbook of Agriculture, federal
    government's annual, 97
Yorkey, D.G., 388n2

Ziegler, Ron, 168

Window on Congress
A Congressional Biography of
Barber B. Conable Jr.

Barber B. Conable Jr. served as a Republican congressman from western New York from 1965 to 1985. He is recognized as one of the most respected members of the House of Representatives in recent years. This biography explores his twenty-year congressional career, focusing on his remarkable educational abilities as a gifted teacher-legislator. Using excerpts from Conable's private journal, his newsletters and news columns, and from personal interviews, James S. Fleming has crafted a book that enables readers to appreciate why Conable was held in high regard by his constituents, his colleagues, the press, and congressional scholars. Political scientist Charles O. Jones expressed the opinion of many when he observed that "Barber Conable was just about everybody's idea of what a congressman should be."

Recognizing the importance of Conable's western New York heritage, James Fleming traces Conable's story from his childhood in Warsaw, New York, to his election to the historic Eighty-ninth Congress of 1965–1966. Fleming's chronicle of Conable's subsequent legislative career offers a window on Congress and on an historic period in American history. As the fourth-ranking Republican leader in the House, Conable played a critical role in the Watergate investigation that led to the resignation of President Richard M. Nixon. As the ranking Republican leader of the Ways and Means Committee, he was a key contributor to the tax legislation passed during the Ford, Carter, and Reagan administrations. The highlight of his legislative career was his crucial work in solving the 1983 Social Security crisis. Fleming concludes the biography with a look at Conable's service as World Bank President and his retirement to his beloved western New York home.

In his foreword the renowned congressional scholar, Richard F. Fenno Jr. writes, "Barber Conable was an especially admirable United States Representative; and Jim Fleming has written an especially admirable congressional biography. This book is, therefore, a special gift."

James Fleming is Professor of Political Science at the Rochester Institute of Technology.